ENTERTAINMENT LAW: MUSIC
(Or, How to Roll in the Rock Industry)

By

Stephen Wade Nebgen, Esq.

&

Wendy Kemp Akbar, Esq.

With Special Contributions
By
Taylor Rivich
Les Scott

BODY ELECTRIC PRESS, LLC
SCOTTSDALE, ARIZONA
SECOND EDITION

BODY ELECTRIC
PRESS, LLC

Photo Courtesy - Zach Carmichael

<u>DEDICATIONS</u>

"Everything, always, for Jill, Austin, and Lindsay."

"To Jan, for bringing back the light."
-   Stephen

"With thanks to my (musical) accompaniment:
Josh, Alex, and Phoebe."
-   Wendy

The section on Blockchain is contributed by:	Taylor Rivich
Research & Copy Editors:	Taylor Rivich Leslie Scott Hanson Amir Jahan Sadeghi Spree Lawrence
Cover Design/ Interior Layout:	Joshua Jaymes Wood Anthony Noyes Sean Newman
Mr. Nebgen's Photo: **Ms. Akbar's Photo:**	Pete Schulte Erin McDonald

<u>ACKNOWLEDGEMENTS</u>

Stephen Wade Nebgen: Mom and Dad; Austin and Lindsay Nebgen; Jan Caraway; Mark Nebgen and Susan Cosley-Harvey; Don, Pam and Qin Nebgen; Matt, Brenda, Drew, and Hailey Nebgen; Steve & Joy Carmichael; Pete Schulte; Rob Davis; Rev. James and June Hagen; Carl R. Sword, Psy.; Dave Feldman; Peter Grahame & Henry Seale; Prof. David S. Sokolow; William F. Connell, Esq.; Michael Norman Saleman, Esq.; David Keneipp, Esq.; Maria Crimi Smith, Esq.; Ken Waissman; Peter Angelus; David Saline; Les Scott; Dan Bush; Don Salter, Ellen Canacakos; Pete Schulte; and Kirt Hamm, Robert Brock, Glen O'Hara, my colleagues, and my students at the Conservatory of Recording Arts and Sciences.

Wendy Kemp Akbar: To my parents, Bruce and Barbara Kemp, for encouraging me in anything and everything; Joshua Akbar, Esq. and our two shared perennial 'clients', Alexander Peter and Phoebe Amelia, who we try to encourage in anything and everything; and my colleagues at VENJURIS/Campillo Logan Meaney PC.

Rights and Permissions:

Ordering Information:

For permission requests, write to the publisher, addressed "Attention: Permissions Coordinator," at the address below.

Body Electric Press, LLC
3370 N. Hayden Road, Suite 123-565
Scottsdale, Arizona 85251
(480) 215-6305
snebgen@azentertainmentlaw.com
www.azentertainmentlaw.com

Quantity Sales.
Special discounts are available on quantity purchases by corporations, associations, faculties, students, and others. For details, contact the publisher at the address above.

Printed in the United States of America.

TABLE OF CONTENTS

INTRODUCTION

"I know. It's only rock'n'roll but I like it!"
- Mick Jagger & Keith Richards.[1]

To thrive in the ever-changing music industry - from the romantic aspects of authorship and performance to the more practical legal and business perspectives - it is important to understand how music developed into the vast enterprise it is today.

Music has been an essential part of the human experience. Archeologists have uncovered crude flutes tens of thousands of years old.[1] Poetry and art have celebrated the charms of music for just as long. Music can, by turns, "stir" or "sooth" the savage beast. It can give us the most sublime moments (for example, Richard Wagner) and some of the most ridiculous (again, Wagner).

But with the industrial revolution and the technology that flowed from that movement, the music industry - indeed all of entertainment - changed forever. The appearance of the phonograph in 1877 allowed once ephemeral and one-time-only performances to be recorded and preserved forever. The radio, also invented in the late 1800s, could broadcast that recording around the world. A person at home could then listen to that performance by phonograph or radio.

As radios expanded into more homes and entered the workplace, the audience expanded as well. People listening to records or to the radio started to develop favorites, leading to the emergence of impresarios and stars. One of the first impresarios, (*i.e.,* a person who organizes and often finances concerts or other musical performances) was Nils T. Granlund (1882-1957). Mr. Granlund created the first movie preview, filmed the first commercial, was the first to broadcast a live sports event, and, as a popular radio personality, introduced the Jazz Age to America via his broadcasts from Harlem's Cotton Club.[2]

Impresarios were nothing without talent, however. The *people performing* on the radio drew the listeners, *not* the person behind the scenes *who put the performer on* the radio. Among the first big radio stars was Rudy Vallée. The singers were deemed "crooners" because they could croon into the microphone and did not have to belt out the song.[3] Later singers like Frank Sinatra and Bing Crosby, though termed "crooners," hated the label and disavowed it.[4] But despite a backlash against the term and the music associated with it - which was even labeled by some as the devil's work - the genie was out of the bottle.

In the 1930s and 1940s, easy listening, Broadway musicals, or classical music ruled the airwaves. Then came the 1950s, a decade of musical experimentation and change. Musicians began mixing rhythm and blues, country, and gospel music, resulting in Rock 'n Roll, Doo Wop, Rockabilly, and the beginnings of Soul. Songs on the R&B stations gained popularity, and then crossed over to the pop charts in the late '50s. Stars like Chuck Berry, Bill Haley, Buddy Holly, Little Richard, and Jerry Lee Lewis emerged, generating huge record sales. Country music as well had its own big stars such as Hank Williams Sr., Johnny Cash, and Ray Charles.

Above all, there was the King - Elvis Presley. In the 1950s, no bigger star existed. Elvis sold the most records, threw the biggest concerts, and acted in movies and television. But far more important than the financial success was his influence - and *sex*! Girls could *swoon* at Sinatra or Crosby, but they *screamed* at Elvis – when Elvis shimmied, the girls shivered. Through Elvis, "white America" embraced a new type of music that broke barriers and taboos. It was fun and wild! As before, the establishment immediately attacked Elvis and rock and roll as subversive and anti-American.[5] But the outrage only fueled the interest of the younger generation.

Unfortunately, Elvis created another template for a rock star: the out-of-control but pampered artist whose self-destructive actions led to an early death. Elvis' manager, Colonel Parker, ignored the signs of Elvis's drug addiction and Elvis died in 1977, on a toilet in his bathroom at the age of only 42.[6]

As the 1950s gave way to the 1960s, a new influence seeped into the music - drugs. Drugs have always been a part of the music scene - but it was a secret kept hidden by the musician and other members of the band/artist (see Elvis above). As the Beats gave way to the Hippies, drug use came out into the open. By the end of the '60s, drug use was (unfortunately) championed and glorified as a means to a deeper understanding of both music, and the universe. The Doors took their name from the famous book by Aldous Huxley, "The Doors of Perception" that chronicled Huxley's experimentation with mescaline.

If Elvis was the standard-bearer for the '50s, The Beatles had that mantle during the '60s. As with Elvis, after The Beatles nothing would ever be the same again. As with Elvis, sex was upfront. But now adolescents were the ones screaming and shaking.[7] Musically, The Beatles stretched the term "album" and expanded the instrumentation and orchestration of a "rock" record. Before The Beatles, an album was treated like a collection of short stories - each song told its own story but was not related to the song before or after it. The Beatles started to treat the album as a novel, more correctly as a symphony. Each song became part of a larger narrative - a movement in a symphony, laying out themes and then building upon those themes with subsequent songs. The Who, of course, took it to the next level with the rock operas "Tommy" and "Quadrophenia." The Beatles also played with technology such as looping a short burst of sound or by playing the tape of a guitar solo backward.

A final aspect cannot be overlooked – the fans of The Beatles' music were experimenting with drugs and those fans looked for symbolism in the music. Conjecture fueled the interpretation that The Beatles' music was steeped in drug references and influences. "She's a Woman" was among the first Beatles' song to be interpreted as having a reference to drugs - "Turn me on when I get lonely." Connections were also made in at least two other songs: "Norwegian Wood" ("So I lit a fire, isn't it good . . ..") and "Lucy in the Sky with Diamonds" (although The Beatles denied the connection - capital letters equaled LSD; various drug references in the song, and the use of psychedelic imagery).

In the late 1960s and into the 1970s, record sales tripled. Music marketers began analyzing audiences for their "sales demographics."[8] Radio stations that previously played a variety of musical styles began programming only one style. Disco, punk rock, heavy metal, and new wave music grew in popularity. Even opera and the classics benefited.[9]

The 1970s was a decade where rock and roll matured somewhat - not in the sense of settling down, but in the sense of mastering the many influences that created it. Led Zeppelin, based upon a blues sensibility, brought a deeper edge to the music, and hence, created something new. David Bowie emphasized theatre influences, androgyny, and a constantly changing image. Alice Cooper injected horror into the mix with the further twist of having a female first name.

Black artists also flourished during this period. With Motown leading the way, artists such as Stevie Wonder, Marvin Gaye, and Diana Ross and the Supremes shared the charts with white artists. And, of course, there was Jimi Hendrix – who forever changed what it meant to play electric guitar. Jazz also gained greater acceptance and musicians like Charlie "Bird" Parker, John "Trane" Coltrane, and Miles Davis gained worldwide fame and fortune. Also, a new form of music was emerging – rap/hip-hop. Seminal artists like The Last Poets, led by Jalal Mansur Nuriddin, who released their album in 1970, and Gil Scott Heron who gained a wide audience with his 1971 track "The Revolution Will Not Be Televised", combined spoken word and music to create a kind of "proto-rap" vibe.[10]

The 1980s brought disco, for good or ill. The interplay of funk and blues led to a beat-dominated music good for dancing. Although held in disdain, the influence of disco is still clearly present. But the '80s also brought the next paradigm-changing performer - Michael Jackson. Again, as with Elvis and The Beatles, the dynamic changed.

Michael Jackson had released prior solo albums, including the immensely popular *"Off the Wall."* Then, on November 30, 1982, Jackson released *"Thriller."* It became the biggest selling album in history with sales north of 30 million copies in North America alone and estimates of approximately 110 million copies worldwide.[11] Seven singles were released from the album and each one of them reached the top 10 on the Billboard Hot 100.[12]

Jackson helped to break down racial barriers. He was the first black artist to get a rotation on MTV; he met with President Ronald Reagan at the White House (echoing Elvis with Nixon); and he was one of the first to use music videos as a successful promotional tool. The music video for "Thriller" cost approximately $500,000.00 to produce, but it was worth it: the video itself sold in the millions and was hugely influential on other artists in producing their own videos.

Unfortunately, one bad thing resulted from "Thriller" - the emphasis on blockbuster albums. Budgets exploded for albums, albums became fat and bloated with mediocre music, and sales were lackluster. Even Jackson succumbed to this phenomenon. "Bad," the follow-up album to "Thriller," while selling over 30,000,000 copies worldwide, was considered a "failure" for not matching its predecessor.[13] Jackson also, unfortunately, followed the model of Elvis, becoming yet another example of the out-of-control but pampered artist destined for early death. Jackson died as a result of a heart attack after an overdose of drugs administered by his doctor, causing his death at age 50, right as he was poised to launch a long-awaited comeback.

The 1990s showed a further maturation of rock and roll. The '90s exploded with new genres such as grunge, alternative, industrial, house, hip-hop, techno, and trance. Artists such as Eminem, Nirvana, Sonic Youth, The Pixies, Pearl Jam, R.E.M., Blues Traveler, Phish, and Beck sold side by side with Whitney Houston, En Vogue, NSYNC, TLC, Mariah Carey, and Britney Spears. Rap/hip-hop became particularly dominant into the new millennium with influential artists like NWA, 2 Live Crew, Tupac Shakur, LL Cool J, Drake, and many others dominating the charts.

In the new millennium, the main development so far is

in technology. In general, the sale of compact discs (CD's) has dropped precipitously. However, one area of growth is in vinyl sales. 2013 had sales of $146 million, a 43% increase over the year before.[14] In the first quarter of 2015, sales increased by 53% over the previous year of 2014.[15] Data on vinyl album sales in the United States from 1993 to 2019 shows consistent growth since 2006, and in 2019 a total of 18.84 million vinyl albums were sold, up 14.5 percent from the previous year.[16] Despite that fact, however, downloads of singles to devices such as iPhones, iPads, and computers have become the main delivery medium for sales. It is common to see the chart leader on Billboard Album charts with sales under 100,000 copies. Yet that same artist could have a million downloads of a particular song.

Who is harmed the most? The recording artist and the record companies. As discussed below, the *author* of a song has many rights and protections under the Copyright Code. The *performer* of the song has almost none. The author will participate in performance royalties and other revenue streams from music publishing. The performer used to rely on record sales as a major revenue stream – now touring is the most important revenue stream. The same is true for the record company - it made money by selling records. Consequently, for both the performer and the record company, no record sales mean no money.

But the music industry has adapted, albeit slowly, and is still generating significant sums of money. Here are some numbers as of the end of fiscal year 2021 and into early 2022: (i) *Global* revenue from recording music was $28.8 Billion[17]; in the *United States,* the largest music market in the world, the figure was $15 Billion[18]. The three major labels reported the following numbers: (i) Universal Music Group (the largest label in the world) reported revenue of $2.7 Billion for the 2nd Quarter of 2022[19]; (ii) Sony Music grossed $2.03 Billion in the 2nd Quarter of 2022[20]; and, (iii) Warner Music Group grossed

$1.43 Billion in the 2nd Quarter of 2022.[21] And music publishing also continues to generate significant income with a robust figure of $4.7 Billion in 2021 for just the United States![22]

Conclusion

The purpose of this book is to provide an overview of the ever-changing music industry, the important legal considerations to keep in mind, and counsel on how best to manage a career. It is a guide, not a full legal treatise or commentary. The book's structure gives the reader: (i) an introduction to intellectual property (Copyright and Trademark); (ii) the revenue streams from your intellectual property; (iii) an overview of business formation; (iv) important concepts and structure of contracts; and (v) important agreements in the music industry. Both a musician and a businessperson should find this book informative and useful. However, the music industry continually evolves, and the reader is urged to monitor industry sources and legal developments for new updates.

CHAPTER 1

INTELLECTUAL PROPERTY OVERVIEW

For the creative artist, few things are as important as protecting your intellectual property. In music, intellectual property can consist of any number of things, including your song (lyrics, music, or both combined), the name and logo of your band/artist, and your cover art or insignia. The reader may want to skip ahead to what might be considered "the good stuff" - how to make money! But before you can start making money, it is important to understand the contracts that protect your rights, as well as how to set up your own business and how to protect yourself from overreaching Digital Distribution Service Providers, managers, distributors, and agents.

In the music industry, *the music comes first.* There is nothing to contract away or bargain with if you have not adequately protected your creation. To do that, you need to understand intellectual property. It is the sun around which the rest of entertainment law - the planets of contracts, royalties, licenses, bands, unions, and agent relationships, and so on - revolve. Without the sun, there would be no gravitational force. The planets would lack momentum. They would be still.

To begin with, the law recognizes three types of property:

1.   **real property** - dirt (land) or a building;

2.   **personal property** - tangible items such as your car or your computer; and,

3.   **intellectual property** - intangible items, such as your brand, your creations, or your ideas. However, unlike a building or a car, you cannot touch or feel an "idea." Consequently, in general the idea must be turned into something that we *can* see and touch - it must be turned into a "fixed" and "tangible medium of expression" to be subject to legal protection.

There are four main types of Intellectual Property: (i) Copyright; (ii) Trademarks, which also includes Service Marks and Trade Dress; (iii) Patents; and (iv), Trade Secrets. Each covers an area of creative expression, although "creative" is not necessarily synonymous with "artistic" in the context of Intellectual Property. A person can be creative in the field of inventions - that is covered by **Patent Law.** A person can be creative in branding products, services, and business in the stream of commerce - that is covered by **Trademark Law, and Trade Dress**. A person can be creative in the arts and sciences - that is covered by **Copyright Law.** And a person can be creative in these or other ways but seek to keep the resulting ideas and creations secret rather than reveal them to the public -

that is most often covered by **Trade Secrets.** Often, items that could otherwise be subject to Copyright or Patent Law, for example, wind up classified as Trade Secrets because a person prefers for them to remain unknown (*e.g.,* the secret recipe for Coke) rather than make them public as is usually required to obtain Patent, Trademark or Copyright protection.

Copyright, Trademark/Trade Dress, Patent, or Trade Secret?

It is important to know the differences between the five major types of Intellectual Property.

A *Copyright* protects works of authorship, such as writings, music, and works of art "reduced to a fixed and tangible medium of expression."[23] A copyright holder has six exclusive rights: (1) to reproduce the work; (2) make derivative works; (3) distribute copies; (4) publicly perform the work; (5) publicly display the work; and (6), which is exclusive to the owner of a Sound Recording, the ability to turn it into a digital audio transmission for public performance.[24] Additionally, the copyright holder has the right of "first use" of the copyrighted material. Examples in the music world could include songs, lyrics, arrangements. Note that the songs, lyrics, and arrangements are referred to as a "Musical Composition."[i]

It is important to note that there is also a copyright in the Sound Recording. A Sound Recording is defined under the Copyright Code as "works that result from the fixation of a series of musical, spoken, or other sounds, but not including the sounds accompanying a motion picture or other audiovisual work."[25] So, the best practice is to file a copyright application for both the Musical Composition and the Sound Recording.

A Copyright exists from the moment a work is created, so registration is not required.[26] However, registration with the U.S. Copyright Office allows copyright holders to be eligible to sue for infringement, obtain mechanical royalties, and be awarded statutory damages and attorneys' fees in a Copyright infringement suit.[27] For works created after January 1, 1978, a Copyright generally lasts for the life of the author plus an additional seventy years.[28]

A *Trademark* is a word, phrase, symbol, and/or design that identifies and distinguishes the source of the goods of one party from those of others.[29] For example, the familiar "A" with a star in the center, inside a circle surrounded by wings with the word AEROSMITH stamped on front in unique font, identifies the band/artist Aerosmith and its music. A *service mark* is a word, phrase, symbol, and/or design that identifies and distinguishes the source of a service rather than goods. The term "Trademark" is often used to refer to both Trademarks and

---

[i] The third edition of the Compendium is a great source of Copyright info/guidance. This is the absolute best source to refer to on anything copyright related: https://www.copyright.gov/comp3. Updated January 28th, 2021.

service marks. Although Trademark rights are acquired simply by adopting and using the mark such that registration is not required, registration with the U.S. Patent and Trademark Office makes it easier to prove and enforce those rights. Once registered, if the Trademarks are renewed as required, they can last indefinitely. But it is important to note that to have a "worldwide" trademark, you would need to register in every country that you wish to protect the mark.

Then there is *Trade Dress*. Trade Dress covers the distinctive *packaging* of the product, together with Trademark protection, which covers the name and/or logo. Together these protect the "brand."

A *Patent* is a limited duration property right relating to an invention, granted by the United States Patent and Trademark Office in exchange for public disclosure of the invention.[30] A patent grants property rights on inventions, allowing the patent holder to exclude others from making, selling, or using the invention. Unlike Copyrights and Trademarks, you can *only* obtain a patent in the United States by filing for one with the U.S. Patent and Trademark Office. There are three types of patents. A *utility patent* (the most common) covers any process, machine, article of manufacture, or any new and useful improvements thereof. To qualify, an invention must be novel, non-obvious, and have some usefulness. A *design patent* covers any new, original, and ornamental design for an article of manufacture. A *plant patent* covers any new variety of asexually produced plant. A design patent lasts fourteen years from the applicable filing date, and a utility or plant patent twenty years from the applicable filing date.

And finally, there is *Trade Secret*. A trade secret is a formula, process, device, or other business information that companies keep secret to give them an advantage over competitors - for example, customer lists, business methods, recipes, survey results, and computer algorithms. Unlike the other types of intellectual property, you cannot obtain protection by registering your trade secret - nor do you want to. Instead, protection is automatic, but lasts only as long as you take the necessary steps to keep the trade secret . . . secret: you need to control disclosure and use of the information. Businesses use confidentiality or non-disclosure agreements, non-compete agreements, restrict access to confidential information, require post-employment restrictive covenants, and use other security practices to maintain trade secrets.

There is often an overlap between the various types of intellectual property. For example, some copyrightable items (say, album cover art) might also be eligible for Trademark protection. Likewise, items that qualify as trade secrets can sometimes be patentable or copyrightable, so people and businesses often need to make an important decision on how to protect their intellectual property: internally as a trade secret, or externally by filing for a Copyright, or Patent to cement ownership and exclusivity for a period of time, at the expense of secrecy.

For example, a musician might build a revolutionary new guitar with shape and strings precisely calibrated to emit a unique sound. The musician could choose to file a patent on the new guitar. The patent would publicly explain how the guitar works and how to make it, announcing her ownership to the world. However, while patents provide ownership rights for up to twenty years, history is replete with those who try to tweak the invention disclosed in a patent *just* enough to get out of potential infringement. So, if the musician did not want anyone else to reproduce the invention and compete with the band/artist using a similar sound or have to police the patent to make sure someone does not try to "design around" it, the musician might wish to keep secret the guitar's makeup, within the artist, or within the company that houses the artist. In that case, it is treated as a trade secret.

An important point to remember is that your song is *property* - like a piece of dirt. But it is *valuable* dirt! In the following chapters, we will be focusing on two of the five major types of intellectual property: COPYRIGHTS and TRADEMARKS.

CHAPTER 2
COPYRIGHT

"Only one thing is impossible for God:
to find any sense in
any copyright law on the planet.
- Mark Twain's Notebook, 1902-1903

History of Copyright Code

Over the years, Congress[ii] has revised the Copyright Code multiple times. The original Copyright Code became law

---

[ii] It is important to remember that Copyright is governed completely by Federal Law. In the United States, the Federal legal system is broken down into three levels of courts: lower-level district courts, appellate-level Circuit courts, and the U.S. Supreme Court. Each state has from 1-4 Districts, depending on size and population density; thus, the District of Alaska is the only District in that state, while New York has Southern, Northern, Western and Eastern Districts. The district courts in nearby states clump together to form into a total of twelve Circuits and the D.C. Circuit for the District of Columbia. Thus, for example, the Ninth Circuit hears the

in 1790, was revised in 1831, and again in 1909. Currently in place is the Copyright Act of 1976 **(the "1976 Code")**.

The 1976 Code provides the basic framework for the current copyright law and was enacted on October 19, 1976, and went into effect on January 1, 1978. It was a comprehensive revision of the copyright law in Title 17. There have been amendments since then, a few of the biggest being: (a) the Digital Performance Right in Sound Recordings Act of 1995 **(the "DPRSRA")**, enacted November 1, 1995; (b) the **Sonny Bono Copyright Term Extension Act**, extending the term of copyright protection for a flat twenty years, enacted October 27, 1998; (c) the Digital Millennium Copyright Act **(the "DMCA")**, amending §108, §112, and §114 of Title 17, and enacted on October 28, 1998.

But a major addition to the Copyright Act was the Music Modernization Act **(the "MMA")** enacted in 2018. "The Music Modernization Act is an attempt to repair the fissures created as the digital revolution bloomed, and to balance the interests of artists and the tech giants who need them," states Andrew Flanagan.[31]

Up until then, the system for licensing the songwriters' copyright (known as "mechanical rights" for historical reasons) was a mess. Streaming services have had trouble identifying the owners of music rights, which has led to songwriters not getting

---

appeals from district courts in the single-district states of Alaska, Arizona, Guam, and Hawaii, along with those in each of the Central, Eastern, Northern and Southern Districts of California. Some of the more important circuits for the music industry include: (i) the Second Circuit composed of district courts in Connecticut, Massachusetts, and New York, -- including New York City (within the Southern District of New York); (ii) the Sixth Circuit which includes Nashville, Tennessee; and (iii) the Ninth Circuit, which includes the district courts across California, including in Los Angeles (within the Central District of California). Because many prominent music-related companies and individuals reside or work there, these areas tend to see the most music-related litigation.

paid and streaming services periodically getting sued for non-payment.[32]

The Music Modernization Act aims to establish a modern system for licensing mechanical rights. The new organization will offer streaming services "one stop shopping" for getting songwriters' licenses for all the songs they want to stream, with the database helping to get the funds to the appropriate songwriters and Publishers.[33]

The law is organized into three key titles: Title I—Music Licensing Modernization; Title II—Classics Protection and Access; and Title III – Allocation for Music Producers.[34]

• <u>Title I - Music Licensing Modernization:</u> The Music Licensing Modernization allows a more efficient music-licensing process and makes it easier for rights holders to get paid when their music is streamed online. It reforms Section 115 to ensure songwriters are being compensated in a timely manner by ending the bulk Notice of Intent (NOI) process, creating a single Mechanical Licensing Collective (MLC) funded by the digital services, and providing a publicly accessible database for song ownership information. It also repeals Section 114(i) which will allow courts setting public performance royalty rates for mechanical licenses to consider rates for Sound Recording royalties.

> Meredith Rose from Public Knowledge told The Verge: Streaming presented its owns challenges. Streaming deals with two different systems of copyright protection for streaming a song online: protection for (a) the Composer or Songwriter, and (b) a separate copyright for the Sound Recording. Services like Pandora and Spotify typically need licenses for both

types of rights in order to stream a song online.[35]

"It . . . does a thing which you couldn't really do with these kinds of licenses before: obtain a blanket license. You can license the whole corpus of Musical Compositions, and before you [didn't have] an entity that was allowed to license everything. So, if Spotify was starting today they'd be able to jump in and say, 'Okay, I want all of it,' write one check, and then just kind of go about their business," Mr. Flanagan concludes.[36]

- Title II—Classics Protection and Access: The Compensating Legacy Artists for their Songs, Service, & Important Contributions to Society (CLASSICS) Act extends protection for pre-1972 Sound Recordings.

On October 15, 1971, legislation to protect, under the Copyright Act, Sound Recordings – the particular series of musical, spoken, or other sounds fixed on a tape or record album and the performance embodied therein – was enacted, effective February 15, 1972[37]. Prior to this date, Sound Recordings were protected solely by state common law or criminal statute. It became an issue with the controversy surrounding a series of cases concerning the 1960's rock band, The Turtles.

In the California case, *Flo & Eddie Inc. v Sirius XM Radio Inc.*, et al., CV 13-5693, Flo and Eddie, founding members of The Turtles, had sued Sirius XM Radio, Inc. ("SiriusXM") for violation of Flo and Eddie's rights granted to Copyright owners under the Copyright Code. Flo and Eddie brought assorted claims, but the two (2) significant ones were: (i) the playing of the Sound Recordings violated their *"performance"* royalty; and (ii) when SiriusXM made copies of the Sound Recordings to facilitate its operations, it violated their *"reproduction"* right. The Court found that summary judgment was appropriate on the first issue.[38] Subsequent decisions in Florida and New York merely continued to muddy the waters surrounding the status of pre-1972 recordings.

The CLASSICS ACT: (i) closes the pre-1972 loophole by establishing federal copyright protection that will guarantee compensation for artists who recorded music before February 15, 1972; (ii) codifies SoundExchange's longtime practice of honoring "Letters of Direction" from artists who want to share royalties with studio producers and other creative participants who work with them; (iii) creates a new process that will allow eligible participants in recordings made before the digital performance right was enacted in 1995 to share in digital royalties for those recordings; and (iv) establishes a "willing buyer, willing seller" rate standard that will require all digital platforms to pay fair market value for music; and

- Title III – Allocation for Music Producers: The Allocation for Music Producers (AMP) Act helps to improve royalties for producers and engineers from SoundExchange. SoundExchange is the body that monitors digital or extraterrestrial outlets. Most importantly, this is the first time that producers would be covered by copyright law.[39]

What Is Covered By Copyright?

Section 102 of Chapter 1 of the Copyright Code lists what can and cannot be copyrighted.

§ 102. Subject matter of Copyright: In general

(a) Copyright protection subsists, in accordance with this title, in original works of authorship fixed in any tangible medium of expression, now known, or later developed, from which they can be perceived, reproduced, or otherwise communicated, either directly or with the aid of a machine or device. Works of authorship include the following categories:

1. Literary works;

2. Musical works, including any accompanying words;

3. Dramatic works, including any accompanying music;

4. Pantomimes and choreographic works;

5. Pictorial, graphic, and sculptural works;

6. Motion pictures and other audiovisual works;

7. Sound Recordings; and

8. Architectural works.

(b) In no case does Copyright protection for an original work of authorship extend to any idea, procedure, process, system, method of operation, concept, principle, or discovery, regardless of the form in which it is described, explained, illustrated, or embodied in such work.

For musicians, § 102(a)(2) and (7) are important. Clause (a)(2) covers the lyrics of a song, the music, and the combination of both - this is a *"musical work"* or a **Musical Composition**. Clause (a)(7) covers the **Sound Recording** of the musical work. Generally, the Copyright for the Musical Composition is held in the name of the authors of the song, while the Copyright in the

Sound Recording is held by the recording company (or whoever fixed the sounds in a tangible medium of expression, e.g., the producer or the performer, who generally have a work-for-hire agreement in place putting the copyright in the hands of the record label).

So, it is important to remember that multiple Copyrights can exist in one piece of intellectual property. Keep in mind our analogy of a piece of land or a house. The owner of a piece of real estate holds a variety of rights in that piece of land. There are air rights, surface rights, and mineral rights. The same can exist in a song: there can be a Copyright in the lyrics, a Copyright in the music, and a Copyright in the lyrics and music together as a Musical Composition. In addition, there can be a Copyright in the Sound Recording - the actual wave form – that is contained on vinyl, tape, or a digital file, which are termed "Phonorecords."[40]

Section 102(a) says, it "must be an *original* work of authorship" (emphasis added).

> "The sine qua non of copyright is originality." *N.Y. Mercantile Exch., Inc. v. Intercontinental Exchange, Inc.,* 497 F.3d 109, 113 (2d Cir. 2007). While this is "a low threshold . . . [t]he law requires more than a modicum of originality" and the Copyright Act "has been interpreted to require a distinguishable variation that is more than merely trivial." *NYC Image Int'l, Inc. v. RS U.S., Inc., 10 (S.D. N.Y. 2020)*; *Waldman Pub. Corp. v. Landoll, Inc.*, 43 F.3d 775, 782 (2d Cir. 1994).

Furthermore, it must be "fixed in a tangible medium of expression." The Statute lists items such as an idea, procedure, process, system, method of operation, concept, principle, or discovery that will not be granted Copyright protection.[41] Also, you cannot copyright the idea of a song about a boy and girl from warring families who fall in love and have a tragic end – remember the doctrine of *scenes a faire*. That is too general an idea and the public interest is not served by locking up such a general idea.

Likewise, you cannot Copyright the principle of gravity or Copyright the discovery of a new planet in the solar system. Such facts are so fundamental that, again, no public interest is served by denying the use of such discoveries and principles.

How Do You Get a Copyright; Rights Granted

Your copyright comes into existence the minute, indeed even the second, that you put your idea into a "fixed and tangible medium of expression."[42] Upon "fixation," six rights are created:

§ 106. Exclusive rights in copyrighted works: Subject to sections 107 through 122, the owner of copyright under this title has
the exclusive rights to do and to authorize any of the following:

(1)   To **reproduce** the copyrighted work in copies or phonorecords;

(2)   To **prepare derivative works** based upon the copyrighted work;

(3)   To **distribute** copies or phonorecords of the copyrighted work to the public by sale or other transfer of ownership, or by rental, lease, or lending;

(4)   In the case of literary, musical, dramatic, and

choreographic works, pantomimes, and motion pictures and other audiovisual works, to **perform** the copyrighted work publicly;

(5)   In the case of literary, musical, dramatic, and choreographic works, pantomimes, and pictorial, graphic, or sculptural works, including the individual images of a motion picture or other audiovisual work, to **display** the copyrighted work publicly; and

(6)   In the case of sound recordings, to perform the copyrighted work publicly by means of a **digital audio transmission**.[43]

Here are brief descriptions of each of the rights.

Clause 1 and 3 - Reproduction and Distribution. Clause (1) and Clause (3) work together. Clause (1) allows the copyright holder to make copies and Clause (3) allows the copyright holder to distribute and sell the copies. Record companies will generally hold this right for the Sound Recordings. As part of a recording agreement, the recording artist will assign the rights in the Sound Recording (NOT the song) to the record company. The record company will then be able to exploit the Sound Recording by making copies (generating a mechanical royalty for the Composer) and selling them (generating a record royalty for the recording artist).

Clause 2 - Derivative Works. Musicians often overlook Clause (2), but it brings in significant revenues and should not be ignored. The copyright holder of a song is the only person that can make a "derivative work," *i.e.,*

> ". . . a work based upon one or more preexisting works, such as . . . a musical arrangement . . . a

24

Sound Recording . . . or any other form in which a work may be recast, transformed, or adapted. A work consisting of editorial revisions, annotations, elaborations, or other modifications, which, as a whole, represent an original work of authorship, is a 'derivative work'." Copyright Code; § 101. Definitions.

In other words, a derivative work is a new work that includes major, Copyright-protected elements of an original, previously created first work (the underlying work). The derivative work becomes a second, separate work independent from the first. But note, the copyright only extends to the new material in a derivative work.

Some examples of derivative works would be:

(i)   leaving the bridge out of your recording;

(ii)   altering the order of the verses/choruses; or

(iii)   replacing ANY lyric with another lyric.

A perfect example of this is when an advertiser wants to use a famous song (and recording) in their commercial but wants to change the lyrics. There are three separate licenses required, not two. Note that there could potentially be four, but we'll stay with these three.

You will need:

(i)   a license to use the song (a "Synchronization "License");

(ii)   a license to use the Sound Recording (a "Master Use License"); and

> (iii)   a license to make a derivative by changing the lyric (a "Mechanical License").

Other examples of the benefit of this right come to mind. One is Green Day creating a musical from the song and album "American Idiot!" The resulting "American Idiot" musical played on Broadway for over a year and a half, grossed almost $40 million dollars, was seen by over 500,000 people, and continues to generate revenue from an American tour of the show.[44] The second example is "The Beatles LOVE," the Cirque du Soleil production of The Beatles catalogue running in Las Vegas, which generates huge revenues for the estates of each respective Beatle.

Samples

Clause 2 also has an effect on the use of "samples." Steve Vondran defines sampling as "the actual copying of sounds from an existing recording for use in a new recording, *even if accomplished with slight modifications such as changes to pitch or tempo"* (emphasis added).[45] Thus, using an unlicensed sample in your own new work is a derivative work, and violates Clause 2.

Many creative people believe they can get away with using Samples without being caught if they: (i) alter the frequency pitch of the sample; (ii) alter the timing; (iii) chop up and move around various elements of the sample; or by (iv) adding other sounds directly on top of the sample. Technology is now developed to the point that nothing is undetectable; the copyright holder can "strip" the layers and plug-ins and get down to the actual sound wave.

But, over the last two decades, a conflict has existed regarding the use of the "de minimis" defense as to the use of software to manipulate the original sampled Sound Recording.

Our previous discussion on the Federal Circuit legal system now comes into play (See Footnote 2; Pg. 13). The conflict began with a case at the District Court level in the Sixth Circuit entitled *"Bridgeport Music, Inc. v. Dimension Films, Inc.,* 230 F.Supp.2d 830 (Mid-Ten 2002) *("Bridgeport")*. In *Bridgeport,* the action concerned the use of a sample from the Musical Composition and Sound Recording of *"Get Off Your Ass and Jam"* ("Get Off") in the new song *"100 Miles and Runnin"* ("100 Miles"). In the initial action, the United States District Court for the Middle District of Tennessee granted summary judgment to the defendant on the grounds that the alleged infringement was *de minimis* and therefore not actionable.[46] The Plaintiff, Bridgeport, then appealed to the Sixth Circuit Court of Appeals.[47]

The Sixth Circuit Court of Appeals reviewed the case and then overruled the District Court. The Appeals Court made a key distinction at the outset of its opinion – the *de minimis* exception is not applicable to determining the issue of a sampling of a Sound Recording.[48] Next, the Court of Appeals stated that its analysis begins and ends with § 114(a) and (b) of the Copyright Code. After analyzing § 114, the Court of Appeals got to the heart of the matter:

> "If you cannot pirate the whole Sound Recording, can you "lift" or "sample" something less that the whole[?]. Our answer to that question is in the negative."[49]

The Court of Appeals made three key comments: (i) get a license or do not sample; (ii) the market will control the license price and keep it within bounds; and (iii) sampling is never accidental.[50]

And a final nuance was articulated by the Sixth Circuit:

the taking of a piece of a Sound Recording was a "physical" taking, not an "intellectual" taking, i.e., a Sound Recording is a physical piece of property, while a Musical Composition is an intellectual piece of property.[51]

For many years, the *Bridgeport* decision was the controlling case on the use of the Sound Recording of a sample and whether there was a *de minimis* defense. Then, in 2016, the Ninth Circuit Court of Appeals issued its decision in *VMG Salsoul, LLC v. Madonna Louise Ciccone*, 824 F.3d 871 (9th Cir. 2016) ("VMG Salsoul"). And all hell broke loose.

In *VMG Salsoul*, the case concerned a sample from a song entitled *"Ooh I Love It (Love Break)"* (*"Love Break"*). *Love Break* had come out in the 1980's and was produced by Shep Pettibone ("Pettibone"). VMG Salsoul claimed that Pettibone, who was also the producer of Madonna's hit song, *"Vogue"* ("Vogue"), which had come out in the 1990's, had sampled a 0.23-second segment of horns from *Love Break*.[52]

The Ninth Circuit Court of Appeals held that the *de minimis* exception *did* apply to infringement actions concerning copyrighted Sound Recordings.[53] The Ninth Circuit stated that it "reflects the legal maxim, *de minimis non curat lex* (often rendered as, 'the law does not concern itself with trifles'").[54] It further stated that *"a general audience would not recognize the brief snippet in Vogue as originating from Love Break."* *(emphasis added)*.[55] In other words, if you take just a little bit and the average audience member does not detect it, you are free to steal!

The Ninth Circuit Court of Appeals cited other cases and doctrines from other Circuits that supported their position that the *de minimis* defense applied to Sound Recordings.[56] However, the dissent in the case stated, "It is no defense to theft that the thief made off with only a *"de minimis"* part of the victim's property."[57] The dissent continued, "Accordingly, the pertinent inquiry in a sampling case is not whether a defendant sampled a little or a lot, but whether a defendant sampled at all."[58] Another aspect of the decision is that as much as the "de minimis" exception is settled law, so is the fact that copyright infringement is a "strict liability law." As stated by Janet Fries and Jennifer T. Criss,

> The U.S. Copyright Act is a strict liability statute. In other words, following a "rule" that you believe to be true, but which turns out to be a myth will not excuse you from liability for infringement. Under certain circumstances, it is possible to plead "innocent infringement," but even that only serves to reduce the amount of damages you may owe and does not excuse your infringement.[59]

The Ninth Circuit decision was in direct contradiction to the decision in *Bridgeport*. Consequently, there is now a split in the Circuits as to whether the *de minimis* exception applies to Sound Recordings. As of the date of the printing of this book, the Supreme Court has not stepped in to settle the dispute.

Clause 4 – Publicly Perform. Clause (4), together with Clause (6), protects the copyright holder's *performance* right. Clause (4) pertains to the songwriter. Only the copyright holder in the song, generally the songwriter, can perform the song in public. If anyone else performs the song in public, a royalty must be paid. It is important to note that the actual performer of the song does NOT get a performance royalty, except in extremely limited cases discussed further below. When a Frank Sinatra record plays, such as "New York, New York" the songwriter gets the performance royalty. In the old days, Sinatra would get his money from a royalty on the record sales.

However, this model has broken down with the drop of record sales due to new technologies that have changed the way we acquire and listen to music.

The revenue generated from Clause (4) is accounted for by the performance rights societies - the biggest ones in the United States being ASCAP, BMI, and SESAC, with a new entity, GMR, entering the mix. Chapter 3 on Music Publishing will go into more depth of the performance royalty and performance rights societies.

Clause 5 – Publicly Display. Clause (5) does not have a significant effect for musicians. Clause (5) gives the copyright holder the exclusive right to publicly display the work. Its general application is to cover artists of the "plastic arts" – for example, photography, graphic design, and sculpture. It overlaps with the performance right in Clause (4). Clause (5) would cover the situation where the actual notes of John Lennon's "Imagine" are put on display. Only John Lennon, or his heirs for a period of seventy (70) years from his death (1980), can put those notes on display.

Clause 6 – Digital Performance. In the pre-1995 version of the 1976 Code, § 106 was comprised of only Clauses (1)-(5). However, due to the increase in the availability of downloads and streaming of music on the internet and other devices, the Digital Performance Right in Sound Recordings Act of 1995 (**the "DPRSRA"**) created a limited performance right for the copyright holders of a Sound Recording in digital audio transmissions. In the DPRSRA, a Sound Recording is defined as:

> works that result from the fixation of a series of musical, spoken, or other sounds, but not including the sounds accompanying a motion

picture or other audiovisual work." Common examples include recordings of music, drama, or lectures.[60]

The DPRSRA protected two elements of the Sound Recording: (i) "the contribution of the *performer(s)* whose performance is captured" on the Sound Recording; and (ii) "the *contribution* of the *person or persons responsible for capturing and processing the sounds to make the final recording.*" (emphasis added)[61]

Consequently, on extraterrestrial platforms such as Pandora, Spotify, and SiriusXM, each of the following could receive a royalty: the performers, the producers, and arrangers, etc.[62] The royalty is ridiculously low, as will be discussed below.

Finally, as mentioned above, while §106 of the Copyright Code enumerated the various copyright holder's rights *generally,* § 114(a) specifically addresses Sound Recordings. In doing so, it limited the rights of a copyright holder in a Sound Recording to only those rights found in § 106(1), (2), (3), and (6), and specifically excludes Clause (4), performance, and Clause (5), publicly display.

Section 114(b) provided for a statutory licensing scheme for non-exempt subscription services and eligible non-subscription digital audio transmissions.[63] The main point here is the distinction between what is or is not "interactive." The closer to "interactive" the transmission is, the more likely the transmitter should negotiate separate licenses with the stakeholders.

Who Owns The Copyright?

Section 201 of Chapter 2 of the Copyright Code addresses the issue of ownership of a Copyright.

Initial Ownership.

§ 201(a). Ownership of Copyright

(a) INITIAL OWNERSHIP. — Copyright in a work protected under this title vests initially in the author or authors of the work. The authors of a joint work are co-owners of Copyright in the work.

Using the analogy to a house, there can be a builder, a government agency that issues a piece of paper, and an owner of the house. The same is true when it comes to Copyright. Under Copyright law, the person who wrote the song is the Author (the person who built the house) and the six rights came into existence the minute the songwriter put the song into a "fixed medium of expression." The Copyright Office issues the registration of the work (like the County Recorder on a house), and the person who owns the Copyright is the Claimant (the person that owns the house). Oftentimes the Author is also the Claimant, but sometimes that is not the case. As discussed more fully in the chapter on recording agreements, common clauses in such agreements will require that the Copyright in Sound Recordings be transferred from the Author to the record company, and the music publishing be transferred to the record labels music publishing division. They then become the Claimant.

Joint Ownership

The second sentence of § 201(a) on Joint Ownership is especially important and can cause a lot of grief among members of a songwriting team. It is rare that every single member contributes equally to each aspect of a song: the lyrics, the music, and so on. Often, one writer contributes the lyrics, while another takes the first pass at the music. What happens then? Does one writer own the Copyright on the music, one on the lyrics, and both or only one of them own the Copyright on the Sound Recording? What happens if one writer wants to make a deal contrary to an equal split? The answer to these issues comes down to two inquiries: (1) Is it a joint work? (2) If so, was any arrangement other than an equal share, memorialized properly?

A "joint work" is defined as ". . . a work prepared by two or more authors with the intention that their contributions be merged into inseparable or interdependent parts of a unitary whole." [64] There are several key concepts here. First, to be a joint author, a co-author's contribution must be "independently copyrightable" - not, for example, making typographical edits to finalized songs or lyrics. [65] Second, the parts of a work are "interdependent" when they have some meaning standing alone, but achieve their primary significance because of their combined effect, as in the case of the words and music of a song.[66] Third, the "intention" of the parties at the time the work is made, controls the issue of ownership. The requisite intent to create a joint work exists when the putative joint authors intend to regard themselves as joint authors.[67] It is not enough that they intend to merge their separate contributions into one unitary work.[68] As Georgia K. Harper comments:

> No matter how many collaborators, the work will only be a jointly owned work if the collaborators intended, at the time of creation, that their contributions would be joined into a unified whole and that they would be joint authors. Many times, collaborators agree on the first point, but they really haven't thought about the second point. This makes intent an excellent issue to bring up for discussion at the beginning

of a project.[69]

Even when the existence of a joint work is undisputed, problems can develop. Band members may take for granted that they are all contributing to a combined work - a song and album. Some members may assume each person owns the piece they created (lyrics or music). Others may assume the band or artist owns everything in equal shares, regardless of which portion each member contributes. This is precisely why Copyright Law is subject to the Statue of Frauds.[70] The default position under the Copyright Code and case law is that given joint authorship, each writer shares equal percentage ownership in all aspects of the work (lyrics and music) unless there is an agreement to the contrary. And under § 204 that agreement must be in writing. An agreement such as a "Split-Letter" or "Song Authorship Agreement" or Collaboration Agreement will fulfill the writing requirement.

As one example, a writer may informally discuss that one writer member, who founded the band and contributed the lion's share of the music, will receive 70% of the songwriting credit while the other three members each receive 10%. Being good friends and desiring to go ahead and make music, they may not want to get attorneys involved to write up a contract and may not see the need to write a simple one-page "split-letter" or fuller Song Collaboration Agreement among themselves to memorialize the arrangement. But bands are notorious for having growing pains. If things go sour and one band member later wishes to leave, he or she might deny the informal agreement ever occurred, or might repudiate it, and demand an equal share – 25% rather than 10%. Without a written agreement, the departing member might prevail. The example points out the importance of a written agreement, and of not relying on informalities and friendship.

Finally, the above example and concept of joint works

underscores why writers should consult with an attorney during the songwriting process - and not necessarily the same one. Absent an agreement in which "we share everything equally; a shared attorney may not be enough to make sure each individual writer member's interests are adequately protected. If one or more writers are receiving either more, or less, than others, each writer should ideally consult with their own attorney, at least briefly, to make sure they understand the implications of the arrangement.

Works Made For Hire.

§ 201(b). Ownership of Copyright

(b) WORKS MADE FOR HIRE. — In the case of a work made for hire, the employer or other person for whom the work was prepared is considered the author for purposes of this title, and, unless the parties have expressly agreed otherwise in a written instrument signed by them, owns all of the rights comprised in the Copyright.

Section 101 of the Copyright Act defines a "work made for hire" in two parts:

A.   A work prepared by an employee within the scope of his or her employment;

Or

B.   A work specially ordered or commissioned for use

    1.   as a contribution to a collective work;

    2.   as a part of a motion picture or other audiovisual work,

3.   as a translation,

4.   as a supplementary work,

5.   as a compilation,

6.   as an instructional text,

7.   as a test,

8.   as answer material for a test, or

9.   as an atlas,

if the parties expressly agree in a written instrument signed by them that the work shall be considered a work made for hire.

Determining whether a work fits under this doctrine is not always easy. The first step of the analysis is to review the definition of a "work made for hire" - if an employee creates it then § 101(1) would clearly control. To determine if someone is an employee one looks at how close the relationship fits with the factors that make up a traditional employer-employee interaction:

1.   <u>Control by the employer over the work</u>: For example, the employer dictates how the job is done, it is accomplished at the employer's place of business, and the employer provides supplies or other equipment.

2.   <u>Control by the employer over the employee</u>: For example, the employer controls the schedule, can assign the

employee other duties, determines the method of payment, or has the right to hire, veto, or dictate the terms of the employee's assistants.

3. The employer's conduct and status: For example, the employer is in business to produce works of this type, gives the employee benefits, and/or withholds taxes.

The closer the relationship comes to fitting the traditional employer-employee paradigm, the more likely the creation at issue is a "work for hire." And it is imperative to remember that a "work for hire" agreement *must* be signed *before* commencing the work.[71] Since the copyright comes into existence at the time of creation, and the author is the original owner, any "work for hire" agreement entered into subsequent to the creation of the work will not meet the factors listed above.[72]

§ 101(2) lists situations where "work for hire" exists:

(i) contribution to a collective work,

(ii) part of a motion picture or other audiovisual work;

(iii) a supplementary work;

(iv) a compilation; or

(v) if the parties expressly agree in a written instrument signed by them that the work shall be considered a work made for hire.

Examples of a "work made for hire" are: (i) an artist hired to draw cover art for a band/artist's CD; or (ii) a musician hired to create an appropriate theme song for a television show. Depending upon the contract, the Composer will get a flat fee and sign away all the rights to the person that contracted with the Composer.

The doctrine of "work-for-hire" is an important one to keep in mind, both as an artist and as a businessperson. The person creating something under a "work-for-hire" scenario is often expected to show up at a certain time, work for a set period of hours, and at the direction of a supervisor. In film, this has long been the case with screenwriters and composers. However, rarely does the "work-for-hire" doctrine apply in music. Imagine the record company telling Mick Jagger and Keith Richards to show up at 8:00 a.m. in the morning, and please have "Satisfaction" completed by the end of the day!

However, it is IMPERATIVE that songwriters and performers know about this doctrine, especially because of the termination rights found in § 203 (discussed below), which allows a songwriter to snatch back a Copyright license after a certain period of time elapses. If a work is deemed a "work-for-hire," however, these § 203 rights are not available to the creator of the work.

Another term that is used is "phonorecords." It is important to remember that a "Sound Recording" is not synonymous with "phonorecords." The phonorecord is "the physical object in which works of authorship are embodied."[73] Therefore, CDs, vinyl records, and cassette tapes are each Phonorecords, which carry a Sound Recording.

Registration

Even though Registration is voluntary, there are extra benefits by registering your copyright with the Copyright

Office. For example, a copyright holder cannot bring a lawsuit to protect the copyright *unless* it has been registered with the Copyright Office.[74] You might also have trouble licensing your work absent an official Copyright, as others may be unwilling to pay for something that does not have that federal protection dating back across a period of time.

A good analogy for your Musical Composition or Sound Recording is to liken it to a house or your car. With your house, the deed comes from the land office; with your car, it comes from the state motor vehicle division; and with Copyright it will *only* come from the Copyright Office of the Library of Congress. It does NOT come from the Writer's Guild of America. It does NOT come from sending yourself a self-addressed stamped envelope. It does not come from ASCAP, BMI, or SESAC.

To obtain a Copyright, an application must be filed. The application can be filed online or by mail. The Copyright Office prefers e-filing, so the filing fee (as of March, 2022) is generally only $45.00 for a "single application" (one author, one work); $65.00 for a regular application done on-line, and $125.00 for mailing the application.[75] Even though you do not get the Certificate of Registry for a while (it is not unusual for the Certificate to take 3-6 months to issue) your protection will relate back to the date and time the Copyright Office received all the material to be copyrighted.[76] Thus, it is important to have your materials ready when you begin the online application process.

Recently, the Copyright Office added two new forms of application. The first is GRAM: Group Registration for Works on an Album of Music. There are several unique benefits to using this form (providing the copyright owners can answer yes to all the requirements for using this new type of registration). Some requirements include:

(i)   You can file up to twenty works within one fee of registration;

(ii)   All works within the body of work are not required to be included in order for you to use the form (e.g., you could register tracks 1-4, omit 5, register 6-10, omit 11-14, etc.).

(iii)   You can include other types of work in the same GRAM registration, e.g., you can include the artwork that goes along with your musical album.

(iv)   You cannot use the GRAM registration if the work(s) have not been published. They must be published prior to registering through GRAM.

(v)   You can only include items that you own the rights to, NOT anything you've licensed.

Example - A Band who is planning to register their new musical album wants to use GRAM. They own all Musical Compositions, Sound Recordings, and additionally own the artwork for the album (by specially commissioning a graphic artist as a work-made-for-hire). The one issue is that one of the art pieces is "licensed" to the Band, not owned, so the Band can still include everything owned as long as they don't include that "licensed" piece in their registration.

A question that arises is "can someone register a copyright of a Musical Composition within a "Group" or "GRAM" and also register that same Musical Composition in a separate "single" Musical Composition registration?" The answer is NO, a copyright can only be registered once - you cannot make more than one registration for a work. Of course, there might be a scenario where the copyright is sold or transferred to another, in which case, the registration is revised, meaning there's still not a second registering of the work.[77]

The second new application is "Group Registration of Unpublished Works" (GRUW). On March 15, 2019, the Copyright Office implemented a group registration option for unpublished works. This option is called Group Registration for Unpublished Works (GRUW) and may be used to register up to ten unpublished works for a single fee. This option replaced the prior accommodation for registering multiple unpublished works as part of an "unpublished collection" using an online application or a paper form.[78]

Applicants are required to use a new application form specifically designed for this group option and must submit the application and required a digital deposit copies through the electronic Copyright Office (eCO) registration portal.

Copyright Terms

The 1976 Code also changed the length of the copyright terms.[79] The MMA will significantly shorten the term of protection of older music published between 1923 and 1954, which under the current law, could take until 2067 to fall into the public domain.[80]

For *Sound Recordings*, works will fall into the following broad categories:

• For recordings first published before 1923, the additional time period ends on December 31, 2021.

• For recordings first published between 1923-1946, the additional time period is 5 years after the general 95-year term.

• For recordings first published between 1947-1956, the additional time period is 15 years after the general 95-year term.

• For all remaining recordings first fixed prior to February 15, 1972, the additional transition period shall end on February 15, 2067.[81]

These new additional time periods listed above relate only to the *Sound Recordings*.

The length of the copyright in the *Musical Composition* are based on the following time periods.

(a)   Works Created before January 1, 1964.

To get a copyright for a Musical Composition, you needed to register or publish the work. Any work by a U.S. national published or registered before January 1, 1964, must have been renewed by an application for registration in the 28th year following the original date of publication or registration to continue its term of protection. It is important to note that there may be a difference regarding whether the "registration" date or the "publication" date control. Make sure to confirm which date is used in the particular Circuit that you filed the litigation.

(b)   Works Created Between January 1, 1964, and December 31, 1977.

To get a copyright, you needed to register or publish the work. Copyrights in works registered or published between January 1,1964, and December 31, 1977, have an automatic renewal for a full 95-year term of protection. But an initial filing still must have been submitted to the Copyright Office.

(c)   Works Created on or after January 1, 1978

Under the 1976 Code, on or after January 1, 1978, a copyright automatically comes into existence upon a work being created and fixed in a tangible medium of expression.

The duration of the Copyright is from the moment of its creation and lasts for the author's life, plus an additional 70 years.[82] Regarding Joint Works – the term is the life of the last surviving author, and 70 years after such last surviving author's death. And for Anonymous Works, Pseudonymous Works, and Works Made for Hire - a term of 95 years from the year of its first publication, or a term of 120 years from the year of its creation, whichever expires first.[83]

Termination.

Section 203

Songwriters, and all artists in general, need to be aware of the tremendous power and benefits of Section 203. It reads:

> **§ 203. Termination of transfers and licenses granted by the author.**
>
> (a) CONDITIONS FOR TERMINATION. — In the case of any work other than a work made for hire, the exclusive or nonexclusive grant of a transfer or license of Copyright or of any right under a Copyright, executed by the author on or after January 1, 1978, otherwise than by will, is subject to termination under the following conditions:
>
> (1) In the case of a grant executed by one author, *termination of the grant may be effected*

by that author or, if the author is dead, by the person or persons who, under clause (2) of this subsection, own and are entitled to exercise a total of more than one-half of that author's termination interest. In the case of a grant executed by two or more authors of a joint work, termination of the grant *may be effected by a majority of the authors who executed it;* if any of such authors are dead, the termination interest of any such author may be exercised as a unit by the person or persons who, under clause (2) of this subsection, own and are entitled to exercise a total of more than one-half of that author's interest.

Section 203 only applies to works created on or after January 1, 1978. In sum, ***after a period of 35 years, the original copyright holder can terminate the grant of its material to a third-party***. On January 1, 2013, the first termination rights matured. Authors filed notices for the musical works behind enduring songs like Charlie Daniels' "The Devil Went Down to Georgia," Pat Benatar's "Hit Me with Your Best Shot," Tom Petty's "Refugee," Steven Greenberg's "Funkytown," and Gary Morris' "The Wind Beneath My Wings."[84] Additionally, Bob Dylan, Bryan Adams, Loretta Lynn, Kris Kristofferson, and Tom Waits have also filed termination notices for songs written soon after the effective date of Section 203.[85]

A major legal landmark was established when the songwriters of "YMCA" got their rights to the song back. [86] That is no little matter - a song like YMCA can generate hundreds of thousands of dollars a year in royalties. Imagine what will happen when "Thriller" is eligible for termination.

As mentioned above, if the work is deemed a "work-for-hire," § 203 is not available to the original author of the work, and in some artistic fields such as motion pictures, the effect on licensees may not be too drastic. However, in the universe of music, where the "work-for-hire" concept has found little if any traction, such termination rights create the ability for a songwriter to have a "second bite at the apple."

To effect the termination, the copyright holder must follow §§ 203(3) and (4):

> (3) Termination of the grant *may be effected at any time during a period of five years beginning at the end of thirty-five years from the date of execution of the grant*; or, if the grant covers the right of publication of the work, the period begins at the end of thirty-five years from the date of publication of the work under the grant or at the end of forty years from the date of execution of the grant, whichever term ends earlier (emphasis added).

> (4) The *termination shall be effected* by serving an *advance notice in writing*, signed by the number and proportion of owners of termination interests required under clauses (1) and (2) of this subsection, or by their duly authorized agents, upon the grantee or the grantee's successor in title.

> (A) The notice *shall state the effective date of the termination*, which shall fall within the five-year period specified by clause (3) of this subsection, and the *notice shall be served not less than two or more than ten years before that date.* A copy of the notice shall be recorded in the Copyright Office before the effective date of termination, as a condition to its taking effect

(emphasis added).

(B) The notice shall comply, in form, content, and manner of service, with requirements that the Register of Copyrights shall prescribe by regulation.

There are two important periods to keep in mind to execute the termination: (i) when the termination is effective; and (ii) when to give notice of the termination.

Pursuant to Clause (3)(A), the *effective date* of the termination must be within a five-year window, beginning 35 years after the date of the grant. For example, if the grant was made on January 1, 1980, the copyright holder would be able to give a termination date in the notice of anywhere from January 1, 2015, up to January 1, 2020.

Pursuant to Clause (4)(A), the notice shall be served not less than two or more than ten years before that date. So, the notice with a termination date of January 1, 2015, could be sent as early as January 1, 2005 (ten years prior) and as late as January 1, 2013 (two years prior).

Section 203 is a huge benefit for copyright holders who may have provided grants before the real value of their music was known. It is certain to spawn litigation as the record companies fight like the dickens to retain their valuable Copyrights in recordings.

Section 304

Sir Paul McCartney has opened a new front in the battle for composers to get the rights back to their music. Sir Paul's attack centers on the rights found in Section 304 of the Copyright Act. This section is different than the rights under Section 203.

For songs that are in their initial or renewal period *prior* to January 1, 1978, Section 304(c) allows songwriters to terminate grants after a period of fifty-six (56) years.

§304(c) reads:

Termination of Transfers and Licenses Covering Extended Renewal Term.—In the case of any copyright subsisting in either its first or renewal term on January 1, 1978, other than a copyright in a work made for hire, the exclusive or nonexclusive grant of a transfer or license of the renewal copyright or any right under it, executed before January 1, 1978, by any of the persons designated by subsection (a)(1)(C) of this section, otherwise than by will, is subject to termination under the following conditions . . . .

To effect the termination, Section 304(c)(3) states:

(3) Termination of the grant may be effected at any time during a period of five years beginning at the end of fifty-six years from the date copyright was originally secured, or beginning on January 1, 1978, whichever is later.

McCartney is trying to regain the rights to a long list of The Beatles' hits that he either wrote or co-wrote with John Lennon. He argues that the 1976 Copyright Act should allow him to start reclaiming ownership of the songs from Sony/ATV.[87]

There is a convoluted history regarding the catalog of the early Beatles' songs. Sony and entertainer Michael Jackson formed Sony/ATV in 1995, a decade after the King of Pop paid over $40 million to acquire the ATV catalog, which included many Beatles songs. Jackson outbid McCartney to clinch the deal.[88] Sony took full control of Sony/ATV after Michael Jackson's estate agreed to sell its 50% stake for $750 million.

In 2008, McCartney began sending Sony/ATV "termination notices" that would start taking effect on Oct. 5, 2018. The first song on the list is "Love Me Do."[89] In order to avoid costly litigation, the parties settled, and McCartney regained the rights to "Love Me Do." As any of The Beatles' songs become available for termination, he is reclaiming the rights to his songs.[90]

But there is a twist to the story that can create some complications. Duran Duran attempted to file termination notices in England based upon the United States Copyright Code. However, the English court denied Duran Duran's claim reasoning it to be a breach of contract.

Strategically, McCartney brought his case in the American court of the Southern District Court of New York (remember any and all claims under copyright are only heard in a Federal Court.) In June of 2017, Sony/ATV and McCartney settled the dispute.

> The parties have resolved this matter by entering into a confidential settlement agreement and jointly request that the Court enter the enclosed proposed order dismissing the above-referenced action without prejudice," writes McCartney attorney Michael Jacobs in a . . . letter to U.S. District Judge Edgardo Ramos.[91]

The details of the deal are unclear, but the order specifies that the New York federal court will "enforce the terms of the parties' Settlement Agreement, should a dispute arise."[92]

Fair Use.

Although the government wants to promote creative expression, there are situations where the absolute monopoly given to a copyright holder hinders the dissemination of information for the public good. The biggest such exception is the doctrine of "Fair Use."

§ 107. Limitations on exclusive rights: Fair Use·

Notwithstanding the provisions of sections 106 and 106A, the fair use of a copyrighted work, including such use by reproduction in copies or phonorecords or by any other means specified by that section, for purposes such as criticism, comment, news reporting, teaching (including multiple copies for classroom use), scholarship, or research, is not an infringement of Copyright. In determining whether the use made of a work in any particular case is a fair use the factors to be considered shall include—

(1)   The purpose and character of the use, including whether such use is of a commercial nature or is for nonprofit educational purposes;

(2)   The nature of the copyrighted work;

(3)   The amount and substantiality of the portion used in relation to the copyrighted work as a whole; and

(4)   The effect of the use upon the potential market for or value of the copyrighted work.

> The fact that a work is unpublished shall not itself bar a finding of fair use if such finding is made upon consideration of all the above factors.

Another factor that has been created by case law is whether the user acted in "good faith" in trying to meet the factors.[93]

For musicians, "fair use" most commonly arises in areas such as "sampling" and "mash-ups." *Sampling* is the use of a pre-existing track in the track of original music.[94] A *"mash-up"* is a song or Musical Composition created by blending two or more pre-recorded songs.[95] An informative article regarding sample clearances is found at BeatStars (www.beatstars.com). A beatmaker will create a BeatStars account, pay a subscription fee and upload their Beats (aka Samples) for the public to license. As part of their service, BeatStars provide their subscribers (beatmakers) with a License Template. The Template allows the beatmaker to modify the Template as to personalize their particular terms (such as: on a non-exclusive basis, an exclusive basis or possibly a complete purchase of copyright(s)).[96]

Under the fair use doctrine, such Musical Compositions *may* be protected but it must be on the plus side of the four factors listed above. If that occurs, the author of the original Musical Composition is out of luck. Each factor receives equal weight and no one factor will prove positive or dispositive of the issue.[97] *Sampling* receives a much stricter review than *parody* - and *parody* is different than *satire.*

Parody is defined as: (i) a literary or musical work in which the style of an author or work is closely imitated for comic effect or in ridicule; (2) a feeble or ridiculous imitation."[98] *Satire* is defined as "a way of using humor to show that someone or something is foolish, weak, bad, etc.; humor that shows the weaknesses or bad qualities of a person, government, society, etc."[99] Parody may fall under the doctrine of "fair use," whereas satire generally does not gain protection.

The seminal case is *Campbell v. Acuff-Rose Music*.[100] The rap group 2 Live Crew used the Roy Orbison hit *"Pretty Woman"* as the source of a parody about hairy women and the singer's attraction to them. The Supreme Court held that parody is protected under the "fair use" doctrine.[101] Importantly, the Supreme Court also stressed that the lower court had erred in giving more weight to the first factor than to the other three.[102]

The Court stressed that parody needs the underlying work to make its point.

> Parody needs to mimic an original to make its point, and so has some claim to use the creation of its victim's (or collective victims') imagination, whereas satire can stand on its own two feet and so requires justification for the very act of borrowing. See Ibid.; Bisceglia, Parody and Copyright Protection: Turning the Balancing Act Into a Juggling Act, in ASCAP, Copyright Law Symposium, No. 34, p. 25 (1987).[103]

The first factor, **the purpose of the use,** is whether the previously copyrighted material is being used to help create something new, or is it merely copied verbatim into another work. When taking portions of copyrighted work, ask the following questions:

1. Has the material you have taken from the original work been transformed by adding new expression or meaning?

2. Was value added to the original by creating new information, new

aesthetics, new insights, and understandings?[104]

Education is an area that the courts will allow a broad grant of use of copyrighted material - a not-for-profit entity that wants to use music, photos, or footage that shows the effects of a drought is given much more leeway than a producer who wants to use the footage as "b" roll in her next big-budget blockbuster.

The second factor, **the nature of the copyrighted work,** addresses the nature of the previously copyrighted work being used: the old work should help the new work aid in the dissemination of facts or information that benefits the public. Thus, a person has more leeway to copy from factual works such as biographies than from fictional works such as plays or novels. Similarly, the new work would have greater protection if the material copied is material from a published work rather than an unpublished work - an author has the greater right to control the first public appearance of his or her expression.[105]

The third factor, **the amount and substantiality used,** addresses how much of the underlying copyrighted material is being used. Simply, the more you take, the less your protection. Mashups start to fail here since they use a substantial portion of any underlying song without any new redeeming value. Parody gets a freer hand.

The less you take, the more likely it is that your copying will be deemed fair use. However, this is *not* a hard and fast rule. If you take the very heart of a song, protection will be weak. For example, it would probably not be a "fair use" to copy the opening guitar riff and the words "I can't get no satisfaction" from the song "Satisfaction" (but a Mechanical License, which will be discussed in greater depth below, may allow you to make your own version of "Satisfaction").[106]

The rule - less is more - is not necessarily true in parody

cases. A parodist may borrow quite a bit, even the heart of the original work, to conjure up the original work.[107] That is because, as the Supreme Court has acknowledged, "The heart is also what most readily conjures up the [original] for parody, and it is the heart at which parody takes aim."[108]

That factor is one of several reasons why separate Copyrights should be filed on the Musical Composition and the Sound Recording of a band/artist song. What if another artist copied one hundred percent of the lyrics to a song, and created completely different music? Or vice versa, like Weird Al Yankovic. If you assert infringement of a Copyright containing the Sound Recording, only fifty percent of the total has been copied. If you assert the Copyright containing only the lyrics, one hundred percent of the copyrighted material has been infringed! This can make a big difference on the issue of infringement and damages.

The fourth factor, **the effect of the use on the market,** concerns whether the use deprives the Copyright owner of income or undermines a new or potential market for the copyrighted work. In Rogers v. Koons, 960 F.2d 301 (2d Cir. 1992), an artist used a copyrighted photograph without permission as the basis for wood sculptures and used all the elements of the photo in the sculpture.

After the photographer sued, the artist argued his sculptures were a fair use because the photographer would never have considered making sculptures. The court disagreed, stating that it did not matter whether the photographer had considered making sculptures; what mattered was that a potential market for sculptures of the photograph existed.[109]

Again, *Parody* is given a slightly different fair use analysis in regard to the impact on the market. It is possible that a parody may diminish or even destroy the market value of the original work - the parody may be so good that the public can never take the original work seriously again.[110] It is not the same type of loss as when an infringer merely appropriates the work. As one judge explained, "The economic effect of a parody with which we are concerned is not its potential to destroy or diminish the market for the original—any bad review can have that effect—but whether it fulfills the demand for the original." (*Fisher v. Dees*, 794 F.2d 432 (9th Cir. 1986).[111]

In short, fair use is a great tool for songwriters but it must be used carefully and judiciously. Not all use is fair use, and a use that would otherwise fail the four factors cannot be transformed into "fair" merely by taking remedial measures - for example, acknowledging the source material (giving credit to the original songwriter whose lyrics were taken) or using a disclaimer stating that you are not associated with or licensed by the original songwriter. These factors might in some small part weigh against finding non-fair use, but in and of themselves they will not "save" an otherwise infringing use.

The Creative Commons

A second source of copyrighted material that can be used for free is the Creative Commons. The Creative Commons is an organization that allows copyright holders to *voluntarily* put their material into the public domain. However, there are restrictions on what and how to use material through the Creative Commons.

There are six different license types, listed from the most to the least permissive:

(i)   CC BY: This license allows re-users to distribute, remix, adapt, and build upon the material in any medium or format, so long as attribution is given to the creator. The license allows for commercial use.

(ii)   CC BY includes the following elements:
-     BY – Credit must be given to the creator.

(iii)   <u>CC BY-SA</u>: This license allows re-users to distribute, remix, adapt, and build upon the material in any medium or format, so long as attribution is given to the creator. The license allows for commercial use. If you remix, adapt, or build upon the material, you must license the modified material under identical terms. It includes the following elements:
-     BY – Credit must be given to the creator.
-     SA – Adaptations must be shared under the same terms.

(iv)   <u>CC BY-NC</u>: This license allows re-users to distribute, remix, adapt, and build upon the material in any medium or format for noncommercial purposes only, and only so long as attribution is given to the creator. It includes the following elements:
-     BY – Credit must be given to the creator.
-     NC – Only noncommercial uses of the work are permitted.

(v)   <u>CC BY-NC-SA</u>: This license allows reusers to distribute, remix, adapt, and build upon the material in any medium or format for noncommercial purposes only, and only so long as attribution is given to the creator. If you remix, adapt, or build upon the material, you must license the modified material under identical terms. It includes the following elements:
-     BY – Credit must be given to the creator.
-     NC - Only noncommercial uses of the

work are permitted.

- SA - Adaptations must be shared under the same terms.

(vi) <u>CC BY-ND</u>: This license allows reusers to copy and distribute the material in any medium or format in unadapted form only, and only so long as attribution is given to the creator. The license allows for commercial use. It includes the following elements:
- BY– Credit must be given to the creator.
- ND – No derivatives or adaptations of the work are permitted.

(vii) <u>CC BY-NC-ND</u>: This license allows re-users to copy and distribute the material in any medium or format in un-adapted form only, for noncommercial purposes only, and only so long as attribution is given to the creator. It includes the following elements:
- BY – Credit must be given to the creator.
- NC – Only noncommercial uses of the work are permitted.
- ND – No derivatives or adaptations of the work are permitted.[112]

What Happens When the Term Expires – the Public Domain

When all copyright protection has expired, the work goes into the "Public Domain." "[C]opyright law . . . grants the public the right to copy without attribution once a copyright has expired, e. g., *Sears, Roebuck & Co. v. Stiffel Co.*, 376 U. S. 225,

230; *Daystar Corp. v. Twentieth Century Fox Film Corp., et al,* 539 U.S. 23 (2003).

This means:

- Nobody can ever own this work again; and

- Anybody can use the work without having to pay royalties (since nobody owns it anymore).

Examples of things that are in the Public Domain include:

(1) The duration of copyright in the work has expired;

(2) The work was produced by the U.S. federal government; or

(3) The work isn't fixed in a tangible form.[113]

Also, be aware that attempting to create a copyright in a piece of music that is in the public domain, that also contains a new piece of music, will not work. The copyright in the new work only extends to the new work, *not* to the work that was in the public domain.

The adaptation of a work in the public domain may have copyright protection for its own original additions but not for the underlying work in the public domain. Adaptations, translations, amended versions, and annotated versions are examples of source material that might be in the Public Domain.[114] As mentioned above, "[i]n the case of a derivative work based on an underlying work that is in the public domain, only the material added to the underlying work is protected by copyright." *NYC Image Int'l, Inc. v. RS U.S., Inc.* (S.D. N.Y. 2020); *Waldman Publ. Corp.,* 43 F.3d at 782.

For example, Shakespeare's "Romeo and Juliet" is in the public domain, but a new version with annotations or illustrations may have copyright protection in these new parts of the work. Copyright protection does not extend to "scenes a faire," or devices, elements, or sequences of events that "necessarily result from the choice of a setting or situation." *NYC Image Int'l, Inc. v. RS U.S., Inc. (S.D. N.Y. 2020)*, *Williams v. Crichton,* 84 F.3d 581, 587 (2d Cir. 1996) (internal quotation marks omitted); *See* also *MyWebGrocer, LLC v. Hometown Info, Inc.*, 375 F.3d 190, 194 (2d Cir. 2004) (scenes a faire are "unprotectible elements that follow naturally from a work's theme rather than from an author's creativity").[115]

All terms of copyright run through the end of the calendar year in which they would otherwise expire, so a work enters the public domain on the first of the year following the expiration of its copyright term. For example, a book published on March 15, 1925, will enter the public domain on January 1, 2021, not March 16, 2020 (1925+95=2020). It is important to be aware that different countries have different copyright terms, so be careful of using material from other countries that might still be under copyright protection.

In January of 2019, for the first time in twenty years (remember the Sony Bono Copyright Term Extension Act added a flat twenty years to the term of copyright), published works began to enter into the public domain. Also, the enactment of the Orrin G. Hatch-Bob Goodlatte Music Modernization Act in 2018 radically changed the calculus for pre-1972 published Sound Recordings. As of the beginning of 2020, George Gershwin's *Musical Composition* of "Rhapsody in Blue" went into the Public Domain. But the particular *Sound Recording* of the Musical Composition may not be in the public domain. So be careful in using the Musical Composition versus the Sound Recording.

Infringement.

It is important for an artist always to be aware of what constitutes Copyright infringement - both to avoid doing it and to prevent others from doing it to you. Chapter 5 of the Copyright Code addresses infringement.[116]

To prove infringement the copyright holder must prove two things: (i) the plaintiff owns the Copyright or Copyrights at issue[iii]; and (ii) the third-party infringed the Copyrights by unauthorized copying or distribution.[117] If the plaintiff cannot provide direct evidence of copying, the second element can be satisfied with facts showing that defendant had *"access"* to the plaintiff's work and that the two works are *"substantially similar."*[118]

The Ninth Circuit confirmed in *Antonick v. Elec. Arts, Inc.*, 841 F.3d 1062 (9th Cir. 2016), that a court should employ a two-part test for determining whether one work is substantially similar to another: (i) The *"extrinsic test"* is an "objective comparison of specific expressive elements." The *"intrinsic test"* is "a subjective comparison that focuses on whether the ordinary, reasonable audience would find the works substantially similar in the total concept and feel of the works."[119]

As mentioned above, you do not need to file an actual Copyright application for your Copyright to come into existence. *However,* you *must* file with the Copyright Office if you want "standing," *i.e.*, the ability of bringing a lawsuit to protect your property.

Also, and this is very important, if you have filed the

[iii] When citing court cases, the book will generally cite cases from the jurisdictions that encompass New York City, New York and Los Angeles, California. The reason is that these two cities and the attendant jurisdictions are the center of the entertainment industry in the United States.

Copyright, you do not have to prove that you were damaged by the infringer's actions.[120] Statutory damages will kick in, which can be substantial. The minimum amount in damages is $750.00 per work, and the court has the discretion to go up to $30,000.00 per work.[121] Furthermore, if the court finds that the infringement was *"willful"*, it can raise the award up to $150,000.00 per work.[122] But as stated above, if you do not have a registered federal Copyright, you have no right to these statutory damages.

The moral of the story is, *always file for your Copyright, and do it sooner rather than later!*

The "Blurred Lines" Decision

Recently, a federal jury seated in the U.S. District Court in Los Angeles handed down a $7.4 million verdict against Robin Thicke, Pharrell Williams, and Clifford Harris, Jr. regarding their song "Blurred Lines."

Ironically, Thicke, Williams, and Harris had filed a preemptive suit against the Marvin Gaye estate in a California court, seeking a ruling to establish that "Blurred Lines" does not plagiarize Gaye's 1977 song, "Got to Give It Up." (*Williams v. Bridgeport Music, Inc.*, CV13-6004-JAK). The heirs of Marvin Gaye then filed their lawsuit claiming that "Blurred Lines" did improperly infringe on "Got to Give It Up."

The jury found for The Gaye Estate. It will receive $1.7 million from Thicke and $1.6 million from Williams and an additional $4 million in punitive damages (Harris had been dismissed from the suit on appeal). As important, the Gaye Estate gained an injunction to prevent the song from being played or any distribution of the song, which gave them leverage to negotiate royalties going forward.

After playing the two songs back-to-back, it is clear the jury was wrong in its decision. There is certainly a similarity in the "feel" of the song. And that seems to be where the jury hung its hat. However, a "feel" or a "style" is not protected under copyright law.

As R. J. Lehmann comments,

The two songs are quite dissimilar in their construction. "Blurred Lines" is in the key of G and its basic chord progression over eight bars is GGGGDDDD. "Got to Give It Up" is in the key of A, and its progression is basically just AAAAAAAA. They're both 4/4 at 120 beats per minute, but that's true of an overwhelming proportion of the popular canon, as well.

The lyrics don't betray any obvious similarities, either. Gaye's song tells the story of a former wallflower who learns to dance and have fun at parties. Thicke's is a notoriously "rapey" ode to a woman who, the singer believes, enjoys rough sex.[123]

As many have commented, the reasoning of the jury is not supported by copyright law. In major cases in the past, such as when George Harrison was found guilty of infringement with "My Sweet Lord" from the Chiffons' "He's So Fine," there was a clear similarity between the two Musical Compositions. As seen above, that is not the case here.

And yet the appeals court has upheld it. The Ninth Circuit has refused to rehear the case *en banc*, though it has issued a slightly amended opinion, removing a single paragraph concerning the "inverse ratio rule" of whether or not greater access to a song means you don't have to show as much "substantial similarity."[124]

The case has the potential for creating real chaos in the music industry with a chilling effect on songwriters because they will feel threatened that a sound that has the same "feel" could open them up to potential copyright claims. Copyright law is not meant to protect "style." If so, Bo Diddley is owed money by thousands of musicians who copied his distinctive rhythmic style. As Kal Raustiala and Christopher Jon Sprigman of Slate comment, "The 'Blurred Lines' verdict may end up cutting off a vital wellspring of creativity in music—that of making great new songs that pay homage to older classics."[125]

Infringement in Digital Transmissions.

The area of digital transmissions is a hotbed for litigation. Beginning with Napster, through Grokster, and into LimeWire, the owners of copyrighted material have fought the encroachment of digital downloads ferociously. A very important case in this area is *UMG Recordings, Inc. v. Shelter Capital Partners LLC.*[126] In the case, Universal Music Group **("UMG")** filed suit against Veoh, a self-publishing video service like YouTube, for direct and secondary Copyright infringement. In the past, users of Veoh's service had been able, without UMG's authorization, to download videos containing songs for which UMG owned a Copyright.

The case originated with a claim by UMG that Veoh was infringing on its Copyrights. The district court granted summary judgment to Veoh after determining that it was protected by the Digital Millennium Copyright Act **("DMCA")**, 17 U.S.C. § 512(c). That clause provides a "safe harbor" for service providers and limits their liability for "infringement of Copyright by reason of the storage at the direction of a user of material that resides on a system or network controlled or operated by or for the service provider."

The Court of Appeals for the Ninth Circuit (which

includes California) affirmed the district court's determination on summary judgment that Veoh was entitled to section 512(c) safe harbor protection. The Appellate Court also affirmed the district court's dismissal of the claims of secondary liability against the Investor Defendants.[127] Even though held to be engaged in a legal activity, the cost of the litigation drove Veoh out of business.

Since technology will continue to change, the revenue streams will constantly change. When the revenue streams change, stakeholders will always scramble to make sure they get their share.

It is important to keep in mind, with the proliferation of websites created by musicians, that a person who hosts a website can be liable for contributory infringement.[128] However, as mentioned above, certain "safe harbors" are provided for internet service providers (**an "ISP"**). The four safe harbors provided by Congress, in the following subsections of Section 512 are:

1. Transitory digital network communications;

2. System caching;

3. Information residing on systems or networks at the direction of users; and

4. Information location tools.[129]

The safe harbors are not absolute but if you qualify your liability is greatly reduced or eliminated. Many elements must be met to qualify for a safe harbor. Among them are:

1.	You must be a "service provider" (**an "ISP"**);

2.	The ISP needs to designate an agent to receive notification of claimed infringement from a Copyright owner and register that agent with the Copyright Office;

3.	If there is infringing material on site, the ISP cannot have actual knowledge that the material is infringing;

4.	Also, the ISP must not be aware of facts or circumstances from which the infringing activity is apparent;

5.	If it gets notice or knowledge, the ISP must act "expeditiously" to remove or disable access to the infringing material; and

6.	The ISP cannot have received a financial benefit directly attributable to the infringing activity, if the ISP has the right and ability to control such activity.[130]

So, when starting a website for the band/artist, consider limiting the ability of third parties to post information or content. Additionally, consider using safeguards: there is technology out there that, if used properly, makes it more difficult to copy photographs or music from a website. If all else fails, have an attorney send a powerfully worded cease-and-desist letter to a website infringer demanding removal and retroactive license payments - and threaten to send a DMCA notice to the website's ISP if the infringer does not comply.

Because the website's ISP is motivated to avoid liability, upon being notified of a possible infringement they will take the infringing website offline - either the offending sub-page or perhaps the full site. If the infringing work is on a prominent enough location on the site, such a move could be damaging to the infringer.

Conclusion.

EVERY creative person, including songwriters, needs to be aware of the protections afforded by the Copyright Act. If not, a composer can inadvertently lose millions of dollars. Spend the fee and get protected!

CHAPTER 3

TRADEMARK

"Use It or Lose It!"
\- General Rule

In the Middle Ages, local trade guilds began using marks to identify the source and content of their products.[131] Other notable trademarks used for an extraordinarily long time include Stella Artois, which claims use of its mark since 1366[132], and Löwenbräu, which claims use of its lion mark since 1383.[133] As the marks became well-known, they became valuable. The holders of the marks then grew concerned as people began to infringe on the mark (although it wasn't called that yet).

Britain established a Trademark statute in 1875 and the office that administered the new act opened on January 1, 1876. In a story that may be apocryphal, an employee from Bass Brewery, then the largest brewery in the world (with over a million barrels sold annually) queued himself in line the day before the office opened and camped there overnight (much like many concertgoers would in the future.) When the office opened the next morning, the employee was the first to register a Trademark - the Bass Red Triangle for the company's pale ale.[134]

Differences Between Copyright and Trademark.

Copyright and Trademark law are both critical to protecting the interests of a brand for a performer or a band/artist. But they are *vastly different* as to purpose and scope. They are complementary to each other - the yin and the yang, each playing its own distinct role. Copyright protects your artistic expression, (*e.g.,* the song, the film, or the book). However, the actual title of the film, song, or book cannot be copyrighted. Trademark law steps in and protects the brand in the stream of commerce. For example, there can be two songs entitled "Blowing in The Wind" as long as they have different subject matter. Woody Guthrie may write one about the Oklahoma Dust Bowl, and Bob Dylan could write one about civil disturbance. What sets the two apart is the look and style of the album cover, the font, and the cover art – the Trademark and the Trade Dress. The album cover of Woody Guthrie's song cannot mimic the cover art of Bob Dylan's album, and vice versa.

What is the reason for the differences between Copyright and Trademark? The reason is that each serves a different purpose. The "policy considerations" underlying Copyright are to promote the arts and sciences because it brings many economic and cultural benefits to society. The "policy considerations" underlying Trademark are to identify the source of goods and services in the stream of commerce to promote accurate identification so that society can reward good providers and penalize bad providers.

So, there are numerous differences between Copyright and Trademark, some of which are listed below.

Cost and Process: *Copyrights* are inexpensive. The application fees can range from $45.00 to $125.00, and it is a one-time cost. Most of the time, the application is automatically granted resulting in a Copyright registration. In other words, the U.S. Copyright Office is not going to send multi-page back-and-forth legal briefs arguing why the subject matter at issue is not copyrightable and ask the applicant or their attorney to respond accordingly.

By contrast, *Trademarks* are more time-consuming and expensive. As of early 2022, the fee for an initial application for the mark ranges from $250.00 - $350.00. Go to http://www.uspto.gov/teas for more information.

Goods and services are sorted into "International Classes," and each International Class above the first one requires a separate filing fee. There are 45 "International Classes," each with a large number of subclasses of goods and services to choose from. International Classes 1-34 cover goods, while International Classes 35-45 cover services. You can list as many of the subclasses as you want within each International Class without extra cost; however, because each Class adds another $250-$350 to electronic filings, filing fees can quickly approach two thousand dollars.

For example, Class 9 encompasses instruments for recording, transmission or reproduction of sound or images. Some subclasses are "series of pre-recorded video and audio cassettes, and a series of pre-recorded phonograph records and compact discs featuring musical performances," and "downloadable music files." By contrast, Class 15 covers musical instruments and has an extensive selection of subclasses corresponding with various types of instruments. Class 16 covers paper goods and printed matter, and includes subclasses that cover posters, tour books relating to musical performances, and concert programs, stickers, and decals. On the services side, for example, Class 41 covers entertainment as well as sporting and cultural activities, education, and providing training.

Currently, there are two types of TEAS filings: TEAS Plus, and TEAS Regular. **TEAS Plus**, at $250 per class, offers the lowest filing fee but is the most cookie-cutter, with less personalization. In a TEAS Plus application:

1. You are largely limited to the pre-set subclasses listed in the USPTO Trademark ID manual for each International Classification and cannot author your own.

2. You must commit to certain statements regarding the mark, if applicable (claim of ownership, color claim and description). Often times these are not an issue, as these sub-listings within International Classifications are extensive, and you can usually find multiple listings that correspond with the goods and services at issue.

3.   All of the costs are to be paid up-front, most notably the cost for any International Classifications over and above the first one.

4.   The USPTO must be able to send correspondence to you by e-mail concerning the application, throughout the process, and certain filings must be done electronically as well.

If you have an easily classified good or service and are only filing for one International Classification, a TEAS Plus application is often the best option. Sub-listings within International Classifications are extensive, and you can usually find multiple listings that correspond to the goods and services at issue.

The second application process is the **TEAS Standard** ($350/class) application. With TEAS Standard you pay one application filing fee with your initial application and the rest later in the process. And you can write the description of your goods and services (rather than use the cookie-cutter descriptions provided by the USPTO), but it's still essential to accurately describe your goods and services. TEAS Standard is more commonly used when the goods and services covered by the mark are atypical, and not covered by the extensive sub-descriptions provided by the USPTO. Note that the USPTO is constantly updating its descriptions to refine existing ones and add more to account for emerging technologies and other developments.

In addition to the application fees, there are also the attorneys' fees for the preliminary "clearance" of the mark (running searches on the USPTO database and to otherwise determine whether there are obvious conflicting marks out there) as well as for completing and "prosecuting" the application. Some applicants are lucky - the Trademark Office Examiner assigned to the application may find no objection to the mark and place it on the fast track to official registration. When that happens, the mark is "published" for a short period of 30 days (to give anyone in the public a chance to contest it), and only minimal fees remain.

However, if the Examiner determines that potentially confusing marks exist, and then issues what is termed an "Office Action" - a legal brief of sorts - making a reasoned argument as to why it would be inappropriate to grant the application for the mark, a response is needed to keep the application alive. An Office Action requires the attorney to respond with a similar legal and factual argument to the contrary to keep the application alive and give it a chance to obtain approval and mature into a registered Trademark. Sometimes, the Examiner will agree and grant the registration; other times, more back-and-forth is required. Thus, in cases with Office Actions and responses, attorneys' fees can easily climb to four or five figures over the course of a year or two. Even then, it is possible that the Examiner will not be swayed, and the mark will never be approved for registration.

Use: With Copyrights (at least for works created on or after January 1, 1978), once you have it, you do not need to do anything to preserve your rights. You can put the song on the shelf, and you never need to use it. Trademark is drastically different - you will not get onto the Registrar of Trademarks until you have used the mark and established it in the stream of commerce.

Length of Protection: With Copyright, once you receive the Certificate of Registration, the length of the Copyright for works created after January 1, 1978, is the life of the author plus 70 additional years. In the case of an anonymous work or a corporation's rights, which will arise in the context of "work for hire," the length of the Copyright is 95 years from the year of first publication or 120 years from the year of its creation, whichever expires first. (However, the length of protection for works first published before 1978 depends on different factors). And, except under special circumstances found in § 203 or § 304, nothing can take the Copyright away from you.

Trademarks are radically different. In general, the mark must be used in commerce, establish its prominence, protect its prominence once gained, and the owner must file statements of continued use accompanied by minor maintenance fees, at specific durations. This is because it is unfair to keep a mark out of the public domain if you are no longer using it. If you do not "monitor" the use of your mark, cease to use it, or allow others to infringe upon it without protest, you can lose the mark.

Copyright/Trademark Comparison Chart

Element	Copyright	Trademark
Cost:	$45.00 Filing, possibly up to $125.00; No further costs.	$250-$350 Filing Fee $250-$350 Filing Fee for Each Category. Further filing fees 1-2 times per decade.
Application Formalities:	File once online. Must upload the Deposit Copy.	File On-Line. Must up-load Deposit Copy.
Use:	Do not have to use once get Copyright protection.	MUST use in stream of commerce. File declaration of use every five (5) years. MUST police brand; if allow infringement can lose the mark.
Length of Protection:	Individuals: Life of the author plus 70 years. Corporation: if published, 90 years; if not published, 120 years.	Perpetual IF maintain use and protect the mark. If do not protect and use, can lose the use of the mark.

Subsequent Formalities:	No further formalities.	Must file Declaration of Use 1-2 times per decade.

Copyright protects the specific way you artistically express yourself - the Musical Composition, the Sound Recording which is the "wave form" of the Musical Composition, and the Phonorecord, such as a CD, a vinyl record or a digital file that contains the Sound Recording of the Musical Composition. Trademarks protect your logo, name, slogan, and your brand in the marketplace. When it comes to Copyrights, the rule is that you do not show anyone your work until you have filed. With Trademarks, however, you must use the mark in commerce before you will get protection.

So, what does Trademark cover and how do you protect it? In the United States, a *Trademark* is a brand name. A Trademark or *service mark* includes any word, name, symbol, device, or any combination, used or intended to be used to identify and distinguish the goods/services of one seller or provider from those of others, and to indicate the source of the goods/services. [135]

The U.S. Supreme Court summed up the purpose of Trademark Law in 1995 in the case of *Qualitex Co. v. Jacobson Products Co.*:

> [T]rademark law, by preventing others from copying a source-identifying mark, 'reduce[s] the customer's costs of shopping and making purchasing decisions,' for it quickly and easily assures a potential customer that … the item with this mark … is made by the same producer as other similarly marked items that he or she liked (or disliked) in the past. At the same time,

the law helps assure a producer that it (and not an imitating competitor) will reap the financial, reputation related rewards associated with a desirable product.[136]

First, it is important to note that the term **"Trademark"** is often used to refer to four different things: trademarks, service marks, trade names, and trade dress:

- A *Trademark* is a word, phrase, symbol, logo, slogan, design, or any combination thereof, that identifies and distinguishes the source of the goods of one party from those of others.

- A *Service mark* is a word, phrase, symbol, and/or design that identifies and distinguishes the source of a service rather than goods.

- A *Trade name* is the official or fictitious name under which a company does business. It is also known as a "doing business as" or "d/b/a" name. Trade names are often conflated with Trademarks because it is possible to use and register a trade name AS a Trademark - *i.e.,* use it in association with the goods as well as the company. Coca-Cola, for example, is famous for using its trade name in its Trademark.

- *Trade dress* is a product's physical appearance, including its size, shape, color, design, and texture. In addition to a product's physical appearance, trade dress may also refer to the manner in which a product is packaged, wrapped, labeled, presented, promoted, or advertised, including the use of distinctive graphics, configurations, and marketing strategies. It is the distinctive packaging containing the goods .

Marks do not have to be registered but, as with Copyright, there are significant advantages to doing so. By registering, the Trademark holder: (i) is giving notice to the public of its claim of ownership of the mark; (ii) has a legal presumption of ownership nationwide; and (iii) has the exclusive right to use the mark on or in connection with the goods or services set forth in the registration.[137] Trademarks can be registered at the state level and on the federal level. Whether it is more appropriate to register in one forum, or both, often depends on various factors such as the mark, where the goods and services are advertised and sold, and the expected zone of eventual geographic expansion.

On the state level, Trademark registration is simple and obtained by filling out a one-page form obtained from the website of the state's Secretary of State or other appropriate authority. Sometimes samples of the mark in use are required, but little else is needed. Unless an identical Trademark has already been filed, the user will likely receive the mark, which is then protected within that state only. However, because state Trademarks are so easily granted, the protection they provide is not strong. Moreover, federal registrations trump state registrations, so if someone else received a federal registration for the same mark, that registration will most likely supersede the state registration. It is possible, however, that the state filer might reserve the right to use the mark in that state only . . . *if* the owner of the federal mark has not and will not in the near future expand to that state.

On the federal level, the United States Patent and Trademark Office **(the "PTO")** is responsible for the review and issuance of Trademarks. There, unlike the Copyright Office or at the state level, the application process is more complicated and the level of review more stringent. Filing an application does not mean that one will actually receive the Trademark registration. Rather, the PTO conducts its own search for potentially conflicting marks, and it can often take several back-and-forth correspondences between the PTO Examiner for the application, and the party (and their counsel) filing the mark before the Examiner is convinced that the mark should be issued. Even if there are no conflicting marks, the PTO also looks at other factors, such as whether the mark is too descriptive or generic to be granted trademark protection. Even after some back-and-forth, the mark may still be considered too similar to other pre-existing marks, or too descriptive or commonplace, in which case the PTO Examiner will refuse to issue a registration or require the mark to be listed on the "supplemental" rather than "principal" registry for Trademarks - receiving some but not maximum protection.[138]

Ultimately, whether to file for one or more state registrations, for federal registration, or both, is something that depends on the goods, services, and company at issue.

𝄽 𝄽 𝄽 𝄽

What You Can't Trademark.

The Trademark statute lists items that cannot be trademarked. The statute lists the following items that will not receive trademark protection:

No trademark by which the goods of the applicant may be distinguished from the goods of others shall be refused registration on the principal register on account of its nature *unless* (emphasis added) it—

(a) Consists of or comprises immoral, deceptive, or *scandalous* (emphasis added) matter; or matter which may *disparage* (emphasis added) or falsely suggest a connection with persons, living or dead, institutions, beliefs, or national symbols, or bring them into contempt, or disrepute; or a geographical indication which, when used on or in connection with wines or spirits, identifies a place other than the origin of the goods and is first used on or in connection with wines or spirits by the applicant on or after one year after the date on which the WTO Agreement (as defined in section 3501(9) of title 19) enters into force with respect to the United States.

(b) Consists of or comprises the flag or coat of arms or other insignia of the United States, or of any State or municipality, or of any foreign nation, or any simulation thereof.

(c)   Consists of or comprises a name, portrait, or signature identifying a particular living individual except by his written consent, or the name, signature, or portrait of a deceased President of the United States during the life of his widow, if any, except by the written consent of the widow.

(d)   Consists of or comprises a mark which so resembles a mark registered in the Patent and Trademark Office, or a mark or trade name previously used in the United States by another and not abandoned, as to be likely, when used on or in connection with the goods of the applicant, to cause confusion, or to cause mistake, or to deceive: Provided, that if the Director determines that confusion, mistake, or deception is not likely to result from the continued use by more than one person of the same or similar marks under conditions and limitations as to the mode or place of use of the marks or the goods on or in connection with which such marks are used, concurrent registrations may be issued to such persons when they have become entitled to use such marks as a result of their concurrent lawful use in commerce prior to (1) the earliest of the filing dates of the applications pending or of any registration issued under this chapter; (2) July 5, 1947, in the case of registrations previously issued under the Act of March 3, 1881, or February 20, 1905, and continuing in full force and effect on that date; or (3) July 5, 1947, in the case of applications filed under the Act of February 20, 1905, and registered after July 5,

1947. Use prior to the filing date of any pending application or registration shall not be required when the owner of such application or registration consents to the grant of a concurrent registration to the applicant. Concurrent registrations may also be issued by the Director when a court of competent jurisdiction has finally determined that more than one person is entitled to use the same or similar marks in commerce. In issuing concurrent registrations, the Director shall prescribe conditions and limitations as to the mode or place of use of the mark or the goods on or in connection with which such mark is registered to the respective persons.

(e)   Consists of a mark which (1) when used on or in connection with the goods of the applicant is merely descriptive or deceptively misdescriptive of them, (2) when used on or in connection with the goods of the applicant is primarily geographically descriptive of them, except as indications of regional origin may be registrable under section 1054 of this title, (3) when used on or in connection with the goods of the applicant is primarily geographically deceptively misdescriptive of them, (4) is primarily merely a surname, or (5) comprises any matter that, as a whole, is functional.

(f)   Except as expressly excluded in subsections (a), (b), (c), (d), (e)(3), and (e)(5) of this section, nothing in this chapter shall prevent the registration of a mark used by the applicant which has become distinctive of the applicant's goods in commerce. The Director may accept as prima facie evidence that the mark has become distinctive, as used on or in connection with the applicant's goods in commerce, proof of substantially exclusive and continuous use thereof as a mark by the applicant in commerce for the five years before the date on which the claim of distinctiveness is made. Nothing in this section shall prevent the registration of a mark which, when used on or in connection with the goods of the applicant, is primarily geographically deceptively misdescriptive of them, and which became distinctive of the applicant's goods in commerce before December 8, 1993.[139]

Note, however, that two Supreme Courts cases have struck down portions of what cannot be trademarked due to conflicts with the First Amendment.

The first case is *Matal v. Tam*, 582 U. S. ——, 137 S.Ct. 1744, 198 L.Ed.2d 366 (2017). In this case, the Supreme Court held §15 U.S. Code § 1052(a), the Anti-Disparagement Clause, violated the First Amendment's Free Speech Clause. The Court found that the clause constituted impermissible viewpoint discrimination.[140]

In *Matal*, a dance-rock band's application for federal trademark registration of the band's name, *"The Slants,"* was rejected for being defamatory of people of Asian descent. The band was comprised of Asian–American musicians. The band members wanted to take the pejorative term as the name of their group, hoping to "reclaim" the term and drain its denigrating force.

To determine whether a trademark is disparaging, the PTO would apply a "two-part test": (i) The examiner first considers "the likely meaning of the matter in question, taking into account not only dictionary definitions, but also the relationship of the matter to the other elements in the mark, the nature of the goods or services, and the manner in which the mark is used in the marketplace in connection with the goods or services."[141]

Depending upon the decision on the first prong, the examiner will turn to the second part of the test: asking "whether that meaning may be disparaging to a substantial composite of the referenced group."[142]

After applying the two-part test, the PTO denied the application under the anti-disparagement clause. However, the Supreme Court overruled the PTO because the disparagement clause discriminated on the bases of "viewpoint." As a result, after analyzing the facts in light of the First Amendment, the Court held:

> "The Patent and Trademark Office (PTO) denied the application based on a provision of federal law prohibiting the registration of trademarks that may "disparage ... or bring ... into contemp[t] or disrepute" any "persons, living or dead." 15 U.S.C. § 1052(a). *We now hold that this provision violates the Free Speech Clause of the First Amendment. It offends a bedrock First Amendment principle: Speech may not be banned on the ground that it expresses ideas that offend."* (emphasis added)[143]

To summarize, the case held that: (i) if a trademark registration bar is viewpoint-based, it is unconstitutional; and, (2) the disparagement bar was viewpoint-based.

The second case is *Iancu v. Brunetti*, No. 18–302, 588

U.S. ___ (2019). In this case the Supreme Court held that the bar on registering "immoral or scandalous" marks is an unconstitutional restriction of free speech.[144]

In *Brunetti*, a clothing designer had a shirt that used the word "fuct." The proposed mark invoked another of the Lanham Act's prohibitions on registration: marks that "[c]onsist[ ] of or comprise[ ] immoral[ ] or scandalous matter." § 1052(a).[145] The PTO applies that bar as a "unitary provision," rather than treating the two adjectives in it separately.[146]

As the Supreme Court states, "To determine whether a mark fits in the category, the PTO asks whether a "substantial composite of the general public" would find the mark "shocking to the sense of truth, decency, or propriety"; "giving offense to the conscience or moral feelings"; "calling out for condemnation"; "disgraceful"; "offensive"; "disreputable"; or "vulgar."[147] The PTO said the mark failed this test.

The Court framed the issue: "If the "immoral or scandalous" bar similarly discriminates on the basis of viewpoint, it must also collide with our First Amendment doctrine. . . . [s]o the key question becomes: Is the "immoral or scandalous" criterion in the Lanham Act viewpoint-neutral or viewpoint-based?" The Court succinctly stated, "It is viewpoint-based."[148] Additionally, the Court stated, "in any event, the "immoral or scandalous" bar is substantially overbroad."[149]

It is going to be very interesting to see the ramifications of these two cases, particularly with the way that band/artist names tend to push the envelope of propriety.

Types of Marks.

When forming a band and trying to name the band, trademarking the name and logo is mandatory. But how likely is a particular name or logo likely to receive federal protection?

Trademark law lists four types of marks, and each receives a different level of protection. However, two types of marks are lumped together: arbitrary and fanciful. But each is a distinct mark, and we will break out "arbitrary" from "fanciful." From the weakest to the strongest, the four (actually five) types are: (i) generic; (ii) descriptive; (iii) suggestive; and (iv) arbitrary/fanciful.[150]

A *generic* mark is a generic term for a type of product. It consists of words or symbols that describe the product or service itself as a category, rather than distinguish between competing versions of them.[151] Generic terms therefore **cannot** be Trademarked since the point of a Trademark is to promote an association with the source, or owner, of the product or service. But it begs the question – what about a name such as *"The Band"*? As will be discussed, that could gain protection from the second class of trademark – a "descriptive" mark.

Granting a Trademark on a generic name would be akin to granting a monopoly on the description of the product at issue, such that competitors could no longer accurately describe what they sell. Examples of terms found generic and not protected include: (i) "Lite" for a low-calorie beer; (ii) "Safari" for hunting expedition clothes; and (iii) "Super Glue" for a strong-bonding glue.[152] Other well-known examples of products that have become generic over time are "videotape" (originally Trademarked by Ampex Corporation), and the term "App Store."

A case that pushed the envelope of whether a "generic" term could gain Trademark protection regards the word "how."[153] As Jonathon Mahler comments in his piece in The New York Times,

> No, that's not a line from a Dr. Seuss book or
> an Abbott and Costello routine. It's the question
> at the center of a bitter legal battle pitting a best-

selling author and management guru against America's largest Greek yogurt manufacturer.[154]

The battle is between author Dov Seidman and yogurt company Chobani. Mr. Seidman is the author of a series of business law books centered around the question "how?" One example is "How: How We Do Anything Means Everything."[155] Chobani started in 2005 and had an ad campaign that featured the slogan "how matters."[156] Mr. Seidman is claiming Trademark protection for his use of the word in his brand.

Mr. Mahler notes that James D. Weinberger, a Trademark lawyer at Fross Zelnick Lehrman & Zissu, feels that Mr. Seidman is on weak legal ground.

> The strongest Trademarks, [Mr. Weinberger] notes, cover words that have no other meanings (think Kodak), or that are being used in an unusual way (think Apple). Mr. Seidman may be using "how" in a particular context — and in noun form — but he is still using it "in connection with its ordinary meaning," said Mr. Weinberger. "I think these rights are very weak conceptually."[157]

Another very recent case, is *USPTO v. Booking.com B.V.*, 140 S. Ct., 2298, 2020 USPQ2d 10729 (2020) (Booking.com), decided in June of 2020.[158] The case concerned the use of the generic extension of ".com". The case arose from the USPTO's refusal to register the proposed mark BOOKING.COM on the ground that it is generic as applied to the identified hotel reservation services, or, in the alternative, that it is merely descriptive and has not acquired distinctiveness.[159] The Supreme Court held that "[w]hether any given 'generic.com' term is generic ... depends on whether consumers in fact perceive that term as the name of a class or, instead, as a term capable of distinguishing among members of the class."[160] Therefore, under Booking.com, a proposed mark composed of a generic term combined with a generic top-level domain, such as ".com," is not automatically generic, nor is it automatically non-generic.[161] The effects of the case are going to be quite interesting. Remember the question on *The Band*? Now, stick a ".com" behind it and you might have a registrable mark.

A *descriptive* mark describes the ingredients, qualities, features, purpose, or characteristics of a product or service. These marks are not inherently distinctive, and thus do not receive Trademark protection *unless* they acquire that distinctiveness through *secondary meaning*. Specifically, a descriptive mark does **not** gain protected status **until**: (i) there has been a period of exclusive use[162]; and (ii) it has developed acquired distinctiveness, or "secondary meaning."[163]

"Secondary meaning" refers to the fact that the mark not only has a first meaning, (*i.e.,* the descriptive, dictionary term), but also has a secondary meaning, (*i.e.,* a strong association with the source of the product or service). Here is where *The Band* could gain protection. Consumers in the marketplace must exclusively associate the mark, as used on the goods or in connection with the services at issue, with a particular source (*i.e.* the Trademark owner).[164] Some examples of marks with secondary meaning are: (i) "Honey-Baked Hams" (both descriptive and a protected brand name); and (ii) "Vision Center" (both descriptive and brand name).[165] However, even when a descriptive mark qualifies for Trademark protection, they are the weakest marks possible, and do not receive the same level of protection as suggestive, arbitrary and fanciful marks.

A *suggestive* mark suggests rather than describes the qualities of the underlying goods or services. It "requires[s] imagination, thought, and perception to reach a conclusion as to the nature of the goods." A suggestive mark is the type of mark an individual sees, thinks about, and then has an "ah-ha!" moment as they "get" the connection.[166] Suggestive marks already have acquired distinctiveness, so a showing of secondary meaning is not necessary. Examples of suggestive marks are: (i) "Citibank" (suggests banking and identifies its urban-based nature.); (ii) "Playboy" (suggestive of a lifestyle and identifies the magazine); and (iii) "Chicken of the Sea" for tuna fish. In music, the band/artist name "Metallica" could be considered suggestive: the "ah-ha" moment comes when the connection between the name (Metallica) and product (metal music) is recognized.

The final types of Trademark, *fanciful and arbitrary*, are generally the strongest. Similar to suggestive marks, no showing of secondary meaning is required for these marks. A person choosing a fanciful or arbitrary mark will have less competition in the marketplace and an easier time acquiring distinctiveness and protection - simply because no one else out there uses the mark on similar goods and services.

An *arbitrary* mark consists of terms that exist in popular vocabulary, but the mark has no direct connection to the product being identified.[167] An example is "Apple" for a music company or the maker of computers, or *The Cure* for a band/artist. In each case, there is no direct correlation between the mark and the product, (*e.g.,* no obvious connection between apples and a computer or record company). The company or band members arbitrarily chose the name. In music, many band names are arbitrary.

A *fanciful* mark is a "coined-up" phrase or word that has no dictionary meaning.[168] Examples of fanciful marks are: (i) EXXON; (ii) KODAK; and (iii) ROLEX.[169] In music, many band names are fanciful: *The Beatles* (unusual spelling); *Aerosmith* (made up word) or *Metallica* (made up word).

It is not always simple to determine into which category a given Trademark falls. Indeed, during Trademark litigation a plaintiff usually tries to argue for a stronger category (suggestive or arbitrary/fanciful) while the defendant often tries to argue that the mark is merely descriptive. It can be a very subjective determination (as described below), one that ultimately winds up before the jury.

The same is true during registration of the mark with the U.S. Patent & Trademark Office: an Examiner may respond stating that the mark is merely descriptive; the applicant (usually through counsel) will then make arguments as to why the mark either has secondary meaning, lifting it out of the merely descriptive category, or arguments as to why it is suggestive rather than descriptive.

Registration of a Mark.

Compared with Copyright, where generally there are no rights until you file, Trademark rights can be established by use of the mark in commerce, even without a federal registration. However, as with Copyright, owning a federal Trademark registration on the Principal Register provides several advantages, including:

- *Public notice* of your claim of ownership of the mark;

- A *legal presumption of your ownership* of the mark and your exclusive right to use the mark nationwide on or in connection with the goods/services listed in the registration;

- The *ability to bring an action*

concerning the mark in federal court;

- The use of the U.S. registration as a basis to obtain registration in *foreign countries* by way of the Madrid Protocol, as discussed below;

- The ability to record the U.S. registration with the U.S. Customs and Border Protection (CBP) Service to *prevent importation of infringing foreign goods;*

- The right to use the *federal registration symbol* ®; and

- Listing in the United States Patent and Trademark Office's online databases.[170]

"Use in Commerce" versus "Intent to Use" Basis for Filing.

A Trademark application can be filed under two categories: (i) an Application under Section 1(a) - meaning the mark is already being used in commerce[171]; or (ii) an "intent to use" Application under Section 1(b) - meaning the mark is not yet being used, but the owner has a bona fide intent to use it in commerce.[172]

Which type of application is filed depends on whether you have started to use the mark on all the goods/services at the time the application was filed, or only have an intent to use it. If you have already used your mark in commerce, you may file under the "use in commerce" basis. If the mark has not yet been used, but there is a bona fide intent to use it in the future, then you should file under the "intent to use" basis. An "intent to use" basis requires filing an additional form and fee that are unnecessary if you file under the "use in commerce" clause.[173]

Use in Commerce.

For applications filed under Section 1(a), the use in commerce basis, you must be using the mark in the sale or transport of goods, or the rendering of services in "interstate" commerce between more than one state or U.S. territory, or in commerce between the U.S. and another country. For goods, the mark must appear on the goods (*e.g.,* tags or labels), the container for the goods, or displays associated with the goods. For services, the mark must be used in the sale or advertising of the services.[174]

To properly establish use in commerce, the applicant will need to provide the date of the first use of the mark anywhere and the date of the first use of the mark in commerce. Additionally, the application must include a specimen, or a sample of how the mark actually was used in commerce on your goods or services.[175] A specimen is different from the drawing. The drawing shows only your mark, such as a computer-generated image, whereas a specimen shows the mark "in action" as your purchasers encounter it in the marketplace (*e.g.,* on the labels or on your website).[176] In other words, the specimen will show the actual goods, and the labeling or packaging for the goods. For example, a specimen may be a tag or label displaying the mark, or a photograph showing the mark on the goods or packaging. The specimen may not be a "mock-up" of these items, such as a computer-generated t-shirt with the mark superimposed on it but must be a sample of what is actually used.[177]

Intent to Use.

If the mark has not been used but the holder of the mark plans to do so in the future, the Application may be filed based on a _good faith_ or _bona fide intent_ to use the mark in commerce. A _bona fide intent_ to use the mark is more than an idea and less than market ready. For example, having a business plan, creating sample products, or performing other initial business activities may reflect a bona fide intent to use the mark.[178]

Section 1(b) applications are common when a business is just starting up and wishes to get a head start on protecting its mark before it launches, or when a band/artist is about to release an album and wishes to protect the album and song names before its release.

However, filing a Section 1(b) application does not change the fact that the owner MUST use the mark in order to obtain the benefit of Trademark protection. Unlike Copyright where a song can be left on the shelf without losing protection, a Trademark must be used, or you will lose it. Thus, for applications that are filed under Section 1(b), an official Trademark registration will not issue - even if the Trademark Office clears the mark for registration - until the owner has certified through a Statement of Use that the mark is now being used in commerce. The owner can put this off for up to three years after the Trademark Office Examiner approves the mark for registration, by repeatedly filing for six-month extensions.

Filing Date.

If a Trademark application is filed over the internet through the TEAS (Trademark Electronic Application System) or TEAS PLUS system, the filing date is the date the transmission reaches the USPTO server, in Eastern Standard Time. If the Application is filed by paper, the filing date of an application is the date the USPTO receives the application. The date can become VERY important since the USPTO relies on a filing date to assess priority among competing applications.[179]

To obtain a Trademark, the application must comply with all the requirements and overcome any refusal(s) issued by the assigned USPTO Examiner during examination.[180]

Information to be Included.

A Trademark application must contain the following information, at a minimum:

1. The owner of the mark, including whether it is an individual or a type of entity;

2. An address for the owner, as well as a name and address for correspondence, usually an attorney;

3. A depiction of the mark by itself, either stand-alone words or a depiction of the image, logo, sound or other representation of the mark. (**the "Drawing"**);

4. A description of the goods or services that are at issue, usually by choosing sub-listings under one or more International Classes; and

5. The application filing fee.[181]

6. If filing an "in use" mark, a "specimen" of the mark as used in commerce, for the specific goods or services the application is being filed under. For an

"intent to use" mark, the specimen must be filed before official registration can occur, even if the mark has been accepted. This could be, for example, a screenshot from a website, or the mark on a t-shirt (if filed for use on clothing), and so on.

Every application must include a Drawing – a clear image of the mark. The USPTO uses the Drawing to upload the mark into the USPTO search database and to print the mark in the Official Gazette and on the registration certificate.[182] There are two types of Drawings: **"standard character"** and **"special form."**

A "standard character" drawing is commonly submitted when the mark consists solely of words, letters, or numbers. A standard character mark will give you greater protection since the mark is the wording itself and is not limited to a specific font, style, size, or color.[183] A standard character drawing must have the following characteristics:

- No design element;

- No stylization of lettering and/or numbers;
- No letters and words in Latin characters;

- No numbers in Roman or Arabic numerals; and

- Only common punctuation or diacritical (accent) marks.[184]

The USPTO has created a standard character set that lists letters, numerals, punctuation marks, and diacritical marks that may be used in a standard character drawing. The set is available on the USPTO's website at http://teas.uspto.gov/standardCharacter Set.html.[185]

"Special Form" Drawing.

A **"special form" drawing** is required when a mark consists of more than simply unformatted letters (*i.e.,* contains a "logo" or design, alone or with wording, or if the particular style of lettering or particular color(s) is important).[186] Rather than simply typing in the words on the online application, an image of the mark in .jpg format must be uploaded into the TEAS form. Unless a specific color or colors are claimed as a feature of the mark, the mark image should be pure black-and-white.[187] As a general rule of thumb, however, a black-and-white drawing is fine even if the actual mark is in color, because a black-and-white drawing covers use of a mark in any color, which will provide broader protection for the mark. Thus, generally only if coloring is such an integral piece of the mark will there be a need to submit a color drawing. If color is an integral part of the mark, it may be prudent to submit a colored drawing (*i.e.,* you may not be able to enforce the mark against someone using a similar version with different coloring).

Once You Get It, Who Owns It

The Trademark Office presents the following examples. These are some common ownership scenarios for an individual artist or a band/artist:

- You're a solo musical performer and want to register your personal or stage name . . . file your application in your name as an individual applicant using your personal name as the applicant.

- You're in a musical group with more than one member and want to register your brand name . . . your application must identify the owners as joint individual applicants, with each member of the band listed as an individual applicant.

- You're in a musical group with more than one member and the band has formed a partnership . . . the application must identify the business name as the owner of the trademark.

- If the partnership has not been organized under a business name, list the names of the general partners as the partnership name.

- You're in a musical group with more than one member and the band has set up a corporation or limited liability company (LLC) to manage the business or own the trademark rights. The application must identify the corporate or LLC name as the owner of the trademark.[188]

Maintaining a Federal Trademark Registration.

One of the main differences between Copyrights and Trademarks is that you must *maintain* the Trademark registration once you have it. To do this the Trademark holder *must* file its first maintenance document before the end of the sixth year after the registration date, and other maintenance documents approximately every five years thereafter. It is interesting to note that the USPTO previously did not send out reminder notices. It does so now and that alleviates a tremendous burden on the holder of the Trademark. But it is still advisable to have an attorney help you keep track to make sure that the Declaration of Use is timely filed.

This requirement highlights another key difference between Copyright and Trademark. Under Copyright, there is a definite term and you do not have to do anything to maintain the Copyright. Under Trademark, if you have maintained the use of the mark, the rights in a federally registered Trademark can last indefinitely.

The mark holder must file a:

• Declaration of Continued Use or Excusable Nonuse under § 8; and

• Combined Declaration of Continued Use and Application for Renewal under §§ 8 and 9.

A § 8 declaration is due before the end of the 6-year period after the registration date or within the 6-month grace period thereafter. Failure to file this declaration will result in the cancellation of the registration.

A combined §§ 8 and 9 must be filed before the end of every 10-year period after the registration date or within the 6-month grace period thereafter. Failure to make these required filings will result in cancellation and/or expiration of the registration.[189]

There is one more optional filing, which is usually done in concert with the initial § 8 declaration filed between the fifth and sixth year after issuance. This is the § 15 Declaration of Incontestability, certifying that the mark has been in continuous use in commerce for five or more years. Filing a § 15 Declaration means the mark is incontestable, and immune from challenge except if it has become a generic term for the goods or services, the registration was acquired under fraudulent conditions, or the mark was abandoned due to nonuse. A § 15 declaration need only be filed once. Often a Combined § 8 and 15 Declaration of Continued Use and Incontestability is filed between the fifth and sixth year after registration; thereafter, a Combined § 8 and 9 Declaration is filed at each 10-year mark from the date of registration.

International Trademark Registrations.

Occasionally, a band/artist or song becomes so popular that it receives international exposure, or a band/artist decides to include international venues such as Canada, Mexico or beyond in their touring schedule. In that case, or in other select instances, it may be prudent to file for international protection on Trademarks (and perhaps even Copyrights) as well as federal registrations. For example, it is not unheard of for a band/artist or company to become successful in the United States, at which time an opportunistic individual or organization files for the same Trademark in China. The opportunistic individual or entity will then attempt to leverage that brand equity or hold it hostage so that you will then purchase it from them - for more money than it would have cost you to register it in that country yourself.

Even if your Trademark is officially registered with the U.S. Patent & Trademark Office, protection overseas is still not guaranteed. The mark may have a meaning in a foreign language that poses problems, or someone might already be using the mark in that country for a similar purpose. Thus, a search is usually recommended before filing an application. Once ready, however, there are several ways to file foreign Trademarks that can save money. Rather than filing *ad nauseum* in every country you think your music or band/artist might make an appearance, you can do the following:

- **Utilize the "Madrid Protocol" to file internationally**. The Madrid Protocol consists of a group of close to 100 countries, including most of the major industrial nations, who have agreed to certain Trademark rules. Through the Madrid Protocol, you can take your existing U.S. Trademark application and extend it to other countries within the Protocol. While you still need to pay the requisite filing fees for each country, this method saves time and money.

- **Apply for a Community Trademark (CTM) throughout the European Union** in one application, rather than filing within each country that is a part of the EU. The downside is that if the mark does not clear in *any one* country in the EU, the CTM will be denied and you will have to file in each country you want protection in, to obtain similar protection.

International protection is also becoming increasingly important in the age of the internet - where music can be downloaded and played anywhere in the world at a press of a button. If you think that your music may receive international exposure, then exploring Trademark protection beyond the four corners of the United States may be warranted.

♪ ♪ ♪ ♪

Domain Name and Website Protection from Cybersquatters and Typosquatters.

A band/artist will undoubtedly have a presence on the internet, including its own website, such as www.ourband.com, that utilizes the band/artist's Trademarks. To protect both the website and the band/artist's Trademark, it is prudent also to register the same domain name in similar top-level domains: such as .net, .org, .biz, .co, and others that are growing in popularity. If the band/artist expects to receive international exposure, it may be worth registering country-specific domain names as well, such as .CA (Canada), .FR (France), and so on. This will prevent 'cybersquatters' from registering your domain name in these top-level domains, and then try to sell them back to you or use them to promote unsavory businesses that the band/artist does not wish to be associated with.

Likewise, if there is a popular misspelling of your band/artist's name, you may wish to register that domain name as well. For example, at one time typing in www.nirvanna.com brought you to a site whose content was typically spam-ish: a single page that, amidst a smattering of advertisements, provides a handful of links to sites described as "Nirvana Shop," "Nirvana Merchandise," "Cupcake Cult" and "Nirvana Heart Shaped Box." Clicking on one gives you a Google-like list of hits for that item. And of course, the website owner is being paid for each click and search, making money off the band/artist's goodwill (note that none of the items listed are actually spelled "Nirvanna," demonstrating that the site's owner knows that people reaching the site are those who are searching for but misspelled "Nirvana."). Chances are, Nirvana itself would prefer to own this website, and have it link back to its own home site. By contrast, www.slayer.net appears to be owned by Slayer, along with www.slayer.com. And typing in www.u2.org

automatically reroutes the user to U2's main page at www.u2.com.

Infringement and Damages.

Section 32 of the Trademark Code provides the remedies for damages due to infringement. It reads:

§ 32 (15 U.S.C. § 1114). Remedies; infringement; innocent infringers

(1)   Any person who shall, without the consent of the registrant—

(a)   use in commerce any reproduction, counterfeit, copy, or colorable imitation of a registered mark in connection with the sale, offering for sale, distribution, or advertising of any goods or services on or in connection with which such use is likely to cause confusion, or to cause mistake, or to deceive; or

(b)   reproduce, counterfeit, copy or colorably imitate a registered mark and apply such reproduction, counterfeit, copy or colorable imitation to labels, signs, prints, packages, wrappers, receptacles or advertisements intended to be used in commerce upon or in connection with the sale, offering for sale, distribution, or advertising of goods or services on or in connection with which such use is likely to cause confusion, or to cause mistake, or to deceive, shall be liable in a civil action by the registrant for the remedies hereinafter provided. Under subsection (b) hereof, the registrant shall not be entitled to recover profits or damages unless the acts have been committed with knowledge that such imitation is intended to be used to cause confusion, or to cause mistake, or to deceive.

In short, Trademark law protects a Trademark owner's exclusive right to use a Trademark when use of the mark by another would be **likely to cause consumer confusion** as to **the source or origin** of goods or services.

To establish a violation of the Lanham Act for either a registered mark under 15 U.S.C. § 1114, or an unregistered mark under 15 U.S.C. § 1125(a), the plaintiff must demonstrate that:

1.   It has a valid and legally protectable mark;

2.   It owns the mark; and

3.   The defendant's use of the mark to identify goods or services causes a likelihood of confusion.[190]

"Use" of a Trademark by an alleged infringer must be established as a threshold matter. Any number of activities may be "in commerce" or create a "likelihood of confusion." However, such activities do not violate the Lanham Act absent the use of a Trademark.[191]

To satisfy the **"in commerce"** requirement, the plaintiff must demonstrate that the allegedly infringing activities have a substantial effect on interstate commerce. Examples of acts that will meet the "in commerce" requirement are: (i) advertising by the alleged infringer in more than one state; (ii) interstate movement of goods bearing an infringing mark from manufacturer to seller; (iii) sending a product to another state for the purpose of registering a Trademark; and (iv) advertising in newspapers that have interstate distribution, on billboards near interstate highways, or on radio or television stations with an interstate broadcasting range.[192]

The most important factor in the infringement analysis, however, is **"likelihood of confusion."** A "likelihood of confusion" exists if the relevant consuming public is likely to be confused or mistaken about the source of a product or service sold using the mark in question.

Trademark law proactively prevents consumer confusion; thus, it does not require proof of actual consumer confusion for a legal "infringement" finding. A Trademark owner must simply prove that a hypothetical, "reasonably prudent" consumer would likely be confused by the same or similar Trademark on potentially competing products. (Such a hypothetical purchaser is expected to view the mark as a whole and is not expected to make detailed side-by-side comparisons or have perfect recall.) In determining likelihood of confusion, courts evaluate numerous factors. The factors considered can differ depending on what Circuit the dispute is in. No one factor is determinative, and the relative importance of each depends on the individual situation, although the first two factors are often the most heavily weighed. The most commonly considered factors are:

- **Similarity of marks.** Whether the marks are similar in appearance, phonetic sound, or meaning.

- **Similarity of goods/services.** Whether or not the goods or services are so closely related that they are being marketed through the same stores or channels of distribution.

- **Level of competition.** Whether or not the goods or services using the same mark compete with one another. There is a distinction in the courts between likelihood of confusion for directly competing, as opposed to non-competing, goods. *See* <u>A&H Sportswear, Inc. v. Victoria's Secret Stores, Inc.</u>, 237 F.3d 198 (3rd Cir. 2000). When the alleged infringer and the Trademark owner deal in competing goods or services, the court rarely needs to look beyond the mark itself. Infringement will usually be found if the two marks at issue are sufficiently similar that consumer confusion can be expected. If the goods in question are completely unrelated, confusion is unlikely, and infringement will generally not be found. Even where the plaintiff's products are not exactly similar, however, in some cases the court may consider how likely the plaintiff is in the future to sell similar products.

- **Intent.** Whether or not the alleged infringer intended to trick consumers in order to ride on the coattails of the plaintiff's business reputation or good will.

- **Consumer sophistication.** How careful the consumer is likely to be prior to purchase. The more sophisticated the consumer (*e.g.,* savvy business owners versus children), or the more expensive the product, then the more discriminating the consumer is assumed to be, and the more difficult it is to prove confusion.

- **Similarity in customer base.** Whether or not the companies have or reach out to overlapping customer bases. For example, if both companies market and sell primarily to heavy metal fans or musicians, there is more likely to be consumer confusion.

- **Similarity of marketing and trade channels.** Whether the marks are advertised, promoted, or found in the same or different places – on the internet, for example, in a brick-and-mortar store or in live concert venues, or on the same streaming platforms.

- **Strength of the mark.** This factor has to do with the type of mark at issue - whether the mark is weak (generic or descriptive) or stronger (suggestive, arbitrary, or fanciful). The stronger the mark - greater the public recognition of a mark as a source identifier - the more likely that similar uses will be confusing.

- **Whether any actual confusion occurred.** Actual confusion is not necessary to find a likelihood of confusion. Moreover, even if there is some actual confusion, alone does not mean that you will necessarily win. Rather, the existence (or not) of actual confusion must be weighed together with the other factors.

- **Zone of likely expansion.** This factor looks to whether the owner of the mark is likely to expand either geographically, or in terms of types of goods and services.

One way to better understand this test is to realize that Trademark law is focused on protecting *consumers,* even more than protecting the Trademark owner and their business interests. Trademark law is designed to give a business incentive to obtain and police the exclusivity of their Trademark. This incentive, in turn, allows the consumer to easily find the brand they like without worrying about being tricked with a "bait and switch" tactic, and having to carefully read ingredient labels or scrutinize packages. Thus, the analysis focuses on whether a consumer is going to be confused and deprived of an ability to make informed purchasing decisions.

An interesting case regards the use of the name "Van Halen."[193] Eddie and Alex Van Halen had trademarked the family name. In 1984, Alex married Kelly Carter; twelve years later they divorced. Realizing the worth of the Van Halen surname, Kelly kept her name as "Kelly Van Halen." Alex had to sue Kelly for using it in personal business ventures since she had trademarked the name of her construction and interior design company with "Van Halen." In 2015, they settled whereby Kelly was allowed to use her full name, but not on "music-related services." The key consideration was the issue of consumer confusion; consequently "music-related services" was carved out of any use by Kelly. She was allowed to use it in relation to her construction and interior design company but with restrictions.

Finally, an additional form of infringement is *dilution*. Dilution is a "whittling down" of the identity or reputation of the mark.[194] Dilution occurs due to the corrosive nature of the wrong - it "blur[s] [the] production identification or . . . damage[s] positive associations that have attached to it."[195] It is possible to have separate legal claims both for Trademark infringement and for Trademark dilution. A federal dilution claim, however, requires that the mark be "famous." The association between the product/service and the Trademark owner must be strong to prevail on a dilution claim. Additionally, dilution usually occurs when someone is using a famous mark on *non-competing* products, which makes the mark more common by stretching it beyond its original use and association by the Trademark owner.

There can be dilution by blurring or dilution by tarnishing. One example of dilution by "blurring" is if someone started using the mark METALLICA to sell wall paint with a metallic sheen. An example of dilution by "tarnishing" is when someone used the mark METALLICA to sell cute baby dolls wearing pink dresses, or as the name of a child porn magazine. In either case, and for different reasons, neither is an image the band/artist would want associated with its brand.

Remedies.

Similar to Copyright, relief sought for infringement can include monetary compensation, but the main relief is injunctive

- *i.e.,* ideally making the other side stop using their infringing mark, even if they have to re-brand to do so. The remedies for infringement under the Lanham Act are statutory and consist of: (i) injunctive relief; (ii) an accounting for profits; (iii) damages, including the possibility of treble damages when appropriate; and (iv) attorneys' fees in "exceptional cases" with costs.[196] These remedies are cumulative, meaning that a successful plaintiff may recover the defendant's profits in addition to any damages, or other remedies awarded.

Need for an Attorney.

Unlike patent applications, there is no requirement that an attorney or other licensed professional prepare and file a Trademark application. It is therefore possible for an individual or company to file the application on their own. But why would you want to? While this may appear to save expense in the short-term, the risks are high and the costs could end up being far greater - both in terms of money, and in terms of the value and registrability of the Trademark. For example:

> An attorney can "clear" the mark: conduct a comprehensive full search for potentially conflicting marks and provide an educated assessment about your ability to prevail before the USPTO on your Trademark application. If the attorney feels the mark is too descriptive, too close to another mark (such that their owner could come after you for trademark infringement) or has other problems, you have saved the cost of trying to register something that is

not likely to succeed. Moreover, the attorney may be able to recommend a change that could make the mark much more likely to pass USPTO scrutiny.

- Trademark law and the application process are highly technical and complicated. While filling out the application may appear easy, many legal and practical decisions must be made as to what International Classes to file under, which sub-listings under each Class are appropriate, whether the application needs to distinguish the goods and services from another, similar mark in order to succeed, whether the application should be filed as a Section 1(a) "use" or Section 1(b) "intent to use" mark. An attorney can also help you decide when and whether to file for multiple International Classifications under a single application, or whether to avoid putting all your eggs in one basket and instead file multiple applications, each for a single class.

- Responding to a Trademark Examiner's "Office Actions" setting forth reasons why he or she considers your mark unregistrable can be complicated. This often involves citing to legal cases and regulations, applying them to your situation, and making cogent arguments responding to each of the Examiner's specific points. You may also need to decide if or how you might want to narrow the scope of your mark to get around the Examiner's objections. Without knowing the law in these areas, what the Examiner's argument really means, and what your options are, it is difficult - if not near impossible - to convince an Examiner they are incorrect.

- Everything you say in the application and in a response to an Examiner's office action, is public record and binding. It can be used against you later if you are sued (or sue someone else) for Trademark infringement. So, for example, if you tell the Examiner that your mark is only meant to apply to X type of products, and not to Y and Z, and you later sue someone for using a similar mark on products Y and Z, you will almost certainly not prevail.

You might ask: "what's the worst that could happen if I file without an attorney?" The answer is that you will pay $250.00 or $350.00 to give it a try, and then simply not get the mark. But in truth the consequences could be far worse.

Even if you do not obtain the registration, your application is now in the public domain. The same is true if you do obtain a registration. Someone with prior rights to the name can find you, which could expose you to liability. You could be forced to pay damages and be enjoined from using the mark again, which will force you to engage in the costly process of re-branding. Thus, while an attorney is not *required,* it is highly recommended to at least consult with counsel before going ahead and filing an application. The best and safest course of action, however, is to hire a Trademark attorney to shepherd your mark through the process.

Conclusion.

A Trademark is an important tool that works hand-in-hand with Copyright, to protect an artist's valuable intellectual property. All artists need to be aware of the value in a Trademark and take the necessary steps to protect that value. Such protection consists not only of obtaining a federal and/or state registration for their Trademark(s), but also, once obtained, continuing to police the mark. Failure to watch out for potential infringers and protect the Trademark against unlicensed use will make it difficult, if not impossible, to obtain remedies from an infringing user later. **In short, Trademark owners cannot ignore infringing uses of their mark**. Letting others use similar marks, especially for similar goods or services, dilutes the Trademark and increases the likelihood that consumers will be confused. Since a Trademark is supposed to tell a consumer that they are buying from a specific source, companies who allow infringing uses of their mark risk losing all their rights if a third-party challenger claims the company abandoned their mark by not enforcing it. Thus, you must enforce your mark against anyone that is infringing.

CHAPTER 4

REVENUE STREAMS CREATE THE REVENUE RIVER

"Every time it rains, it rains
Pennies from Heaven"
- Johnny Burke & Arthur Johnston.[197]

Before turning to the central issues of forming your business and signing contracts concerning your music, it is extremely important to have a thorough understanding of the revenue streams that create the cash flow river - and they are available to both the songwriter and the performer. These revenue streams represent ways to monetize the intellectual property rights discussed in Chapter 1 and Chapter 2: Copyrights and Trademarks.

For a songwriter, revenue can come from the lyrics, the music, or the music and lyrics together. As Les Scott comments, "When it comes to making money in the music business, unless the Performer is famous, the writer (Composer) is the ONLY person (not the performers or master owners) to make money."[198] For example, "even a very famous, worldwide recording such as Frank Sinatra's version of "New York, New York", the songwriter will earn 20-30 TIMES more money than the performer in that famous Sound Recording."[199]

The reason underscores the different treatment of royalties in the rest of the world. In the vast majority of the world, performance royalties are paid to the master owners and performers on those Sound Recordings. However, in the U.S., performance royalties were only paid to the Composer, not on the Sound Recordings, to the performer, or to the master owner. The performers and master owners complained to Congress.

Finally, in 2003, Congress created SoundExchange - an American non-profit collective rights management organization founded in 2003. It is the sole organization designated by the U.S. Congress to collect and distribute digital performance royalties for sound recordings. It pays featured and non-featured artists and master rights owners for the non-interactive use of sound recordings under the statutory licenses set forth in 17 U.S.C. § 112 and 17 U.S.C. § 114. However, it only collects in the U.S. and only for a very limited (non-terrestrial) category. The earnings collected are miniscule compared to the earnings created on behalf of the underlying song.[200]

For a performer, particularly a band/artist, touring and the logo and slogan of the band/artist are the sources of revenue (merchandising - think *"KISS"*).

The following chapter examines the major revenue streams available to musicians. The website "Artist Revenue Streams" provides an exhaustive list of 45 sources of revenue available in the music world, whether you are a songwriter, in a band, or merely a sideman musician.[201] Ari Herstand, in his book "How to Make It in the New Music Industry," discusses the ways to make sure you can participate in all the revenue streams available to both an "artist" (the performer of the Musical Composition) and Composer (the person(s) who actually wrote the Musical Composition.[202]

This book will not attempt to describe all of these sources but will address the major ones. By understanding the money at stake, the songwriter or band member can make a more informed decision about what business entity to form, and the terms addressed in a Band Agreement.

Keep in mind, however, that with the diversification of the recording industry, the opportunities for "big" money are getting harder to find. The take-away message is that with today's easy electronic access to free music, musicians must make every penny count! To do that, musicians must proactively protect their legal interests from day one.

*Nebgenism #1: You MUST **act as if** there is a million dollars on the table!*

*Nebgenism #2: Because **when there is** a million dollars on the table, people change!*

REVENUE STREAMS.

As touched upon in the previous chapters, a bundle of rights is conferred upon a copyright holder. (You see, we told you intellectual property would be relevant!) In a Musical Composition, the author of the song is the original copyright holder in the song. There can be more than one songwriter for a song. When that is the case, each copyright holder has a pro-rata interest in the Copyright. Thus, for example, if there are two songwriters, each has a fifty percent share of the Copyright. Additionally, the Copyright is broken into the "lyrics" and the "music." It can get confusing: generally, the lyricist gets one hundred percent of the fifty percent of the lyric portion, and the Composer of the music gets one hundred percent of the fifty percent of the music portion. If there are multiple lyricists, the portion going to the lyricists is pro-rated based upon the number of lyricists; the same with the music side of the equation. Additionally, songwriters must keep in mind whether they want to consider the song to be a "joint work" or not.

Always remember, however, that there is a distinction between *ownership* and *control*. To use a real property (land) analogy, ownership entitles a person to participate in the profit of a piece of land. Control entitles a person to determine the use of the land. In land, each party has a *fifty percent ownership* in the land, but each has a *one hundred percent right to use* the land. However, if one person uses the land, he must account to and pay any portion of profit to the other landowner.

The same principle is at work in Copyright. Each author has a fifty percent ownership right and each author has the right to use one hundred percent of the Copyright. Do not forget to keep in mind the discussion from above regarding joint authorship. Without an agreement stating otherwise, one owner can license the Copyright to someone without getting permission from the co-owner, as long as the profits are shared.

A highly contentious battle between the Department of Justice (the "DOJ") and BMI and ASCAP, performing rights organizations ("PRO's"), had erupted regarding which of two systems will be used to determine the rights of authors with respect to licensing joint Musical Compositions. The PRO's, such as BMI and ASCAP, are working under Consent Decrees negotiated back in the 1940's, since amended from time to time, after the DOJ asserted concerns about anti-trust effects. "The consent decrees establish rules of the road to ensure that [the benefits of blanket licenses] are balanced against the power that comes from a few companies controlling rights to a majority of music in the cannon," states David Balto of Law Offices of David Balto.[203]

The controversy concerned the issue of "fractional licensing." As discussed above, the long-established practice was to treat the co-writers of a song as "tenants-in-common", a term from property law, that allows the co-owners to each have an independent right to use or license the use of a work, subject to a duty of accounting to the other co-owners for any profits.[204]

The DOJ's alternative was "fractional licensing." Such licensing "essentially forces music users to assemble 100 percent of the interests of songs from multiple owners . . . ."[205] This would make it much harder to gain access to songs if the permission of each songwriter is required.

Not that the "tenants-in-common" scheme does not have drawbacks – it does. Imagine if one heavy metal band member licensed a band song without the knowledge of the other band members, to a store that sells frilly women's handbags. The other band members might have an objection to their music being associated with that type of image, even if they do share in the licensing profits.

Then, on August 14, 2016, the U.S. Department of Justice closed its review of the issue and disseminated a statement deciding not to the change music licensing rules and leave intact the prior process.

As Balto states, "Fractional licensing would not be good for the U.S. music industry. The Justice Department made the right decision when it chose not to change the consent decrees for ASCAP and BMI."[206] Some of the elements of the license are:

(i)   it can ONLY be a non-exclusive license;

(ii)   A Co-writer/Co-Owner cannot outright "sell" the copyrights in and to the "work." This comes into play when a co-author has entered into a non-exclusive publishing or license agreement that contains a performance clause setting several thresholds, one being that if the publisher achieves a certain amount of activity, that non-exclusive turns into "in perpetuity", thereby becoming a "Sale" (which is not permitted); and

(iii)   All Owners receive their shares of income.

Only in the U.S. does a Co-Writer have the *non-exclusive* right to license a co-written song. In the rest of the world, all writers must sign the license. Consequently, an important consideration in songwriting agreements and band agreements is how the Copyright of the various pieces of property can be exploited, under what conditions, and by whom.

A look at each of the rights of § 106 of the Copyright Act reveals the potential sources of revenue and how to protect them.

I. *RECORD ROYALTIES.*

§ 106(1) - Provides the right to reproduce the Copyrighted work in copies or phonorecords.

§ 106(3) - Provides the right to distribute copies or phonorecords of the copyrighted work to the public by sale or other transfer of ownership, or by rental, lease, or lending.

As part of a recording agreement with a record label, the recording artist will typically have to assign the (Copyright) rights in the Sound Recording to the record company. The two major rights are: (i) the right to make copies (§ 106(1)); and (ii) the right to distribute those copies (§ 106(3)).

However, if the recording artist is not the author of the song, the recording artist must get a license from the author of the song to record the song, generally from the Harry Fox Agency (more below), or through the Mechanical Licensing Collective. The reason is that the author of the Musical Composition is the only person who can perform the song, such as on a Sound Recording.

In exchange for assigning the rights to the record company, the record company will pay royalties to the recording artist. A *record royalty* is the percentage paid to the recording artist from the sales of the Sound Recording. Generally, a recording royalty will be around 16% of the suggested retail price.

Before the explosion of digital technology and the internet, record royalties were a significant part of a recording artist's compensation. In those "old days," a record company would provide records to a radio station free of charge. The radio station would play the records (paying a performance royalty - more below), attract listeners, and sell advertising. The radio station created demand for the songs played. The recording artist and record label would then make money from the sales of the record. Everyone was happy. Now, however . . . no more. Record sales are almost an afterthought for songwriters and performers - they are now a "loss leader." That does not mean that anyone should ignore this area of compensation. It just does not carry the financial importance it used to.

Pre-1972 Recordings.

Over the past few years, various rulings occurred that effected pre-1972 Sound Recordings. It began with a ruling in a huge case in the Central District of the Southern District of California. The case, <u>Flo & Eddie Inc. v Sirius XM Radio Inc., et al.</u>, CV 13-5693 (RZx) **(the "Case")**, created a potential bonanza for songwriters and record labels, and a potential huge liability for entities such as SiriusXM, Pandora, and Spotify.

The key issue was and is the date of the Sound Recordings: Sound Recordings made prior to 1972 were specifically exempted under the Copyright Code of 1976,

> With respect to Sound Recordings fixed before February 15, 1972, any rights or remedies under the common law or statutes of any state shall not be annulled or limited by this title until February 15, 2067...no Sound Recording fixed before February 15, 1972, shall be subject to Copyright under this title[.][207]

However, Congress allowed the states to enact their own laws regarding this area of Copyright law. The Court noted, and actually quoted, the language of Section 301 (capitalization of "Sound Recordings" added):

> When Congress passed the Federal Copyright Act in 1976, it carved out pre-1972 Sound Recordings as a limited area of Copyright law unaffected by the new federal law and within the domain of the states:

> With respect to Sound Recordings fixed before February 15, 1972, any rights or remedies under the common law or statutes of any state shall not be annulled or limited by this title until February 15, 2067...no Sound Recording fixed before February 15, 1972, shall be subject to Copyright under this title[.] Id. § 301(c).

> Accordingly, California statutory and common law presently governs the rights that attach to pre-1972 Sound Recordings because the Federal Copyright Act does not apply to those earlier recordings and explicitly allows states to continue to regulate them. Id. Flo & Eddie's Sound Recordings were fixed prior to February 15, 1972 (DSGF ¶¶ 4, 7); therefore, its rights to those recordings depend solely on whatever rights are afforded to Sound Recording owners under California law.[208]

This decision created chaos in the music industry. However, the CLASSICS Act (which is part of the Music Modernization Act) resolved the problem by giving federal protection to Sound Recordings made before 1972.

II.   *DERIVATIVE WORKS*

§ 106(2) - Provides the right to prepare derivative works based upon the copyrighted work.

As mentioned in Chapter 2, above, a derivative work is ". . . a work based upon one or more preexisting works, such as . . . a musical arrangement . . . a Sound Recording . . . or any other form in which a work may be recast, transformed, or adapted. A work consisting of editorial revisions, annotations, elaborations, or other modifications, which, as a whole, represents an original work of authorship, is a "derivative work."[209]

Derivative works are important for many reasons, but two are prominent: one positive and one negative. The positive aspect of derivative works is the ability to generate new revenue from old, copyrighted material. The negative aspect is that the right to make derivative works is a potential source of Copyright infringement. Green Day, mentioned above, is a perfect example of increasing revenue from previously copyrighted material for its musical adaptation of the song and album "American Idiot!" Regarding the second issue, most people do not realize that the Copyright owner is the only one that can create a sequel, prequel or a "spin-off." Consequently, many Copyright infringement cases arise from someone infringing on the copyright holder's right to create derivative works.

Films have long been an obvious derivative work for songs. In rock, Elvis took songs and made movies around them - "Heartbreak Hotel" is one that immediately jumps to mind. Many rock acts followed with *The Beatles* releasing "Hard Day's Night," "Help," and "Magical Mystery Tour," *The Who* releasing "Tommy" and "Quadrophenia," and *Pink Floyd* releasing "The Wall."

Newer areas of derivative works include Broadway musicals and live theatre events. As already mentioned, Green Day went to Broadway. The Beatles' music was adapted for a stage production, "Love," by Cirque du Soleil. Another phenomena is the "juke-box" musical - a musical made up of the songs of a particular artist or genre. Some examples include "Jersey Boys," which was based on the music of Frankie Valli, "Rock of Ages" based on rock anthems, and "Smokey Joe's Café" based on the music of Lieber and Stoller.

III. *PERFORMANCE ROYALTIES.*

§ 106(4) - Provides the right, in the case of literary, musical, dramatic, and choreographic works, pantomimes, and motion pictures and other audiovisual works, *to perform* (emphasis added) the copyrighted work publicly.

§ 106(6) - Provides the right, in the case of *Sound Recordings*, *to perform* the copyrighted work publicly by means of a *digital audio transmission* (emphasis added).

The author of the song is the *only* person with the right to perform the song publicly. This performance right is one of the most valuable rights. If anyone else wishes to perform the song, the author must be paid. The payment generally takes the form of a royalty (whether a "performance" royalty or a "mechanical" royalty). However, sometimes it can be a flat fee license - this is common for using a popular song for a movie, television show, or commercial. It is so important that it is *not* one of the rights granted to a record company.

Regarding a flat fee, it is important to note that it will not affect the writers' or master owners' performance royalties, it only pays for the grant from the owners for permission to incorporate the music into the film/show/etc. There are exceptions to this scenario where the flat fee also covers the future performance royalties but "fortunately" it isn't the standard way to obtain licenses, yet.

It is important to note that this performance royalty covers what are now termed "terrestrial" mediums – television and radio that have their primary source in a physical station on the ground. However, internet downloads and audio streaming, and then radio delivered from satellites in space, complicated matters. The result was Section 106(6) - the public performance right related to digital transmissions.

Performance Royalties. The biggest source of income for a songwriter comes from performance royalties. These royalties are generated any time the song is performed, in any medium, anywhere in the universe. Every radio station, television station, performance venue, restaurant, club, and bar, with some limited exceptions, must pay for the right to play/perform the song in his or her venue. Each of these entities will need to negotiate a license with either (a) the Publisher or (b) an entity like Muzak that has the right to grant a broad license at a set fee.

And yes, "anywhere in the universe" includes outer space. A video of Canadian astronaut Chris Hadfield performing David Bowie's "Space Oddity" on the International Space Station during his 2012-2013 tenure was posted on YouTube, went viral, and was viewed by over 22 million people. Before the video went up, however, and even before he made the recording, Hadfield spent months negotiating a one-year lease of the song with Bowie, NASA, and both the

Canadian and Russian space agencies (Hadfield knew he would not be in the United States-owned portion of the station when he played the song, so U.S. law did not apply). Twelve hours before the license expired, The Washington Post even warned readers to view it now or lose the chance forever.[210]

As mentioned above, Performance Rights Organizations (**a "PRO"**) will track, compute, and distribute these royalties. The biggest of the PRO's in the United States are, in order (a) BMI (Broadcast Music, Inc.), (b) ASCAP (American Society of Composers, Authors, and Publishers), and (c) SESAC (Society of European Stage Authors and Composers). BMI and ASCAP must take a songwriter if they apply for admission. SESAC, in comparison, will only accept songwriters that they have "invited" to join. The authors of the song AND the Publisher of the song will register with a particular PRO. Both the author and publisher must be registered with the same PRO.

IV. *LICENSES:*

Licensing Revenues. Significant monies are possible from the licensing of a Musical Composition. A license allows the licensee to use the song in certain ways. A *Synchronization License* allows the licensee to use the Musical Composition and match it up with a visual image, whether still or moving (*e.g.,* a motion picture). A *Master Use License* allows the licensee to use the <u>master recording</u> of the song to synchronize with the visual image. If a filmmaker wants to use "Satisfaction" in the movie, the filmmaker must first get a Synchronization License to use the Musical Composition. If the filmmaker then wishes to use the Rolling Stones version, a Master Use License must be obtained to use the actual Sound Recording, and even a particular phonorecord of the musical recording.

Some considerations in getting these licenses include:

(i)   Is the song (or master) publicly known?;

(ii)   Is the artist publicly known?;

(iii)   Will it be used as the Theme Song?,

(iv)   Will it be used to drive the story (or scene) forward? This is called a "Featured" performance: there is no dialog happening, and the music is supporting and driving forward the mood of the scene;

(v)   Is it a featured vocal or a background vocal?;

(vi)   Is it an instrumental? Instrumentals typically pay an upfront fee half of what a "vocal" performance would receive.

(vii)   Note that the backend performance royalties are much lower for an instrumental use, vocal performances pay more (except for at ASCAP);

(viii)   How long is the music used? (over 45 seconds pays almost 4x more performance royalties than under 45 seconds);

(ix)   On what network or what country are the performances being performed?; and

(x)   What time of day? Primetime pays approx. 4x daytime.[211]

Another term that has significant importance is the concept of "All In." The term refers to the fact that the upfront payment is not only paying for the use of the song but also covers the payment for the use of the master Sound Recording. Mr. Scott comments:

In almost every case, (with the exception of major labels or famous songs/artists), those entities that want to license a song/master expect that the administrator of the song also controls the rights of the master Sound Recording. These types of administrators come in a few forms such as: a publisher, a sync agent, a licensing agent, the author, or a master owner themselves. Production companies are leery (and rightfully so) of making transactions with the artist/songwriter themselves because of the many legal issues that could easily arise (which is why the Production Company/Music Supervisor uses their trusted sources for obtaining the music.)[212]

Revenues from these licenses can be very, very lucrative. In 1995, it is generally accepted that Microsoft paid Jagger and Richards $3 million to use "Start Me Up" for the launch of Windows 95. Just recently, Mercedes-Benz used "Sympathy for the Devil" in a car commercial. The price paid has not been revealed as of the publishing of this edition, but it is rumored to have been in the range of $1.5 million.

Mechanical Royalties. Heather McDonald describes mechanical royalties as a "royalty paid to a songwriter whenever a copy of one of their songs is made. For instance, when a record label presses a CD of your song, you are due a mechanical royalty."[213] Ms. McDonald continues: "In addition to an agreement to pay royalties on the sales of the album [the Record Royalty], the label must also obtain a mechanical license for the music on the album and pay those mechanicals. For this reason, there can be several mechanical licenses tied to a single album, depending on how many songwriters contributed music to the release."[214]

Here is chart from the MLC that describes the process.

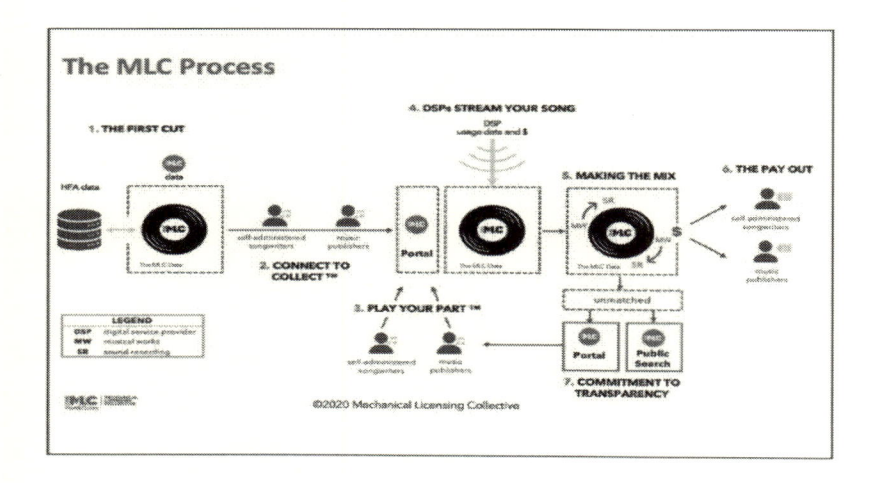

So, mechanical royalties can be generated for a songwriter by a performing artist's Sound Recording, paid by the record label to the songwriter. However, be aware of a "Controlled Musical Composition" clause in the recording agreement; this allows the record label to pay a discounted amount of the statutory rate. The statutory rate is discussed below, and the issue of Controlled Musical Compositions will be discussed in greater depth in the chapter on a record label agreement.

Once a song is *"published,"* mechanical royalties are also generated whenever any other person makes her own version of the song - *a "cover."* "Publication" is a term of art and is defined as:

> . . . the distribution of copies or phonorecords of a work to the public by sale or other transfer of ownership, or by rental, lease, or lending. The offering to distribute copies or phonorecords to a group of persons for purposes of further distribution, public performance, or public display, constitutes

publication. A public performance or display of a work does not of itself constitute publication. *See* U.S. Copyright Office - Definitions (FAQ)https://www.copyright.gov/help/faq-definitions.html.

The MLC has started to issue and administer blanket mechanical licenses for eligible streaming and download services (digital service providers or DSPs) in the United States.[215] The MLC will collect the royalties due under those licenses from the DSPs and pay songwriters, composers, lyricists, and Publishers. On January 1, 2021, it began issuing blanket licenses for digital audio delivery systems such as Pandora, Spotify, and other entities.[216]

Grand Rights: An often-over-looked source of revenue for songwriters is what is termed "Grand Rights." Grand Rights are invoked when someone wants to license music for the live theatre.[217] Whereas to use music with a photograph or moving image, you need a Synchronization License, with live theater you will need to negotiate a Grand Rights Agreement. The Grand Rights are *not* controlled by the PROs. The Grand Rights must be negotiated with and issued by the Publisher or the Composer.[218]

Grand Rights can generate significant revenue for the songwriter, particularly when connected with a hit theatrical production. So, as mentioned above regarding derivative works that result in a stage play, the producers of "American Idiot" had to get the Grand Rights to use the music in a live theatrical production. This includes opera, choreography with music, and other live performances where music is used.[219]

🎷   🎷   🎷   🎷

Tribute Bands/Artists.

Tribute Bands/Artists have become a cottage industry of the music business. Tribute Bands are "a group that plays the songs of a band/artist they admire, often dressing in the style of the original band/artist members."[220] The same definition can be applied to a Tribute Artist. And, both Copyright and Trademark issues are raised by Tribute Bands/Artists.

The Copyright issue is usually handled easily - the Tribute Band/Artist will need to get clearances for permission to perform the songs of the original band/artist. However, that is generally covered by the venue's performance rights license granted by a PRO or an entity like Muzak.

The bigger issue is Trademark - the Tribute Bands/Artists will often deliberately design their logo, costumes, and makeup to mimic the look of the original band/artist. Technically, this could be Trademark infringement.

Similar to Copyright, however, the courts have applied a "fair use exception" to Trademark law (based on the First Amendment granting of free speech), that can protect Tribute Bands/Artists (among others). The Tribute Bands/Artists conduct[221] is termed a "nominative fair use," since the Tribute Bands/Artists use the original Trademark as the starting point for its own product.[222] To determine if it is "fair use," the court will apply a three-part test:

1.   Whether the product/service in question is readily identifiable without use of the Trademark;

2.   Whether only so much of the Trademark is used as is "reasonably necessary" to identify the product or service; and

3.   Whether the user does anything that

would, in conjunction with the Trademark, suggest sponsorship or endorsement by the original Trademark holder.[223]

If the Tribute Bands/Artists can stay on the positive side of these factors, they should be okay as to the Trademark issue. However, keep in mind that just because Tribute Bands/Artists believe they are operating under the fair use doctrine, the original band/artist or its heirs might believe otherwise and could send a cease-and-desist letter or sue in court.

A final consideration regarding tribute bands is the right of publicity. The right of publicity varies from state to state. Depending upon the state, a celebrity's likeness is protected from unauthorized use. "[B]ut overall first amendment free speech protection will generally protect an impersonator entertainer and not prevent the individuals that make up a famous entertainment act from shutting a band/artist down."[224]

V. *Digital Downloads & Streaming Services.*

Section 106(6) created a Performance right in music delivered from a digital platform. The Performance right is only held by the owner of the Sound Recording. It is a new revenue stream that resulted from technology expanding the types of delivery systems through which music could be delivered. Over the last two decades, digital technology, the internet, and new playing devices have sounded the death knell for the classic "album" as well as CD sales.

Most people now purchase their music from one of two sources: (i) downloads from services such as iTunes; and/or (ii) listening to streaming services such as Spotify or Pandora. As Ben Sisario reported in the *New York Times*, "A decade after Apple revolutionized the music universe with its iTunes store, the music industry is undergoing another, even more radical, digital transformation as listeners begin to move from CDs and downloads to streaming services like Spotify, Pandora and YouTube."[225]

The most popular sites in 2020 were: Amazon Music; Spotify; Apple Music; Pandora; Tidal; Deezer; YouTube Music; Soundcloud; Sirius XM; and iHeartRadio.[226] Many of the services have different payouts. Here is a list of the provider and the royalty paid:[227]

Entity	Payout	Comments
Amazon Music	$0.0082 per stream	Among the highest royalty payments for music streaming services globally
Spotify	$0.003 and $0.005 per stream	Spotify has accounted for some of the lowest royalties paid in the industry.
Apple Music	0.00783 per stream	A song will earn $1 after streaming roughly 128 times.
Pandora	0.00133 per stream	752 streams to earn one dollar on the platform.
Tidal	0.0125 per stream.	Specialty service for high-quality rap, hip-hop, and R&B. Founded by Jay Z.
Deezer	$0.0011 per stream	Has unique user-centric payment system.

You Tube	minimum of $0.00087; $0.00164 on streams from their own channels; $0.008 per stream on YouTube Music	The platform offers video and a variety of streaming possibilities.
SoundCloud	$0.0025 to $0.004 per stream	On average is roughly $.003275 per stream.
iHeartRadio	$0.017 per stream	iHeartRadio also shares a small percentage of ad revenue and paid subscription profit to the artists with music on the platform.

As William Glanz comments, "The growth of streaming is almost too incredible to believe. Using on-demand audio and video services, music fans in the U.S. streamed 403.4 Billion recordings in the first half of 2018, according to Nielsen Music. That's up from 284.8 Billion a year ago – a stunning 41.6 percent increase."[228]

SoundExchange is entrusted by The U.S. Library of Congress to collect and distribute these digital performance royalties from: (i) satellite radio (such as SIRIUS XM); (ii) internet radio; (iii) *cable* TV music channels; and (iv) streaming Sound Recordings. In March of 2022, SoundExchange announced that it had distributed over $9 Billion Dollars since 2003.[229]

However, these revenue streams still have a great deal of improvement before they become very profitable for the artist. Spotify and Pandora are becoming billion-dollar businesses (but are still running in the red due to a negotiated settlement that forces them to pay anywhere from 45% to 60% of their gross revenue to the major record labels), but artists are receiving pennies. The numbers paint a stark picture of what it is like to be a working musician these days.

Here are some examples of how hard it is to be profitable on Spotify and Pandora. The *New York Times* reported on Zoe Keating, an independent musician from Northern California.[230] After her songs had been played more than 1.5 million times on Pandora over six months, she earned $1,652.74. On Spotify, 131,000 plays last year netted her just $547.71, or an average of 0.0042 cent a play.[231] But there are benefits. Ms. Keating's music has been featured in various commercial ventures and she reached #1 on the *Billboard* Classical charts.[232]

Another example is Desmond Child – a name you might not recognize but who is responsible for some of the biggest hits in rock, including "Livin' On A Prayer" performed by *Bon Jovi*. The song was played 6.5 million times on Pandora and he and his follow songwriters split $110.00 (and that is *not* a typo)![233] The article that reported Mr. Child's situation was entitled "Songwriters: Spotify Does Not Pay Off . . . Unless You're Taylor Swift." Ironically, Taylor Swift quickly thereafter pulled all of her recordings off Spotify![234] She subsequently relented and put her music back up but not before going through intense negotiations.

Attorney Andy Urias points out that:

[I]n 2014, Bette Midler tweeted that she earned only $114.11 in royalties from 4,174,149 streaming plays over a three-month period on

Pandora. Around the same time, Grammy-nominated Composer and recording artist Armen Chakmakian claimed that he earned $4.20 from over 14,227 digital spins of music he owned the copyrights to (meaning he did not have to share royalties with a record label, publisher, or co-writer) via streaming platforms.[235]

Another concern in this area is the growing controversy of the big players such as SiriusXM and Pandora to make deals directly with the record companies, thus bypassing Sound Exchange and the attendant royalty schedule.[236] In addition, there is a growing sentiment to level the playing on both sides of the equation. On the provider side, there is a wide discrepancy between what the entities pay - Sirius pays 8% of its revenue to record companies and artists while Pandora's fees amounted to about 54% of its revenue.[237] And on the artist side, there is growing discontent that Pandora and Spotify are making millions, even billions, while the artists themselves are at their mercy, being paid pennies.[238]

In late 2012, the Internet Radio Fairness Act (**the "Bill"**) was introduced in the House of Representatives (HR6480) and the Senate (S3609). The Bill, among many items, "[a]mends the Digital Millennium Copyright Act with respect to the standards applied by Copyright Royalty Judges (**the "CRJs"**) to establish compulsory licensing royalty rates for the public performance of Sound Recordings by non-interactive digital audio services."[239] It would allow the CRJ's to set rates that are more equitable for performance royalties over the internet. But as can only happen in Washington, no one likes the Bill. The traditional "terrestrial" companies don't like it because it will allow for the continuing erosion of their market share. The artists do not like the Bill because it keeps the royalties very low, allowing the providers to become rich while the artists continue to starve.[240]

As of the printing of this book, the Bill had been assigned to Committee but had not reached the floor for debate.

VI.   _Blockchain Technology & the Music Industry_

As this book has stressed, revenue streams tend to work in everyone's favor…except the artists. Recording agreements with record labels are notoriously one-sided, and streaming services like Pandora often pay artists little in royalties.[241] Taylor Swift's recent dispute with Big Machine Records over her masters should make new artists at least stop and think before signing away the rights to their songs[242] (not to mention their freedom to be as creative as they want to be throughout the recording process). Fortunately for artists, this traditional route is no longer the _only_ one.

Artists now have access to technology that allows them to record whole albums at home. Websites like Kickstarter or Go Fund Me make it possible for bands to crowdfund (more on this below) the money necessary to record, market, and distribute their own music. Although, crowdfunding has become a bit _passe'_, it cannot be ignored. Fans who invest in a band/artist's success can receive free merchandise, backstage passes, or other perks. And, because investor-fans have a personal stake in the band/artist's success, they are more likely to share the band/artist's music with family and friends.

New, disruptive technologies are fundamentally changing how people buy music, how artists interact with their fans, and, of course, _how artists get paid_. Entertainment attorneys in the digital age should strive to stay abreast of these developments. Blockchain technology is becoming increasingly important to understand. Since 2014, around twenty music streaming platforms have been created on blockchains. Artists can utilize blockchain technology to sell, not only their music, but tickets, merchandise, and even the copyrights to their songs.[ii]

What Is Blockchain Technology?

A blockchain is essentially a decentralized network used for storing data and rapidly processing transactions between users. A mysterious individual called "Satoshi Nakamoto" is credited with inventing blockchain in 2008, originally for the purpose of transferring Bitcoin.[iii] Nakamoto created the Bitcoin blockchain after losing confidence in traditional fiat currencies, as well as the third-party intermediaries that were required to handle every-day transactions. In Nakamoto's own words:

> The root problem with conventional currency is all the trust that's required to make it work. The central bank must be trusted not to debase the currency, but the history of fiat currencies is full of breaches of that trust. Banks must be trusted to hold our money and transfer it electronically, but they lend it out in waves of credit bubbles with barely a fraction in reserve. We have to trust them with our privacy, trust them not to let identity thieves drain our accounts. Their massive overhead costs make micropayments impossible.[243]

Essentially, Nakamoto wanted to cut out the middleman and conduct business on a "peer-to-peer" basis. That is what blockchain achieves. Whenever any user transfers Bitcoin to another user, the blockchain validates the transaction, transfers

---

[ii] In the latter part of 2022, the Copyright Office and the Patent and Trademark Office announced that they would be reviewing the interaction between non-fungible tokens and Copyright and Trademark Law.

[iii] Or is it a group of individuals? The identity of "Satoshi Nakamoto" remains unknown.

the funds, and timestamps and records the transfer. It does this in a way that is incredibly resistant to hackers, who are unable to make subsequent changes to any data block. The blockchain thus serves as an accurate record of the exact amount of digital currency always held in every user's crypto wallet. The Bitcoin blockchain can accomplish all this in as little as ten minutes,[244] in stark contrast to traditional banks, which can take several days to process a single transaction. Blockchain technology goes far beyond Bitcoin; blockchains can be programmed for just about anything. For example, in the securities context, investors can program a blockchain to automatically buy or sell a stock when share prices hit a certain value, without relying on brokerages. In the real estate context, buyers could transfer funds to sellers, without escrow companies. Similarly, artists can distribute their music to fans *directly*, without assistance from record labels.

Blockchain Music Platforms

There are around twenty blockchain music platforms that allow fans to purchase music directly from artists with cryptocurrencies.[245] So how do they work?

Artists or labels upload their music the same way they would with a traditional streaming platform. After music is uploaded, the metadata is run through external databases, like AcoustID, to ensure that the music is original.[246] Original tracks are given unique digital fingerprints, so that no one other than the track's owner will be able to later upload the same track.[247] This distinguishes blockchain music platforms from older file sharing systems like Napster and LimeWire, which allowed anyone to upload songs, regardless of whether the user owned the rights in them. A copy of the digital fingerprint is then stored on a side chain, so that any user can look up the owner of any track.[248]

There is real controversy on the issue of "fingerprinting" and "watermarking." "Fingerprinting" takes a very small sample of the audio wave and matches it against what audio is on file. "Watermarking", in comparison, embeds a unique catalog identifier within the Sound Recording. It allows many sources to market the work. The proper source has its own identifier, and all the correct parties will be accounted for (and no one who has proper rights will receive a "take-down" notice). Mr. Les Scott comments, "This relieves ALL confusion and eliminates all "Authorized" licensees from receiving the take-down notices (and "strikes" [negative status resulting from take-down notice] against that Licensee's account)."[249] Mr. Scott continues,

> Fingerprint is horrible and has been the cause of massive confusion regarding ownerships and rights throughout the entertainment industry. There are tons of errant take-down notices sent out every day, [which] causes rightful licensees, content owners, and administrators nothing but distress, time, and confusion.[250]

The problem regarding "fingerprinting" comes from someone rushing to upload an audio sample of the work with one of the detection services (e.g., Rumblefish) and has registered themselves as the owner (or sole controller) of that content. Mr. Scott continues, "So every time the work shows up being uploaded or performed by others (under that detection service's system), a "take-down" notice is sent out and someone gets a strike on their account (such as someone's use of YouTube). Three strikes, you're out."

Non-Exclusive

A problem arises because, in many cases, the owner of the content has granted a "non-exclusive" license to several different parties wherein they each have the permission to upload and potentially market the owner's content. Under fingerprint detection, even though these different licensees all possess the right to upload, monetize, etc., typically, all but one will receive "take-down" notices (because the fingerprint matches).

Watermark is the answer

A watermark embeds a unique catalog identifier within the Sound Recording. It allows many sources to market the work, the proper source to have its own identifier, and all the correct parties will be accounted for, so that anyone who has the proper rights will not receive a "take-down" notice. It will help prevent an authorized user from receiving "strikes" against that its account.

Payment and Downloads

Users can stream tracks and, upon payment, can download them.[251] When a user transfers the requisite amount of Bitcoin, Ether, or other cryptocurrency, the owner of that track receives payment almost instantly. Further, because blockchain is a "trustless" system, artists never have to worry about auditing a label's or personal manager's records, to ensure they are paid what they are owed. But not all blockchain music platforms are created equally; different platforms offer different payment structures and levels of control to artists. Here are few of the different features, but this chapter will just scratch the surface.

One of the most interesting aspects of the Bittunes model is that it facilitates micropayments to previous purchasers of songs. For example, if a track sells for $1, the artist is paid 40 cents, Bittunes is paid 20 cents, and the remaining 40 cents is divided between five previous purchasers of the track. The five previous purchasers are selected using an algorithm that focuses on "Good Citizen Behaviour" (i.e., logging in often, rating songs, etc.).[252] Thus, Bittunes incentivizes people to purchase music directly from artists and then actively try to boost their popularity. Unlike Bittunes, which lives in the Bitcoin ecosystem, other platforms, like Audius, live in the Ethereum ecosystem.[iv]

Audius works similarly to SoundCloud. $AUDIO is the primary token used. Not only do $AUDIO tokens allow users to unlock content, but they are also used to determine voting power for blockchain governance purposes, like stock in a corporation.[253] Audius also addresses one of the biggest concerns with cryptocurrencies: price volatility. Audius anticipates that, soon, users will be able to purchase content with "stablecoins" (i.e., cryptos whose values are tied to a relatively stable asset, like gold or the U.S. dollar).[254]

Price stability is a big deal, for a couple of reasons. First, the value of cryptos can be extremely volatile. Assume that an artist becomes popular on Audius and brings in $100,000.00 worth of $AUDIO. The next day, the value of the coins could plummet, and all that $AUDIO in the artist's crypto wallet might be worth thousands of dollars less than the day before. The possibility of huge fluctuations in value forces artists to speculate about when their tokens will be worth the most before cashing out. Similarly, users might be hesitant to spend their

---

[iv] The Ethereum blockchain is the second largest blockchain in the world, next to Bitcoin. Also, just recently, the market saw the collapse of FTX with losses in the billions.

tokens when the token value is high or expected to rise. Using stablecoins would solve both problems by taking speculation out of the picture. Lastly, stablecoins are highly divisible, which gives artists and users greater flexibility in transactions and promotes the free flow of digital currencies.

In 2018, PeerTracks chose the SounDAC blockchain, which is a music-specific blockchain designed to manage royalty payments.[255] However, it is unclear what blockchain it is currently using. Whatever blockchain is being used, like other streaming platforms, artists are registered on the blockchain as the owners of their uploaded tracks. Whenever a song is streamed through any SounDAC-connected platform, the owner of the song earns RYLT (Royalty) tokens equal in value to the performance royalties owed. It is like a P.R.O. that pays artists in real time for digital streams. If a track has two or more authors entitled to royalties, PeerTracks splits the royalties according to any co-author agreement submitted by them at the time the track was uploaded.[256] Obviously, it is hugely beneficial for artists to receive royalty payments in real time. Additionally, because no record label is involved, the royalties will not be deducted to reimburse a label for production costs.

In 2019, PeerTracks introduced the PeerTracks Radio Live Stream, which was essentially an ad-free radio station playing top songs on the blockchain.[257] However, as of March 2021, it seems to have been taken down. Audius has a similar radio feature called "trending," which plays the most popular songs on the blockchain of the week, month, and all-time.[258]

Non-Fungible Tokens

Kings of Leon recently became the first band/artist of their caliber to ever release a full-length album in the form of a "non-fungible token (NFT)."[259] A non-fungible token is a token which gives its holder rights to a particular asset, and they can be *very* profitable for sellers. Digital artists can now sell their artwork as NFTs, and, if the public thinks the work is valuable, the digital artist can sell their work for just as much as a traditional paint and canvas artist. Mike Winkelmann just sold a piece of digital art for almost $70 *million*.[260]

Kings of Leon sold three different types of NFTs. The first NFT was a digital copy of the album, "When You See Yourself," which included moving cover art and a limited-edition vinyl record. The second type of NFT was "golden tickets." Each golden ticket holder receives front row tickets for each tour, including a personal chauffeur, hangouts with the band/artist, and one of everything from the merchandise booth, *for life*. The third type of NFT was collectible Kings of Leon digital artwork.[261] A colleague managed to get the first type of NFT (digital downloads and vinyl record), and, although it is exciting to see high-caliber artists breaking new ground in this way, he noticed significant drawbacks for consumers who might want to purchase NFTs.

The purchasing and redeeming process is quite complex. Before you can start, you need to set up a crypto wallet, like MetaMask. When you set up a crypto wallet, you are provided a password (a series of twelve words) that you can never change or recover, so you must write the phrase down and keep it safe or you will be locked out of your wallet forever. Kings of Leon uploaded its music to YellowHeart and sold its NFTs on OpenSea. The NFT was listed on OpenSea for 0.035 ETH (about $60 in March 2021). MetaMask uses Transak to convert your cash to crypto and add that amount to your wallet, however, you must use a debit card, because credit card companies like Capital One are still hesitant about their funds being used to purchase crypto. Once you have the funds, you can navigate to OpenSea and make the purchase. However, the transaction cost could be closer to 0.085 ETH ($150), because of the "gas" required to carry out the transaction (Yes, you might pay more in gas than you pay for the actual NFT, but this might change with the introduction of "rollups" in Ethereum 2.0). Because of the gas required, you should make sure you add twice the Ether to your wallet than you think you need, in order to avoid multiple withdrawal fees from Transak. Once you own the NFT, you must connect your wallet to YellowHeart, which, as of March 2021, does not support mobile connections, so you must install your crypto wallet's browser extension on a desktop computer and connect to the blockchain that way. With your wallet connected, YellowHeart can verify that you own the NFT and allow you to download the album as .mp3 or .wav files. After the sale period ends, you then need to join YellowHeart's Discord server to prove that you are human and provide your shipping information.

You could do all this, or you could just stream the album for free through Amazon Prime. Still, despite the greater expense and complexity, Kings of Leon made over $2 million from its two-week sale of NFTs.[262] Their success proves that the system works. Other artists could even take it a step further and use blockchains to sell fractions of the underlying copyrights, which, for the right artists, could easily turn that seven-figure profit into an eight-figure profit.

Kings of Leon created *artificial scarcity* by limiting the sale to a two-week period, destroying any vinyl that was not sold, and storing other unlisted works of digital art, which were part of the same series, in a "vault," to be sold later.[263] But any number of people could have purchased the NFTs, and once sold, the files can be easily copied. My colleague was not the *only* person who could listen to the new Kings of Leon album. It is the *token* that is scarce, so that is what is valuable to collectors. Selling copyrights, on the other hand, would create *real scarcity*. There are only so many fractions of a copyright you can buy before you own the whole copyright, and the pieces cannot be duplicated. Imagine if Machine Gun Kelly wanted to sell 75% of the copyright to *"my ex's best friend."* He could list, hypothetically, one thousand NFTs, each one representing one one-thousandth of the 75% portion. Keep in mind, copyright holders are entitled to a portion of future royalty payments. How much would each NFT go for? If each NFT sells for $10,000.00, MGK could make $10,000,000.00 (equal to his current net worth). Ditto Music currently offers artists the tools to sell fractions of copyrights through its Bluebox blockchain.[264]

Artists should experiment with this formula. What if Taylor Swift sold 50% of the copyright to the title track of her next album *before* she releases the album to the public? The song is guaranteed to be good, which means the royalties will also be good. What if Michael Jackson's estate sold 100% of the copyright to "Thriller," with the proceeds going to improving the lives of youth in Jackson's hometown of Gary, Indiana?

New artists can take advantage of this revenue stream as well. Fans already invest in new artists by helping them raise funds through crowdfunding sites. New artists looking for more capital, and do not want to sign away the rights to all their music, can sell fractions of their copyrights to fans while maintaining their autonomy.

Venues can also use NFTs to improve the ticketing process. Because ticketing blockchains, like YellowHeart, create an immutable record of ownership, venues can easily verify authentic tickets and detect fraudulent ones.[265] That is good for event security, because venues can easily keep track of who is in attendance. Additionally, blockchains can be programmed to prevent "scalping" (when people use bots to buy tickets for the sole purpose of reselling at a much higher price).[266] For example, blockchains could be programmed to limit the number of tickets one person may buy or even put a ceiling on the price at which a ticket may be resold. These same protocols, which control the number of NFTs that one user is permitted to hold and the resale price, will also prevent the new copyright market from being dominated by hedge funds. Lastly, the resale of tickets on the secondary market could become yet another revenue stream for artists, because the blockchain can be programmed to give artists a percentage of any resale price.[267]

Legal Issues

On the one hand, the trend toward self-publishing could mean less work for transactional attorneys, because there could be fewer recording agreements in demand. On the other hand, perhaps artists' newfound ability to self-publish gives artists greater bargaining power with record labels. A great entertainment attorney might be able to get a label to bend further than ever before.

On the litigation side, blockchains are introducing questions of first impression in many courts. For example, it is not entirely clear which theories of liability will work against blockchains. Imagine that a programming error causes unintended results and thousands of artists file a class action suit. The problem is: who can be held accountable when the defendant is a decentralized network?

Various theories of liability against blockchain developers have been considered. The problem with a breach of contract theory is that any member of the public may become a token holder without signing an agreement.[268] If tokens are subject to securities regulations, then the Securities Exchange Commission **(the "SEC")** could pursue a claim, but not all cryptocurrencies qualify as "securities."[269] The Consumer Financial Protection Bureau could get involved, but there is the argument that users voluntarily assumed the risk when they chose to participate.[270] Perhaps a claim in tort law would be the most likely to succeed, if the plaintiffs can prove that the blockchain developers owed a fiduciary duty to future users at the time they designed the platform protocols.[271] This seems unlikely though. At the bare minimum, one would hope that plaintiffs could win on an equitable, detrimental reliance theory, in the scenario that the platform developers intentionally deceived users.[272]

If none of these theories of liability stick, and public policy dictates that someone be held accountable for programming errors that cause people to lose a lot of money, then an act of Congress seems to be the only real solution. For example, Congress could create an agency to regulate the largest public blockchains and oversee the licensing of programmers, who agree to be subject to liability and to purchase malpractice insurance.

Either way, the slight risk of a catastrophic programming error, with no one to be easily held accountable, is something that entertainment attorneys should keep in mind when counseling clients. At least with record labels, if something goes wrong, it would probably be easier to secure a judgment.

Entertainment attorneys also need to understand how securities laws will affect clients hoping to utilize blockchain technology. Courts apply the *Howey* test to determine if an investment contract is a security subject to SEC regulations.[v] A security exists if individuals invest their funds in a common enterprise and expect profits solely from the efforts of a third party. Clearly, crowdfunding meets the definition. As will be explained in the chapter on Business Formation, the JOBS Act allows startups to solicit investors without going through the

---

[v] The Howey test is defined as an investment contract exists if there is an "investment of money in a common enterprise with a reasonable expectation of profits to be derived from the efforts of others." https://www.findlaw.com/consumer/securities-law/what-is-the-howey-test.html. Further discussion follows on Page 139.

expensive formal registration process. What about cryptocurrencies?

Cryptocurrencies are often found to be securities, but not always. Do artists sell unregistered securities on blockchain music platforms? I think the answer is clearly no. No one who purchased the Kings of Leon tokens expected future profits, aside from resale, which would not require any further effort from Kings of Leon. Selling fractional copyrights as NFTs poses the more difficult question.

If fans are engaged in a "common enterprise" when they purchase an artist's crypto-copyright, and they expect to profit from that purchase, then the *Howey* test might be satisfied. It is difficult to predict the likely outcome of this hypothetical litigation with any degree of certainty. Circuit courts apply different tests for determining whether *Howey* is satisfied. For example, some courts look for "vertical commonality," while other courts look for "horizontal commonality," when analyzing the "common enterprise" factor. And, because it is a question of first impression, Courts, the SEC, or Congress might be inclined to create new rules at any time, based on whatever seems like good policy.

Ultimately, the best decision is that courts should hold that crypto copyrights are not securities. First, applying the *Howey* test, there is probably not an "investment," but a sale. At least with the bigger artists, the goal of listing the crypto copyrights is not to raise funds to finance operations and grow as a brand. The goal is simply to sell the song. People sell copyrights all the time, so why should selling smaller pieces of your copyright to the general public be treated any differently? Second, the crypto-copyright holders will earn future profits without the artist performing any further work. One could argue that profits depend on the artist maintaining a good public image post-sale, because bad press for the artist can affect the value of the copyright, the same way bad press for a corporation can affect that company's stock prices.

The better position, though, is that artists finish working on songs upon their release (or maybe even when a song is recorded or fixed in its first tangible medium of expression). Third, people will probably be motivated to buy crypto copyrights, not to become entitled to a tiny fraction of royalty payments, but simply because they value the artist's work. Although, this could depend on the context. Perhaps a court would be more likely to find a security if the copyright is sold before the song is released, because, in that scenario, the purchasers seem more like venture capitalists, investing money in a project with hopes of an even greater return.

Conclusion

Blockchain music platforms seem poised to disrupt the music industry just as much as digital streaming did at the turn of the century. These new platforms are great for artists who want to get paid a higher percentage of the revenue generated by their creativity and interact with fans in new and exciting ways. But there are at least two legal drawbacks to consider: the difficulty of suing a blockchain platform and the uncertainty about how securities laws will apply. As always, the law varies from circuit to circuit. Entertainment attorneys need to stay up to date on case law addressing blockchain technology, because nowadays such decisions could have a major impact on the music industry.

VII. *Touring.*

Music publishing will flow to the songwriters. However, not all the members of a band are songwriters. Elvis Presley and Frank Sinatra, to name just two, wrote little, if any of the hits that are associated with their stardom. Consequently, the biggest revenue stream for *performers* will come from touring. Despite all the hype around online streaming and radio services, the live show still drives non-recorded music revenue at Warner Music Group, the world's third largest music company.

Currently, the highest grossing tour is Ed Sheeran's "+ Tour", with a total gross of $775,046,937.[273, vi] The second is U2's "360" Tour grossing over $735,000,000.00.[274] The Rolling Stones have not had a top-ten hit since "Mixed Emotions" in 1995. However, as of the printing of this book, they have two of the top ten grossing tours in history.[275] The "Bigger Bang" Tour grossed $558,255,524 and the "Voodoo Lounge" Tour grossed almost $320 million. The Grateful Dead had only one (1) top-ten hit ("I Will Survive") in its entire career, but until Jerry Garcia's death in August of 1995, it had stayed among the top-ten grossing acts every year. Phish has never had a top-ten hit (the closest was "Free" in 1996 at #11) yet has grossed over $175 million in the last twenty (20) years due to touring.[276]

Of course, one major event caused all of the live

---

vi Although the final numbers are not in, the current Elton John tour, *Farewell Yellow Brick Road Tour*, has already earned over $800 million dollars and still going. *See* Eric Frankenberg, *Elton John's Farewell Yellow Brick Road Tour Is the Highest-Grossing Concert Tour of All Time*, Billboard, Jan. 30, 2023, *https://www.billboard.com/pro/elton-johns-farewell-yellow-brick-road-tour-highest-grossing-concert-tour-all-time/#recipient_hashed=003533ec81a8b78ada12c0964285f7064895d575d 4da8c3d6708494b7fcd88ef&recipient_salt=5da25472e76b7f3d6fe755bce8 f7b23b2a6e812b45f0743003482484b631007f&utm_medium=email&utm_s ource=exacttarget&utm_campaign=billboard_BreakingNews&utm_conten t=409984_01-30-2023&utm_term=12238381.*

performance revenue to go into the toilet – Covid-19. For almost two years, there were no live concerts. However, in 2022 the live concert event came roaring back; it will be interesting to see the figures that come from the built-up demand of concert goers getting out again.

VIII. *Merchandising.*

Many artists overlook the revenue streams that can come from merchandising. We have already talked about the importance of the band logo and slogan. Licensing deals for hats, t-shirts, and other types of memorabilia generate major revenue for artists.

Merchandising can also be based upon a person's *right of publicity*. The right of publicity "prevents the unauthorized commercial use of an individual's name, likeness, or other recognizable aspects of one's persona" - yet another category, although less regulated, of intellectual property. It gives an individual the exclusive right to license the use of their identity for commercial promotion.[277] And it covers the distinctiveness of a celebrity's voice: Ford attempted to use a sound-alike to record a Bette Midler-sounding recording for a commercial. The court held that the sound-alike violated Midler's right to publicity and prevented Ford from using the commercial.[278]

The right of publicity is not protected on a federal level - there is no federal law or code that protects such a right (see more below on the Right of Publicity). Generally, it is left to the states - either through the common law or by statute. Currently, nineteen states have recognized the right of publicity in statutes; an additional twenty-eight (28) recognize the right via the common law.[279]

The band/artist KISS has become almost a cliche for its merchandising efforts - but the revenues generated are certainly no laughing matter. Given the value of the KISS brand, it is important to address merchandising in a Band Agreement.

Gene Simmons and Paul Stanley have merchandised anything and everything possible. A KISS fan can have KISS paraphernalia from birth (cradle, onesies, baby bibs) to death (a KISS coffin!).[280] In 2011, KISS offered a special cruise package to Israel. According to Steve Strauss in an article for Inc. magazine, "Kiss has licensed its name to more than 3,000 product categories, from lunch boxes and comic books to credit cards and condoms to become nearly a *one-billion-dollar* brand." (*emphasis* added)[281]

Every rock band and solo performer has branched out to merchandising, although admittedly not to the level of KISS. Artists such as Lady Gaga, Madonna, and the Rolling Stones all have significant merchandising arms as part of their overall operations. Toby Keith and Rascal Flatts have licensed their names to restaurant chains. Metallica sells baby "onesies" on its website. It is almost *de rigueur* for a rap artist to have a clothing line, (*e.g.,* Jay-Z, and Kanye West.) Performers even have perfumes and jewelry lines. The list goes on. However, remember, a record company will usually participate in merchandising under the terms of the recording agreement, so the artist does not receive the full amount of profit.

In fact, as part of the new and increasingly standard "360° deals" recording agreements, a record company now participates in all aspects (*i.e.,* 360° in all directions) of an artist's career and revenue.

IX.   *Rights After Death.*

When an artist dies, the revenue spigot does not automatically turn off. Remember, the songwriter has a Copyright that lasts the life of the artist *plus* 70 years. As a result, the heirs of an artist will receive the royalties for 70 years after the artist dies. For instance, John Lennon died in 1980, so Yoko Ono (or Yoko's heirs) is receiving the various monies generated by his songs and will receive those monies until 2050 and beyond. The heirs of Jimi Hendrix are still generating significant revenues from the release of studio tracks that Hendrix did while alive.[283]

Also, remember the § 203 and § 304 Termination rights that were discussed in the chapter on Copyright. The right can be exercised by the heirs of the artist pursuant to the terms of § 203 or of § 304 of the Copyright Act. Consequently, Yoko could exercise termination rights for certain Musical Compositions and Sound Recordings and have the ability to renegotiate those original deals.

X.   *Right of Publicity.*

As mentioned above, the right of publicity can be a source of revenue during the musician's lifetime. The right to publicity can also generate post-death revenue. However, not all states recognize the right of publicity after death. Only about a dozen states recognize that the right of publicity survives death.[283] It is telling that the first states to recognize the survivability of the right of publicity were Tennessee (home to Elvis) and California (home to so many celebrities). Consequently, what state the artist decides to call home can have a huge effect on the after-death earnings.

The revenue an artist's heirs can receive is considerable. The first year after an artist's death can revitalize the sales of the catalogue of the deceased artist. Michael Jackson, although trumpeting a comeback, was in a deep decline before his tragic death in 2009. In the next year, 2010, Michael Jackson was the top-earning dead celebrity, with revenues of $275 million.[284]

Likewise, in the year after Elvis Presley's death, his heirs received $60 million and the year after John Lennon died, his heirs received $17 million.[285] In 2013, the top grossing dead musical celebrities were: (i) Michael Jackson with an estimated $210 million; (ii) Elvis Presley with an estimated $55 million; (iii) Bob Marley with an estimated $18 million; and (iv) John Lennon with an estimated $12 million.[286] In 2021, among the top grossing dead musical celebrities were: (i) Prince with an estimated $120 Million; (ii) Michael Jackson with an estimated $75 Million; (iii) Bing Crosby with an estimated $33 million; (iv) Elvis Presley with an estimated $30 million; (iv) Bob Marley with an estimated $16 million; and (v) John Lennon with an estimated $12 million.[287]

Conclusion.

Many revenue streams are available to create a revenue river for a solo performer or a band/artist. Particularly in the band/artist context, it is mandatory to have certain legal documents in place. As discussed below, issues such as (a) the proper business form, (b) a proper band agreement, and (c) a clear understanding of the rights of the partners, are mandatory. A key point to remember is that band members are partners. As such, they will have obligations and responsibilities to each other. Partnerships can quickly come undone when it comes to money. Having the rights and obligations clearly set out will both prevent problems from arising and will make it easier to resolve issues as they do come up.

♪   ♪   ♪   ♪

CHAPTER 5

BUSINESS FORMATION

"There's no business like show business."
- Irving Berlin[288]

When starting a career in the entertainment industry, no matter which area of the arts, implementing the proper protections and structures is crucial. Having covered the basics of Intellectual Property, the next step is to determine the proper business form for the artist.

There are five major business forms (**the "Five Forms"**), and the analysis of which business form to use entails five factors (**the "Five Factors"**). This chapter will examine the Five Factors and then apply them to the Five Forms.

THE FIVE FACTORS

Formalities.

An initial consideration in forming a business is how complicated is it to create and run. Generally, unless there are significant factors for choosing a complicated form of business, a simple process is preferable. Some aspects to consider include: (i) where you file; (ii) what you file; and (iii) whether there are any follow-up formalities in maintaining the business form. For example, with a corporation there are high formalities such as annual meetings and annual reports. With a sole proprietorship or a general partnership, there are very few - and sometimes none. In many cases a major factor in determining the form of business is how many people are involved and whether they want equal management and voting rights in what happens with the business.

Investment.

The second factor, *investment*, works hand-in-hand with the third factor, *control* (more below). A business owner must determine how to bring money into the company without sacrificing control. There are five basic sources for a company to obtain money at *start-up*:

1. Partnership capital;

2. Debt;

3. Sponsorships/Barter;

4. Crowd funding; and

5. Investment.

The first method, *Partnership Capital,* comes from the partners in the enterprise - they dig into their own pockets, put their own money into the company, and then run the company themselves. Other than proper accounting practices and good faith in operating the business, the government does not care about protecting the partners since it is their money, they are active in running the company, and they can protect themselves.

The second method of obtaining money is through *Debt* - the company goes to the bank and gets a loan, or the company might issue a bond. Again, the government does not care about protecting the parties since they are in a position to protect themselves: the bank can take security in the form of collateral, and the partners are receiving the money and are liable for its repayment.

The third method of *Sponsorships/Barter* is a possibility but will generally be for in-kind items – a trade of equipment for branding rights to the sponsor.

The fourth method is *Crowdfunding* from such sources as Indiegogo and Kickstarter. Crowdfunding is "the practice of funding a project or venture by raising many small amounts of money from a large number of people, typically via the Internet."[289] The rock band Marillion is an example of a band/artist that used crowdfunding to help finance an album – they asked their fans to pre-pay for the album.[290] The band raised $100,000.00, was able to bypass the record company, and retained complete control over its music.[291]

The final method - *Investment* - sets off red lights and sirens! The issue of how to take investment into a company is broad and complicated. Crossing over into the dreaded land of the *"improper solicitation of securities"* can occur without warning and through the most innocuous of acts.

In the first three situations above, the party providing the money can take care of itself - the partners are running the company, the bank protects itself by taking a security in collateral, and a sponsor can sue for breach of contract if there is no delivery of a purchased product. An investor has none of these protections. By law, an investor must take a "hands-off" approach to her investment - she puts her money in and expects profit from another person's effort.[292]

The general rule on investment is that any investment offered to the public MUST be "filed" *and* "registered" with the Securities Exchange Commission.[293] Registration is an expensive and onerous task. Legal fees can easily reach tens of thousands of dollars. However, most small businesses could not afford the legal fees in a "public" offering, so the SEC developed certain exemptions to the general rule.

The exemptions to the public offering rule are found in Regulation D, and Rules 504 and 506. Rule 505 was rescinded since Rule 504 "swallowed" it up with the revisions to Regulation D in late 2016 and early 2017.

The basic rule remains the same - you must "file," but the securities do not need to be "registered." Each rule creates a specific exemption to the public offering rule. Rule 504 allows a person to raise a maximum of $5,000,000.00, but the offeror can only solicit "accredited investors."[294] An "accredited investor" is: (a) an individual who has an annual income of at least $200,000.00 or a married couple that made $300,000.00; or (b) a person with liquid assets totaling $1,000,000.00.[295] Rule 506 allows an unlimited amount of money to be raised, BUT you can only sell to 35 purchasers AND each one must "either alone or with the purchaser's representative(s) ha[ve] such knowledge and experience in financial and business matters that he is capable of evaluating the merits and risks of the prospective investment, or the issuer reasonably believes immediately prior to making any sale that such purchaser comes within this description."[296]

In 2012, President Obama signed into law the Jumpstart Our Business Startups Act **(the "JOBS Act")**. Under the JOBS

Act, crowdfunding was extended to allow investment. Prior to the JOBS Act, funds raised through such entities as Kickstarter had to be a "sale" transaction, (*e.g.,* pre-sales or reward packages). The person would purchase a special package for a price, but the person purchasing had no right to profits. The JOBS Act extended Rule 506's limited exemption to soliciting investors through online internet sites.

In the latter part of 2015, the SEC finally published rules and regulations regarding such activities over the internet. And the states have also stepped in to allow *intrastate* solicitation. The list of states that have legalized equity crowdfunding as of the printing of this edition included: Alabama, Colorado, Georgia, Idaho, Indiana, Kansas, Maine, Maryland, Michigan, Tennessee, Washington, and Wisconsin. [297]

Just as with the exemptions above, an issuer must follow strict rules to use an internet site as a tool for raising investment. The issuer: (i) must make the offering through a registered broker or "funding portal" (defined in the Act) that complies with certain requirements; (ii) must comply with the amount an investor may invest dependent upon the investor's annual income and net worth (Ex: a person who has an annual salary of $100,000.00 or less is limited to only investing the greater of (a) $2,000.00 or 5% of the investor's annual income or net worth[298]); and (b) the issuer can only raise up to $1,000,000.00 in a 12-month period.[299]

In late 2015 the SEC proposed the Rules and Regulations to govern how to implement the law. The new rules address three (3) major areas: (i) the limits on the amount to be raised; (ii) the Disclosure Requirements; and (iii) the need for crowdfunding portals that are registered with the SEC.[300]

The rules followed the examples of the states. Here is a quick overview of the rules:

(i)   Permits a company to raise a maximum

aggregate amount of $1 million through crowdfunding offerings in a 12-month period;

(ii)   Permits individual investors, over a 12-month period, to invest in the aggregate across all crowdfunding offerings up to:

(a)   If either their annual income or net worth is less than $100,000, than the greater of: $2,000 or 5 percent of the lesser of their annual income or net worth;

(b) If both their annual income and net worth are equal to or more than $100,000.00, 10 percent of the lesser of their annual income or net worth; and

(iii)   During the 12-month period, the aggregate amount of securities sold to an investor through all crowdfunding offerings may not exceed $100,000.00.

You must be very careful in the areas of securities in general and be particularly vigilant in the area of crowd funding. Investment is one of the biggest areas of danger for a start-up business - *HERE BE MONSTERS!*

Control.

The third factor, *control*, is linked with the factor of investment. One of the disadvantages of the corporate business form is that if an investor buys fifty percent +1 shares of the stock, that investor owns the company. The original owner, who often times started the company, is now out. By comparison, in the limited liability company **("LLC")** business form, a person who has started and built a company, can take investment but retain control by being named the "Manager" of the LLC. Thus, the choice of business entity is very important when it comes to control.

Taxes.

The fourth factor to consider is the tax treatment of the business form. See *"Taxman"* by The Beatles! Some business forms have *"double-taxation,"* (*i.e.,* a tax at the business form level and a tax at the individual level). An LLC, if taxed as a partnership, will have *"flow-through"* taxation, (*i.e.,* only a tax event at the individual level.) Choosing one versus the other tax regime can lead to millions of dollars in tax savings.

Liability.

Finally, the main reason for choosing a business form is to get out of the possibility of personal liability. The great disadvantage of a sole proprietorship or general partnership is that the owner or owners of such entities is/are personally on the hook for the company's liabilities. Consequently, if the owner is found at fault, the owner's personal house, car, and assets are at risk of being taken for the payment of the liability.

One disadvantage of a Limited Partnership business form **(the "LP")** is that the General Partner of the LP is personally liable for the debts of the LP (discussed in more depth below). Consequently, when the LP business form is needed, it is best to get an LLC into the position of the General Partner, not an individual.

♪   ♪   ♪   ♪

THE FIVE FORMS

The five major forms of business are sole proprietorships, general partnerships, corporations, limited partnerships, and limited liability companies. Each has its own advantages and disadvantages. Choosing which entity to adopt is a fact-intensive decision based on how the Five Factors affect an artist's unique situation.

Sole Proprietorships.

There are many definitions for the term "sole proprietorship." In this book, a *sole proprietorship* shall mean a business owned by one person who receives all the profits, assumes all the debts, and assumes all the liability for the business. In applying the Five Factors, the sole proprietorship is the simplest and fastest form of business. There are no formalities in setting up the company, the tax treatment is "flow-through," and there are no issues of investment or control since the owner is the only one putting in capital.

However, there is no limited liability in the sole proprietorship or the partnership. As mentioned above, the owner of these types of entities has its own personal assets at stake. Such a situation would be a major reason to forgo this business entity.

General Partnerships.

A general partnership consists of two or more people coming together in an expanded sole proprietorship. Similar to the sole proprietorship, there are few, if any formalities, which can actually be a disadvantage - if a group of guys forms a band, starts rehearsing, and does a performance or two, they have created a general partnership without even knowing it! Thus, it is always preferable to have a partnership agreement – in our context, a Band Agreement. The general partnership will have "flow-through" taxation. However, the partnership still has personal liability, and, since there are at least two partners, there is an issue of control.

The partners can address the issue of control by executing a simple partnership agreement. However, nothing will remove the aspect of personal liability. Again, the lack of limited liability would be a reason to forgo this type of business entity.

Corporations.

The corporate business form came into existence in response to the need for limited liability. The general impression is that corporations are a relatively recent business form, with the 1800s and the 1900s seeing an explosion of corporations and their attendant power. "[A]ctually they are very ancient - so ancient that their actual point of origin is lost in the legend of Numa Pompilius and beyond," says Bruce Brown.[301] "The oldest surviving business corporation in the universe is probably Sweden's Stora Kopperberg, which was founded in 1288 and is now known as StoraEnso. The oldest surviving corporation of any sort is the Benedictine Order of the Catholic Church, which was founded around 529 A.D."[302] In America, the first major corporation was the Boston Manufacturing Company, established in 1813.[303]

The corporation has a distinct terminology. *Shareholders* own the shares of the company. *Directors* literally direct the corporation and have ultimate legal responsibility for the actions of the corporation and its subsidiaries, officers, employees, and agents. *Officers* are generally appointed by the Directors to take care of day-to-day operations and have legal authority to act on the corporation's behalf.

While the LLC has replaced the corporation as the preferred business entity, corporations are still dominant with significant capital and assets under their control. Moreover, not-for-profit businesses must be a corporation.

Limited Partnerships.

The limited partnership came into existence in 1916 with the Uniform Limited Partnership Act (**the "ULPA"**).[304] The drafters of the ULPA had a small *local* business in mind in which capital was invested from *local* investors.[305] However, larger limited partnerships developed due to both (i) the advantages of "flow-through" taxation, and (ii) the fact that limited liability extends to passive investors.[306]

Like the corporation and the LLC, distinct terms are used in relation to the parties of a limited partnership. *General Partners* have the ability to run the partnership and make decisions for the partnership. But there is a major drawback - the general partners can be liable to third-parties or to the other limited partners.[307] *Limited Partners* have no liability *unless* they "take . . . part in the control of the business."[308]

Limited Liability Company.

In industry, including entertainment, the preferred business form is the LLC. LLCs are, compared to the other business forms, relative newcomers. The first LLC law is generally attributed to a German law of 1892.[309] In 1977, Wyoming became the first American state to enact a true LLC act, which was modeled after the 1892 German Code. In addition to limited liability, the Wyoming Act has four basic characteristics: (i) a form of the word "limited" must be in the entity's name; (ii) the entity is given full juristic (legal) personality; (iii) the partnership concept of *delectus or intuitus personae* that permits a partner to control admission of new partners to the partnership, is present; and (iv) LLCs are dissolved by death of a member and provide for probate or sale of a deceased's share. Most LLC acts have followed this lead.[310]

An LLC is comprised of *Members*, who own the *Membership Interests* (not "shares") of the LLC, and *Managers* (not "officers") who run the daily operations of the company. Sometimes, the Members will want to run the company and that is a *Member-Managed* LLC. Sometimes, the Members will appoint a Manager to run the company and that is a *Manager-Managed* LLC.

Between 1988 and 1993, more than thirty states passed some form of a limited liability act.[311] Now the LLC is the preferred form of business entity and is recognized in virtually all states. The reason was that the IRS issued a ruling that LLCs would be taxed as partnerships and not as corporations.[312] The combination of limited liability, "flow-through" taxation, the power to determine who is in the company, and the power to retain control even though others may own the company has caused the LLC to be the most popular form of business entity in modern business.

Conclusion.

Given the advantages of the LLC, most clients should consider this business form first. The only reason to consider one of the other forms is if the law or circumstances demand it. An example of the law demanding a business form is the IRS requirement that an entity filing for a not-for-profit status must be in the corporate business form. An example of circumstances dictating what form to use, particularly in film and theatre, is when investors are used to seeing an LLC as the parent company, with subsidiary LLCs to take investment in a particular project. Other than the special circumstance of forming a not-for-profit company, the LLC should be the starting point in the discussion of what form of business entity to create.

CHAPTER 6

CONTRACTS - PART 1

*"A verbal contract is not worth
the paper it's printed on!"*
-        Samuel Goldwyn

A *written* contract is the foundation of all relationships in the entertainment industry - a verbal contract, by comparison, is almost worthless. When we talk about "contracts," most people think of a piece of paper that reflects an agreement by and between two or more people. However, under the law, a contract refers to a *promise* made by one person that is *enforceable* by another person.[313] The word "promise" implies something in the future. The law is concerned with enforcing a promise for some future action - "[t]he critical issue is whether . . . there was an enforceable promise to sell. . . ."[314] For the promise to be enforceable there has to be an exchange - "I will do "A" if you will do "B.""[315]

No system can declare that every promise creates a contract. Therefore, we need to distinguish between those promises that we will enforce and those we will not. There are two philosophical approaches to determine which promises to enforce: (i) all promises are enforceable, but there are exceptions for promises that are not enforceable; or (ii) all promises are unenforceable, but there are exceptions for those promises we want to be enforced.[316] Both the Romans and English common law adopted the second choice.[317]

The Romans were the first to give life to the idea that a promise may be the foundation for a legal duty; however, that is not the true notion of a modern contract.[318] To the Romans, only promises that fell into certain categories received protection.[319] The Romans had three types of contracts:

1. *the "stipulation",* a formal ceremony of swearing through a set litany of questions and answers, but only one person was bound;

2. *the "real" contract* that required a person to turn over a piece of property, creating a promise by the other party to return it when demanded (though in this scenario one person had already performed, so this contract did not address the issue of when both parties have to make a promise); and

3. *the "consensual" contract,* which was more flexible but still limited to only four situations: (a) sales, (b) hire, (c) partnership, and (c) mandate.[320]

After the Roman Empire dissolved, two distinct systems of law emerged in its place:

1.   the **common law** system in England; and

2.   the **civil code system**, derived from the Romans, now present on the European continent.[321]

Generally, the "common law" is not codified: there is no comprehensive compilation of legal rules and statutes. It is largely based on "precedent," or a legal decision made in a prior case ("common cases make common law"). Common law functions as an adversarial system, *(i.e.,* a contest between two opposing parties before a judge who moderates).[322] Judges (or juries) gather facts and then apply prior precedents to determine the holding in the case. Judges and juries consequently have an enormous role in shaping American and British law.

The common law dominates in America *except* in Louisiana, which follows a civil code regime. One might ask, "*why* Louisiana?" Because Louisiana was settled by the French, and the French followed the civil law system. Louisiana retained the civil law system.

The "civil law" is codified: it is comprised of "comprehensive, continuously updated legal codes that specify all matters capable of being brought before a court, the applicable procedure, and the appropriate punishment for each offense."[323] The judge's role is to bring the formal charges, investigate the matter, and decide the case within the framework of a codified set of laws. Under a civil law regime, the judge's role is less important than the decisions of legislators and legal scholars who will actually draft the code.[324] The civil code regime dominates on the European continent, particularly in France.

Offer and Acceptance.

To enforce a contract, a contract must first be made. Marvin A. Chirelstein comments, "In a very real sense, the role of contract law in this context is (a) to distinguish the culminating moment of agreement from all the bargaining activity that has gone before and (b) to protect the agreement thus arrived at from any effort by either party to start the bargaining process up again."[325] The first prong is addressed by the concepts of *offer, acceptance,* and *consideration.* The second prong is addressed by doctrines such as *mistake, duress, the Statute of Frauds,* and *the Parol Evidence Rule.*

Offer.

Under the law, an *offer* is "a manifestation of assent to enter into a bargain made by the offeror to the offeree, conditioned on a manifestation of assent in the form of some action (promise or performance) by the offeree."[326] Simply put it means "I will do "A" if you do "B." It is important to note that a person making an offer can retract the offer at any time prior to acceptance by the offeree. Once the offeree has accepted the offer, however, the offeror is then bound to stand by the offer.[327]

A key doctrine to remember is the "*mirror-image rule*" - "a statement of assent is effective only if it exactly mirrors the offer and expresses unconditional assent to all of the terms and conditions imposed by the offeror."[328] An offer made by the offeror must be accepted by the offeree *exactly as the terms are described* by the offeror or the original offer is dead.[329] The offeree's requested changes to the original offer creates a counteroffer. The counteroffer kills the original offer, and the counteroffer now becomes the offer. The offeree becomes the offeror, and the original offeror becomes the offeree!

One of the important questions with an offer is: when is a communication an "offer" versus merely an "invitation to deal?"[330] An explicit statement such as "I will sell this car for $500" is clearly an offer to sell. But what about a statement such as, "I am thinking of selling my car but not for less than $500"? In that case, the court will look to the series of negotiations between the parties to determine whether there was an offer or merely an invitation to deal.

An interesting case arises when someone makes a promise in jest or in drunken boasting. In the classic court case *Lucy v. Zehmer*[331], the defendant offered to sell his farm for $50,000 to the plaintiff. Zehmer then claimed that he was (a) drunk, (b) kidding, and (c) that Lucy knew that. However, the Supreme Court of Virginia found for Lucy, holding that there was a written agreement, Zehmer had written the agreement, and Lucy had taken the offer seriously, even going as far as to leave to get the money.

A few years ago, a similar situation came up between the television comedian Bill Maher and billionaire Donald Trump. Prior to his election to the presidency, Trump had been vociferous during President Obama's presidency in demanding that President Obama reveal his birth certificate. Maher demanded that Trump provide his birth certificate to prove that Trump's parents were not orangutans, and if Trump would do so, Maher would give $5 million to any charity of Trump's choice. Trump provided the birth certificate and made demand on Maher to send the $5 million to certain designated charities. Maher said he was kidding, and Trump sued. Trump later withdrew the suit but said he was withdrawing it in order to amend the complaint and refile it at a later date.[332] As of the date of the printing of this edition, Trump had not refiled the suit.

What about an advertisement in a paper? In *Lefkowitz v. Great Minnesota Surplus Store,*[333] a store advertised a mink coat for the price of $1.00 to the "first person in line" (it did not specify a "woman"). The first person in line happened to be a man, Mr. Lefkowitz. The store, however, would not sell the mink coat to him because they claimed the advertisement was for women only. The court ruled against the store and the store had to sell the mink coat to Lefkowitz for the advertised price. Despite this case, however, the general rule is that an advertisement in a paper, a flyer, or on television, is an invitation to deal. The person who buys the shirt is actually making the offer to the storeowner.[334]

Termination of Offer.

Another issue must be kept in mind: when can the offer be terminated? An offer can be terminated four ways:

1. <u>Revocation by the offeror</u> - the offer can be terminated by the offeror at any time before acceptance by the offeree, usually by sending a revocation in writing;

2. <u>Death or incapacity of the offeror;</u>

3. <u>Lapse of the offer</u> - the offeror can set a time limit during which the offer remains open, after which it lapses; or

4. <u>Rejection of the offer by the offeree</u> - the offeree can terminate the offer by rejecting it *or* making a counteroffer.[335]

<u>*Acceptance.*</u>

Acceptance is "the action (promise or performance) by the offeree that creates a contract (*i.e.,* make the offeror's promise enforceable)."[336] Again, simply put, in this case "B" says, "Yes, I will do "B" if you do "A." Acceptance can take many forms but generally, acceptance is (i) a return promise or (ii) performance.

There are two philosophical approaches to determine whether assent occurred: (i) "the *subjective* approach which looks at the actual or subjective intentions of the parties"; or (ii) "the *objective* approach which looks to the external or objective appearance of the parties' intentions as manifested by their actions."[337] The objectivist position is the generally accepted theory today.[338] If there is a dispute on language, the court will look to common and normal usage, and to the circumstances surrounding the negotiations.

Under the law, the "offeror is the master of his offer" - the offeror can dictate how acceptance is to be manifest.[339] The offeror can tell the offeree to accept in writing or to accept by beginning performance - it is up to the offeror. And the general rule is that only the offeree can accept the offer, unless the offeror indicates otherwise.[340] For offerees, it is important to remember that an offer can be accepted by silence[341] - so answer your mail!

Remember the mirror-image rule from above - if the offeree changes the terms of the original offer, it becomes a counteroffer, and the original offeror is now the offeree. If the offeree does change the terms and creates a counteroffer, the original offer is dead, and the offeree cannot try to resurrect the original offer.[342]

Consideration.

Along with offer and acceptance there is one other element to address regarding whether a contract has been made - *consideration.* For example, even if A promises to give B $500 (makes an offer) and B agrees to take it (acceptance), no contract exists if B does not have to do anything to receive the money. Why? Because it is a *nudum pactum* - a promise without consideration - the parties did not make a contract because the *bargain* was not supported by *consideration.* Thus, the transaction entails a gift - not a contract. There is no benefit to A to give B the $500 - A received nothing in return, and B received no *detriment* in making the promise to receive the money. If B's promise to receive the money came in return for giving something to A, even a peppercorn, it would become a contract.

Consideration is now expressed in the "bargain theory" - something is bargained for if it is sought by the promisor in exchange for the promise and is given by the promisee in exchange for that promise.[343] In plain English, both parties have to give up something and each must get something. One big consequence of this new theory was that judges now did not concern themselves with the substance of the exchange but rather focused on whether it was the result of a "bargain."[344]

So, what can be consideration? Anything and everything, even something nominal with very little value. The classic example is that something with the worth of a single peppercorn can be consideration for a contract.[345] Consideration can also take the form of (a) a promise, (b) performance, (c) cash, or (d) goods. The same consideration can support a number of promises within one bargained for exchange.[346] Also, note that consideration can "move" - one person can guarantee the performance of another.

Flaws in Formation.

As discussed above, to determine whether a contract was created it is essential to determine whether: (i) was there was an offer; (ii) was there acceptance; and (iii) was it supported by consideration. However, what happens if, on the surface, those three elements are met but there is still a problem? There are many ways that a flaw in the formation of the contract can occur - a few of the more prominent ones are briefly reviewed below.

Ambiguity.

The parties have agreed on the transporting ship, the price paid, and when to deliver the goods - EXCEPT the parties have different ships in mind! That is what happened in the seminal case of the *Peerless.*[347] There were two ships named *Peerless* - one leaving in October, one in December. When the goods arrived on the December boat instead of the October boat, the defendant refused to pay since, to his mind, the goods were late.

The problem was *ambiguity* - the parties to the contract were not clear on which ship *Peerless* was being discussed.[348] Another aspect was *mistake*, which we discuss below. The parties did not understand each other. The court held for the defendant - there had been no *consensus ad idem* - no agreement on the same thing, or "no meeting of the minds." The main issue between the parties was not the cotton, but the time of the delivery of the cotton. The parties were betting on the market price of cotton at a particular time: one for the market price in October and one for the market price in December. Since they did not agree on which *Peerless* was the correct one, there was no contract.

The moral of the story - *make sure which ship you are talking about!*

Mistake.

Mistake can arise in two ways: (i) mutual mistake, and (ii) unilateral mistake. *Unilateral mistake* requires only a quick comment, as courts are generally reluctant to undo a contract in those circumstances. *Unilateral mistake* occurs when "only one (1) of the parties has an erroneous belief as to the facts."[349] Unilateral mistake often arises in cases concerning a general contractor making a bid on a construction contract. Contractors will often wait to the last minute to submit bids, and in doing so, make mistakes as to the actual costs of the project. Upon winning the bid, the contractor realizes that he has made a mistake as to the costs. In limited circumstances and as long as the other party has not already relied on the bid, the contractor might be able to revoke the bid.[350]

Far more common is the second category of mistake - mutual mistake. *Mutual mistake* "occurs when both parties are under substantially the same erroneous belief as to the facts."[351] As compared to ambiguity, in mistake both parties understand each other but both are mistaken about a fact that is part of the understanding.

Sherwood v. Walker[352] is a case that all law school students get familiar with in their contracts class. In *Sherwood*, a farmer and a buyer agreed on the sale of a cow they both knew as "Rose 2d of Aberlone." Both the farmer and the buyer thought that the cow was barren and could not have calves. However, before the exchange they discovered the cow was pregnant. The farmer sought to cancel the contract, as Rose was now worth far more than the low contract price for a barren cow. The court agreed.

The Restatement (Second) of Contracts lists three requirements for a contract to be avoided on grounds of mutual mistake: (i) the mistake concerns a basic assumption on which the contract was made; (ii) the mistake has a material effect on the agreed exchange of performances; and (iii) the mistake is not one of which that party bears the risk.[353] Each of the three (3) elements was present in *Sherwood*: (i) both thought the cow was barren; (ii) the cow being barren was a key element as to the price; and (iii) neither party had been obligated to make sure the cow was indeed barren.

The moral of the story - *see if your cow can have a cow: or in other words, make sure you know what you are contracting for!*

Duress.

In the next scenario, offer and acceptance as well as consideration exist, and the parties have agreed on the subject matter of the contract. However, one party was threatened into signing the agreement with physical or financial harm.

One of the major requirements of a contract is that the parties must agree *voluntarily* to the bargain that they negotiate.[354] Thus, "while a gun to the head will almost always compel an affirmative response from the victim, the law, for reasons too plain to require discussion, treats the resulting 'agreement' as void."[355] A person signing a contract with a gun pointed to her head has not voluntarily made the bargain. As Marvin Chirelstein comments, "Promises extorted by violence or threat of violence are obviously not enforceable."[356]

Generally, the elements for duress are:

1. there must be a threat;

2. the threat must be improper;

3. the threat must induce the victim's assent to the contract; and

4. the threat must be serious enough to justify the victim's assent.[357]

As with most tenets of contract law, however, the rules of

different states can vary - sometimes slightly, sometimes widely. In New York, for example, the elements for a claim of duress are: "A valid claim of duress has two components, (1) threats of an unlawful act by one party which (2) compels performance by the other party of an act which it had a legal right to abstain from performing."[358]

Generally, the remedy for a contract made under duress is that the contract is voidable at the discretion of the victim.[359] In New York, "A contract is voidable on the ground of duress when a party establishes that he was forced to agree to it by means of a wrongful threat which precluded the exercise of his free will."[360]

Simply put, *no consent, no contract.*

Unfairness; Unconscionable.

A contract might be set aside as *"unfair"* or *"unconscionable."* One example is a seller attempting to get a buyer to waive warranties in exchange for a "good" such as a car or a refrigerator. Unconscionability can arise in form contracts, which often have draconian clauses that are hidden or placed in very small type. In *Williams v. Walker-Thomas Furniture Co.*, 350 F.2d 445 (C.C. Cir. 1965), a customer, Ms. Williams, had purchased a variety of household items over several years from the store, Walker-Thomas Furniture. Each purchase had required Williams to sign a new contract, and each contract contained a "cross-collateral clause" (*i.e.,* if Ms. Williams failed to pay on one (1) item, ALL of the items could be taken back by Walker-Thomas Furniture). The print was small, the language was confusing, and it was not brought to Ms. Williams' attention. Ms. Williams defaulted on the stereo payments and Walker-Thomas Furniture came and repossessed certain items of Ms. Williams. On one (1) item Ms. Williams only owed three cents and, on another item, only 25 cents.

The lower court, feeling that it had no statutory authority to overturn the contract, reluctantly held for the company but condemned the conduct of the store. On appeal, the Court of Appeals overturned the decision and returned it to the lower court instructing it that no statutory authority was needed to invoke the doctrine of unconscionability, since the doctrine was in the common law. Furthermore, the Court of Appeals established a two-element test for unconscionability: (i) an absence of meaningful choice on the buyer's part, and (ii) the contract contains terms that are unreasonably favorable to the seller. Applying the factors, the lower court held for Ms. Williams and set aside the contract.

Another example of unconscionability is when there is uneven bargaining on both sides. For example, one side is a large company represented by a team of attorneys from a top-ten firm, while the other side is a lone individual representing himself. The importance of using an attorney to negotiate contracts cannot be understated. Such unevenness in the bargaining process can sometimes (although rarely) be grounds for unconscionability. Consulting with an attorney so that you do not wind up in the position of having to argue unconscionability after the fact, however, is preferable to taking the big risk of proceeding alone and hoping everything will work out.

The moral of the story - *read the fine print!*

Fraud & Misrepresentation.

Sometimes a contract is achieved by fraud or a material misrepresentation - for example, the forty acres of "beach property" is actually forty acres in the desert, or that bridge in

Brooklyn is not actually for sale. In these cases, the law will allow the contract to be voidable at the discretion of the person receiving the misrepresentation.[361] Two types of misrepresentations exist under the law: (i) misrepresentations that go to the *"inducement"* of entering into the contract; and (ii) misrepresentations that go to the very heart of the contract, the *"factum"* or in the *"execution."*[362] An example of misrepresentation in the "inducement" is when a seller misrepresents the quality of goods - the buyer is "induced" to enter into the transaction based upon a misrepresentation about the goods. An example of misrepresentation in the "factum" or in the "execution" is when someone is told that a paper being signed does not have any legal effect.[363]

However, certain elements must be met before the recipient can void the contract, and one well-known contracts' scholar places them into four major categories:

1.   The assertion made was <u>not in accord with the actual facts</u> (as opposed to mere opinion);

2.   The assertion made must be either "<u>fraudulent" or "material</u>." In tort, where money damages are sought, fraudulent assertions are needed; in a contract action seeking to void the contract, only material assertions are needed[364];

3.   The assertion must be <u>relied upon</u> by the recipient in manifesting assent – it was part of the reason why the recipient agreed to the deal[365]; and

4. The reliance by the recipient must be justified - a person cannot rely upon the misrepresentation that the sun will not rise tomorrow. It is not justified to rely upon such a statement.[366]

Again, different states can have slightly different rules. In New York, for example, the elements for common law fraud or misrepresentation are: (i) a plaintiff must allege a misrepresentation of a material fact; (ii) the falsity of the misrepresentation; (iii) scienter; (iv) plaintiff's reliance on the alleged misrepresentation; and (v) injury resulting from the reliance.[367]. A new term is introduced in these elements: *scienter* - "a term used in pleading to signify an allegation (or that part of the declaration or indictment which contains it) setting out the defendant's previous knowledge of the cause which led to the injury complained of, or rather the person's previous knowledge of a state of facts which it was the person's duty to guard against and his omission to do which has led to the injury complained of."[368]

The moral of the story - *check it out before you buy the bridge!*

Capacity.

A final item to be aware of is whether the person entering into the contract has the "capacity" to execute the agreement. The issue of "capacity" arises in a variety of situations, such as: (i) minors attempting to sign a contract; (ii) a mentally ill person signing a contract; and (iii) a person without authority to make the agreement signing the contract.

Minority. In the music industry, the issue of minors entering into agreements arises frequently. It is mandatory that all signatories to an agreement be of "majority" age, which in most jurisdictions is 18 and over. California law allows parties to seek court approval of entertainment industry contracts involving minors.[369] The advantage of taking the time and energy to do this is that the minor's right to cancel the contract will become limited.[370] The State of New York will also allow a party to seek judicial approval of an entertainment contract with a minor.

However, one major difference exists between California and New York. In New York, a judge has authority to deny approval of a contract until the parents (if entitled to the minor's earnings) *or* the minor (if entitled to the minor's own earnings) agree to put a portion of the earnings under the control of a guardian. In addition, under New York law, most terms of the minor's employment contract cannot exceed three years from the date of approval of the contract. The California law regarding minors does not have such a limit. A different part of California law will impose limitations on the term - California Labor Code § 2855 limits the term of any personal service contract to seven years.[371]

A case in 2007 underscored the importance of getting judicial approval of contract that involved a minor. The case of *Berg v. Traylor*, 148 Cal.App.4th at 809, involved the child actor, Craig Traylor. Traylor became a star on the television show *Malcolm in the Middle*. Prior to that, his mother had entered into a personal management contract with a Personal Manager for a fifteen percent (15%) commission. Traylor, only ten years old at the time, did not see or sign the contract. The contract also contained an express provision that if Craig Traylor disaffirmed the contract, his mother would be personally liable for the payments due to the Personal Manager.

Then came the problems - two years into the contract, Mr. Traylor got the *Malcolm in the Middle* job. Four months before the expiration of the contract for that show, the mother fired the Personal Manager. The Personal Manager sued, won a judgment for $600,000.00 in arbitration, and the award was upheld by the trial court.[372] However, since the contract had not gained court approval, the Court of Appeals overturned the trial court verdict as to Mr. Traylor - no court approval, so he could disaffirm.[373] The mother, however, was still on the hook and the judgment was affirmed as to her.

Mental Infirmity. One clear legal principal is that a person who is mentally ill or mentally incompetent cannot make a contract. As Marvin Chirelstein states, if "[a] party lacks or can be presumed to lack the attributes of informed volition, then the customary basis of contract is in doubt."[374] Allan Farnsworth points to dictum in a variety of cases that states, "Perhaps no branch of jurisprudence is more elusive than that dealing with one's mental capacity to contract."[375]

Mental infirmity, although initially concerned with "insanity," now includes mental retardation, mental illness, brain damage, brain deterioration from old age or dementia, and the use of mind-altering drugs including alcohol.[376] However, the infirmity must exist at the time of signing of the contract. If it arises after the contract is made, it does not invalidate the contract.[377] The test to determine mental infirmity is the *cognitive test*, which inquires whether the party knew what they were doing and the consequences of their actions.[378]

Originally, the remedy for a contract made by a mentally incompetent person was to void the agreement[379] given the lack of any "meeting of the minds." The more modern view is that the agreement is only voidable, not void, by the mentally incompetent party (similar to a minor).[380] In other words, the mentally incompetent person can declare the contract void or can elect to let it stand.

Authority (or lack thereof). A final area of capacity is when a person without authority or power signs an agreement. The determination regarding whether a contract should be void due to lack of authority of the signer "must be decided by a court."[381]

The situation of someone signing without authority is a constant problem in the entertainment industry. The authors have seen numerous instances of clients coming in with agreements made by a person wishing to be involved with the band/artist. One particular case concerned a major metal band/artist whose Musical Compositions have appeared in various mediums and whose albums were re-released without the band/artist's permission. A person with a prior relationship with the band/artist had misrepresented its position to a variety of parties. Those agreements are being contested and the unauthorized signer faces millions of dollars in damages.

Statute of Frauds.

One way to address the issue of flawed contract formation and disagreement regarding the terms is to force the parties to put their agreement in writing. The *Statute of Frauds* (**the "SOF"**) requires that certain types of contracts *must* be expressed in a writing - *i.e.,* they cannot be oral:

1.   a contract of an executor or administrator to answer for a duty of his/her decedent (*the executor-administrator provision*);

2.   a contract to answer for the duty of another (*the suretyship provision*);

3.   a contract made upon consideration of marriage (*the marriage provision*);

4.   a contract for the sale of an interest in land (*the land contract provision*); and

5.   a contract that is not to be performed within one year from the making thereof (*the one-year provision*).[382]

Goods used to be covered by the Statute of Frauds but are now covered under the Uniform Commercial Code (**the "UCC"**). In the music industry, the UCC comes into play in Distribution Agreements for sales of records, CDs, and other tangible goods. The UCC covers:

1.   a contract for the sale of goods for the price of $500 or more (Uniform Commercial Code § 2-201);

2.   a contract for the sale of securities (Uniform Commercial Code § 8-319);

3.   a contract for the sale of personal property not otherwise covered, to the extent of enforcement by way of action or defense beyond $5,000 in amount or value of remedy (Uniform Commercial Code § 1-206).[383]

An important clause in the SOF that affects the

entertainment industry is the *one-year provision* that requires any contract that takes longer than a year to complete to be in writing. In determining the one-year time period, two key points in time are relevant: (i) the time of the making of the contract; and (ii) the time for performance.[384] Mr. Farnsworth gives the example of a ten-month agreement: (a) if performance is to begin at once and be completed before the year expires, it is NOT within the statute; however, (b) if the performance of the contract does not begin for three months, and then takes ten months, that is more than one year and IS within the statute.[385]

In the music industry, all recording agreements, distribution agreements, and personal management agreements MUST be put in writing. Why? Because generally each of these types of contracts will be for a period that is longer than a year. Record agreements tend to last for multiple years, as do personal management agreements. So, if someone makes a verbal agreement in these areas, the other party to the contract can argue against enforcement of the contract.[386] Other remedies may be available depending upon the level of performance and reliance by the party arguing the failure to abide by the Statute.[387]

Parol Evidence Rule.

Another way that the law has addressed the issue of flaws in contracts is the *Parol Evidence Rule* (**the "PER"**). Under the PER, once an agreement is reduced to a writing, the use of an extrinsic writing (a writing that is outside the agreement) may be barred.[388] There are exceptions to the general rule, but once the parties have created a written contract, they are held to the terms of the contract.

As mentioned, the PER is not an absolute rule. The PER will give precedence to subsequent agreements over *prior* negotiations and *prior* agreements. But what about the situation where one of the parties to the agreement argues that the agreement does NOT reflect what the parties actually agreed upon leading up to the signing? The law will look to whether or not the parties to the agreement *intended* to make the agreement a final and complete expression of their agreement.[389] If the parties DID intend the written agreement to be a final and complete expression, the agreement is considered *"integrated."* If they did not, it is considered *"unintegrated,"* and the PER does not apply.[390]

If the court determines that the agreement is *integrated*, the court will then look to determine if the agreement is *"fully integrated"* or only *"partially integrated."*[391] Specifically, the courts look to see if the agreement itself gives any indication, whether by the completeness of its construction or by an explicit clause in the agreement.

If the agreement is determined to be fully integrated, even then parol evidence is allowed to show that the agreement was NOT a final expression of the terms of the contract.[392] If the agreement is determined only partially integrated, a new consideration arises: is the evidence of the prior negotiations being used to *contradict* the terms of the written agreement? If so, the court will not allow the evidence. However, if it is being used to "explain" or "supplement" the original writing, the court may allow it.[393]

The PER will allow evidence: (i) of subsequent negotiations to the written agreement; (ii) that there was no agreement; and (iii) that assists in the interpretation of the contract.[394] The modern trend in the law is to allow parol evidence. "The writing cannot prove its own completeness and accuracy."[395]

Breach & Damages.

Breach. Breach is the term used when one party to a contract has failed to perform. Most contracts contain a clause regarding breach and cure: the party that is injured must give notice to the breaching party demanding the cure of the breach. If the breaching party does not cure, the injured party can litigate. The law passes no moral judgment on breach - money damages are deemed adequate and, generally, there are no criminal penalties or punitive damages.[396]

Damages. Three different *"interests"* can be harmed by the breach of a contract, and remedied with its own type of tailored relief:

1. the *"expectation interest"* of the injured party - the goal is to put the injured party in as good a position as that party would have been in had the contract been performed if there had been no breach[397];

2. the *"reliance interest"* - the goal is to put the injured party back in the position in which that party would have been had the contract not been made[398];

3. the *"restitution interest"* - if the party in breach has gained a benefit before the breach, that benefit must be returned;[399]

There are a couple of ways to break down damages: (i) *"specific"* - relief that "is intended to give the injured party the very performance that was promised"; and (ii) *"substitutional"* - relief that is intended to give something to the promisee in substitution for the promised performance."[400] A second way to categorize damages is: (i) *"legal"* - to remedy a breach of a promise by payment of money (similar to substitutional); and (ii) *"equitable"* - to remedy a breach of a promise by requiring specific performance of the contract (similar to specific relief).[401] Different types of damages address different interests.

Expectation Interest. Generally, courts look to the *expectation interest* first - trying to put the injured party in as good a position as that party would have been in had the contract been performed without breach.[402] These damages consist of: (i) the value the injured party lost by reason of the default; and (ii) any expenditure made by the injured party in carrying out its own obligations.[403] The UCC will apply the same general rule to breaches of a contract for goods.[404]

It is important to remember that expectation damages are not guaranteed. If the injured party does not take steps to *mitigate* (lessen) their damages, the law will not reward ignorance or negligence. If you know the ship is the wrong ship, you cannot just stand around - you have to try and find another ship. However, the party that is breaching cannot assert that *any* ship will do; nor can the injured party claim that *only* the exact same ship will do.

A famous case in show business illustrates the issue of mitigating your damages and at the same time demonstrates that one job does not replace another. Back in 1965, before she was a star, Shirley MacLaine, signed a contract with Twentieth Century-Fox Film Corp. (**"Fox"**) to play the lead role in a movie, "Bloomer Girl," in which she would act, sing, and dance for $750,000.00.[405] Fox decided to cancel the movie but, in an attempt to mollify Ms. MacLaine, they offered her an inferior part in another movie. Ms. MacLaine refused to take the role and sued.

The Supreme Court of California held for Ms. MacLaine, reasoning that an employee does have a duty to take new employment but does NOT have to take inferior employment. The "other employment" had to be comparable and not "of a different or inferior kind."[406]

Reliance Interest. Sometimes expectation damages are inadequate or unfair. The court will then look to protect the *"reliance interest"* - put the injured party back in the position in which that party would have been had the contract not been made.[407] There are two types of reliance expenses: (i) *"essential reliance"* - monies spent by the injured party to perform under the contract; and (ii) *"incidental reliance"* - monies spent by the injured party that were in furtherance of the essential aim of the contract. Mr. Farnsworth gives the example of a contract to build a store: (i) essential expenses were architect plans, labor, and materials - those are essential to building the store; but (ii) store goods and hiring of employees would be incidental to building the store.[408]

Restitution Interest. A third way to protect someone in the case of a breach is to protect the party's restitution interest. The purpose of restitution is different - the court looks to prevent unjust enrichment (*i.e.,* put the party that breached back in the position the party that breached would have been in if there had been no contract).[409]

Here is an example of the three interests. A recording artist has hired a musician to play guitar on certain tracks of an album. The guitar player is to get $10,000.00 a track and will be playing on ten tracks (a very nice gig!). The guitar player figures it will cost her $5,000.00 a track for costs (travel, equipment, and other related costs), so she will make $5,000.00 per track in profit. If the guitar player does ten tracks, she *expects* to make $50,000.00 in profit. However, after playing on five tracks, the recording artist drops the album and becomes a recluse. The guitar player's *expectation damages* would be $50,000.00 because that is what she expected to make from the agreement. If she had spent $40,000.00 in preparing for the recording sessions, those would be her *reliance damages*. In addition, since the guitar player actually did do five tracks, the guitar player should get that value back from the recording artist as *restitution damages* - even if the reclusive recording artist does not use the recordings, he still has tracks that are worth some money.

In most cases, damages take the form of money. In protecting the expectation and reliance interests listed above, the court would generally look to *"substitutional"* or *"legal"* remedies - the payment of money to correct the wrong.[410] Sometimes, however, money is not enough - the court then looks to an *equitable* remedy.

The most important "specific" or "equitable" remedy is *"specific performance"* - "to produce, as nearly as is practicable, the same effect as if the contract had been performed."[411] The classic cases that require specific performance are: (i) contracts for the purchase of land; (ii) orders of specialty goods; and (iii) the provision of special personal services. If someone contracts to buy a piece of land and the seller backs out at the last minute for a better offer, the court will sometimes force the sale, even though the benefit to society might be better because of the breach. Another example is specialty goods - you order a special set of crocodile cowboy boots, and the bootmaker uses inferior leather. The court may order the bootmaker to make the boots as originally ordered. And regarding special services, a contract for a certain band/artist to record albums for a label might require the recording artist to fulfill its obligations under the recording agreement.

Another form of an "equitable" remedy is an *injunction* - "a writ granted by a court of equity whereby one is required to do or to refrain from doing a specified act."[412] As the definition indicates, the injunction can either be (a) to stop doing something or (b) to order someone to perform a certain act. If the injunction is to refrain from something that the person is already supposed to refrain from, that becomes, in effect, specific performance.[413]

What most people think of as an injunction is when someone is restrained from doing an action inconsistent with the agreement.[414] In show business, there is the case of *Lumley v. Wagner*.[415] Johanna Wagner (1826-1894), a famous opera singer of the time, had made a contract with a theatre owner, Benjamin Lumley, to sing only at Mr. Lumley's theatre. Another promoter, Fredrick Gye, enticed Ms. Wagner to break her contract with Lumley, and come and sing at his theatre. Lumley obtained an injunction and Ms. Wagner appealed. The court held for Lumley, the judge stating, "It is true that I have not the means of compelling her to sing, but she has no cause of complaint if I compel her to abstain from the commission of an act which she has bound herself not to do, and thus possibly cause her to fulfill her engagement.[416]

Liquidated Damages: A final way to address damages is through *"liquidated damages"* - damages predetermined by the parties, usually in the contract.[417] The courts have generally upheld liquidated damages since they help to avoid litigation costs and conserve judicial resources.[418] However, the court will look at two factors: (i) are liquidated damages appropriate for the breach being contemplated, *i.e.*, are they being used in an area where the damages are easy to calculate and (ii) are they excessive. If the damages are easy to determine, such as in a

Copyright infringement case where there are statutory damages that are easy to calculate, those damages will be awarded in place of the amount provided for in the liquidated damages provision. The court will also want to make sure that the damages are "reasonable in light of the anticipated or actual loss caused by the breach and the difficulties of proving loss."[419] If the court finds the damages excessive in relation to the actual harm, the court will deem them a "penalty" and reduce the amount or use the more customary methods of determining damages.[420]

Liquidated damages are commonly inserted into agreements concerning show business. One prong of the analysis is generally always met - the inability to accurately forecast damages. The second prong, however, is problematic - how to value the breach of an agreement that concerns a performing artist? Nevertheless, it is generally better to attempt to have a liquidated damages clause in the agreement.

Conclusion.

For better or worse, America is a litigious society. When you add in the volatility and instability of the artistic temperament, written agreements become imperative. Heed Mr. Goldwyn's wise advice and get things in writing!

CHAPTER 7

CONTRACTS - PART 2

Driftwood: It's all right, that's, that's in every contract. That's, that's what they call a 'sanity clause'.
Fiorello: Ha ha ha ha ha! You can't fool me! There ain't no Sanity Clause!
-        A Night At The Opera[421]

The construction of a contract itself - its language, its organization and thoroughness - can indicate the quality and professionalism of the party who drafted it and the completeness of the agreement. If certain important clauses are missing or the structure of the contract is poor, you must immediately think: "If it doesn't *look right*, it probably is not *written right!*" This chapter describes important clauses that must be in an agreement.

Preamble.

The preamble is that first block of text at the very beginning of the contract. People may presume (never assume!) that it is not very important - it just has the names and the date. *NO!* The preamble contains much more than just names and the date. The preamble is important because it says *"who"* is entering into the contract.

A proper preamble contains the following: (i) the name of the document; (ii) the date; (iii) the name of the first party to the contract; (iv) whether the entity is an individual or a company; (v) if a company, the type of company; and (vi) the address of that party. It then turns to: (vii) the second party to the contract; (viii) whether the entity is an individual or a company; (ix) if a company, the type of company; and (x) the address of that party. In drafting the preamble, it is customary to use "by and *between*" if there are two parties to the agreement, and to use "by and *among*" if there are three or more parties.[vii]

Each of these pieces of information is very important. The names and addresses should be correct for purposes of notice and litigation. The date must be clear because this could

---

[vii] Many attorneys are eliminating the "by and between" and are simply going with "between." The author uses the traditional "by and between."

be another key point in litigation. The type of entity is important to make sure a person with proper authority signs the agreement.

If you do not see a proper preamble, this should be a red flag that things are not right with the agreement. Additionally, when defining a term, be sure to be consistent with how the term is defined and then is used within the agreement.

Recitals.

The Recitals are another very important block of text in an agreement - one that is often eliminated, to the detriment of the parties involved. The Recitals tell *"why"* the parties are making the Agreement. The Recitals will give the reader context for the reason to do the contract and can be evidence of the parties' intent.

Remember that Recitals are not dispositive, *i.e.,* they do not create an obligation or duty, or establish any rights. The parties are attempting to make it clear "why" they are entering into the agreement - not the "what" behind the agreement's actual terms.

As an example, a music producer will produce masters and the artist will sing and perform. Why is this important? Because initial arrangements tend to grow and metastasize into bigger and bigger duties and obligations - and the line can grow very fuzzy if there is no clear-cut agreement. A person starts out as the producer of a record, then grows into managing the artist's career, all without a formal agreement. The producer asks for a commission and the artist says no. The recitals in the agreement between the two would support the artist's position that the parties never contemplated management services as part of the agreement.

Statement of Consideration.

The Statement of Consideration, although seemingly redundant, is important because it explicitly states that the parties have an agreement, and the terms of the agreement are reflected in the following writing. It is also important because it can create a rebuttal presumption that there is consideration.

All law students are introduced to *Wood v. Lucy, Lady Duff-Gordon.*[422] In that matter, the plaintiff, Otis F. Wood, a top New York advertising agent, sued Lucy, Lady Duff-Gordon, otherwise known as "Lucile" (her couture label), a leading designer of fashions for high society as well as for the stage and early silent cinema. Lady Duff-Gordon signed a contract with Wood giving him the exclusive right to market garments and other products bearing her endorsement for one year beginning on April 1, 1915. The parties would split the profits 50/50 - Wood's only duties under the contract were to account for monies received and secure patents, as necessary. There was no explicit duty to market the garments, only the agreement that if he did, they would split the profits.

Around the same time, Duff-Gordon came up with an idea to market a line of clothing "for the masses." She broke the agreement by endorsing products sold by Sears Roebuck and Wood sued. Duff-Gordon defended by claiming that no valid contract existed since Wood had not made an express promise to do anything - there was no consideration. The trial court disagreed with her argument and found for Wood. The Appellate division reversed the trial court, and Wood then appealed to the Court of Appeals of New York, the highest court in the state.

The Court, in an opinion by Judge Benjamin N. Cardozo, made new law by determining that a promise to exclusively represent the interests of a party constituted sufficient consideration to require enforcement of an unstated duty to use reasonable efforts to live up to that promise. Cardozo wrote, "A promise may be lacking, and yet the whole writing may be 'instinct with an obligation,' imperfectly expressed."[423] In a short and concisely written opinion, Judge Cardozo established a duty of good faith on a party to perform an implied promise. Judge Cardozo explicitly dispenses with formality in order to enforce a promise that was implied when viewed in the context of numerous aspects of the agreement - and as a result, an implied promise is sufficient to constitute consideration.[424]

Conditions Precedent.

After you have reviewed the Preamble, the Recitals, and the Statement of Consideration, the next thing to do is to confirm if any *"conditions precedent"* exist in the agreement. The modern trend is to use only the term *"condition"* since the Restatement (Second) of Contracts has eliminated the term "subsequent condition."[425]

A *"Condition"* is "an event, not certain to occur, which must occur, unless occurrence is excused, before performance under a contract becomes due."[426] More simply put, a condition is something that needs to happen before a party is obligated to perform under a contract. For example, a condition precedent in a record producer contract is that certain musicians will be signed to play on the record - no musicians, no producer.

Some conditions can be *"express"* - explicitly listed in the agreement - such as a condition that a studio must be booked before the producer becomes obligated; or *"implicit"* - when a court will step in to create a condition for some subsequent act.[427] Implied conditions are those that the court presumes were intended to be included in a contract.

Although almost any event can be a condition, the

Restatement excludes three types of situations: (i) events that must occur before a contract is even in existence (*e.g.,* offer and acceptance, consideration); (ii) events that are certain to occur (*e.g.,* the passage of 30 days before having to pay); and (iii) events that extinguish a duty after its performance has become due (*e.g.,* if a party is required to give notice to an insurance company for a claim and does not do so, thus eliminating insurance company's obligation to pay).[428] These cannot be used as a condition.

In drafting such clauses, it is important to remember a few rules of construction: (i) use "must" in the context of conditions section and (ii) use "will" in the context of covenants (discussed below). Also, the modern trend is to eliminate the word "shall" - it is misused so often that it has become confusing and ambiguous.[429]

Note that conditions may appear within a clause and are not always separated into their own provisions. For example, the requirement to give notice and a chance to cure (to rectify the breach) before suing on a breach is a condition. This is yet another reason it is always important to review contracts carefully - a provision with a seemingly innocuous heading may contain a condition that is anything but.

Substantive or Action Provisions.

Services. It is shocking how often a contract will not adequately describe the terms and conditions of what each party is to do under the contract. The same is true for the jobs, or credits, given to each party. In the music industry, this can become very important. One's position and duties, (*e.g.,* a "producer" versus an "engineer") will determine that person's status to participate in revenue streams and become eligible for awards. A producer may be able to participate in music publishing and record sales royalties; an engineer generally gets a flat fee and no further compensation. However, with the implementation of the Mechanical Licensing Collective **(the "MLC")**, for the first time a right to royalties was given to Producers, Engineers, and Performers. The MLC will be discussed below.

Term. The "term" of the agreement is another neglected clause - how long does it last? It may seem obvious that such a term must be included - but many poorly drafted agreements address the issue in broad and loose terms, and sometimes not at all.

In the entertainment industry, the term becomes very important. Remember, in California an agreement for personal services cannot be longer than seven years. In New York, it cannot be longer than three years. Thus, failure to address the term of the contract can have very different effects depending on what state's law governs it.

Compensation. Two types of compensation exist in the entertainment industry: (i) *fixed* and (ii) *contingent*. *"Fixed"* compensation is a fee or a salary - compensation that is fixed in amount and with a set schedule of payment. *"Contingent"* compensation generally takes the form of a royalty and is "contingent" on certain goals being achieved. In that way, contingent compensation can function as a condition precedent - an event must occur for the compensation obligations to kick in. One example of contingent compensation is an arrangement where the band/artist can start receiving royalty checks only after the record has recouped its production costs. Royalty amounts can also be contingent on performance (.*e.g.,* X amount of concerts) or other benchmarks (receiving X amount of ticket or CD sales).

The main consideration when negotiating for contingent compensation is whether it deals with "gross" (the total amount earned) or "net" (the total amount minus expenses). *It is axiomatic in the entertainment industry that a person NEVER negotiates for a royalty based on "net."* In the creative accounting of the entertainment industry, there will never be a "net" profit - so agreeing to royalties on net amounts is agreeing to a percentage of zero!

More often compensation is based upon the *"modified gross receipts"* - certain agreed-upon expenses are deducted from the gross and the remaining amount is subject to the royalty. In the end, the deal will depend upon your market position - whether you are a famous band/artist or have other leverage. In other words, Taylor Swift will get a deal that Taylor Slow will not.

Accounting. Whenever there is an element of contingent compensation, such as a royalty, there should be a "sister" clause allowing for the review and audit the books and records of the party paying the royalty. The royalty is the "brother," and the accounting clause is the "sister." It is imperative to have both.

Payment. Payment of the compensation, whether fixed or contingent, is a very important part of the contract. Obviously, if there is no clear date, time, or form of acceptable payment, the party that needs to pay has plenty of wiggle room for delay.

Terms in the payment clause should include: (i) when the payment is due (*e.g.,* first day of recording, delivery of the masters); (ii) how much is due (*e.g.,* 1/3 of compensation); (iii) what form of payment is acceptable (*e.g.,* cash, check); (iv) when dealing with royalties, the procedures for reviewing the books and records; and (v) all royalties should be paid in United States Dollars.

Status of the Parties. It is important to make clear whether the parties are entering into a contract that creates an employer-employee relationship, or whether the arrangement is only an independent contractor arrangement (such as a "work-for-hire" situation). Many consequences can arise if the relationship is not clearly stated. For example, a breach may affect taxes, disability, termination, and the remedies available.

The status also affects who owns the intellectual property created during the relationship. Absent provisions in the contract stating otherwise, the employer rather than the employee that actually created the work is presumed to own intellectual property generated during the course of the employer-employee relationship. This is because of the *"work-for-hire"* doctrine already discussed at length. By contrast, absent a "work-for-hire" provision in the agreement, which must be signed *before* work begins, an independent contractor can claim ownership of the work that is created. From the point of view of the person creating a work, then, where intellectual property ownership is paramount, it is usually better to be considered an independent contractor rather than an employee.

Finally, even if it is two entities making the agreement it is still important to clarify the relationship of the parties. Again, different liabilities and obligations will arise if the agreement is termed a "joint venture" or a "partnership agreement."

Representations & Warranties; Covenants.

The following clauses address the issue of insuring that the party entering into the agreement is authorized to do so and that there are no impediments to completing the deal. These clauses deal with *"I have the ability/authority/age/rights to do this."* There are three types of clauses: representations, warranties, and covenants. While they may seem similar, the key difference is a temporal one - past and present for representations, and predominantly future for warranties and covenants.

Representations and Warranties. A representation is an assertion by the party making it that the statement is true. Warranties generally are promises that appear on the face of the contract, such as promises that a proposition of fact is true at the time of the contract and will be true in the future. Contracts often use the two in tandem, providing that parties "represent and warrant" various things. Important representations and warranties include: (i) the person is of legal age to enter into the agreement; (ii) the person signing has the authority to sign; (iii) there are no outstanding obligations, liens, or legal proceedings that would delay or make impossible, performance under the agreement; and (iv) of great importance in entertainment, that the person signing has the rights to the intellectual property at issue.

Covenants. Covenants, by contrast, are generally undertakings to do or not do something in the future. Covenants come in two forms: (i) covenants within the agreement, such as agreeing to split the costs on an item or agreeing that one party will keep the books and records; and (ii) covenants that govern post-agreement behavior, such as the *"covenant not to compete," "covenant of non-solicitation"* or, the *"covenant of confidentiality."*

The covenants within the agreement are unique to each contract. In contrast, the covenants that govern post-agreement behavior are more standard but deserve special comment.

Non-Compete. The covenant not to compete is a clause that record companies and the like always attempt to insert into every entertainment agreement.

Two main elements are at issue in a non-compete clause: (i) the term of the clause (how long does it last); and (ii) the scope of the clause (what geographic territory does it cover). In New York, for example, the law does not like non-compete agreements and views them as an unreasonable restraint of trade.[430] As a result, a non-compete in New York can be reasonable only if it: (i) is no greater than required to protect an employer's legitimate protectable interests; (ii) does not impose undue hardship on the employee; (iii) does not cause injury to the public; and (iv) is reasonable in (a) duration and (b) geographic scope.[431] This is yet another example of why the state law that governs the contract can be extremely important.

The last two elements are most important: duration and geographic scope. As to duration, courts generally will allow a non-compete that is six months in duration and will start to frown when it is for more than a year. Any duration longer than two years will almost certainly be struck down. As to geographic scope, the decision comes down to the particular facts of the situation. If a person is a sales representative for a national computer company, the court may allow a restriction that covers the country. However, if the company only has a presence in the state of New Mexico, a national restriction would be struck down.

Non-Solicitation. A non-solicitation clause is also very important in entertainment contracts. The non-solicitation clause prevents the producer, or others, from taking all of the record company or recording studio's employees with him. The record company has invested much time and money in its employees and does not want someone to steal them away. Furthermore, the departing employees may have secret information of the company. To address that issue, there is a confidentiality clause.

Confidentiality. Just as a record company does not want a band/artist to leave the label and record for another label, the record company likewise does not want the band/artist to take its sensitive information. Consequently, a party will be bound to keep secret the information possessed by a company; it is generally termed a *"trade secret"* The Uniform Trade Secrets Act (**the "UTSA"**) defines a trade secret as: (i) information, including a formula, pattern, compilation, program, device, method, technique, or process; (ii) that derives independent economic value, actual or potential, from not being generally known to or readily ascertainable through appropriate means by other persons who might obtain economic value from its disclosure or use; and (iii) is the subject of efforts that are reasonable under the circumstances to maintain its secrecy.[432] One of the most famous trade secrets in the universe is the recipe for Coca-Cola.

A Trade Secret is like Trademark – if you take steps to keep the information secret and continue to use the secret in business, the protection is perpetual. The court will look to three essential elements to uphold a trade secret claim:

(i)   the subject matter involved must qualify for trade secret protection (*i.e.,* it must be the type of information trade secret was intended to protect, and it must not be generally known);

(ii)   the holder of the trade secret must establish that reasonable precautions were taken to prevent disclosure of the secret information; and

(iii) the trade secret holder must prove that the information was wrongfully acquired by another (*i.e.,* misappropriated).[433]

The use of a trade secret that belongs to another does not always create liability for the user. A trade secret may be used if it is discovered through: (i) independent discovery (different people have the same idea at the same time); (ii) reverse engineering (taking it apart and seeing how it works, then building a new one from scratch based on those observations); or (iii) inadvertent disclosure (the trade secret holder did not take steps to protect the secret).

Breach; Cure; Termination.

Breach. The issue of damages resulting from a breach was covered in Chapter 5. The discussion here focuses on *what* is a breach. There are two types of breaches: (i) immaterial, and (ii) material. Immaterial breaches are generally technical in nature - such as when a party missed a payment by one day. Immaterial breaches generally do not generate damages. The harm is relatively minor, and it is easy to rectify. Material breaches, on the other hand, are ones that go to the heart of the bargain.[434]

Cure. Given a breach that is material, the next question is what steps must be taken by the parties in order to correct the breach. A *cure* provision in an agreement establishes the process whereby a breach is declared and what to do to correct it. Generally, a cure provision will require that the party claiming a breach: (i) give notice of the breach to the other party; (ii) describe the breach; and (iii) demand the breach be cured within a certain period of time, (*e.g.,* ten days). If the breach is not cured within that ten-day period, the other party can terminate the agreement.

Termination. A termination clause is very important in any agreement, but particularly one that deals with personal services. There are three types: (i) termination according to the agreement's terms; (ii) early termination; and (iii) termination for cause.

Termination according to the agreement's terms will occur when the term expires (*e.g.,* the agreement is for two years and the two years are up), or some act needed to occur and it did not (a sales goal is not met).

Early termination can occur when the parties agree to terminate an agreement prior to the completion of a project or prior to the expiration of a term. The termination can be unilateral (either party can terminate with notice) or bi-lateral (both parties must agree to the early termination). Early termination clauses allow parties who see that the deal is going badly to get out with little pain. However, be aware of unilateral provisions that give one party the power to terminate early or even "at will" - try to stay away from such clauses unless it is impossible to avoid (or unless, of course, you are the one with the powers of early termination).

Termination for *"cause"* is an important type of termination and must be addressed in any agreement. Termination for cause is defined by the parties and includes items such as termination for fraud, embezzlement, revealing a trade secret, or violating a conduct policy such as sexual harassment. Termination for cause will generally constitute grounds for the immediate termination of the agreement. When negotiating a contract, the parties must be clear regarding the consequences of a termination for cause.

Boilerplate.

The term "boilerplate" refers to the clauses that generally are at the end of the agreement and is defined as "a description of uniform language used normally in legal documents that has a definite, unvarying meaning in the same context that denotes that the words have not been individually fashioned to address the legal issue presented."[435] Many people will only give a cursory glance to the boilerplate, believing - similar to the preamble - that boilerplate terms are not important. Nothing could be further from the truth!

Boilerplate will include clauses regarding: (i) _"assignment"_ - the agreement can only be assigned to a third-party if both parties agree; (ii) _"waiver"_ - if you waive a clause that does not mean you waive it forever; (iii) _"severability"_ - if one clause is found to be unenforceable, only that clause is taken out, and not the whole agreement); (iv) _"entire agreement"_ - basically incorporating the parol evidence rule such that no outside evidence can be examined when trying to construe the contract or its terms); (v) _"amendment"_ - any change in the agreement must be in writing); (vi) _attorneys' fees_; and (vi) _represented by counsel_ - both parties have had a chance for legal counsel to review the documents). Other potential boilerplate clauses include a clause stating that electronic signatures are permitted, or that the parties may execute the document by signing on their signature line on separate signature pages (say, if they are in different states).

The three most important clauses are:

1.   attorneys' fees;

2.   choice of law, venue, and jurisdiction; and

3. a provision on how to give notice.

Attorneys' Fees. By far the most important boilerplate clause is one that concerns attorneys' fees. The attorneys' fees clause addresses who will pay the costs of litigation if it is needed to enforce the agreement. Such a clause is very, very important – it has two purposes: (i) make a plaintiff "whole" in winning a lawsuit; and (ii) to prevent frivolous litigation by penalizing someone who brings a baseless claim with the costs of the litigation. In New York, an attorneys' fees clause must be in writing *and* if it is not in an agreement, can be a basis for a malpractice claim against the attorney![436] It is also imperative that the demand for attorneys' fees be in the Prayer for Relief in the Complaint.

Note that in some cases, courts can award attorneys' fees even if the contract does not call for it – for example, in an "exceptional" case involving trademark infringement.

Choice of Law; Jurisdiction; Venue. The second most important clause in the boilerplate section is the choice of law provision. The choice of law provision deals with what law will control the contract - generally which state law will be applied to the agreement. In the entertainment industry, most contracts will be governed by California or New York state law. The choice of law becomes particularly important when it comes to litigation - you want to be on your home court. Why? Because if there is litigation it is better to have the law be one with which you are familiar. You also make the other party have to travel to your state.

Note, however, that some contracts stay away from courts altogether and mandate that all disputes will be subject to binding mediation or arbitration. This is often the case with larger organizations who would rather not have their disputes publicized in an open courtroom that is easily accessible by the press.

It is also important to address the issues of jurisdiction and venue. A Choice of Law clause governs which state's "substantive" law applies to litigation (*e.g.,* law of New York or California on contract formation), jurisdiction and venue determines *where* the litigation will occur and therefore which state's "procedural" law will occur. Even if New York law applied, absent a jurisdiction or venue provision, a California recording company might try to sue in California district court and ask the California court to apply New York law. That way the recording company gets the benefit of its home state (which can save on expense and help elicit jury sympathy), and of its home "procedural" law. The jurisdictional and venue provision states *where* an action can be brought if litigation arises, such as "in the state and federal courts of the state of California," and states that the parties agree to personal jurisdiction in this venue for purposes of disputes arising out of the agreement. A party can only be sued in states where there is personal jurisdiction over them - (*i.e.,* where they have sufficient contact and connections with that state). Just because a contract states that New York law applies, does not necessarily mean that a musician can sue a California record company in New York and obtain personal jurisdiction over them.

What if the record company never set foot in New York - it has not done business there? It can take significant motion practice and attorneys' fees just to litigate the personal jurisdiction issue before the merits of the case are even touched. As a result, it is always prudent to state what venue (what state, and whether federal court, state court or both) will apply and that both parties have consented to jurisdiction for that purpose.

Notice. Proper clauses on how to give notice - whether about breach, payment, or otherwise - is paramount. If notice is not properly given, it can be a basis for ignoring or even dismissing a claim against someone for breach. The notice provision should give the addresses, state how notice should be given (*e.g.,* certified mail), and it should be set out so that it is easy to find.

Letter of Intent (The Pre-Contract "Contract").

Before concluding our discussion of contracts, it is worth briefly addressing the letter of intent. When a musician agrees to sign a recording contract, a "letter of intent," or deal memo, is often drawn up by the company and signed by the musician prior to signing the actual agreement. This letter of intent usually sets forth the key terms of the arrangement and affirms that the musician will sign with the label once a contract is formalized. It holds the status quo while the actual agreement is drafted.

Such a letter of intent may at first glance seem safe to sign, especially as the language is usually looser and informal than an actual contract. And at this point, a musician is so excited at the prospect of being signed that they will do just about anything not to rock the boat. However, it is often very hard to get out of a letter of intent if a contract never materializes.

For example, once a band/artist signs the letter of intent, they are largely under an obligation to conclude a deal with the label. If the label then presents them with a contract that the band/artist does not want to sign, the label can stall forever. These letters of intent usually have no dates of termination, so the band/artist remains bound until a contract is signed, no matter how long it takes. The band/artist may not be able to sign with another label or even put out their own music unless released from the letter of intent, which rarely happens. The band/artist eventually has no choice but to sign a contract that is not favorable in terms of royalties or other provisions. In short, once a band/artist has signed a letter of intent, they must either eventually sign a contract that suits the label, or they will find themselves perpetually in limbo, and likely will break up.

Consequently, if a letter of intent must be signed, it is usually prudent to insist on a limited term for its effectiveness. For example, if no contract is signed within a mutually agreed upon number of months, the letter of intent is no longer in effect unless the band/artist agrees (or both parties do) to renew it for another mutually agreed upon number of months.

Conclusion.

It is good advice to clients that "If it does not look right, there is good chance that it is not right." Always with the attendant statement - "Merely because it looks right does not make it right." These two statements mean: (i) if you take a quick review and do not see, for example, an attorneys' fees clause, you know that something is missing; however, (ii) even if you see the attorneys' fees clause, your work is not complete. There could still be significant flaws in construction or missing terms.

CHAPTER 8

UNIONS

*"If any man tells you he loves America,
yet hates labor, he is a liar.
If any man tells you he trusts America,
yet fears labor, he is a fool."*
- Abraham Lincoln

As with so many industries, unions are major players in the entertainment industry. In the music industry, there are multiple unions that are relevant:

1. the American Federation of Musicians (the **"AFM"**);

2. the International Brotherhood of Teamsters, Chauffeurs, Warehousemen and Helpers of

America (**the "Teamsters Union"**);

3. The International Alliance of Theatrical Stage Employees, Moving Picture Technicians, Artists and Allied Crafts of the United States, Its Territories and Canada (the **"IATSE"**). In late 2021, it went on strike against the Studios. But the strike was resolved, and a new three-year agreement was reached[437]; and

4. The Screen Actors Guild/American Federation of Television and Radio Artists (**the "SAG/AFTRA"**). A band/artist (or songwriter) can sometimes receive a payment from SAG-AFTRA even though they're not an actor or a Union member. A songwriter (not affiliated with any Union) can still receive a SAG-AFTRA "one-time" payment if their song is incorporated into certain types of uses (e.g., a TV Show).

Each union covers a particular aspect of creating and performing music. The AFM controls the musicians. The Teamsters Union controls numerous other occupations including drivers and trucks that move equipment, sets, and goods such as CDs and DVDs. And IATSE covers stagehands, grips, gaffers, and other occupations backstage and behind the scenes.

AFM.

The story of the need for a union for musicians is all too familiar. Musicians were being taken advantage of on numerous sides including theatre owners, cabaret owners, and producers and impresarios. As a result, the AFM was formed in 1896 and chartered by the American Federation of Labor.[438] In 1913, AFM and IATSE signed an agreement of mutual support during negotiations and strikes with theatrical producers and theatre owners.[439]

In the late 1800's music boxes, mechanical orchestras, and player pianos were popular, but these machines did not seriously affect the ability of musicians to earn their livings. Things changed drastically with Edison's invention of a voice recording on tin foil in 1877.[440] The Sound Recording caused a revolution in all aspects of the music industry. Everything from vaudeville sketches to the classical repertoire was being recorded. The resulting perfect storm - the increase in recorded music along with the economic effects of World War I - caused a fall in employment for musicians.[441]

Another development in technology also had an effect on employment for musicians: sound came to the movies and musicians were no longer needed to play accompaniment to the silent pictures.[442] Within three years, 22,000 theater jobs for live musicians were lost, and only a handful found jobs by performing on soundtracks.[443]

Of course, the advent of technology was not all bad. In the 1930s, technology continued to advance, with a positive benefit - the workplaces of musicians became increasingly diverse.[444] Technology allowed musicians from all genres to work with electronic instruments that were of increasing sophistication, yet low in cost.[445]

As the AFM moved into its second century it realized

that the music industry had continued to evolve. It was imperative that AFM agreements change, especially in the area of electronic media.[446]

The AFM renewed its emphasis on public relations to create greater awareness of the activities of the union among musicians, to the public, and for politicians.[447] The AFM has been successful, especially in the area of legislative advocacy where the AFM is a major player in such areas as performance rights.

However, many working musicians do not benefit from the AFM; in fact, union membership might actually be detrimental. But, artists such as musicians on Broadway, that play in Symphonies, or that go on tour might receive some benefits.

TEAMSTERS.

The Teamsters Union is the largest private-sector labor union in the United States, representing truck drivers and workers in related industries (such as aviation).[448] Its origins began in 1901 when exploited drivers formed the Team Drivers International Union **(the "TDIU")**, with an initial membership of 1,700.[449] In 1902, a rival group was formed - the Teamsters National Union.[450]

The early decades of the twentieth century heralded a period of aggressive organizing.[451] Membership increased, and the types of team drivers covered by the union included "gravel haulers, beer wagon drivers, milk wagon drivers, and deliverymen for bakeries."[452] The Teamsters quickly moved into representing drivers of the new "motor trucks."[453]

The Teamsters have great power in the music industry due to the large amount of trucking services required in that world. For example, every tour that travels across America needs to deal with the Teamsters regarding the trucks and drivers required to get the sound equipment and the set to the next performance venue. The Teamsters may also control the workers at the venue that unload and load the equipment off and on the trucks. To make matters even more confusing, multiple unions can be involved regarding what may appear to be the same occupation.

For example, the "local" union for Southern California is Joint Council 42, which is the parent body to 23 Teamster Local Unions with members in Southern California, Southern Nevada, Guam, Saipan, and Hawaii.[454] Joint Council 42, through the Local 399, will have jurisdiction for labor matters regarding music, film, and television.

IATSE.

IATSE was founded in 1893. Stagehands from eleven cities sent representatives to New York, and together they pledged to support common efforts to establish fair wages and working conditions for their members. IATSE evolved to represent workers in all entertainment mediums, support craft expansion, technological innovation, and to promote geographic growth. [455]

Today IATSE is the largest union representing workers in the entertainment industry. Members work in all forms of live theater, motion picture and television production, trade shows and exhibitions, television broadcasting, and concerts as well as the equipment and construction shops that support these areas of the entertainment industry. As a result, IATSE represents virtually all the behind-the-scenes workers - from a motion picture animator to a theater usher.[456]

In California, the local IATSE is **Local 33** - it covers workers in theater, television, video, arena shows, digital media, conventions, and outdoor events.[457] Local 33 provides workers protection in set construction, lighting, sound, props, special effects (including pyrotechnics), rigging, camera operation, drapery, fly-rail operation, automation, and stage management.[458]

In New York, the local IATSE is **Local 1,** and it is responsible for the workers that construct, install, maintain, and operate the lighting, sound equipment, scenery, and special effects for Broadway shows, Radio City Music Hall, Madison Square Garden, Carnegie Hall, The Metropolitan Opera, and Lincoln Center. Local 1 also handles the workers on television networks, PBS, and cable TV studios, major corporate industrials, and special events.[459]

SAG/AFTRA.

SAG-AFTRA represents approximately 160,000 actors, announcers, broadcast journalists, dancers, DJs, news writers, news editors, program hosts, puppeteers, recording artists, singers, stunt performers, voiceover artists and other media professionals.

SAG-AFTRA brings together two great American labor unions: the Screen Actors Guild and the American Federation of Television and Radio Artists. Both were formed in the turmoil of the
1930s, with rich histories of fighting for and securing the strongest protections for media artists.[460] SAG and AFTRA merged on March 30, 2012.

Conclusion.

Dealing with unions is inevitable and inescapable in the entertainment industry. It is imperative to know which unions represent which types of workers. While it is easy to criticize unions, it is because of unions that workers in the entertainment industry are guaranteed a living wage, health, and pension plans, as well as rules and regulations that increased worker safety.

CHAPTER 9

BAND AGREEMENTS

"Which one's Pink?"
-        Roger Waters[461]

Previous chapters in this book addressed Copyright, Trademark, revenue streams, business forms, and contracts. Starting with this chapter, discussion will now focus on applying those concepts to real situations and real agreements.

The first agreement addressed is the Band Agreement. Unless the musician is a solo performer, the Band Agreement is generally the first agreement that needs to be executed because, generally, the first thing that is going to happen is that a person will want to form a band. In this chapter, we will look at certain important issues regarding forming the band and bringing a new member into the band. In the next chapter, we will look at what happens when the band decides to break up.

As was discussed in the chapters on contracts, it is very important to do a quick "sight" test of the agreement. For example, is there a proper preamble and proper recitals? The following chapter will look at important clauses of the Band Agreement by examining the provisions of a sample agreement. However, the below agreement may not necessarily apply to any and all situations, as relevant issues and factors can differ widely between bands and their members.

Services.

As previously discussed, a contract should attempt to follow the logical process or order of the proposed transaction. Consequently, in an agreement for personal services, it makes sense to lay out the services to be provided.

Services

(a)   Commencing on the date hereof, Group (*Note: "Group" would have been defined up above in the Preamble or Recitals)* hereby engages Member to render during the Term hereof (defined below) Member's exclusive services as a member of the Group in any and all areas of the entertainment industry upon the terms and conditions herein set forth, and Member hereby accepts such engagement and will keep and perform all of the duties, services, obligations, and covenants herein set forth. Member will perform and render the services required to be rendered hereunder conscientiously, and to the best of Member's ability at all times, wherever reasonably required or desired by Group and as instructed by Group in all matters.

(b)   As a member of the Group, Member will render services as, without limitation, a performer, vocalist, and/or musician in the production, exploitation, and/or performance of, without limitation, phonograph records, videos, television programs, concerts, tours, and radio programs, and will render services in such other related artistic or creative aspects of the entertainment industry, as Group will specify.

(c) During the Term (defined below) hereof, Member will render such services at such places throughout the world, at such times and in such a manner as Group will from time to time reasonably require or as Group will be contractually committed to provide. In this regard, Member will perform vocal and/or instrumental services to the best of Member's ability during all of the Group's performances in which Member participates, including, without limitation, rehearsals, performances in connection with recording masters, video recording sessions, live concerts, and otherwise.

(d) Member agrees to render Member's services hereunder during the Term hereof in compliance with such rules and regulations as Group or the Group's management may establish and with the Group's management's instructions, directions, and requests, consistent with this Agreement.

(e) Without limiting the generality of the foregoing, Member agrees to punctually report and attend all of the Group's activities, for the duration thereof, in which Member is required by Group or the Group's management. Member shall participate, including, without limitation, Group meetings, Group rehearsals, audio and video recording sessions, sound checks, in-store and radio appearances, at the times and places as Group or the Group's management may designate. Member further agrees to perform Member's vocal and/or instrumental services in connection with such musical materials as Group and/or the Group may select. If requested by the Group to do so, Member will re-record any such material until a commercially satisfactory master is accepted by Group and by the Record Company, respectively.

(f) During the Term hereof, Member will perform recording services in connection with recording master quality recordings commercially and technically satisfactory for the production, manufacture, and sale of phonograph records ("Masters"), pursuant to the terms and provisions of the Recording Agreement (defined below).

(g) During the Term hereof, Member is solely responsible for procuring, maintaining, and insuring Member's musical equipment. The Group will not be responsible for any loss or damage of any kind to a Member's Musical equipment.

These paragraphs clearly establish what is expected from the Member: (i) she is accepted into the Group; (ii) she will perform whatever is needed on whatever medium the Group decides to perform; (iii) she will be on time; (iv) she will take care of her own equipment; and (v) she will follow the rules of the Group. The Member will know exactly what is expected of her.

Term.

The next clause is the "Term" - how long the agreement will be in force. Remember the constraints on the limits of the length of the term (New York; California) regarding agreements that provide for personal services.

Term; Renewal; Extension.

(a) Term. Subject to the earlier termination of this Agreement as herein elsewhere provided and without limiting the generality of the foregoing, Member hereby agrees to render, subject to the terms hereof, services as a musician for a period commencing as of the date hereof and ending on the later of one (1) year from the effective date hereof (the "Term").

(b) Renewal. The Term of this Agreement shall renew automatically for a period of one (1) year, unless otherwise terminated pursuant to the terms and conditions herein. In no event will the Term hereof extend beyond seven (7) years from the date hereof. At the conclusion of any continuous seven (7) year period, _i.e.,_ the Term has not been suspended or tolled, the parties shall renegotiate a new Agreement, in good faith, similar in terms and conditions to the current Agreement.

(c) Extension. Notwithstanding the foregoing, if within such one (1) year period following the termination or expiration of a Recording Agreement (defined below) and Group enters into a subsequent Recording Agreement, then the Term hereof will run concurrently with the Term of such subsequent Recording Agreement, and any renewal, extension, or substitution thereof.

As used herein, the Term "Recording Agreement" means any agreement entered into between the Group and a recording company. In the event that the Group enters into any new, replacement, or successor recording agreement(s), such agreement(s) and recording company(ies) will be deemed substituted hereunder in the place of the Recording Agreement and the Record Company.

Within these clauses, the Term, and any extensions and options, is clearly laid out. It is very important for Group members to be clear on these terms. The Agreement gives the Group a series of options to have the Member continue in the Group. Note that the total years of the Agreement does not exceed seven years.

And be aware of additional time periods that might be imposed on the Member from a third-party. For example, if a Recording Agreement is signed, the Member might be bound to the Group for the further time periods contained within the Recording Agreement. A Member might be under the impression that he is in the Group for one year but could be "in the Group" for the additional period of the Recording Agreement.

Compensation.

We now get to where the rubber meets the road - money! As outlined in the chapter on revenue streams, multiple areas need to be addressed when it comes to Compensation. The next clause dealing with royalties is a "brother clause" to the "sister clause" of accounting (which we will discuss further).

Compensation.

(a)   As   full   and   complete   consideration   for

Member's services and the rights granted by Member hereunder, Group will cause Member to receive the compensation specified in the following paragraphs, subject to Member's full and complete compliance with all the terms and conditions of this Agreement and the performance of Member's services in a first-class manner hereunder.

(b)   Advance. No advance shall be made to the Member.

(c)   Record Royalties. Except as expressly provided otherwise in subparagraph (iii) immediately below, Member will be entitled to receive a *pro rata* portion of the Net Record Royalties (as hereinafter defined) of long- playing records or CD's through normal retail channels in the United States which embody solely Masters recorded pursuant to the Recording Agreement on which Member's performances are substantially embodied ("Record Royalty").

     (i)   The Record Royalty to which Member will be entitled is the Member's "pro rata share" of the Record Royalty Group Share (hereafter defined) of in respect to Masters recorded pursuant to the Recording Agreement on which Member's performances are substantially embodied.

     (ii)   As used herein, the Term "Record Royalty Group Share" will mean that portion of the revenue received by the Group under the Recording Agreement. As used herein, the Term "pro rata share" will mean Member's proportionate interest in the Group, which will be equal to a fraction, the numerator of which is the Record Royalty Group Share and the denominator of which is the number of current members in the Group (including Member).

(iii)   Net Record Royalties shall mean all gross royalties earned and actually received by Group (as distinguished from bookkeeping credit entries), if any, in respect to sales of the respective LPs and any video(s) recorded in accordance with the applicable provisions of the Recording Agreement, after having recouped all advances and other sums paid pursuant to the Recording Agreement in respect to the respective LPs and any video(s) recorded hereunder, including, without limitation, advances against royalties, recording costs, and any other charges permitted hereunder (including, without limitation, tour support, video production costs, and promotional and publicity expenses, if any), less all other charges and adjustments permitted hereunder (including, without limitation; the advance provided for herein and less all costs paid or incurred by Group in connection with the collection of these monies (including, without limitation, legal and accounting expenses and fees), and all other legal, accounting, and management expenses, commissions, or fees.

(iv)   If, after distributing the Group Share of Net Record Royalties to the current members of the Group, a portion thereof remains undistributed, the Group will be entitled to retain the undistributed portion for itself or distribute same in its sole and absolute discretion.

(v)   Notwithstanding anything contained in this paragraph to the contrary, if this Agreement is not otherwise terminated for Proper Cause prior to the expiration of its Term, Member's Record Royalty hereof will continue to be payable after the termination of this Agreement.

(d)   Streaming Royalties. Except as expressly provided otherwise in subparagraph (iii) immediately below, Member will be entitled to receive a *pro rata* portion of the streaming revenues of any digital audio transmission of any digital versions of any Musical Composition and/or Sound Recording sold through any on-line digital distribution platform or service in the United States which embody solely Masters recorded pursuant to the Recording Agreement on which Member's performances are substantially embodied ("Streaming Royalty").

(i) The Record Royalty to which Member will be entitled is Member's "pro rata share" of the Streaming Royalty Group Share (hereafter defined) in respect to Masters recorded pursuant to the Recording Agreement on which Member's performances are substantially embodied.

(ii) As used herein, the Term "Streaming Royalty Group Share" will mean that portion of the revenue received by the Group under the Recording Agreement as results of revenue received from on-line digital streaming. As used herein, the Term "pro rata share" will mean Member's proportionate interest in the Group, which will be equal to a fraction, the numerator of which is the Streaming Royalty Group Share and the denominator of which is the number of current members in the Group (including Member).

(iii) Net Streaming Royalties shall mean all gross royalties earned and actually received by Group (as distinguished from bookkeeping credit entries), if any, in respect to sales of digital streaming, after having recouped all advances and other sums paid pursuant to the Recording Agreement, including, without limitation, advances against royalties, recording costs, and any other charges permitted hereunder (including, without limitation, tour support, video production costs, and promotional and publicity expenses, if any), less all other charges and adjustments permitted hereunder (including, without limitation; the advance provided for herein and less all costs paid or incurred by Group in connection with the collection of these monies (including, without limitation, legal and accounting expenses and fees), and all other legal, accounting, and management expenses, commissions, or fees.

(iv)   If, after distributing the Group Share of Net Streaming Royalties to the current members of the Group, a portion thereof remains undistributed, the Group will be entitled to retain the undistributed portion for itself or distribute same in its sole and absolute discretion.

(v)   Notwithstanding anything contained in this paragraph to the contrary, if this Agreement is not otherwise terminated for Proper Cause prior to the expiration of its Term, Member's Streaming Royalty hereof will continue to be payable after the termination of this Agreement.

(e) Videos. From time to time, during the Term of this Agreement, the Group will have the right to cause the Member to perform at sessions for the purposes of embodying Member's musical and dramatic performances on videotape and/or film and any and all derivatives thereof and reproductions there from (collectively the "Videos" herein) for the production of Videos pursuant to and in accordance with the Recording Agreement. Member hereby consents to Group's production of the Videos at the sessions, and the rights granted with respect to the Masters hereunder will be likewise granted with respect to the Videos recorded (including without limitation the name and likeness rights). The compensation provided to Member herein will be deemed to include full and complete consideration for services rendered and rights granted pursuant to this paragraph, and

Member will not be entitled to any additional compensation for audio visual performances. Member hereby expressly agrees that Group and Group's licensees will have the right to use all Controlled Musical Compositions that appear on the Videos with no payment for the use of such Controlled Musical Compositions in or in connection with the Videos and the exploitation thereof.

(i)   Video Royalties. In respect to any and all commercial exploitation of any Video recorded under the Recording Agreement in which Member's musical or dramatic performance appears, Member's Video Royalty will be Member's "pro rata share" (as hereinafter defined) of the Video Royalty Group Share (hereafter defined) of Net Video Royalties (as hereinafter defined) in respect to Videos recorded pursuant to the Recording Agreement on which Member's performances are substantially embodied.

(ii)   As used herein, the Term "Video Royalty Group Share" will mean that portion of the revenue received by the Group under the Recording Agreement from the sale and exploitation of the Videos. As used herein, the Term "pro rata share" will mean Member's proportionate interest in the Group, which will be equal to a fraction, the numerator of which is the Video Royalty Group Share and the denominator of which is the number of current members in the Group (including Member).

(iii)   Net Video Royalties shall mean all gross royalties earned and actually received by Group (as distinguished from bookkeeping credit entries), if any, in respect to sales of the respective video(s) recorded in accordance with the applicable provisions of the Recording Agreement, after having recouped all advances and other sums paid pursuant to the Recording Agreement in respect to the respective video(s) recorded hereunder, including, without limitation, advances against royalties, recording costs, and any other charges permitted hereunder (including, without limitation, tour support, video production costs, and promotional and publicity expenses, if any), less all other charges and adjustments permitted hereunder (including, without limitation; the advance provided for herein hereof and less all costs paid or incurred by Group in connection with the collection of these monies (including, without limitation, legal and accounting expenses, and fees), and all other legal, accounting, and management expenses, commissions, or fees.

(iv)   If, after distributing the Group Share of Net Video Royalties to the current Members of the Group, a portion thereof remains undistributed, the Group will be entitled to retain the undistributed portion for itself or distribute same in its sole and absolute discretion.

(v)   Notwithstanding anything contained in this paragraph to the contrary, if this Agreement is not otherwise terminated prior to the expiration of its Term, Member's Video Royalty hereof will continue to be payable after the termination of this Agreement.

(f)   Touring. Conditioned upon Member's full and faithful performance of all terms and conditions hereof, in respect of any series of live concert performances, together with Member hereunder (a "Tour") in support of a particular LP, Group will pay to Member an amount equal to Member's pro rata share of the Tour Revenue Group Share of Net Tour Profits (hereinafter defined) earned and received by Group in respect of such Tour. As used herein, for purposes of this paragraph only, a pro rata share will be equal to a fraction, the numerator of which is the Tour Revenue Group Share of the Net Tour Profits and the denominator of which is the number of current members in the Group (including Member.)

(i)   As used herein, the Term "Net Tour Profits" in respect of a particular Tour will mean an amount equal to the gross sums actually received by Group (*i.e.,* paid to Group by the applicable concert promoters or venues) from all personal appearance concerts in which Member performed for the applicable Tour (the "Gross") less all expenses incurred by or on Group's behalf in connection with the applicable Tour, including, without limitation, all stage production, transportation, hotel, lodging and rehearsal expenses in respect of the applicable Tour, all professional fees, agents and management commissions, and any other monies payable to unrelated third parties in connection with the applicable Tour, and less a ten percent (10%) percent administration fee. Any monies payable to Member hereunder will be inclusive of any union fees otherwise payable to Member in respect to Member's services for a Tour.

(g)   Merchandise. Conditioned upon Member's full and faithful performance of all terms and conditions hereof, Group will pay to Member an amount equal to Member's pro rata share of the Merchandise Revenue Group Share (hereinafter defined) of Net Merchandise Profits (hereinafter defined) earned and received by Group. As used herein, for purposes of this paragraph only, a pro rata share will be equal to a fraction, the numerator of which is the Merchandise Revenue Group Share of the Net Merchandise Profits and the denominator of which is the number of current members in the Group (including Member.)

(i)   As used herein, the Term "Net

Merchandise Profits" will mean an amount equal to the gross sums actually received by Group (*i.e.*, paid to Group by the applicable third-parties) from all exploitation of merchandise (the "Merchandise") that features the Member and the Group (the "Gross") less all expenses incurred by or on Group's behalf, including, without limitation, all production, transportation, hotel, lodging, and distribution expenses in respect of the Merchandise, all professional fees, agents and management commissions, and any other monies payable to unrelated third parties in connection with the applicable Merchandise, and less a ten percent (10%) percent administration fee.

(h)   Transportation and Lodging. During any period in which Member is required hereunder to travel at least one hundred (100) miles outside the New York City, New York metropolitan area to perform services in connection with a Tour, Group will provide Member with transportation and lodging designated by Group in Group's sole discretion. Member hereby acknowledges and agrees that Member will be solely responsible for paying any incidental expenses (*e.g.*, telephone calls and room service) incurred by Member during any such period, and that in the event pays any such expenses, Group will have the right to deduct the amount thereof from any and all monies payable to Member hereunder.

(I)   Per Diem. During any period in which Member is required hereunder to travel at least one hundred (100) miles outside the New York City, New York metropolitan area to perform services in connection with a Tour, Group will also pay to Member a per diem for Member's living expenses, the amount of which will be determined in good faith solely by Group.

(i)   Withholding. Group will have the right to

deduct from any monies payable to Member hereunder such portion thereof as may be required to be deducted under the applicable provisions of the Internal Revenue Code, the New York Revenue and Taxation Code, or under any other applicable statute, regulation, treaty, or other law within or outside of the United States, or union or guild Agreement, and Member will execute such forms and documents as may be required in connection therewith.

The first item addressed is whether the Band Member will or will not get an Advance. In the agreement above, the Band Member will not receive an advance. However, in many situations, the Band Member may get some money when joining the Group. The Band Member will get no further compensation until the Advance is paid off. In addition, the Advance may be contingent upon getting a Distribution Agreement, but it does not always have to be that way.

The clause goes on to address how monies will be divided for records, streaming services, videos, touring, and merchandise. In this Agreement, everything will be on a *pro rata* share - each person in the Group gets an equal share. However, this is not set in stone. The Band members can agree on a different distribution of the percentages. A major clause is sharing in Merchandise (remember the comments on KISS from above!). Note that a Leaving Member will continue receiving a Record Royalty during the life of the Copyright for a respective recording that contains the contribution of the Band Member.

The next two clauses deal with living expenses - lodging, transportation, and meals while on the road with the Group. Obviously, the Band Member wants to be taken care of while on the road. It is very important to negotiate this clearly so that there are no surprises while on tour.

The final clause deals with withholding. The issue of withholding can be a major issue - no one wants to be on the hook for a big tax debt at the end of the year. It is imperative to clarify whether the Band Member is an employee or an independent contractor, and, depending upon the status, who will make payment of taxes to the proper authorities.

Statements.

Whenever there are royalties or any other type of contingent compensation, there must be a "sister clause" related to the "brother clause" of contingent compensation. It is so important to be able to confirm that royalties are being paid, accounted for, and how to review the books and records of the Group.

Statements.

(a) **The books of the Group and all other documents relating to the business of the Group will be maintained at its principal place of business and will be available for inspection at reasonable times by any Group Member (or any designated representative of any Group Member). The fiscal year of the Group will end on December 31st. The Group will provide an accounting statement to each Group Member twice a year at the end of June and December.**

(b) **With respect to Record Royalties and Streaming Royalties, Group will send statements as to sums payable to Member hereunder within thirty (30) days after statements are sent to Group by the applicable third-party payors.**

(c) **With respect to Tour Income, Group will send statements as to sums payable to Member hereunder within thirty (30) days after the end of the applicable Tour. Said statements will be accompanied by**

payment of accrued sums, if any, earned by Member hereunder during the applicable accounting period, less all advances and charges to Member under this contract.

(d) Member or an attorney or certified public accountant, on Member's behalf, may, at Member's sole expense, upon ten (10) days' notice to Group, examine royalty statements sent to Group by any third-party provider in connection with record royalties payable to Member hereunder, but solely with respect to those portions of such statements specifically pertaining to royalties payable to Member hereunder. Group's books relating to any particular royalty statement hereunder may be examined as aforesaid only within twenty-four (24) months after the date rendered to Member, and Member will have no right to object to such royalty statement after such period. Group will have no obligation to permit Member to so examine any particular royalty statement more than once. Member understands and agrees that in Group's rendering statements to Member, Group will be relying on statements provided to Group by third parties. Accordingly, notwithstanding anything to the contrary contained herein, the statements which Group renders to Member will to the extent the information is derived from the statements provided by the third-party providers, be deemed accurate.

The first clause is straightforward - the Group will maintain books and records dealing with the Group. The books and records will be kept at a known location and the member is free to inspect them at any time. This clause may appear relatively obvious, but in truth, many bands do not take the time to maintain proper accounts.

The second and third clauses establish when monies will

be distributed - in this case within thirty days of receipt of the monies by the Group.

The final clause is the *"accounting"* clause - it is imperative that such a clause be included. The clause allows a Band Member to audit the books and records of the Group, within certain restrictions. In this clause, the Band Member will be able to review the books and records of the Group with "ten days' notice" to the Group. Also, after a period of two years, the Band Member is deemed to have accepted any statement and cannot contest that statement any further.

Band Artwork.

A major issue of any Group agreement is who will control the name and logo of a Group.

A good case study is Pink Floyd. When Roger Waters, a founding member of the group, left in 1985, he demanded that the Pink Floyd name be retired.[462] However, David Gilmour wanted to continue to use the name for albums and tours. Waters sued, but the High Court in England held for Gilmour, who continued to record and tour under the Pink Floyd name.[463] Although Waters initially was very angry over the decision, he has now come to see that Gilmour and the others were right.[464]

Name & Logo.

(a)   The Group will do business under the name _____ (the "Group Name") as an assumed name and as its Trademark and service mark.

[ ]   The Group also uses the following logo (the "Group Logo") as a Trademark and service mark:

INSERT VERSION OF LOGO HERE.

Each Group Member acknowledges that the Group Name and Logo (if Group Logo exists) is (select one):

[ ] the exclusive property of the Group and not owned by any individual member and, unless otherwise authorized in writing, departing Group Members will have no interest whatsoever in the Group Name and Logo, apart from the limited right to be known as an ex-member of the Group. If the Group dissolves, no individual member will have a right to use the Group Name and Logo, or any confusingly similar name or logo, apart from the limited right to be known as an ex-member of the Group.

[ ] the exclusive property of the Group and not owned by any individual member, except that in the event that _____ and _____ cease to be members of the Group, the Group will cease use of the Group Name and Logo (including "formerly [Group name]" or similar references) and any confusingly similar name or logo, in connection with any offering of entertainment services. Departing Group Members will have no interest whatsoever in the Group Name and Logo, apart from the limited right to be known as a former member of the Group. In the event that the Group dissolves, no individual member will have a right to use the Group Name and Logo or any confusingly similar name or logo, apart from the limited right to be known as an ex-member of the Group.

[ ] **not assets of the Group, but rather are the sole and exclusive property of _____ (name of person who owns Group Name and Logo) and, unless otherwise authorized in writing, will remain that person's sole and exclusive property during and after the Term of this Agreement. The other Group Members will have no interest whatsoever in the Group Name and Logo, apart from the limited right to be known as former members of the Group.**

As seen above, it is imperative to put a specimen of the logo into the Agreement so that everyone is clear on what name and logo is at issue. Also, remember that a logo can be comprised of many different elements, (*e.g.,* a symbol (the "Tongue and Lips" of the Rolling Stones"), the title ("The Rolling Stones"), or a slogan ("The World's Greatest Rock n' Roll Band")). Each element should be inserted into the agreement or attached as an Exhibit. In many cases, the body of the Agreement refers to an "Addendum A" on which is listed each trademark and logo covered by the document.

The clause also will make clear who owns the logo and name - whether the Group or an individual member. Finally, it addresses what are the rights of a Leaving Member. Basically, the Leaving Member can only say he is a former member of the Group.

Ownership of Recorded Musical Compositions.

The administration of the Musical Compositions recorded by the Group is also very important to address. As seen above, music publishing is one of the most important revenue streams that can benefit an artist who is a songwriter. How the

Group wants to assign songwriting credit, who administers the Musical Compositions, and what happens to a Leaving Member must be addressed within the Band Agreement.

Ownership of Recorded Musical Compositions.

(I)   The Group Members (check one) [ ] will [ ] will not create a publishing entity (the "Group Publishing Company") which will own all rights to the following Musical Compositions (the "Recorded Musical Compositions", or alternatively, to the "Controlled Musical Compositions"):

(i)   recorded by the Group;

(ii)   released for sale on Sound Recordings under the Group Name; and

(iii)   which were written or co-written in whole or in part by one or more Group Members.

(II)   Each Group Member agrees to assign any ownership interest in each Recorded Musical Composition or Controlled Musical Composition to the Group Publishing Company and to execute any documents necessary to evidence the transfer of ownership to the Group Publishing Company.

(III)   Division of Publishing Revenue. Revenue from the Group Publishing Company, if such publishing company has been created, will be distributed as follows:

[ ]   All music publishing income derived from Recorded Musical Compositions, *including both writer's and publisher's*

shares, will be *divided equally* among the Group members.

[ ] The Group Members will *share equally* in the *publishing income* from all Recorded Musical Compositions. The *writers* of each Recorded Musical Composition *will receive an equal pro-rata share of the songwriters' income* with respect to each Recorded Musical Composition. By way of example, if two Group Members write a Recorded Musical Composition, each will share equally in the songwriters' income from that song. The publishing income from that song will be distributed equally to all Group Members.

[ ] *All revenue* derived from Recorded Musical Compositions *will be pooled* (whether it is characterized as publishing or songwriter revenue). Each Group Member will receive one credit for performing on each Recorded Musical Composition. The writers of each Recorded Musical Composition will receive one credit for writing. Each Group Member's total number of credits equals the numerator (top number of a fraction). The total number of credits equals the denominator or bottom number of a fraction. Each Group Member then receives this fraction of the song income. By way of example, if four Group Members perform on a song and one Group Member has written that song, the songwriter Group Member

would receive 2/5 of the revenue and the other three Group members would each receive 1/5 of the revenue.

(IV) **Publishing Administration.** The Group Publishing Company, if such company has been created, will have the universal, exclusive right to:

(i) administer and control the Copyright ownership to the Recorded Musical Compositions;

(ii) designate all persons to administer the Copyrights to the Recorded Musical Compositions; and

(iii) enter into agreements to co-publish, sub-publish, or otherwise deal with the Copyrights in the Recorded Musical Compositions.

(V) In the event that a Leaving Member controls a jointly owned Copyright, that Copyright will vest exclusively in the remaining Group Members for the Term of the Group Publishing Company. The Leaving Member's interest in the Group Publishing Company will extend only to those Recorded Musical Compositions that were commercially released for sale during the Leaving Member's period as a Group Member ("Leaving Member Recorded Musical Compositions"). The Leaving Member will receive semi-annual accountings and payments with respect to any income due on Leaving Member Recorded Musical Compositions.

<u>Statutory Licenses.</u> The Leaving Member agrees that Leaving Member will license Leaving Member's share of any Recorded Musical

Composition or Controlled Musical Composition at a rate of Seventy-five percent (75%) of the minimum compulsory statutory rate at the time of the master recording.

(VI) The Leaving Member will be entitled to the Leaving Member's *pro-rata* share of revenues generated by any Musical Composition, based on the Leaving Member's authorship percentage of that Musical Composition. For example, if Leaving Member #1 writes twenty percent of song A, and Group member #2 writes 80% of song A, then the Leaving Member #1 will be entitled to twenty percent and Member #2 will be entitled to 80% of the revenues generated by song A. Member's Authorship Percentage is hereby defined as a Member's percent of ownership in a given Musical Composition. The Member's Authorship Percentages for Musical Compositions composed to date are indicated on Exhibit "A" annexed hereto. With respect to subsequent Musical Compositions, authorship percentages will be determined in writing and signed by all authors, prior to the release of each subsequent LP.

(VII) Authorship percentages for subsequent LP's will be determined as follows:

(i) In the event that Group and Group Member collectively enter into a publishing Agreement with a Publisher for services as composers, each author will share in advances and royalties generated in the same percentage as their Member's Authorship Percentage for any song purchased by Publisher. Notwithstanding anything to the contrary contained in this Agreement, advances and income generated by any such publishing Agreement will only be paid to parties of the

publishing Agreement.

(ii)   Member will receive no compensation with respect to any Musical Composition recorded by the Group during the Term hereof not written or co-written by Member.

The first clause calls for the members of the Group to choose whether they will form a *music publishing company* or whether they will let another music publishing company administer the rights. Remember, the *Publisher* will take fifty percent of the income resulting from the exploitation of the Musical Compositions and the *Songwriter* will take fifty percent. Consequently, many attorneys are counseling their clients to form their own music publishing company or create a D/B/A using the Group LLC (the Group LLC is the company, "doing business as" the Group name). In this way, the songwriters in the Group can get both the fifty percent that goes to the songwriters and the fifty percent that goes to the Publisher. If the catalogue of recorded Musical Compositions becomes large, the Group can make a deal with a Publisher to "administer" the rights. For this, the second music publishing company generally will take twenty-five percent, still leaving the songwriter and the Group with seventy-five percent of the pie.

The second clause deals with the percentages of the various Band Members in relation to the revenues received from the music publishing company. It is argued that equality is a good way to go in a Group. It increases morale and reduces jealousy. But conversely, a good slogan to follow is "Songwriters are songwriters!" Group Members who are not co-writers on a Musical Composition will receive no earnings from such Musical Composition. Mr. Scott comments,

If you want to show appreciation, do it in the form a giving more master Sound Recording share, NEVER give a non-songwriter any songwriting credits or ownership. Ultimately, the Musical Composition will earn 20 to 30X more income than any Master Sound Recording (even if the Master Sound Recording is a hit!).[465]

Song Authorship Agreement (Split-Letter)

As has been emphasized before, it is important to have a written agreement memorializing the agreement between the Members regarding songwriting authorship. The answer is to enter into a Song Authorship Agreement or "Split Letter." Remember, the Copyright Code states that, absence an agreement, the court views co-authorship as "equal shares." Also, in the United States, co-owners (Musical Composition and/or Sound Recording) can exploit the Musical Composition without the other co-owner signing such non-exclusive license. But the writer that makes the non-exclusive deal must account to the other songwriters for their respective portion. It is important to remember that the vast majority of the world requires ALL owners to sign. In those countries, any co-owner can completely stop another from licensing (even on a non-exclusive basis) the work, period. Works can stay in limbo (sometimes forever) wherein no owner can exploit the work (with the exception under U.S. limited exploitation rights (such as but not limited to "mechanicals").

The next paragraph deals with how the members will share in *songwriting* royalties. Very simply, a decision is made as to how to share in the songwriter portion of the music publishing royalties. Generally, the first rule will be that someone had to participate in the writing of the Musical Composition. However, sometimes bands will agree that all members are credited with writing the Musical Composition and all will share equally.

Another key clause deals with mechanical royalties. We will see in the Recording Agreement below that the rate paid for mechanical royalties to a songwriter is seventy-five percent of the statutory rate, (*e.g.,* the statutory rate for mechanical licenses is currently 12 cents per copy sold). So, a Band Member will receive roughly 7.0 cents. The Band Member Agreement mirrors that term from the Recording Agreement.

Use of Likeness.

The ability of and need for the Group to use the likeness and name of the Band Member in promoting the Group is obvious. However, it still must be stated in the Agreement. If not properly addressed, a Leaving Member could prevent any further exploitation of records and other material if it contained the Leaving Member's likeness or name. Imagine the chaos, for example, if the Rolling Stones lost the right to use Mick Taylor's name and likeness on "Sticky Fingers," "Exile On Main Street," or any of the other recordings on which he appeared. Those albums would be relegated to the warehouse, never to be heard or seen again.

Grant of Rights; Use of Likeness.

(a)   Except as otherwise set forth herein, Member hereby grants to Group all rights of every kind and nature in and to the results and proceeds of Member's services and performances rendered hereunder, including,   without   limitation,   the   complete,

unconditional, and exclusive universal ownership in perpetuity of any and all master recordings and audio-visual devices embodying Member's performances in connection with Member's services hereunder. Group will, accordingly, have the sole and exclusive right to Copyright any such master recordings and/or audio-visual devices embodying Member's performances in Group's name, as the sole owner and author thereof, and to secure any and all renewals and extensions of such Copyrights (it being understood that for such purposes Member and all persons rendering services in connection with such master recordings and/or audio-visual devices will be Group's employee for hire). Nevertheless, Member will, upon Group's request, execute and deliver to Group any assignments of Copyright (including any renewals and extensions thereof) in and to such master recordings and/or audio-visual devices, and any and all other documents in connection with the rights granted hereunder, as Group may deem necessary, and Member hereby irrevocably appoints Group as Member's attorney-in-fact for the purpose of executing such assignments in Member's name. Without limiting the generality of the foregoing, at Group's election, Group may refrain from any and all exploitation of the results and proceeds of Member's services and performances rendered hereunder.

(b)   Group will have the exclusive universal right in perpetuity to use and display Member's name, voice, likeness, other identification and biographical material concerning Member for advertising, commercial, trade or publicity purposes and otherwise without restriction in connection with phonorecords (as defined in the Copyright Act of 1976 but limited to audio only or audiovisual) or otherwise in connection with the services performed by Member hereunder, and in connection with products, services and merchandise licensed or otherwise exploited by

Group.

Note that the above represents a very broad grant of rights. The Group can use the name and likeness in every medium, on every recording project, on tour, and in broadcast mediums. For the Group, this is good since it does not want a Group member to have any leverage to prevent or control the ability of the Group to earn a living.

Exclusivity.

The Agreement should also address whether the Band Member can engage in other projects outside the context of the Group.

Exclusivity.

(a) Member will render such services solely and exclusively for Group, and Member will not render such services either for Member's own account, or for the benefit of or on behalf of any other individual or entity without Group's prior written consent. Notwithstanding anything to the contrary contained in this Agreement, Member may continue to render services based on obligations entered into prior to the date of this Agreement, so long as these obligations are disclosed to Group, and approved by Group in writing.

During the Term of this Agreement, Member will not enter into any Agreement or make any commitment which would interfere with Member's performance of any of the terms and provisions hereof, nor will Member perform or render any services for the purposes of making phonograph records or master recordings for distribution in the form of phonograph records, pre-recorded tapes, compact discs, or any other configuration

("phonorecords", as defined in the Copyright Act of 1976) for any person firm or corporation other than Group.

(b)   Further, during the Term of this Agreement, Member will not authorize or permit the use of Group's name, likeness or other identification or voice or other sound effects, for or in connection with the production, sale, distribution, advertising, publicity, or exploitation of phonorecords or by any person, firm, or corporation other than Group, without Group's prior written consent, except to the extent expressly permitted herein.

(c)   After the expiration or termination of the Term of this Agreement, Member will not, directly, or indirectly, perform for any person, firm or corporation other than Group, for the purpose of making phonorecords from any of the Masters made hereunder for manufacture, sale or distribution, any part of the material embodied on the Masters prior to the later of:

(i)   the date five (5) years subsequent to the delivery to and acceptance of the Masters by the Record Company; or

(ii)   the date two (2) years subsequent to the expiration or termination of the Term of this Agreement or of the Recording Agreement, if later; or

(iii)   such date as may be required by the Record Company pursuant to the Recording Agreement, if later. Should Member violate any restriction herein set forth, Group may, in addition to any other right or remedy which Group may have on account of such breach, terminate Group's obligation to pay Member any monies due or to become due thereafter with

respect to any recordings embodying such selection(s) and to seek injunctive relief. Without limiting the generality of the foregoing, Member will not render any musical performances for Sound Recordings for any radio or motion picture or television soundtracks or programs, or as a member of the cast in recording a so-called "cast album", or for any electrical transcriptions except upon prior written notice to Group and pursuant to a written contract expressly prohibiting the use or exploitation of such performances and/or recordings directly or indirectly for phonorecords or videogram purposes.

In this Agreement, the Group has chosen to make the services of the Band Member exclusive. If a musician is a full member of the Group, exclusivity is the general rule. When Ron Wood left Rod Stewart and the Faces to join The Rolling Stones, it was made clear that Wood could not do both. He chose the Rolling Stones and no longer played with Faces.

The agreement also clarifies how long the exclusivity lasts - there is a variety of termination dates such as "two (2) years subsequent to the expiration of termination of this Agreement. . . ." For the Band Member this becomes an important clause since he does not want to be exclusively bound to a group that is no longer in existence.

Credit.

It is amazing how many bands do not address how the members of the Group will be listed and how credit shall be granted.

Credit.

(a)   Group will accord Member credit on, including

but not limited to, labels of records, liner notes, film credits, tour posters, and announcements, and packaging of LP's in all configurations for each medium embodying Member's performance as follows: _____.

(b)   Group member will also be entitled to credit as co-producer of masters embodied on the LP entitled "_____" for which Band Member provided producing services on labels of records and the liner notes and packaging of LP's in all configurations, or any other use involving said masters.

In the Agreement, the Group is giving the Band Member credit in and on all mediums where the Band Member performs. In addition, the Band Member will be given credit if he provides "producing" services.

Addition of Members; Departing Members.

Another area that must be addressed in the Band Agreement is how to add or remove a member of the Group. Numerous examples of litigation exist that involve a Group member arguing that he was improperly terminated from the Group.

Addition of Members; Leaving Members.

(a)   Each new Member entering the Group (an "Entering Group Member") must agree to be bound by all of the provisions in this Agreement. An Entering Group Member will not have any rights to the Group property or assets existing at the time of admission to the Group ("Existing Group Property") or in any of the proceeds derived from the Existing Property (for example, revenue or royalties generated by recorded

Musical Compositions, Sound Recordings or other materials created prior to the new Group Member's admission). An Entering Group Member will have rights only to the Group property or assets existing that come into the Group after the time of admission to the Group ("Subsequent Group Property") and may share in the proceeds derived from the Subsequent Group Property (for example, revenue or royalties generated by recorded Musical Compositions, Sound Recordings or other materials created after joining the Group).

(b)   A Group Member may leave the Group (a "Leaving Member") voluntarily (by resignation) or involuntarily (by reason of death, disability or being expelled). A Group Member who resigns will give thirty (30) days prior written notice. The Group will provide written notice if it expels a Group Member. The Group will have at its option, the right to immediately exclude any expelled Group Members from live or recorded performances during this 30-day notice period.

In the first clause, the Group explicitly states that any Entering Group Member must abide by the rules and regulations of the Group. It might seem redundant, but it is good to make it clear that the Entering Group Member is not allowed to act like a prima donna.

The first clause also creates a clear line regarding the property of the Group to which the Entering Group Member will or will not have a share. In this case, the Entering Group Member will not have any share in the property already accrued by the Group. Therefore, the Entering Group Member will not share in royalties from prior albums, Musical Compositions, or tours.

The second clause deals with departing members. First,

any such Leaving Member that leaves voluntarily must give thirty days' written notice prior to leaving the Group. Regarding the Group, they must give thirty days' written notice to kick the Band Member out, and, during that 30-day notice period, the Leaving Member is relieved of any further activities with the Group.

Ending the Group.

All groups believe that they will last forever. As is clear, this is rarely the case. When The Beatles broke up, the shock was felt far and wide. And it was broader than the fact that there might not be more music from The Beatles - to a whole generation of music lovers they were personal friends, a group of guys that would always be together, and whom fans could turn to in tough times. Alas, as they say, the music ended.

Despite the best of intentions and even in the face of the greatest success, a Group will still break up. The Group members might have grown tired of each other or feel artistically stifled. The next chapter will continue with the provisions of a Group agreement that deals with termination.

CHAPTER 10

DISSOLUTION OF THE BAND

"It is with deep regret that we announce the sudden passing of . . . ."

"Breaking up is hard to do."
- Neil Sedaka and Howard Greenfield[466]

It might seem odd to have just addressed entering into a Band Agreement and starting a new venture, and straightaway talk about breaking up. Unfortunately, it must be addressed right from the start.

Sooner or later, all good things must end. When the Beatles broke up, to those who had grown up with them it was as if some perfect symmetry of the universe had suddenly gone haywire. "Here Comes the Sun" - would it really come after this? Of course, the sun did rise, and the world went on. And as we have seen time after time - and perhaps highlighted best in the throwback movie, *The Wonders* - the break-up of bands is far more common than bands staying together.

With the exception of the Rolling Stones, the bands from the first big generation of rock in the 1960s have not fared well: they are either pale imitations of themselves (The Who – only two members still left) or gone all together (The Beatles, The Kinks). Even the Stones have had various lineups and key founding members leaving the band.

The bands from the 1970s have not fared much better - Led Zeppelin, the Eagles, and other leading chart toppers broke up. In the 1980s, many felt the same sense of disorientation when the Police disbanded. However, some bands who gained fame in the late '70's and early '80s remain pertinent, such as Aerosmith, U2, The Cure, Metallica, and Depeche Mode. From the 1990s, Pearl Jam remains vibrant, but others such as Nirvana and Guns 'n Roses are gone.

If the Band Agreement is drafted correctly, the procedure behind the departure of a member or the breaking up of the entire band should be relatively straightforward.

Some of the main issues when breaking up include: (i) use of the band name, trademarks, and logos; (ii) use of the songs created while with the band; and (iii) future recording commitments with and without the departing member. Below are sample provisions that deal with many of these issues. However, every band has different needs and unique issues that warrant consideration. It is beyond the scope of this book to address every possibility. Just remember - it is not "one size fits all."

Termination.

What if the Band Member is always late, under the influence of drugs or alcohol, or always getting into fights with other band/artist members? What do you do? You must have a termination clause.

Termination Rights.

(a)   Notwithstanding anything to the contrary contained herein, Group will, in addition to any other rights or remedies available to Group, have the right to terminate the Term of this Agreement with or without Proper Cause (as hereinafter defined) by sending written notice to Member at any time.

(b)   In such event, Group will immediately be relieved of any further obligations to utilize Member's services hereunder. In the event Group terminates the Term hereof for Proper Cause, Member's engagement hereunder will terminate as of the effective date of said notice, and Member will be entitled to receive only that contingent compensation due and payable hereunder in respect to Record Royalties earned during the five (5) year period following the termination hereof, together with any other accrued but unpaid compensation due and owing to Member hereunder as of the effective date of termination hereof _less_ any damages to Group which are attributable to Member's actions resulting in the termination hereof.

(c)   In the event Group terminates the Term hereof for any reason other than Proper Cause, Group shall give Member not less than thirty (30) days prior notice of such termination. Group will pay to Member the sum equal to the compensation Member would have otherwise earned during the thirty (30) day period immediately subsequent to the date of Group's such notice to Member, so long as Member fully performs all of Member's obligations hereunder in accordance with the terms and provisions hereof prior to the date the Term of this Agreement terminates pursuant to any such notice to Member, and Member will also be entitled to receive the contingent compensation provided for herein in respect to Record Royalties in perpetuity during which such termination occurs, together with any other accrued but unpaid compensation due and owing to Member hereunder as of the effective date of termination hereof.

(d)   As used herein, the Term "Proper Cause" will mean and include, without limitation:

(i)   Member's failure, refusal, neglect, or inability to render services or to fulfill any obligation hereunder as, when, and in the timely manner required, including, without limitation, Member's failure to appear at times or places requested by Group or the Group's management, such as, but not limited to, any scheduled recording session, filming, videotaping, sound-check, concert, interview, or any other performance or promotional engagement (and any scheduled rehearsals therefore);

(ii)   Member's arrest and/or conviction for any crime, whether a misdemeanor or a felony;

(iii)   Member's involvement in any conduct which Group reasonably deems to be detrimental to the health, safety, welfare or public reputation of Group or any other Group Member; purchase of illegal drugs; Member's use, possession, or sale of illegal substances;

(iv)   Member's abuse of alcohol, especially when such abuse interferes with Member's ability to fulfill Member's obligations hereunder;

(v)   Member's possession of weapons or explosives of any kind;

(vi)   Member's engagement in acts of dishonesty, fraud, theft, or other illegal or unethical behavior;

(vii)   Member's engagement in fighting or other disorderly conduct which may endanger others;

(viii)   Member's engagement in threats, intimidation, or other abusive conduct, including without limitation, harassment, or discrimination of any kind;

(ix)   Member's failure to render performances in a manner consistent with the quality level and standard of the Group as determined in Group's sole discretion;

(x)   Group's failure to enter into the Recording Agreement or the Recording Agreement terminates or expires or is otherwise suspended by the Record Company for a period in excess of six (6) months; or

(xi)   Group is prevented from performing in a substantial portion of Group's obligations hereunder by law, ruling or action of any labor union or guild, court order, force majeure event (as hereinafter defined) lasting longer than a period of six (6) months, or any other cause beyond Group's control, or such

obligations are rendered commercially impossible.

The first clause establishes that the Group can remove the Band Member with or without Proper Cause. A couple of nuances are immediately apparent - the Group can remove a member at any time AND, if for Proper Cause, can do so immediately. The question is - how is it done?

The second clause addresses when termination is for Proper Cause. If the termination is for Proper Cause, the termination can occur immediately. Proper Cause is defined with a variety of examples. Two of the biggest examples are fraud and the inability to fulfill the Member's duties. If the termination is for Proper Cause, the Member will receive the compensation owed to him, but, (a) only for a period of five years from the date of the termination, (b) only after deducting payment for any outstanding advances, and (c) if there are damages from the Leaving Member's actions, only after deducting the damages.

The third clause deals with the situation when the termination is without Proper Clause - the Member must be given thirty (30) days' notice in writing. Under this clause, the Leaving Member will still be able to participate in and receive royalties and other contingent compensation.

Suspension and Force Majeure.

Some of the remedies available to the Group are outlined in this clause.

Suspension and Force Majeure.

(a)   Group will have the right, at Group's election, to suspend the Term of this Agreement and Group's

obligations hereunder upon written notice to Member if:

(i)   for any reason whatsoever Member will become disabled (as such Term is defined herein below),

(ii)   Member will refuse, neglect, or be unable to comply with any of Member's obligations hereunder, or

(iii)   as a result of an act of God, accident, fire, labor controversy, riot, civil commotion, act of public enemy, law, enactment, rule, order or act of any government or governmental instrumentality, failure of technical facilities, failure or delay of transportation facilities, illness or incapacity, or other cause of a similar or dissimilar nature not reasonably within Group's control or which Group could not by reasonable diligence have avoided, Group is unable to conduct or continue as scheduled any engagement or performance which arises hereunder; or

(iv)   Proper Cause.

(b)   Any such suspension will be for the duration of any such event giving rise to Group's right to suspend and, unless Group will notify Member to the contrary in writing, the time periods herein for the performance of any obligations hereunder will be automatically extended by such number of days as equal the total number of days of any such suspension. During any such suspension except for Proper Cause, Member will be entitled to render Member's services in any capacity to any other person, firm, or corporation, subject to Member's being ready willing and able to resume Member's services hereunder upon ten (10) days prior written notice and subject to the other provisions. As used in this paragraph, the Term

"disabled" will mean Member's inability by reason of physical, mental, or emotional illness, vocal impairment, accident, or other incapacity to substantially perform Member's normal and usual employment duties and services for Group, as previously performed by Member.

(c) No suspension as a result of any force majeure event will, in and of itself, suspend Group's obligation to make payments of theretofore-accrued compensation hereunder unless such suspension is due to Member's material breach of this Agreement or Member's refusal or failure to comply with any of Member's material obligations hereunder, or unless the event giving rise to such suspension impairs Group's ability to make such payments.

(d) The Group will not be deemed in default of its obligations hereunder if its performance hereunder is delayed or becomes impossible or impractical by reason of any *force majeure* event.

The first couple of clauses deal with events such a sickness, disability, a refusal to perform by the Band Member, an event of *force majeure* (an act of God), or Proper Cause. The clauses will allow the Group to suspend its obligations to the Band Member until the time of the suspension is ended. Be aware that it requires the suspended member to give ten days' notice to the Group that the Member is ready to resume their obligations before the Member can come back into the Group.

It is important to outline the conditions under which the Band will terminate its partnership.

<u>Ending the Group</u>.

(a) This Agreement and the Group will not

terminate for the reason that a Group Member leaves the Group. If a member leaves, the Group will remain in full force among the remaining members.

(b)   The addition of a new Group Member will not end the Group, and it will remain in full force among the remaining Group Members.

(c)   This Agreement will terminate, and the Group will end, upon the first to occur of the following events:

> **(i) The written agreement of the Group Members to end the Group;**
>
> **(ii) By operation of law, except as otherwise provided in this Agreement; or**
>
> **(iii) If _____ leaves the Group.**

The first clause makes it clear that the Group will not dissolve simply because a member leaves the Group. The second clause –conversely provides that a new member will not end the prior existence of the Group.

The third clause addresses what events might cause dissolution of the Group. First, the Group will dissolve if there is a written agreement among the Band Members to end the Group. Second, the Group will dissolve by operation of law, (*e.g.,* the Articles of Organization say that the LLC will only last for ten years). Third, the Group will be dissolved if a member of the Group is indispensable and that member leaves.

The third situation can create some tricky nuances. Be very careful about giving one individual the power and authority to leave and dissolve the Group. The founder of a Group might rightly demand that if he leaves the Group, the Group dissolves.

If that had been in effect with Pink Floyd, Roger Waters would have been successful in terminating Pink Floyd. Moreover, just because one Band Member might be the founder, does not mean that the public mind will consider, in five to ten years, that Band Member to be the one who best personifies the Band as a whole. A good example is Brian Jones – although Jones was a founding member, it is Mick Jagger and Keith Richards that are considered the important influences of the Rolling Stones.

Distribution of Group Assets after Dissolution.

During the life of a Band much property is acquired - real, personal, and intellectual. It is mandatory that the Band Agreement address how the Group Property is valued and distributed after dissolution of the Group.

Distribution of Group Assets after Dissolution.

(a) **Income and Debts**. After the dissolution of the Group, any income that is owed to the Group will be collected and will be used first to pay off debts to people outside the Group (creditors) and any remaining money will be used to pay debts (loans in excess of capital contributions) to Group Members. If money remains after paying off these debts to Group Members, it will be distributed equally to the Group Members (the "Group Distribution").

(b) **Group Property**. Any property owned or controlled by the Group (for example, musical equipment or real estate) (the "Group Property") will not be sold but will be evaluated, by an accountant if necessary (the "Group Property Value"). The Group Property will then be distributed as nearly as possible, in *pro rata* shares among the Group Members.

(c)   <u>Royalties & Future Income</u>. If at the time of dissolution, the Group is entitled to royalties or owns property that is generating income or royalties, the Group will vote to either establish an administrative trust or designate an individual (for example, an accountant), to collect and distribute the royalties on an ongoing basis to the Group Members according to their respective interests.

(d)   A Group Member that is still a Member of the Group at the time of the dissolution of the Group will be entitled to (a "Dissolving Member"):

(i)   the Dissolving Member's proportionate share of the net worth of the Group as of the date of disassociation; and

(ii)   the Dissolving Member's share of any royalties, commissions, or licensing fees earned from Sound Recordings, which include the Dissolving Member's performance. These payments will be made when actually received by the Group and after subtracting a proportionate deduction of expenses. The Dissolving Member's Record Royalties will only be paid after the record company has recouped the Group's recording costs for the respective recording.

(e)   <u>Determination of Net Worth</u>. The Group Distribution and the Group Property Value will comprise the Group Net Worth. The Dissolving Member's share will be paid in installments starting one month after determining the Group Net Worth and be payable as follows:

(i)   If the share is less than $100,000, it will be paid in 12 monthly installments;

(ii)   If the share is more than $100,000 but

less than $125,000, it will be paid in 24 monthly installments; or

(iii)   If the share is more than $125,000, it will be paid in 36 monthly installments.

(iv)   The payments will include interest at the prime interest rate.

The first paragraph establishes a hierarchy of payment of debts by the Group upon dissolution. Before any monies are distributed to the Band Members, all creditors must be paid off and all loans to third-parties or members of the Group must be retired. After all debts are paid off, the remaining monies will be distributed to the Group, generally on a *pro rata* basis.

The next paragraph establishes that before any distribution, the various items of property owned by the Group will be valued and appraised. The property shall not be sold but divided equally among the Dissolving Members. However, this type of division is not always practical. In that case, the valuations are used to set a price for the property and liquidate it. Also, remember to address what happens with the Band's Trademarks, including their logos and other elements!

The third paragraph states that the Group will establish a trust or escrow account for any future royalties, or other monies received by the Group. Remember, the Group will have established a Group bank account, but that account will be closed as part of the dissolution process. Consequently, a new account must be set up to take care of post-dissolution monies.

The final paragraph deals with how, presuming there are monies to be distributed, the distributions will be made. The paragraph lists various share amounts and how the payments will be made and when made.

Upon the completion of the dissolution process, the

Group will be defunct (not "de-funked"), and each member can pursue his/her career free from the obligations of the Band Agreement.

Conclusion.

It is obvious how important a band/artist agreement is between the members of the Band. Making it clear what the obligations of the Band Members are and, in turn, the obligations of the Group, can prevent much tension and controversy as well as avoid litigation.

CHAPTER 11

MANAGEMENT AGREEMENT

"You ain't got no agreement with Elvis; you got an agreement with the Colonel!"
-     Col. Tom Parker;
Personal Manager of Elvis Presley[467]

"I used to see a management commission as compensation for the relentless time and effort put in by managers on behalf of their clients. However, I now see it more like hazard pay."
-     Pete Angelus
Personal Manager[468]

After creating a band or starting a solo career, the next step is to put together a team that will help guide the band/artist's career. Generally, there are four groups of people that assist the band/artist regarding exposure, jobs, assets, and management:

1. <u>Attorneys:</u> protects the band/artist's legal rights. This is most often an entertainment attorney, although sometimes an intellectual property, employment, labor, or other type of attorney is consulted.

2, <u>Personal managers:</u> oversees and guides the band/artist's career. Although stated in the plural here, generally a Personal Manager will want exclusivity.

3. <u>Agents:</u> finds opportunities for the band/artist to make money. A band/artist can have more than one agent - for example, different agents might take care of tours, engage in book deals, and engage in movie deals.

4. <u>Business managers:</u> an accountant who manages the finances of the band/artist and its members.

This chapter will deal with a Personal Manager Agreement (**the "PMA"**). The Personal Manager's role is two-fold: (i) take care of the minutia of the band/artist's day-to-day affairs; and (ii) most importantly, help guide the band/artist's career. Pete Angelus, Personal Manager who has worked with such groups and artists as Van Halen, The Black Crowes, Jimmy Page, and Hall & Oates states:

There are many different types of management styles, so to speak. Some deal only with the business aspect of management. Some participate creatively as well. I have always been very involved in all aspects of my artists' career.[470]

A great example of a Personal Manager that helped his clients reach the absolute pinnacle of success was Brian Epstein, the Personal Manager of The Beatles. Epstein helped mold some scruffy greasers from Liverpool into the most popular and influential band in rock music history. Many people feel that the death of Epstein was the beginning of the end of The Beatles. Upon hearing of Epstein's death, John Lennon thought "We've fuckin' had it."[471]

Generally, the Personal Manager has a broad grant of authority to oversee a band/artist's career. Consequently, by having this broad authority, there must be an overlap, a checks-and-balances, as to the actions and responsibilities of the lawyers, agents, business manager, and Personal Manager teams, a system of checks and balances should be established and enforced as between the agents, the Personal Manager, the attorneys, and the business manager.

Appointment.

Appointment:

(a)   Band/artist hereby appoints Personal Manager as band/artist's sole and exclusive Personal Manager, representative and advisor, throughout the universe, with respect to all of the band/artist's activities in the Entertainment Industry, and Personal Manager hereby accepts such engagement. In this capacity Personal Manager shall render such advice,

guidance, counsel, and such other services as band/artist may reasonably require to further band/artist's career in the Entertainment Industry, including but not limited to the following services:

(i)   To represent band/artist and to negotiate (in conjunction with band/artist's attorney) the terms of agreements for the use, employment or exploitation of band/artist's services and the products thereof in the Entertainment Industry.

(ii)   To supervise band/artist's professional employment in the Entertainment Industry and to consult with employers and potential employers so as to assure the proper use and promote demand therefore throughout the universe.

(iii)   To be available at reasonable times and places to confer with band/artist in connection with all matters concerning band/artist's career in the Entertainment Industry.

(iv)   To engage and discharge and supervise booking agents that band/artist may elect to utilize for the purpose of securing engagements.

(b)   Band/artist shall advise Personal Manager of all offers of employment submitted to band/artist, in order that Personal Manager may determine in consultation with band/artist whether the same are compatible with band/artist's career. Band/artist shall not engage any booking agent without first consulting Personal Manager. It is expressly understood that Personal Manager is not a licensed talent agent or theatrical employment agent, and that Personal Manager has not offered or promised to obtain, seek, or procure employment or engagements for band/artist.

The first clause of the PMA outlines the obligations and responsibilities of the Personal Manager to the band/artist. Immediately there is a very important nuance - in this particular agreement the Personal Manager is the "exclusive" Personal Manager for the band/artist. There will be no other "personal" managers. The following clauses then list with some particularity the areas of the band/artist's career for which the Personal Manager will provide services.

Clause (a)(i) gives the Personal Manager authority to assist in negotiating agreements regarding *all* aspects of the band/artist's career. It is very broad and could be an area of negotiation. Clause (a)(ii) establishes that the Personal Manager will oversee the performances of the band/artist in order to make sure they are safe and compliant with all laws. Clause (a)(iii) creates an obligation for the Personal Manager to be available to discuss and consult on the band/artist's career. Finally, Clause (a)(iv) gives the Personal Manager the power to engage and fire booking agents.

Term.

The length of any agreement is a key provision. And, even more so with a Personal Manager.

Term:

(a) The initial term of this Agreement shall commence on the date hereof and shall continue for a period of three (3) years from the effective date of this Agreement.

(b) Notwithstanding the foregoing, if band/artist has not entered into a recording agreement (a "Recording Agreement") with a major record company (*e.g.,* Sony Music, EMI, MCA, PolyGram,

Warner Bros., Elektra, Atlantic, and/or BMG or a label associated with or distributed by any of the aforesaid companies) within three (3) years from the date hereof (the period between the date first above written and the date such a Recording Agreement is entered being herein referred to as the "Trial Period"). This Agreement shall automatically terminate three (3) year from the date hereof.

(c) If band/artist's Gross Compensation (as hereinafter defined) during the initial term is at least $_____, Personal Manager shall have an option to extend the term for a further period of _____ years (the "Option Period"), which option shall be exercisable by written notice to band/artist delivered not later than _____ days prior to the expiration of the initial term. In view of the fact that sales of records embodying band/artist's recordings and royalties due to band/artist by reason thereof may not be reported for some time after the date when Personal Manager is to exercise the option, the parties agree to rely upon the projection of the responsible financial officer at the company distributing band/artist's recordings, if such projection is required for the purpose of determining whether the aforesaid Gross Compensation level has been attained during the initial term.

In *any* agreement, it is imperative to make clear how long the Agreement will last. In this Agreement, the initial term is for three (3) years. Many managers will want at least two (2) years, and most will want three (3) years. Why? It takes time for a band/artist to develop into a viable entity. The Personal Manager will want the term to be of a nature that allows the Personal Manager to help shape the band/artist and also continue to participate in the increased revenue from the band/artist's improvement.

Another important point is to put some type of conditions or "benchmarks" that the Personal Manager must meet. In Clause (b), the Personal Manager must get a "recording agreement" for the band/artist. In Clause (c), the Personal Manager must assist the band/artist reach a certain level of revenue.

Such clauses, if they can be inserted, are of great power. Many times, a Personal Manager will take on a band/artist and then leave that band/artist out in the cold. Under this Agreement, the Personal Manager must meet some tangible goals, or the Agreement will terminate at the end of the three (3) year period.

Options.

(a)   **Band/artist grants Personal Manager two (2) consecutive options to extend the Term for one (1) option period of one (1) year per option, the second option period to immediately follow the first, and then only upon the following conditions:**

(i)   **The first option may be exercised by Personal Manager if he is instrumental in securing and has actively cultivated the Record Deal and then, only if it is accepted and signed by band/artist; and**

(ii)   **The second option may be exercised only if the first option was exercised, and then only if Personal Manager has; in the opinion of band/artist, adequately cooperated with the record company in the promotion and or production of the band/artist and any product called for under the record contract, or secured a competent booking agent; secured a tour in support of any record deal supporting a signed nationally known act acceptable to band/artist; and sustained the current level of compensation to band/artist.**

(b) Personal Manager may exercise each such option, so long as the pre-conditions have been fulfilled, by sending band/artist a notice at any time before the end of the period then in effect, and each option period shall commence upon the end of the period then in effect.

If the Personal Manager meets the benchmarks listed in the Agreement, the Personal Manager may extend the term of the Agreement. Under this Agreement, the Personal Manager has two consecutive options. However, the second option only comes into existence if the first option is exercised. Also, the first option can only be exercised if certain benchmarks were met.

Again, this is a great way to impose some responsibility and urgency on the Personal Manager and make him or her feel more personally vested in the band/artist's success.

Personal Manager's Compensation.

This is where the rubber meets the road in an PMA – how much is the Personal Manager going to take for the Personal Manager's services? And for how long will he/she take it?

Personal Manager's Compensation:

(a) <u>Fixed Compensation</u>: Band/artist agrees to pay Personal Manager a monthly fee of _____ Thousand Dollars ($_____) during the term of this Agreement, unless otherwise amended in writing by the parties hereto. The Monthly Fee shall be considered an "advance" against the Personal Manager's commissions and other contingent compensation; and

(b) <u>Contingent Compensation</u>**: Personal Manager shall receive _____ Per Cent (_____ %) of the band/artist's Gross Compensation (defined below) during the Term hereof.**

A Personal Manager may take compensation in two (2) ways: (i) a fixed fee, which could be an "advance" against future commissions; and (ii) contingent compensation, a commission in the form of a percentage of the band/artist's gross income.

The amount of the fixed fee is negotiable, as is whether or not it is considered an advance. When it comes to the contingent compensation, the main thing to remember is that, as compared to an agent, a Personal Manager's percentage is not limited by law. A Personal Manager can ask for, and receive, as much as the band/artist is willing to give (this will be discussed a bit more below). The most extreme example is Col. Tom Parker, Elvis Presley's Personal Manager. By the end of Elvis' career, Parker was taking fifty percent of Elvis' income!

Post-Termination Compensation

One area that will be an area of intense negotiation regards the compensation due and owing to the Personal Manager *after* the termination of the Agreement. It is not uncommon for a Personal Manager to overreach in this area and attempt to receive commissions for things that the Personal Manager did not have anything to do with.

Post-Termination Compensation:

(a) **If this Agreement is terminated other than for "Cause," as that term is defined herein, the Personal Manager shall continue to receive the Commission pursuant to the**

following terms:

(i)   With respect to phonograph records and/or master recordings recorded by band/artist, during the Term hereof, pursuant to a Recording Agreement entered into during the Term hereof, which are released or distributed either through retail outlets or directly to consumers including without limitation by the Internet or by digital downloads or streaming, during the Term hereof ("Term Recordings"), band/artist shall pay Personal Manager twenty percent (20%) of any and all gross monies or other considerations earned from such Term Recordings in perpetuity.

(ii)   With respect to Musical Compositions written or composed in whole or in part by band/artist during the Term hereof which are recorded during the Term hereof by band/artist on a commercial recording under a Recording Agreement entered into during the Term hereof or distributed to retail outlets or directly to consumers by band/artist commercially throughout one or more of the Major Territories during the Term, including but not limited to, by the Internet or by digital downloads or streaming or recorded by a third party on a commercial recording during the Term hereof ("Term Musical Compositions"), band/artist shall pay Personal Manager a twenty percent (20%) commission of any and all gross monies or other considerations earned from such Term Musical Compositions after the Term hereof in perpetuity.

(iii) With respect to Musical Compositions written or composed in whole or in part by band/artist after the end of the Term pursuant to a

Publishing Agreement entered into or substantially negotiated during the Term ("After Term Musical Compositions"), band/artist shall pay Personal Manager ten percent (10%) of all gross monies and other consideration earned from such After Term Musical Compositions during the five (5) year period immediately following the end of the Term. A Musical Composition first released or otherwise exploited within six (6) months after the end of this Term hereof shall be deemed written during the Term.

(iv) With respect to any and all merchandising and tour sponsorships, the agreements for which were entered into during the Term hereof ("Term Merchandise and Sponsorship Agreements"), band/artist shall pay Personal Manager the following percentages of any and all gross monies or other considerations earned after the Term from such Term Merchandise and Sponsorship Agreements:

A. twenty percent (20%) during the period commencing upon the expiration of the Term hereof and ending five (5) years thereafter.

B. When applicable, with respect to any and all concert tours which have commenced prior to the expiration of the Term, but which continue after the expiration of the Term (hereinafter, "Continuing Tours"), band/artist shall pay Personal Manager ten percent (10%) of any and all gross monies earned from such Continuing Tours during the period commencing upon the expiration of the Term hereof and ending one (1) year thereafter, less any advances payable to Personal Manager in connection with such tour.

C. With respect to any activity or property as to which Personal Manager is entitled to a Commission during the Term other than those specified above, Personal Manager shall also be entitled to a commission of ten percent (10%) of gross monies or other considerations earned therefrom after the Term, continuing for five (5) years after the end of the Term.

D. Except as otherwise provided herein, Personal Manager shall receive the foregoing commissions whether or not any employment, engagement, contract, agreement, or other income producing activity shall have been procured by band/artist as a result of Personal Manager's advice, consultation, or other efforts and whether or not the term of said employment, engagement, contract, agreement, or income producing activity shall be effective or continue before, during or after the Term of this Agreement.

E. For purposes of clarification, an agreement shall be deemed "entered into" for purposes of this management agreement even if it is not executed during the Term, provided that an offer in writing is secured by Personal Manager and the material terms thereof have been substantially negotiated and agreed upon during the Term and an agreement resulting from such offer is executed with the same parties no later than nine (9) months after the expiration of the Term.

The term "Recording Agreement," "Publishing Agreement" or other Agreements shall refer to the Agreements as entered into originally and also to all modifications,

amendments, renewals, substitutions, and replacements therefore whether negotiated or entered into during the Term hereof or not.

The key issue within these clauses is to limit the scope of what the Personal Manager will still receive as a commission after the Agreement has been terminated. It is fair to the Personal Manager that he will still receive a commission for deals that were negotiated during the tenure as Personal Manager. However, it is not fair or proper for the Personal Manager to receive a commission for things that are done after being dismissed.

Many of these types of clauses will have a "sunset" provision, *i.e.*, after a certain period of time the payment of the compensation will end. For example, a sunset clause might state that the Personal Manager will get the full commission, let's say 20%, for a period of five years, it will go down to 10% for the next five years, it will drop again to 5% for five years and then be zero at the conclusion of that period.

Expenses and Advances.

Whether the Personal Manager will receive reimbursement for expenses and any type of advance is another area of deep negotiations.

Expenses and Advances:

Band/artist shall be solely responsible for the payment of all fees, costs, and expenses, other than management fees, costs or expenses that are incurred by or on behalf of band/artist in connection with band/artist's career in the Entertainment Industry or in connection with the operation of this Agreement (the "Expenses"). The Expenses include, by way of example and not limitation, the following:

(i)   all of band/artist's wardrobe expenses, recording expenses, publicity and promotion costs, travel and living expenses of band/artist, booking agency fees, and union dues; and

(ii)   all expenses incurred by Personal Manager for the following in connection with the performance of this Agreement: the cost of long-distance telephone calls, postage, photocopying, messengers, and air courier services in excess of per month. If any expenses incurred by the Personal Manager benefit another artist(s) who is being managed by the Personal Manager then that expense shall, with the consent of band/artist, be pro-rated between or among the band/artist and such other artist(s). Absent consent, band/artist shall not be obligated for such expenses.

(a)   The Expenses do not include Personal Manager's overhead.

(b)   Personal Manager shall not be obligated to advance any Expenses or to make any loan to band/artist. Personal Manager may, however, choose to advance Expenses or to make loans to band/artist (such Expenses and Advances are, collectively, the "Advances").

(c)   Personal Manager shall, on a monthly basis, submit a statement to band/artist that itemizes outstanding Advances, and band/artist shall pay Personal Manager the amount of such Advances within ten (10) days after that statement has been submitted to band/artist unless at the time of the Advance another repayment schedule has been negotiated. At the time of any Advance, Personal Manager must inform band/artist of the obligations of this subparagraph as regards to the time of repayment; otherwise, it will be presumed that

another repayment schedule has been negotiated. Personal Manager must, at the time of any Advance, obtain a signed notation from band/artist stating that band/artist has been informed of its obligations hereunder and that band/artist elects to forego negotiation of an alternative repayment schedule.

One area that can generate great tension is determining the definition for "advances," "expenses," and "recoupable."

Under clause (a), the band/artist is responsible for its own expenses, which generally consist of wardrobe, recording expenses, and living expenses. This is a common arrangement for a newer band/artist, which has not proved itself yet. However, if a record company or a Personal Manager believes in the band/artist enough, they may advance certain expenses that will ultimately be recouped from the band/artist's royalty.

Keep in mind clause (a)(ii) - if the Personal Manager is managing other artists (for example, the various members of the band/artist as individuals), the expenses may be prorated across all of the clients. In this agreement, it only occurs if the band/artist gives written permission. Be aware of this practice of amortizing a Personal Manager's costs across a variety of clients - it is highly susceptible to "double-dipping," *i.e.,* the Personal Manager assigning the same cost to multiple clients and getting paid multiple times for one expense.

Clause (d) requires the Personal Manager to provide a monthly accounting. It is a very good practice to require such accountings. If such a requirement exists, do not treat it as merely a formality: do not let the Personal Manager off the hook. There is no better way to find out that a Personal Manager is acting improperly than by getting a consistent stream of reports. It is not foolproof (see Bernie Madoff) but, even if the underlying manipulation of funds remains hidden for a while, the manipulated reports themselves will eventually become evidence against the Personal Manager.

Collection of Income.

Where the money goes is a big negotiating point between the Personal Manager and the band/artist. If the Personal Manager is a major figure, the Personal Manager will want to collect the monies and then forward the band/artist their portion.

Collection of band/artist's Compensation:

(a) All of band/artist's Gross Compensation shall be paid directly to, and collected by, Personal Manager. All monies that are part of band/artist's Gross Compensation shall, immediately after they are collected, be deposited into an account (the "Account"). The Account shall be in the Personal Manager's name, and only the Personal Manager may make withdrawals from the Account. Personal Manager shall maintain the books for the Account. Personal Manager shall promptly furnish band/artist with copies of all deposit slips for the Account after deposits are made.

(b) Any monies collected by the band/artist on behalf of the band/artist shall be delivered to the Personal Manager within _____ days of collection.

(c) "Band/artist's Gross Receipts" shall mean: all revenue received from live performances, fees, television or film rentals, video discs, cassettes or similar devices, advertising accessories, souvenir programs and booklets, merchandise, all sums paid or accrued on account of sales, use, receipts, income, excise, remittance, and other taxes (however

denominated) to any governmental authority, expenses of transmitting to the United States any funds accruing to the band/artist in foreign countries, such as cable expenses and any discounts from such funds taken to convert such funds directly or indirectly into U.S. dollars.

Who collects the monies generated by the band/artist's activities is a "rubber meets the road" issue between the Personal Manager and the band/artist. Most managers will want the funds to go through its offices in order to assure payment of the Personal Manager's commissions. However, a band/artist will want the monies to go through its offices in order to assure that the Personal Manager does not steal money from the band/artist. The resolution of the issue will depend upon Nebgenism #3:

Nebgenism #3 - *the bigger your market position, the better your bargaining position.*

If you are a young band/artist with no track record and Quincy Jones wants to produce and manage the band/artist's career, Mr. Jones' office will control the flow of the funds. If you are a big, established band/artist hiring a young and inexperienced Personal Manager (though why would you?), the band/artist will certainly control the funds.

After determining who will control the funds, the next issue is when the funds will be distributed. The clause above puts the period in days, but it can also be quarterly or even semi-annually.

The definition of what constitutes "Band/artist Gross Receipts" is a very important clause and must be reviewed carefully by both parties. What goes into the definition of "Gross Receipts" is often the subject of intense negotiation.

Books and Records.

It is imperative that proper books and records be kept regarding the activities and monies generated by the band/artist.

Books and Records:

(a)   Personal Manager shall keep books and records of all transactions relating to this Agreement. Band/artist may examine only those books and records that pertain to the statements showing royalties owed to band/artist. Band/artist may make those examinations only for the purpose of verifying the accuracy of the statements sent to band/artist. Band/artist may make those examinations only during Personal Manager's usual business hours, and at the place where it keeps the books and records to be examined. If band/artist wishes to make an examination, band/artist will be required to notify Personal Manager at least ten (10) days before the date when band/artist plans to begin the audit. Band/artist may appoint a certified public accountant to make such an examination for band/artist.

(b)   Personal Manager will pay the band/artist Royalty within thirty (30) days following the end of each such bi-annual period. Personal Manager will send band/artist a statement covering those royalties and will pay band/artist any royalties which are due after deducting un-recouped advances, if any, and chargeable costs under this Agreement and such amount, if any, which Personal Manager may be required to withhold pursuant to the State of _____, the U.S. Tax Regulations or any other applicable statute, regulation, treaty, or law.

(c)   If Personal Manager makes any overpayment to band/artist, band/artist will reimburse Personal Manager for the overpayment; Personal Manager may also deduct it from any payments due or becoming due to band/artist.

(d)   Band/artist may make such an examination for a particular statement only once and only within two (2) years after the date when Personal Manager is required to send band/artist that statement.

(e)   If a discrepancy of underpayment is found greater than ten percent (10%) for the Band/artist, Personal Manager shall bear the cost of the audit.

Although each party may keep their own books and records, under this Agreement the Personal Manager has the primary duty to keep accurate books and records. Obviously, the greater burden is on the party that will control the flow of the funds.

In clause (a), the Personal Manager will keep the books and records, and the band/artist can review the books of the Personal Manager under limited conditions - here, ten days' notice to the Personal Manager. The notice period is a crucial provision - it is a delicate balance between the Personal Manager's ability to get the books in order versus the Personal Manager having time to manipulate the books. Much negotiation can occur regarding this provision.

Clause (b) and (c) deal with making the payments - in this case within thirty days of the ending of the bi-annual period. Clause (c) requires the band/artist to reimburse the Personal Manager if there is any overpayment. Many times, these adjustments will occur in subsequent payments.

Clause (d) gives the band/artist the right to audit a statement only once, and only within two years of the date the statement was issued. If two years pass and the band/artist did not contest that particular statement, the band/artist cannot come back later.

Under clause (e), if an audit is conducted and the discrepancy is greater than ten percent in favor of the band/artist, the Personal Manager will pay for the audit. Again, this is a rather small point, but it can be very important. A band/artist may find a huge discrepancy, but the costs of the audit might cut into whatever recovery it may have. Consequently, if there is a discrepancy greater than 10%, the band/artist will get the initial recovery *and* the costs of the audit. This arrangement gives the band/artist greater flexibility and power to keep an eye on its funds, as well as provide more incentive to the Personal Manager to make sure the books remain in order.

Power of Attorney.

A power of attorney (a "POA") allows a person to take action, such as executing documents, on behalf of another person, for example, when the person granting the POA has become disabled.

Power of Attorney:

(a)   Band/artist appoints Personal Manager, for the Term and throughout the world, as band/artist's true and lawful attorney-in-fact, to sign, execute, and deliver any and all contracts and agreements concerning personal appearances by band/artist, so long as Personal Manager has received the prior consent of band/artist to enter into said contract and agreements. Personal Manager agrees to provide exact copies of all such contracts and agreements to band/artist.

(b)   Band/artist shall, upon Personal Manager's request, sign any and all instruments and other documents which are needed to effectuate the terms of this agreement. Personal Manager may make appropriate disposition of all such documents after providing an exact copy of such documents to band/artist.

A common provision in Personal Manager agreements is for the band/artist to grant a POA to the Personal Manager. The purpose is to allow the Personal Manager to have the ability to timely act on behalf of the band/artist. However, again there is a balancing act in play. The Personal Manager wants to be able to act on behalf of the band/artist when a great deal comes along, but the band/artist does not want the Personal Manager to "timely act" in robbing the band/artist, or in making significant deals or arrangements that the band/artist would normally want to approve of first.

The issue of a POA can arise in two situations: (i) an initial Personal Manager is being hired by a new group or artist; or (ii) an old Personal Manager is being replaced by a new Personal Manager. In both instances, the common problem is trust. In both cases the issue of trust is addressed by (a) notice, (*i.e.,* the Personal Manager must give notice of when the Personal Manager exercises the POA on behalf of the band/artist), and (b) limitation on the areas where the POA can be exercised).

In the clause above, the Personal Manager must give notice to the band/artist before signing any agreements. Also, the Personal Manager can only use the POA in the areas of personal appearances. By implication, the Personal Manager could not exercise the POA in such areas, for example, as executing a contract for the band/artist to be in a film.

Band/artist's Name and Likeness.

The Personal Manager will want to use the likeness of the band/artist in promoting the Personal Manager's reputation for the management services.

Band/Artist's Name and Likeness:

(a)   During the Term, Personal Manager shall have the right to do the following and, after consultation with band/artist, to authorize others to do the following but only insofar as such activity is in full compliance with all appropriate laws:

(i)   to   reproduce,   print,   publish   or disseminate, in any medium, band/artist's name (including each professional and fictitious name by which band/artist is or may become known), pictures, portraits and likenesses, and biographical material concerning band/artist, as news or information and for the purposes of any and all kinds of trade, advertising and promotion; and to engage in publicizing   and   advertising   band/artist   and band/artist's career in the Entertainment Industry.

Under the Agreement, the band/artist will allow the Personal Manager to use its name and likeness in order to promote the band/artist's career. A variety of issues comes together in this clause.

A major issue is that the use of the likeness and image must be closely monitored and strictly limited. The Personal Manager cannot have the opportunity to profit from the likeness and image of the band/artist without the band/artist knowing. Colonel Tom Parker was infamous for getting headshots of

Elvis, selling them at concerts, and pocketing the money from the sales!

A second aspect to this clause is that the band/artist must approve any and every bit of promotional and marketing material. The Personal Manager cannot be in the position to have materials go out that are unflattering to the band/artist or that are contrary to the image that the band/artist wishes to convey.

While the main reason for such oversight is obvious, it is also a tenet of trademark law that a trademark can be considered "abandoned" if the owner fails to control or monitor the quality of the mark's use. If a band/artist turns a blind eye to how its mark is being used or does not put into its contracts any rules about what and when it can and cannot be used for, that can come back to bite it in the future.

Personal Manager Is Not An Agent.

It is important for the Personal Manager to make clear that he/she is not an "agent." The difference is crucial because it affects the amount of commission that can be taken.

Personal Manager, Not Talent Agent:

(a) Personal Manager is not an employment agency, theatrical talent agency or booking agency. Personal Manager will as an incident of the personal management of band/artist and to the extent permitted by law, seek and procure employment or engagements for band/artist. It is Personal Manager's responsibility to assure that she has all necessary licenses in order to fulfill her obligations to band/artist. Personal Manager may engage others to seek and procure employment and engagements for

band/artist with the consent of band/artist as to each additional party so engaged.

The clause may be thought to be unimportant or just a "throw-in," but it is a very important distinction. An "agent" is subject to a different commission structure than a "Personal Manager." Both parties - the band/artist *and* the Personal Manager should be aware of this distinction.

Ownership.

It must be made clear that the band/artist *always* retains ownership of the Intellectual Property that is created during the Term of the Agreement.

Ownership:

(a)   Personal Manager agrees that band/artist shall own all rights in all products, including the intellectual property of band/artist, as well as all documentation, pertaining to the business of band/artist, whether created by Personal Manager or not.

(b)   This Agreement shall not be construed as creating a partnership or joint venture. Personal Manager is an independent contractor. Personal Manager has no legal interest in band/artist, other than as described herein.

These two clauses are so very important. The parties *must* be clear that the band/artist always owns the intellectual property of the band/artist. Many Personal Managers have taken the songs from songwriters and reaped millions of dollars while the band/artist starves. Also, it must be clear that no "partnership" was created by this Agreement and that the parties remain independent of one another.

Maybe the most infamous instance of a person in trust ripping off the artist, is Saul Zaentz, the former owner of Fantasy Records, the record label for which the Golliwogs/Creedence Clearwater Revival ("CCR") recorded. John Fogerty formed the early forerunner of CCR with his older brother Tom, bassist Stu Cook, and drummer Doug Clifford.[472] They called themselves the Blue Velvets, but they signed with San Francisco independent label Fantasy Records, who rechristened them the Golliwogs and made them wear fuzzy white wigs to match their regrettable name.[472] They dropped the name Golliwogs and took the new moniker of "Creedence Clearwater Revival." As CCR, they began to turn out a series of hits that rivaled the Beatles during this period.[473]

At this time, Fogerty was doing everything for the band: Personal Manager, publicist, and producer, among other things. Fading under the weight of the pressure, Fogerty turned to Zaentz.[474] Although not technically the Personal Manager, Zaentz was Personal Manager in everything but name. As the owner of Fantasy Records, he forced Fogerty to sign over the rights to Fogerty's catalogue of songs. Zaentz made millions from the royalties and went on to become a major Hollywood producer.[475]

Then, to add insult to injury, Zaentz sued Fogerty for copyright infringement of Fogerty's own songs after Fogerty wrote "Old Man Down the Road"! Zaentz claimed it infringed on the copyright of "Run Through the Jungle."[476] Zaentz lost and Fogerty turned to writing songs in that inimitable Fogerty style.[viii]

[viii] In January of 2023, Fogerty regained all the Creedence Clearwater Revival publishing after a 50-year fight to get the rights back. *See* Melinda Newman, *"John Fogerty Regains Control Over Creedence Clearwater Revival Songs After Half-Century Fight: Exclusive,"* Billboard Magazine, Jan. 12, 2023.

Termination.

How to get out of an agreement that has gone sour is as important as getting into the agreement.

Termination:

(a) Band/artist may immediately terminate Personal Manager upon discovery of a major breach of this Agreement. A major breach shall include, but not be limited to: (i) fraudulently entering into a contract on behalf of the band/artist; (ii) failure to turnover monies due band/artist; (iii) failure to gain consent for execution of a power-of-attorney; and (iv) any negative comments or press against the band/artist that was generated by or quotes Personal Manager.

(b) Band/artist may not terminate the Term on account of any incidental or minor breach of this Agreement by Personal Manager unless band/artist has given Personal Manager written notice specifying the breach and Personal Manager has failed to cure the breach within ten (10) business days after Personal Manager's receipt of notice.

The Termination clause found here is a concise but effective version.

The first clause addresses breach for "cause." For either party, "cause" should be grounds for immediate termination of the Agreement. The above clause is directed at what "cause" amounts to for the Personal Manager. However, a Personal Manager will usually want similar protections, (_e.g.,_ termination is permitted if the band/artist shows up drunk for a specific number of performances or gets arrested for a crime that would make it impossible for band/artist to perform).

The second clause deals with "minor" or "incidental"

breaches. The language may imply that such breaches are "no big deal." Not true. An "incidental" breach could be a missed payment or failure to give an accounting. Both *are* "big deals," but neither will cause the immediate termination of the Agreement. Rather, the breaching party first has a chance to "cure" - to take care of the breach. However, if the party does not cure the breach, the other party may terminate the Agreement.

The "notice" requirements required in (b) are pursuant to the "Notices" clause typically found in the "boilerplate" language at the end of the Agreement. *If there is no clause addressing how to give notice to the other party, one must be inserted!*

Miscellaneous Clauses (Boilerplate):

As mentioned in other areas of this book, the final clauses of an Agreement are generally "boilerplate" language. Some of the more important ones are:

Attorneys' Fees Clause - it is *mandatory* to have an attorneys' fees clause. Such a clause helps to ward off frivolous lawsuits by making the potential litigant aware that if he does not prevail, he will be paying the attorneys' fees and costs of the other party.

Governing Law - again so important. As a litigant, you want to try to have the advantages of a "home court." Consequently, a party wants to be familiar with the law and wants the practical advantage of literally being at "home" - sleep in your own bed at night, go to your own office, and maintain your own daily routine.

Entire Agreement - such a clause prevents one party from trying to introduce items or statements in an attempt to change the Agreement. If it is not in an Agreement, make sure it is inserted.

Conclusion.

For a band/artist, the choice of a Personal Manager is one with great ramifications. When the band/artist is looking for such a person, it is imperative that the band/artist is aware of the duties and responsibilities of a Personal Manager. The Personal Manager must be someone that the band/artist trusts, who will always have the best interests of the band/artist in mind. When you have found such a person, the band/artist is well-grounded in a bid for success.

CHAPTER 12

RECORD PRODUCER AGREEMENT

"The record producer is the music world's equivalent of a film director."
-        *Phil Ramone* [477]

Once the song is written, the selection of a producer for an artist's record, whether solo or a band, is one of the most important decisions a band/artist will have to make. The Record Producer can make or break a band/artist.

Maybe the most famous example of a beneficial relationship between a producer and a recording artist is George Martin and The Beatles. Martin was put in charge of EMI-Parlophone at the age of only 29. Martin produced a variety of records including classical and regional music, and comedy records.[478] Upon first hearing The Beatles, he was not impressed.[479] Of course his opinion changed and the rest is history.

Legendary producers include people like Quincy Jones (Michael Jackson); Rick Rubin (Johnny Cash; Eminem; Lady Gaga); Pharrell Williams ("Happy"; Robin Thicke); T Bone Burnett (Soundtrack for "O'Brother Where Art Thou?"); and Jimmy Iovine (Bruce Springstein; Tom Petty; U2).

As the quote above states, the Record Producer is akin to a director in the film industry. The Record Producer is responsible for, as George Martin says, "looking after what both the engineer and the artist [are] doing."[480] The Record Producer chooses the studio, books the time, assists with side musicians, and many times helps with the arrangements. In this chapter we will look at a Record Producer Agreement and some of the more important issues and nuances.

Services.

It is imperative to be clear regarding exactly what services the Record Producer will be providing.

Services.

(a)   During the Term hereof, band/artist hereby engages Record Producer, and Record Producer agrees, to render services as producer to record the Musical Compositions and to create those Recorded Tracks as listed on the attached Exhibit "A."

(b)   Record Producer shall oversee the recording process in the recording studio but not the "mixing" or "mastering" of the Recorded Tracks.

(c)   Record Producer shall render production of the Recorded Tracks in cooperation with band/artist, at times and place mutually agreed upon by and

between the band/artist and Record Producer, and agrees to diligently, competently, and to the best of Record Producer's ability, experience and talent perform the services required hereunder.

In paragraph (a) of this Agreement, the Record Producer will only be providing producer services, *i.e.,* oversee the producing process. Paragraph (b) makes it clear that the Record Producer will not do any "mixing" or "mastering." It might seem overkill to be so specific, but it is necessary to protect against "project creep," (*i.e.,* the continual expansion of services that will lead to resentment and anger). Finally, paragraph (c) establishes that the Record Producer and band/artist will mutually agree upon times and places to do the recording session.

A producer is eligible for awards such as the Grammys®; an engineer might not be. Another important point is that the producer will want some type of control, if not complete, regarding musicians to be used and material to be recorded.

Another important aspect to services is a provision on limitations of what the parties can do during the recording process. The biggest consideration is that neither the band/artist nor the producer can exhibit or distribute any work that is not in a finished form.

A final aspect is that the Producer will have archival obligations regarding the recorded tracks and other materials.

Compensation.

As with all of these contracts, a major issue is compensation.

Compensation.

(a) Conditioned upon Record Producer's full and faithful performance of all the terms and provisions hereof, the band/artist shall pay Record Producer the following compensation:

(i) Fixed Compensation. Thirty Dollars ($30.00) per hour for each hour actually spent in the recording studio.

(ii) Contingent Compensation. Band/artist, upon signing a recording agreement with a record company, agrees to:

I. Pay, or cause the record company to pay, to Record Producer a pro-rata portion of band/artist's recording budget received from the record company (the "Recording Budget") for any new master recordings (the "New Master Recordings") created by a record company on which the Recorded Tracks shall appear (the "Record Producer's Master Recording Fee"). For example, if the New Master Recording is to have ten (10) tracks and five (5) of those tracks are Recorded Tracks, and the Recording Budget is $100,000.00, Record Producer shall receive $50,000.00 as the Record Producer's Master Recording Fee.

II. If a Recorded Track shall appear on band/artist's first album, band/artist shall pay, or cause the recording company to pay, to Record Producer the following basic royalties (the "Record

Producer's Album Royalty"):

1 – 5 Recorded Tracks:	1% of the MSRP
6 – 10 Recorded Tracks:	2% of the MSRP
11 or more Recorded Tracks:	3% of the MSRP

The Record Producer's Album Royalty is to be computed, reduced, accounted for, and paid in the same manner as the band/artist's royalty is computed, reduced, accounted for, and paid.

(b) Accounting. Band/artist will account to Record Producer for royalties due under this Agreement in semiannual periods, ending on June 30th and December 31st, respectively, of each year. Within ninety (90) days after the last day of each semiannual period, band/artist will furnish to Record Producer a royalty report specifying the royalties earned by the Recorded Tracks during the semiannual period, and each royalty report will be accompanied by payment of all sums shown to be due by the report, after deduction of any and all advances or other proper deductions.

(c) Band/artist agrees to execute a Letter of Direction in favor of Record Producer in a form acceptable to her record company to have Record Producer's royalties paid directly to Record Producer.

As discussed above, "Fixed" is generally an amount that is guaranteed as a basic minimum for providing the services. "Contingent" compensation will depend upon the success of the sales of the Sound Recordings.

Paragraph (a)(ii) of the Agreement states the "fixed" compensation as a flat hourly rate. Many times, the "fixed" compensation can be in the form of a flat fee per song, (*e.g.*, Three Thousand Dollars ($3,000.00) per track).

Paragraph (a)(ii) of the Agreement outlines the "contingent" compensation and has a tiered structure, dependent upon how many of the recorded tracks are actually used on the "album."

The best deal is for the Producer to receive up to 3% of the first record sold. This is VERY rare.

Option; Buy Out.

A smart Record Producer will always want to make sure that there is an "option" provision and a "buy out" provision. The "option" provision makes sure that the Record Producer has a chance to provide services for any further Sound Recordings. The "buy out" provision makes sure that the Record Producer will get some type of compensation if the option is not exercised.

Option; Buy-out.

(a) Additional Tracks. In the event that band/artist seeks to record additional tracks, band/artist shall give Record Producer a right of first negotiation/last refusal to provide producer services on terms and conditions similar to those set forth in this Agreement, unless the parties mutually agree to substantive changes.

(b) Tracks Re-Recorded. If the Recorded Tracks are re-recorded by a third-party, band/artist shall use its best efforts to negotiate the right for Record Producer to provide producer services in relation to the re-recorded tracks.

(c) Buy-Out. If the third-party refuses to allow Record Producer to provide producer services in relation to the re-recorded tracks, Record Producer

shall receive a buy-out of Fifty Thousand Dollars ($50,000.00) for each Recorded Track that is re-recorded for which Record Producer is not allowed to provide producer services.

In paragraph (c), the buy-out is set at a liquidated amount of Fifty Thousand Dollars ($50,000.00). Remember the points about "liquidated damages" clauses from the Contracts chapters. And, for the Record Producer, the balancing act is to make the buy-out be stiff enough to help tip the scales in favor of using the Record Producer but, if not used, still be remunerative enough to be satisfactory in walking away.

Term

It belabors the point, but it is so important to be clear on the Term of the Agreement, (*e.g.*, when does the Record Producer have to deliver the tracks).

Term.

(a)   The term of this Agreement (the "Term") shall commence as of the date hereof and shall continue until the Recorded Tracks are completed and delivered to band/artist, or, upon earlier termination all pursuant to the further terms and conditions contained herein or as outlined in any previously executed agreement.

In this Agreement, the Term is tied in with delivery of the Recorded Tracks to the band/artist. However, the Agreement can be terminated earlier pursuant to the terms of notice and termination. Termination can be so important once it becomes clear that the recording process is breaking down. There is no worse situation than being forced to work with a producer that you do not want to work with anymore.

Delivery of Recorded Tracks

Timely delivery of the Recorded Tracks is at the heart of a Record Producer's Agreement. The band/artist is hiring the Record Producer to help develop a sound for the band/artist _and_ to put that sound into a form that can be recreated and exploited.

Delivery of Recorded Tracks.

(a) Record Producer shall deliver to band/artist, for each Recorded Track, a digital audio tape or equivalent (the "Delivery Media") on or before _____, 20____.

(b) Said Delivery Media shall be commercially and technically satisfactory to band/artist in the exercise of its sole and absolute discretion, said approval not to be unreasonably withheld.

(c) Said time for delivery of the Delivery Media shall be extended by band/artist, and Producer shall not be in breach hereof, in the event, for any reason whatsoever any session musician's voice or ability to perform as a vocalist or as an instrumentalist shall become materially impaired or if any session musician shall refuse, neglect, or be unable to comply with any recording schedule, or if as a result of an Act of God, accident, fire, labor controversy, riot, civil commotion, act of public enemy, law, enactment, rule, order, or act of any government of governmental instrumentality, failure of technical facilities or equipment, failure or delay of transportation facilities, illness or incapacity of Record Producer or any other key person, or any other cause of a similar or dissimilar nature not reasonably within Record Producer's control or which Record Producer could not with reasonable diligence have avoided.

Paragraph (a) establishes that the Record Producer will deliver the tracks in a "digital audio tape or similar format" on or before a certain date. Both the date and the format of the track is important. For example, even if the Record Producer timely delivers the track but it is not in a usable format, the delivery is moot. And, vice versa, if the Record Producer has the proper format but the delivery is late, it is immaterial about format because deadlines have been missed.

Paragraph (b) gives the band/artist final approval on the acceptance of the tracks but said approval "is not to be unreasonably withheld." Such a phrase can be a bit ambiguous but what it really is getting at is that the band/artist cannot just arbitrarily keep requesting changes or improvements. If there is a "buzz" or certain sections of the recording "drop out" that is obviously not acceptable. But, if the band/artist is merely asking for a remix or hears something that no one else hears, that is unreasonable, and it will be deemed that delivery has occurred.

Paragraph (c) is another example of a *force majeure* clause - the Record Producer is free from delivery if certain "acts of God" occur such as fire, earthquake, and civil unrest.

Other Documents.

Part of the Record Producer's responsibilities is to make sure that all of the paperwork is in order that is related in any way to the Sound Recordings produced under the Agreement.

Other Documents.

Record Producer agrees to obtain from every musician, instrumentalist, vocalist, and any other independent party (including mastering studio), or person to whom payment is made by Record Producer, a Receipt and Release (the "Release") and Record Producer shall indemnify and hold harmless

band/artist and their successors and assigns from any and all claims, damages and matters relating thereto from Record Producer's failure to obtain said Release.

If the Record Producer makes the decision, with the band/artist's approval, to hire certain side musicians or even a "guest star" musician, the Record Producer will make sure all of the proper agreements and releases are executed so that the band/artist will be free to use and exploit the contributions of the side man or guest artist.

Copyright Registration

Ownership of the copyrights in the Sound Recordings is at the crux of this Agreement. As we have seen from the discussion on Revenue Streams, controlling the copyright is mandatory to maximizing revenue.

Copyrights; Registration.

The Musical Compositions shall be registered for copyright by band/artist in the name of the band/artist in the office of the Register of Copyrights of the United States of America at such time as the band/artist, in its best business judgment, deems it necessary.

(a)   Band/artist shall have and is hereby granted the sole, exclusive and world-wide right to administer and exploit the Recorded Tracks, to print, publish, sell, dramatize, use and license any and all uses of the Recorded Tracks, to execute in its own name any and all licenses and agreements whatsoever affecting or respecting the Recorded Tracks, including but not limited to licenses for

mechanical reproduction, public performance, dramatic uses, synchronization uses and sub-publication, and to assign or license such rights to others. This statement of exclusive rights is only in clarification and amplification of the rights of band/artist hereunder and not in limitation thereof.

(b) Each and every Musical Composition embodied in a recorded form, i.e., each and every Recorded Track composed and recorded by Record Producer during the term hereof shall be considered a "work made for hire." All Recorded Tracks delivered hereunder or recorded by Record Producer and the performances contained thereon and recordings derived therefrom shall from inception of their creation be entirely the property of band/artist in perpetuity throughout the world, under copyright and otherwise, free of any claim whatsoever by Record Producer or any other person, and band/artist shall have the right to register the copyrights in such Recorded Tracks and recordings derived therefrom in band/artist's name or in the name(s) of band/artist's designee(s) and to secure any and all renewals and extensions thereof.

(c) Without limiting the generality of the foregoing, Record Producer hereby assigns to band/artist all of Record Producer's right and title to the copyrights in perpetuity throughout the world in and to such Recorded Tracks, recordings derived therefrom and any and all renewals and extensions of such copyrights, and band/artist and its subsidiaries, affiliates, and licensees shall have the sole exclusive and unlimited right throughout the world to manufacture Records, by any method(s) now and hereafter known embodying any portions(s) or all of the performances embodied on Recorded Tracks hereunder; to publicly perform such Records; to import, export, sell, transfer, lease, license, rent, deal in or otherwise dispose of or exploit such Recorded Tracks and Records derived therefrom throughout the world under any trademarks, trade names or labels designated by band/artist; to edit or adapt the Recorded Tracks hereunder to conform to the technological or commercial requirements of Phonograph Records in various formats now or hereafter known or developed, or to eliminate material which might subject band/artist to any civil or criminal action; to use the Recorded Tracks hereunder for background music, synchronization in motion pictures and television soundtracks and other similar purposes, or, notwithstanding the provisions of this agreement, band/artist and its subsidiaries, affiliates and licensees may, at their election, delay or refrain from doing any one or more of the foregoing.

(d)   The initial period of the term of this section shall commence upon the date hereof and shall continue in perpetuity. The rights of the parties hereto in and to each Recorded Track shall extend for the full term of the copyright of said Recorded Tracks and of any derivative copyrights therein in the United States of America and throughout the rest of the world and for the terms of any and all renewals or extensions thereof in the United States of America and throughout the rest of the world.

Paragraph (a) makes clear that the Sound Recordings of any Musical Compositions recorded pursuant to the Agreement are registered in the name of the band/artist. The Record Producer will have no authorship rights in the Musical Compositions or the Sound Recordings.

Paragraph (b) gives the band/artist the music publishing rights in the Musical Compositions to the band/artist and the band/artist is the only one to grant licenses or authorize the use of the Musical Compositions. However, remember the band/artist will most likely be assigning the music publishing to a Publisher.

Paragraph (c) and (d) work hand-in-hand: paragraph (c) establishes that the services of the Record Producer are being provided on a "work-for-hire" basis. As such, the work product of the Record Producer is owned by the band/artist. Paragraph (d) then provides a back-up position: if the work product of the Record Producer is not found to be done as a "work-for-hire" then the Record Producer is assigning all the rights, title, and interest in the work product of the Record Producer to the band/artist. The two paragraphs together will make it clear that the band/artist owns the copyright in the work product of the Record Producer.

Paragraph (e) concludes the section by stating that the rights of the band/artist in the work product of the Record Producer will last for the term of the copyright and, in some instances, for perpetuity.

Services Unique.

It is important to protect the band/artist from a "substitute" producer or from an "assistant" producer that provides the services.

Services Unique.

Record Producer acknowledges that Record Producer's services hereunder are of a unique, innovative, and personal nature and that it is reasonably foreseeable that Record Producer's failure to perform at the times and places required hereunder would cause the band/artist irreparable harm and damages (e.g., the delay and difficulty in finding and working in a suitable replacement). Accordingly, the band/artist shall be entitled to

damages and/or injunctive relief and such other remedies as the band/artist may deem appropriate with proper cause. Neither party hereto shall be deemed in default of its obligations hereunder if performance thereof is delayed or becomes impossible or impractical by reason of any cause beyond such party's control such as war, fire, earthquake, strike, sickness rendering performance impossible, accident, civil commotion, epidemic, or act of government.

When the band/artist retains a Rick Rubin or a Pharrell Williams, the band/artist wants to make sure that Rubin or Williams is the one that actually provides the services. It is a nightmare for a band/artist to be shunted off to the side and the "assistant" to Rick Rubin is suddenly the one that is in the studio and calling the shots. Consequently, it is very important to have this clause so that, to the greatest extent possible, the band/artist works with the Record Producer that it wants.

Credit.

As we have seen in other contracts, the issue of "credit" is very important. It is rather obvious, but the Record Producer will want to receive credit on the tracks that he/she produced.

Credit.

(a)   Band/artist shall give Record Producer a credit on, among other things, any "liner notes" or promotional materials connected with any Sound Recordings of the Recorded Tracks substantially as follows:

"Produced and Recorded by:

"(Originally) Recorded at:

In paragraph (a) the Record Producer will receive credit on the "liner notes" or promotional materials related to the Recorded Tracks. It is important to remember in this day of digital transmissions that "liner notes" do not really exist anymore. So, for a Record Producer, it is important to make sure that the credit is listed on websites, streaming services, and download sites.

Record Producer's Representation and Warranties.

The Record Producer must make certain representations and warranties same as any other party to a contract.

Record Producer's Representations and Warranties.

(a) Record Producer hereby warrants, represents, and agrees that:

(i) no materials, ideas or other properties furnished by Record Producer to the band/artist and utilized by the Record Producer in connection with band/artist's performance of services hereunder or otherwise will violate or infringe upon any common law or statutory right of any person, firm, or corporation, including without limitation, contractual rights, copyrights, and rights of privacy and/or publicity.

(ii) Record Producer hereby agrees to and does hereby indemnify, save, and hold the band/artist harmless from any and all damages, liabilities, costs, losses, and expenses arising out of or connected with any claim, demand or action which is inconsistent with any of the warranties, representations or covenants made by band/artist in this contract. Record Producer agrees to reimburse

the band/artist, on demand, for any payment made by the band/artist at any time with respect to any such damage, liability, cost, loss, or expense to which the foregoing indemnity applies.

The "Rep's and Warranties" section of any agreement, as we have seen, is very important. Paragraph (a) contains one of the biggest representations made by the Record Producer: any work product done for the benefit of the band/artist will be original to the Record Producer and does not infringe on any copyrighted material owned by someone else. If this clause existed in the agreement by and between Robin Thicke and Pharrell Williams, Thicke could have had a cause of action against Williams for breaching this representation.

If anyone should sue the band/artist because of a breach of any representation or warranty made by the Record Producer, paragraph (b) requires the Record Producer to indemnify the band/artist, (*i.e.,* stand in front of the band/artist and protect him). In the Robin Thicke scenario, paragraph (a) would be the breach and paragraph (b) would be remedy that the band/artist would demand from the Record Producer.

Relationship of the Parties.

It is always important to make sure it is clear whether the parties are contemplating a partnership or are remaining independent contractors as to each other.

Relationship of Parties.

(a)   The parties agree that at no time during the term of this agreement will Record Producer be an employee, partner, agent of, or participate in a joint venture with the band/artist for any purpose. Record Producer is and will remain an independent

contractor in relationship to the band/artist. The band/artist is not and shall not be responsible for withholding taxes with respect to the Record Producer's compensation hereunder. Record Producer shall have no claim against the band/artist hereunder or otherwise for vacation pay, sick leave, retirement benefits, social security, worker's compensation, health or disability benefits, unemployment insurance benefits, or any other payments or benefits of any kind except as expressly stated herein.

In this Agreement it is clear that the parties are not creating a partnership or joint venture and are independent contractors in relation to each other.

Conclusion.

The Record Producer is so very important for the band/artist. The recording process is hard, long, boring, and filled with the potential for artistic disagreement leading to conflict and strife. The wrong Record Producer can exacerbate these tensions. Alternatively, a great Record Producer is a god-send to an band/artist.

CHAPTER 13

RECORDING AGREEMENT

"Welcome to the machine!"
-    Roger Waters[481]

Signing a recording agreement is not the "holy grail" it once was, but it still remains an important part of any performer's musical career. The modern recording agreement is now what is termed a "360° Deal." In other words, the record company takes an interest in the entirety (the full 360°) of the band/artist's career.

In today's market, the band/artist really should negotiate for an agreement that focuses on the distribution aspects of the Agreement. The major record labels still excel in one major area - the ability to "break" a record, (*i.e.,* launch a record with great fanfare).

Services:

(a) The band/artist shall, in accordance with the provisions hereof, render to the Company the band/artist's exclusive services as a recording artist throughout the universe (the "Territory") and furnish to Company the services of one (1) or more producers for the purpose of recording Masters (as said term is hereinafter defined) and Delivering (as said term is hereinafter defined) such Masters to Company.

While obvious, it bears repeating that the services to be rendered by the band/artist are to record songs. In this agreement, the record company is gaining the exclusive right of the band/artist as a recording artist. The band/artist cannot record any Sound Recordings for any other record company. As seen below, the rights that the record company acquires include: (i) the right to make copies of the Sound Recordings; and (ii) to distribute those Sound Recordings.

Group Provisions.

Often the record company **(the "Company")** signs a "band" to the Agreement rather than an individual musician. In that case, the following provisions will appear because the Company will have concerns such as what happens if the "star" of the group leaves or if the Band breaks up.

Group Provisions: *(May not need if only signing single artist.)*

(a) This Agreement shall be binding, jointly and severally, on all of the individuals listed as members of the group (the "Group") on the first page or signature page hereof. Notwithstanding any change in membership of the Group, Company will continue to have the right to remit all royalty statements and

payments and all notices under this Agreement to the Group jointly in the name of "_____."

(b) Such individuals agree that, throughout the Term, members of the Group will perform together for the Band. If any individual member of the Group fails for any reason to perform hereunder with the Group or leaves the Group (hereinafter referred to as the "Leaving Member") or the Group disbands (in which case each member shall be deemed a Leaving Member), band/artist shall give the Company prompt written notice thereof (the "Leaving Member Notice").

(c) Each Leaving Member shall remain bound by this, or the Company may, by notice in writing, (i) terminate this Agreement with respect to any Leaving Member(s) or (ii) terminate this Agreement in its entirety, in which event Company shall be relieved of Company's obligations as to all unrecorded or Un-Delivered Masters.

(d) No Leaving Member shall thereafter use the professional name of the Group in any commercial or artistic endeavor; said professional name shall remain the property of those members of the Group who continue to perform their obligations hereunder and whose engagements are not terminated. Band/artist shall consult with the Company concerning the person, if any, engaged to replace the individual whose engagement is so terminated and Company shall have the right to cause such person and any other person who may be added to the Group, as a replacement member or otherwise, to become a party to this Agreement as a condition precedent to his or her becoming a member of the Group.

(e)   In addition, each individual comprising the Group hereby grants to Company, during the Term and throughout the Territory, the exclusive right to the services of such individual for the purpose of making Records other than as a member of the Group, including, but not limited to, solo projects. Without limiting the generality of the foregoing with respect to any Leaving Member, the Company shall have the option to require such individual(s) to record either as a solo artist for the Company or together with other individuals approved by the Company in the event such Leaving Member desires to perform as a recording artist. Said option with respect to any such Leaving Member may be exercised by giving such individual(s) notice in writing within three (3) months after the Company receives the Leaving Member Notice.

(f)   In the event that the Company exercise such option, such individual(s) shall be deemed to have entered into a new and separate agreement with the Company with respect to the Leaving Member(s)' exclusive recording services (the "Leaving Member Agreement") upon all the same terms and conditions of this Agreement except that:

(i)   At Company's request, such Leaving Member(s) shall record and Deliver to Company four (4) demonstration Recordings ("Demos") pursuant to a recording budget therefor approved by the Company in writing; Within ninety (90) days following the Company's receipt of the Leaving Member Notice, or, if the Company has elected to have such Leaving Member record Demos, then not sooner than sixty (60) days following the Company's receipt of the Demos, the Company shall have the option by written notice to require the Leaving Member(s) to record and

Deliver to the Company, certain Masters sufficient to comprise one (1) Album and the right to extend the Term for such number of Renewal Periods as are then remaining under this Agreement, but not less than two (2) such optional Albums;

(ii)   The Recording Fund for the first Album under the Leaving Member Agreement shall be seventy-five percent (75%) of the Recording Fund for the Second Album by the band/artist hereunder, the Recording Fund for the second such Album under the Leaving Member Agreement shall be seventy-five percent (75%) of the Recording Fund for the Third Album required to be recorded by the band/artist hereunder, and so on;

(iii)   The royalties payable hereunder shall be reduced by ten percent (10%); and

(iv)   The Company shall have the right to apply a pro rata portion of any then unrecouped balance of the band/artist's account against the Leaving Member(s)' account and shall have the right to apply a pro rata portion of royalties earned in respect of the Masters made by the band/artist under this Agreement against such individual's or individuals' new account, but otherwise the Company shall maintain separate accounts with respect to Masters by the band/artist and members of the Group subject to this Agreement and Masters made by the Leaving Member(s) in respect of whom Company shall have exercised Company's option.

(g)   The individual members of the Group who are signatories hereto jointly and severally represent and warrant that they are and shall be the sole owners of the Group's professional names and that no other

person, firm, or entity has the right to use said professional names in connection with Records during the Term in the Territory.

Paragraph (a) establishes that the band, as a group, is entering into this Agreement. Royalties and advances are determined on a "group" basis and the entire group is bound by the Agreement.

Paragraph (b) reiterates that the members will be recorded as, and perform as, the band. If a member of the band leaves the group or if the band disbands, the members will give notice to the Company.

Under paragraph (c), the Company may either (a) let a Leaving Band Member go or (b) keep the Leaving Member bound to the Agreement. This decision usually depends on the "star status" of the Leaving Member and the impact he or she has on the band and its image as a whole.

Paragraph (d) limits the right of the Leaving Member to use the name of the band. A classic example of the fights that can occur is Pink Floyd. When Roger Waters left Pink Floyd, he wanted to retire the name of the band. There was a long court fight, with the remaining members of Pink Floyd being victorious. Mr. Waters, although angry at the time, has come to agree with the ruling.[482]

Paragraph (d) contains another requirement - if a new member is elected to join the band, the Company must be given notice and has the right to have the new member sign the Agreement.

Paragraph (e) allows the Company to use the *exclusive* services of each individual band member, whether alone or with the other band members, for Sound Recordings. The key is *exclusive* - the member cannot go and record with other individual artists or bands. The paragraph also extends the rights of the Company to a Leaving Member and its solo records or other recording activities.

Paragraph (f) gives the Company, if they elect the option of paragraph (e), to deem the Leaving Member to have signed a new Agreement, under the same terms and conditions as the original Agreement, *except:* (i) a Leaving Member might be required to do four demo's for the Company; (ii) if the Company desires, the Leaving Member could be required to do an Album; (iii) the recording budget for the Leaving Member's Album will be only at seventy-five percent of the budget for the original band; (iv) the royalties payable to the Leaving Member will be reduced by 10% from those set for the band; and (v) the Company can use royalties from the Leaving Member's Album to reduce any un-recouped amounts from the band.

Paragraph (g) provides a warranty from the band members that the name of the band is unique to them and is owned by them.

Term.

The term of a recording agreement can be very confusing. It is very important to understand the interplay between the following sub-clauses.

Term:

(a)   The Term of this Agreement shall consist of an "Initial Period" (defined below) and for each "Renewal Period" (defined below) for which the Company shall have exercised an option as hereafter provided. The Initial Period and each Renewal Period are each sometimes referred to generally as a "Contract Period."

(b)   The Initial Period shall commence as of the date hereof and shall end ten (10) months following the

Initial Commercial Release by Company of the First Album (as those terms are defined below). The term "Initial Commercial Release" shall mean the date of Company's initial United States commercial release hereunder through physical retail locations of the First Album to be delivered hereunder embodying its collective performances.

(c)   Band/artist hereby grants Company two (2) separate, consecutive options (the "Option(s)"), each to extend the Term for a Renewal Period, exercisable by notice to Company by the later of:

(i)   the expiration date of the Contract Period which is then in effect (the "Current Contact Period"); or

(ii)   within thirty (30) days after band/artist advises Company that such Current Contract Period has expired and that band/artist desires that Company either exercise or waive such Renewal Period.

(iii)   If so exercised by Company, each Renewal Period shall run consecutively, shall commence or be deemed to have commenced upon the expiration of the immediately preceding Contract Period and shall continue until the date ten (10) months following the Initial Commercial Release in the United States of the Album delivered by band/artist in fulfillment of band/artist's Recording Commitment for the Renewal Period concerned, or such fewer number of days of which Company may advise band/artist in writing.

The Initial Period and the Renewal Period require close scrutiny. It may seem at first glance that the initial term is for ten months. But the term begins with the signing of the contract and continues from the time of the Commercial Release for another ten months. The result is that the initial period could be for a period of years. For example, it might take the band/artist a year to record, master, and then deliver the Album. It may take the record company another year to "commercially release" the Album. Then the ten-month period kicks in. So, this Initial Period would run for a total time of two years and ten months!

Another key implication of the above language is that the band/artist must give notice to the Company regarding the exercise of the Option. No - that is not a typo. The band/artist has to tell the Company to exercise the Company's option!

Finally, the Options will run consecutively, (*i.e.,* one after the other). The band/artist must understand what that really means. Under this Agreement, the band/artist could be tied to the Company for up to nine years! There is a reason that Prince went on stage with "slave" written on his cheeks in 1995.

Recording Commitment.

The bottom-line of the Agreement is how many "records" or "masters" does the band/artist need to deliver to the Company? Along with the Term, this arrangement can become a huge point of contention. It is very important for the band/artist to understand what constitutes a satisfactory recording.

Recording Commitment.

(a)   For the Initial Period, band/artist shall record and deliver to Company, at a minimum, Recordings embodying its collective performances (as the sole featured artist thereon) of Musical Compositions, with vocals ("Masters") sufficient to constitute one (1)

long-playing Record of at least forty-five (45) minutes in playing time and containing not less than eleven (11) selections (generically an "Album" herein).

(b) During each Renewal Period, band/artist shall record and deliver to Company, at a minimum, Recordings sufficient to constitute one (1) long-playing Record of at least forty-five (45) minutes in playing time and containing not less than eleven (11) Musical Compositions.

(c) The initial Album that band/artist is required to record and deliver to Company during the Initial Period is referred to as the First Album. The Albums that band/artist are required to record and deliver to Company during the Renewal Periods are referred to as the Second Album and Third Album (in order of their acceptance by Company), and band/artist will Deliver all such Masters to Company (respectively, the "Minimum Recording Commitment") in accordance with all the material terms and conditions hereof.

(d) Each Master shall be subject to Company's approval as technically and commercially satisfactory for the manufacture and sale of Records and at Company's request band/artist shall re-record a Master until it is commercially and technically satisfactory to Company. Each Album recorded, delivered, and accepted hereunder in satisfaction of the applicable Minimum Recording Commitment for a particular Contract Period is sometimes referred generally herein as a "Qualifying Album".

(e) In addition to the foregoing, its Minimum Recording Commitment hereunder shall also include, at Company's election, the recording and delivery to Company of a so called "Companion DVD" of any Album, which such Companion Video shall embody

"Videos" (as said term is hereinafter defined) of Musical Compositions embodied in any such Album. Company shall pay the recording costs of such Videos in amounts mutually agreed by band/artist and Company but shall not be obligated to pay band/artist a separate advance in respect of such Videos.

The first clause of this paragraph establishes the number of "Masters" that will constitute an "Album." In this current era of digital transmissions and CDs, the number of masters might be fluid. However, fluid or not, it must be clear to both parties exactly what is expected.

The next major issue to be aware of is that the Company has final say on approval of the masters that are delivered - namely, whether the masters are acceptable. The reason is to prevent an unhappy artist from dumping inferior music on the Company in attempt to get out of a contract. The band/artist should be careful of such clauses and should ask for language that tempers the Company's absolute right. The band/artist should require that the approval not be "unnecessarily withheld," or similar language.

Finally, even in this day, the Company will demand a DVD from the band/artist. Although videos are really loss leaders now, it is still an important aspect of maximization of revenues and increase in publicity. As discussed below, the choice of director and the amount to be spent on the videos can become key negotiation points.

Recording Process.

The following clause will address the logistics of the recording process. The process may seem rather straightforward. However, as should be obvious by now, *nothing* is straightforward in the music industry.

Recording Process, Creative Approvals:

With respect to all Masters hereunder, no recording sessions shall be commenced unless and until Company shall have approved the applicable recording budget and all other elements of the recording process. In that connection, with respect to each Master, band/artist shall be solely responsible for engaging and paying the producer thereof and such producer shall be mutually approved by band/artist and Company. The respective studio, and times of recording shall also be mutually approved by band/artist and Company. Band/artist agrees that each Master shall consist of a newly recorded studio performance embodying its sole feature performance of a previously unrecorded Musical Composition as shall be mutually approved by band/artist and Company.

As mentioned previously, control over the recording process is very important. In this clause, the Company will control almost all aspects of the process: it will set the budget and control the elements of the recording process. However, the band/artist can choose its producer, subject to the Company's approval, and the band/artist and the Company will jointly agree on times of recording.

One point to keep in mind is that the Company is requiring "previously unrecorded Musical Compositions." The

Company will want to prevent the band/artist from using previously recorded tracks to cut costs or to avoid the onerous delivery requirements.

Ownership.

The issue of ownership of the sound recordings is a key negotiating point. Also, it is important to keep in mind the termination rights of the band/artist under Section 203 of the Copyright Act, 17 U.S.C. § 203.

Ownership:

(a)   Each Master and each Video shall be Company's exclusive property throughout the Territory free from any claims whatsoever by band/artist or any other person, firm or corporation. Each Master and Video shall be considered a "work-made-for-hire" (as defined in the United States Copyright Act) for Company.

(b)   If any such Master or Video is determined for any reason not to be a "work-made-for-hire," the Copyright of that respective Master or Video shall be deemed transferred and assigned to Company by this Agreement, together with all rights in and to such Master(s) and Video(s) (including, without limitation, the worldwide Copyrights therein and thereto along with all renewals and extensions thereof).

(c)   For avoidance of doubt, Company shall have the sole, exclusive and perpetual Copyright throughout the Territory to own and control the Masters and Videos and shall have the unlimited right to sell, lease, license, and otherwise exploit the Masters and Videos and all reproductions derived therefrom in any and all media or forms, whether now

known or hereafter devised, and through any and all channels and means of distribution throughout the Territory (including, without limitation, the right to license each Master for timed synchronization with visual images and for coupling with other recordings), or refrain therefrom, upon such terms and conditions and in such Records, forms and versions as Company may in Company's sole discretion determine.

(d)   Band/artist hereby irrevocably constitutes, authorizes, empowers and appoints Company, and any of Company's officers, its true and lawful attorney-in-fact (with full power of substitution and delegation) in its name, and in its place and stead to take and do such action, and to make, sign, execute, acknowledge and deliver any and all instruments or documents which Company, from time to time, may deem necessary to effectuate the terms of this Agreement and vest in Company, Company's successors, assigns and/or licensees, any of the rights or interests granted by band/artist under this Agreement, including, without limitation, such documents required to secure the Copyright(s) in and to the Masters and/or Videos and the renewal(s) and extension(s) thereof throughout the world, and also such documents as are required to assign to Company, Company's successors, assigns and/or licensees, such renewal Copyright(s), and all rights therein for the terms of such renewal(s) and extension(s) for Company's own use and benefit and/or that of Company's successors, assigns and licensees.

(e)   Band/artist hereby grants to Company (and Company may grant to others) the right in perpetuity throughout the Territory to use its name, photographs, likenesses, and biography for advertising and trade purposes and otherwise in connection with Company's business (including, without limitation, in connection with Records derived from the Masters). During the Term hereof, all photographs, likenesses and biographical material concerning band/artist which Company may desire to utilize for the purposes herein stated shall be subject to band/artist's approval, not to be unreasonably withheld or delayed, and which approval (or disapproval) shall be given to Company within five (5) business days after such photographs, likenesses or biographical material are made available for band/artist's review, failing which the item for which approval shall be sought shall be deemed approved. All photographs, likenesses and biographical material concerning band/artist submitted by band/artist to Company or once approved by band/artist shall be deemed approved by band/artist for all purposes hereof. Any inadvertent failure by Company to seek its approval shall not be a breach of this Agreement by band/artist.

(f) All logos, designs or other merchandising or artwork created by band/artist for use in connection with its name and/or the exploitation of Masters shall belong to Company pursuant to the terms hereof and may not be used by any person or entity other than band/artist without Company's prior written consent, which consent Company may withhold for any reason. Company shall further have the right to use such materials for the sale of items associated with Company's label that are intended generally to promote Company's label as well as Records hereunder. Band/artist shall be entitled to no additional compensation in respect of such exploitations. All costs paid or incurred by band/artist in respect of artwork for the Masters hereunder shall be fully recoupable from royalties otherwise payable to Company hereunder.

(g) Notwithstanding anything to the contrary contained herein, upon its request and reimbursement to Company of fifty percent (50%) of Company's costs of creating and producing any Album artwork, band/artist shall have the right, insofar as Company is concerned, to utilize any such artwork for its own tour merchandising purposes during the Term. Band/artist shall be solely responsible for obtaining any consents and paying any payments that may be required to be obtained from or paid to any third parties, (e.g., photographers), for the use of such artwork, and band/artist shall indemnify and hold the Company harmless from any failure or alleged failure to do so. Any such artwork so used by band/artist shall be accompanied by an appropriate Copyright notice in the Company's name. Notwithstanding the foregoing, in the event that in the creation of any Album artwork Company shall create a logo which band/artist desires to use as its "signature" logo, then, consistent with its payment to the Company as aforesaid, band/artist shall have the general right to use such "signature" logo, subject to any existing rights of any third-party not claiming any right through or from band/artist.

(h) Furthermore, upon its request and reimbursement of one hundred percent (100%) of Company's costs associated with creating and producing merchandising items intended to promote band/artist, Company, and/or the sale of Records hereunder (i.e., T-shirts, hats, stickers), band/artist shall have the right to sell such items solely in connection with its live performances during the Term and band/artist and Company shall split the merchandise revenue 50/50.

(i) Band/artist hereby acknowledges that the sale

of Records is speculative and agrees that Company's judgment with regard to any matter affecting the sale, distribution and exploitation of Records shall be binding and conclusive upon band/artist. Without limiting the generality of the foregoing, Company shall have the right, without limitation, to release Records embodying the Masters and/or Videos on any label Company may choose and through any distribution system(s) Company may choose. Subject to the provisions herein, nothing contained in this Agreement shall obligate Company to make, sell, license, release, distribute or otherwise exploit Records derived from the Masters and/or Videos.

First, the Company retains ownership of the recordings. It may seem unfair at first glance, but it is common since the Company foots the bill for the masters.

Paragraphs (a), (b), and (c) contain a major nuance: the band/artist's work product under the Agreement is considered a "work for hire." In other words, the band/artist is acting as an employee creating works at its employer's (the Company) behalf. The record company will want to characterize the band/artist as an employee engaged in a "work for hire," because in those circumstances the band/artist's termination rights under Section 203 are not available. However, despite this type of language, a Company will have a very high hurdle to be able to get a court to agree that a band/artist is in actuality engaging in work as a work for hire.

Furthermore, even the attempt by the Company to impose such a "work for hire" designation is improper under the Copyright Act - see Section 203(a)(5).[483] Most recently, the author of "YMCA" and other hits from the Village People, won his court case on this issue and the various rights granted to the record company under the recording agreement were returned to the Composer.[484]

Under paragraph (d), the band/artist grants the Company the power-of-attorney to execute whatever documents are needed to perfect the Company's interest in the recordings. The main thing here is to remember the concerns outlined regarding the Personal Manager using a power-of-attorney: make sure the Company is obligated to (and does) give notice of using the power.

Paragraph (e) gives the Company the right to use the likeness of the band/artist. Again, similar to the Personal Manager's agreement, it is important to make sure the band/artist has some control over what is distributed to the public.

Paragraphs (f), (g), and (h) all deal with logos and merchandise. The paragraphs make sense to be together because there is no value in the merchandise if there is no value in the Trademark. If possible, the band/artist should ensure that ownership of the logos, slogans, and any related artwork, be retained by the band/artist. The Sound Recordings will be owned by the Company, and the Company may have other rights to the music and the band/artist's image and use, but the band/artist does have the right to terminate the agreement in certain circumstances. And if that happens, regardless of past recordings, masters, and tours, the band/artist will want to have freedom to use its own Trademarks, name, and logo in the future, with a different company. If ownership vests with the Company, however, this could pose problems.

In paragraph (f), the costs are recoupable from the royalties of the band/artist. If so, it is even more important that the band/artist own the logo. An artist can make a lot of money long after having a hit record. The licensing rights to The Beatles' logo is a license to print money.

Paragraphs (g) and (h) are real doozies. Under paragraph (g), if the band/artist pays for fifty percent of the costs of the promotional materials, the Company will "graciously" allow the band/artist to use the materials on the band/artist's tour! To the extent that the band/artist has any leverage, this type of provision must go. Similarly, under paragraph (h) if the band/artist pays for one hundred percent of the cost of the merchandise, it can sell the merchandise at its concerts but will receive (only) fifty percent of the revenue! Both of these paragraphs are indicative of the over-reaching the Company will attempt to impose on the band/artist.

Finally, paragraph (i) gives the Company the right to choose the distribution mediums. Such a provision is not controversial.

Release Commitment.

The Company has a commitment to release the recordings in a certain timely manner.

Release Commitment:

(a) Provided band/artist is not at any time in breach of this agreement, and specifically provided band/artist has timely Delivered the Masters, satisfactory to Company in accordance with the terms of this Agreement, sufficient to constitute a Qualifying Album ready for Company's manufacture of Records therefrom, Company agrees to commercially release each such Qualifying Album in the United States within one (1) year following its Delivery to Company and Company's acceptance of such Qualifying Album; provided, that if the last day on which Company would be obligated pursuant to the foregoing to release any Qualifying Album hereunder falls between October 1 and January 15 of any year, then Company shall not be obligated to release such Qualifying Album in the United States prior to the

immediately succeeding February 15th (the "Release Commitment").

(b)   If Company shall fail to so release any such Qualifying Album in the United States, band/artist shall have the right, within thirty (30) days following the expiration of said one (1) year period, to notify Company in writing of Company's such failure and of band/artist's desire that the Term of this Agreement be terminated if Company does not, within one hundred and eighty (180) days after Company receives such notice from band/artist, commercially release the applicable Qualifying Album in the United States. It is specifically understood and agreed that if the Company shall fail to fulfill any such Release Commitment, the Company shall have no liability whatsoever to band/artist in respect thereto, and its only remedy shall be to terminate the Term of this Agreement by written notice to band/artist within twenty-one (21) days following the expiration of such one hundred and eighty (180) day period.

(c)   If this Agreement is terminated in accordance with this paragraph, then for a period of sixty (60) days following such termination, band/artist shall have the right to purchase on a quitclaim, as-is basis, without any representations or warranties, the Masters constituting the Qualifying Album which Company failed to so release, by written notice to Company and simultaneous payment to Company of all monies paid to band/artist by Company and/or expended by Company or incurred in connection with such Masters (including, without limitation, all Recording Costs); provided, however, that if, prior to the receipt of such notice and payment, Company commences the manufacture of copies of such Qualifying Album with the intention of releasing such Qualifying Album (and if Company, in fact, thereafter

releases such Qualifying Album within ninety (90) days after receipt of such notice), then such termination and election to purchase shall be of no force.

Paragraph (a) commits the Company to release the Album within one year of delivery by the band/artist. It is imperative for the band/artist to keep track of this because it could be grounds for getting out of the Agreement, if needed. The band/artist does not want the Company to sit on the Album.

Paragraph (b) gives the band/artist the right to give notice to the Company if the Album is not released within the one-year period. The notice must be sent within thirty days and will give the Company one hundred and eighty days to release the Album.

Paragraph (c) grants the band/artist the right to get out of the Agreement if the Company does not release the Album after the 180-day grace period. The band/artist must give notice within twenty-one days of the end of the 180-day grace period. Obviously, the band/artist should track all of these periods carefully and closely.

Paragraph (d) allows the band/artist to buy back the Masters for its own use, by giving notice within sixty days. However, note that if the Company has decided to release the Album prior to getting the notice, the Company retains the right to release the Album.

In general, these clauses are good examples of how slanted these types of Agreements are in favor of the Company.

Recording Costs.

The issue of who pays for the recording and how much is of key concern.

Recording Costs:

(a) For each Album required to be Delivered under this Agreement, Company shall pay the Recording Costs of such Album in an amount not in excess of the applicable recording budget as set forth below with respect to such Album. All Recording Costs paid or incurred by Company in respect of Masters hereunder shall be recoupable from royalties otherwise payable to band/artist hereunder.

Album 1: Twenty-Five Thousand Dollars ($25,000.00);

Album 2: Thirty-Five Thousand Dollars ($35,000.00).

(i) Album 3: Fifty Thousand Dollars ($50,000.00).

(b) Company shall not be required to pay any Recording Costs until Company has approved a written budget setting forth in reasonably sufficient detail the estimated amounts of all Recording Costs to be incurred with respect to the applicable Album.

(c) **Each payment made by Company to band/artist or on its behalf or at its request shall constitute a Recording Cost recoupable from any and all sums payable to Company hereunder. Where band/artist has incurred any liability to Company, whether arising from or under this Agreement or otherwise howsoever arising, Company may, without notice to band/artist, set-off the amount of such liability against any liability of Company to band/artist arising from or under this Agreement, whether either such liability is liquidated or unliquidated, present, or future, accrued or contingent.**

Under paragraph (a), the Company will pay an escalating series of payments for each Album under the Agreement. Notice how little, comparatively speaking, the payments are. The days of getting high six-figure or seven-figure recording budgets are outdated.

Under paragraph (b), the Company does not have to pay any costs unless it has approved a written budget.

And under paragraph (c), any costs the Company expends are counted as part of the recoupable costs that are charged against the band/artist.

Paragraph (d) is one of the most important but overlooked clauses in the entire Agreement, i.e., the Cross Collateralization Clause. Cross collateralization allows the Company to look to alternative sources for repayment of advances and expenses. For example, in the above contract the band/artist has received an advance of Thirty-five Thousand Dollars ($35,000.00). If the first album under this Agreement fails to generate enough revenue for the Company to recoup its costs, the Company can use revenue generated from the second album to pay off the debt remaining from the first album. The upshot of such a clause is that the band/artist will continue to remain in debt until the entire amount is paid off. As pointed out by Mary Ermel, "Cross-collateralization can be particularly harmful if you are signing both a recording contract and publishing agreement with the same company, and both contracts state that advances under either agreement can be repaid from royalties under both."[485] As we saw in the chapter on Revenue Streams, music publishing can be a huge source of revenue for the band/artist. And it can be so disheartening to a band/artist to have a huge hit, but the revenue gets diverted due to prior financial obligations of the band/artist.

Third-party Payments.

In recording the Album, various third-party artists might be hired to help finish the recording.

Third Party Payments:

(a) Band/artist shall be solely responsible for and shall pay all monies becoming payable to producers, engineers and all other third parties rendering services in connection with (or otherwise involved with) the Masters, in respect of sales of Records derived from the Masters or any other exploitation of the Masters, except that Company shall, on its behalf, pay: (i) mechanical royalties becoming payable to the Copyright proprietors of Musical Compositions embodied in the Masters in accordance with the terms hereof; and (ii) all monies, if any, required to be paid to the AFM Music Performance Trust Fund and Phonograph Record Manufacturers Special Payments Fund (or any similar funds) in connection with the manufacture and sale of Records derived from the Masters.

(b) Band/artist shall cause all third parties

rendering services in connection with Masters and Videos to execute written agreements for Company's benefit providing that the results and proceeds of the services rendered by such third-party(ies) shall be works-made-for-hire for Company, and further providing that if such results and proceeds are deemed not to be works-made-for-hire, that all rights, title, and interest in and to same (including, without limitation, the worldwide Copyrights therein and thereto and all renewals and extensions thereof) shall be deemed transferred and assigned to the Company.

(c)   Notwithstanding the foregoing, the Company shall have the right, at Company's sole election, to pay all monies becoming payable to producers, engineers, and all other third parties rendering services in connection with the Masters. Such payments shall be deemed Recording Costs and shall be fully recoupable from royalties hereunder.

The main thrust of this clause is to shift the payments to third parties to the band/artist. So, if you want Eric Clapton to make a guest appearance on your album, his fee is going to be paid by you.

Paragraph (c) provides the Company with the right to pay such third parties directly. Such a payment arrangement is standard and is facilitated with a Letter of Direction informing the Company to pay the third-party directly. Also, if the payments to third parties are advances, those advances are charged to the band/artist.

Royalties.

Now we start to come to some of the real meat of the Agreement - what royalties are paid and at what rate. In particular, a band/artist should be careful to review the deductions that will be applied before any royalty participation is distributed.

Royalties:

Conditioned upon its full and faithful performance of the terms of this Agreement, Company shall pay band/artist the following "all-in" royalties:

(a) United States: For Net Sales of full-priced, top-line, audio-only Records in vinyl, cassette, and compact disc configurations solely embodying Masters through normal retail channels in the United States ("USNRC Net Sales"), band/artist's royalty shall be the following percentages of the applicable Suggested Retail List Price ("SRLP") (as said term is hereinafter defined), less the deductions hereafter provided:

(i) Basic Album Rate: twenty percent (20%).

(b) Singles/ Maxi-Singles/ EP Rate: Notwithstanding the foregoing, for Net Sales of full-priced Singles, Maxi-singles, and EPs (all of which are hereinafter defined) solely embodying Masters and sold through normal retail channels in the United States, its royalty shall be twenty percent (20%) of the applicable Base Price.

(a) **Foreign Rates**:

(i) For Net Sales of full-priced Records solely embodying Masters and sold through normal retail channels outside the United States in the territories specified below, band/artist's royalty shall be the following percentages of the otherwise applicable (*e.g.*, Albums, Singles, Maxi-singles, EPs or Videos) basic (*i.e.*, without regard to escalations) U.S. rate:

(A) Canada & United Kingdom, seventy-five Percent (75%); and

(B) Rest of the world, fifty percent (50%).

(ii) Notwithstanding the foregoing, solely with respect to foreign licenses by the Company or Company's licensees to third parties of Master(s) hereunder for which Company is paid on a flat fee or net receipts basis (*e.g.*, licenses for use in motion picture or television soundtracks), band/artist's royalty shall be the lesser of (A) the royalties provided in subparagraph 9(b)(i) above, and (B) fifty percent (50%) of Company's Net Receipts (as said term is hereinafter defined) in respect of such foreign license.

(iii) Royalties payable to band/artist hereunder in respect to the sales of Records outside of the United States shall be: (i) computed in the national currency in which the Company is paid by Company's licensees or other Record distributors outside the United States; (ii) credited to band/artist's royalty account hereunder at the same rate of exchange as the Company is paid; and

(iii) proportionately subject to any transfer or comparable taxes which may be imposed upon Company's receipts. In the event Company shall not receive payment in U. S. dollars in the United States in respect of any such sales, band/artist's royalties in respect thereof shall not be credited to its royalty account hereunder. However, if Company is able to do so and band/artist's account hereunder shall be in a recouped position, Company shall accept such payments in foreign currency and, at band/artist's expense, deposit the monies in a foreign bank or other depository, in such foreign currency, such portion thereof, if any, as shall equal the royalties which would have actually been payable to band/artist hereunder in respect of such sales had such payments been made to Company in U. S. dollars in the United States. Deposit as aforesaid shall fulfill Company's royalty obligations hereunder as to such Record sales.

(b) **Mid-priced and Budget Records**: For Net Sales of Mid-priced Records (as said term is hereinafter defined) and Budget Records (as said term is hereinafter defined), band/artist's royalty shall be sixty-six and two-thirds percent (66-2/3%) and fifty percent (50%), respectively, of the otherwise applicable basic top-line royalty rate without regard to any escalations thereof. "Mid-price Records" shall mean Records sold in the country in question at less than eighty percent (80%), and more than sixty-six and two-thirds percent (66-2/3%), of the then-prevailing top-line Suggested Retail List Price. "Budget Records" shall mean Records sold at less than sixty-six and two-thirds percent (66-2/3%) of the then-prevailing top-line Suggested Retail List Price. Notwithstanding the foregoing, the Company agrees that it shall not reduce band/artist's royalties in respect of sales of any particular Album with respect to sales of same as "Budget Records" during the first year following the initial release of such Album.

(c) **Premiums**: For Net Sales of Records sold as "premiums" (*i.e.,* Records sold at less than customary prices in connection with the sale, advertising, or promotion of any other product or service), its royalty shall be fifty percent (50%) of the otherwise applicable basic royalty rate. Company shall not sell such Records hereunder as "premiums" without band/artist's prior written consent.

(d) **Government and Educational Sales**: For Net Sales of Records sold to the United States Government, its subdivisions, departments, or agencies (including, without limitation, Records sold for resale through military facilities) or to educational institutions or libraries (collectively "Government Sales"), band/artist's royalty shall be fifty percent (50%) of the otherwise applicable royalty rate.

(e) **Club, TV Advertising, Direct Mail**: Notwithstanding anything to the contrary contained herein, for Net Sales of Records sold through any record club, or any mail-order or other direct-to-consumer method (including, without limitation, any method utilizing television advertising) (collectively "Direct Sales"), band/artist's royalty shall be fifty percent (50%) of the otherwise applicable royalty rate; provided that, with respect to such Records sold by Company's licensees, the royalty shall be one-half (1/2) of Company's Net Receipts. No royalty shall be paid for Records given to record club members as "bonus" or "free" Records unless Company shall receive payment thereon. If Company does, band/artist shall be entitled to receive one-half (1/2) of Company's Net Receipts thereon.

(f) <u>New Technology Configurations</u>:

(i) Sales of Records sold in any New Technology Configuration (as said term is hereinafter defined), band/artist's royalty shall be fifty percent (50%) of the otherwise applicable basic rate, provided that at any time after three (3) years from the date hereof, then upon request of either party, band/artist and Company agree to negotiate in good faith a royalty for Net Sales of Records sold in any New Technology Configuration if Net Sales of Records sold in such applicable New Technology Configuration shall account for twenty-five percent (25%) or more of all Net Sales of all Records in all configurations.

(ii) Notwithstanding the foregoing, or anything to the contrary contained herein, the following provisions shall apply with respect to Net Sales of Records in a digital (i.e., non-physical) format such as via the Internet or other direct transmission to the consumer (any such New Technology Configuration is herein referred to as "Digital Internet Sales"):

(A) In connection with such sales, the applicable base royalty in the United States shall be fifty percent (50%) of Company's Net Receipts and the applicable Base Price shall be the wholesale price charged by Company or Company's distributors to the applicable distributor with respect to such Digital Internet sales and there shall be no container charge or "standard" free goods deductions for such sales. All other applicable royalty provisions hereof shall apply in respect of such Digital Internet Sales.

(g) <u>Flat-fee or Net Receipts or Net Royalty Licensing Receipts</u>: Notwithstanding anything to the contrary contained herein, for all licenses by Company (or Company's licensees) to third parties of Master(s) hereunder for uses not otherwise provided for hereunder and for which Company is paid on a flat fee or net receipts basis (*e.g.,* licenses for use in motion picture or television soundtracks), band/artist's royalty shall be fifty percent (50%) of Company's Net Receipts in respect thereof.

(h) <u>Proration</u>: Notwithstanding anything to the contrary contained herein, as to any Record not consisting entirely of Masters, the royalty rate otherwise payable to band/artist with respect to sales of any such Record shall be prorated by multiplying such royalty rate by a fraction, the numerator of which is the number of Masters embodied on such Record and the denominator of which is the total number of royalty-bearing Recordings embodied thereon (including, without limitation, the Masters). As to any Master embodying band/artist's performances together with the performances of another featured artist to whom Company shall be obligated to pay royalties (a "Joint Recording"), the royalty rate otherwise payable to band/artist hereunder shall be prorated by a fraction, the numerator of which is one and the denominator of which is the total number of royalty artists whose performances are embodied in such Joint Recording (including, without limitation, band/artist), unless Company, band/artist and such other artists agree otherwise in writing. Any group artist (including, without limitation, band/artist) shall be deemed to be one artist for such purpose, unless Company, band/artist and such other artists agree otherwise in writing. In addition, band/artist shall not be required to record so-called Joint Recordings without its prior consent (it being understood that its performances on any such Joint Recording shall be deemed its consent).

(l)   Free Goods: No royalties shall be payable in respect of:

(i)   Records given away, furnished, or distributed on a "no-charge" or "freebie" basis to "one-stops, rack jobbers, distributors, or dealers;

(ii)   Records given away or sold at below stated wholesale prices for promotional purposes;

(iii)   Records sold as scrap, salvage, overstock, or "cut-outs";

(iv)   Records sold below cost; and

(v)   Records for which Company does not receive a payment.

(j)   Receipt of Payment: No royalties shall be payable on any sales by Company's licensees until payment or credit against Recording Costs previously taken has been received by band/artist in the United States.

(k)   Container Deductions: In computing royalties hereunder, Company shall deduct from the Base Price of a particular Record hereunder (or other applicable price, if any, upon which royalties are calculated) a "Container Deduction" in an amount equal to the applicable following percentage(s): (i) ten percent (10%) of the Base Price for single pocket vinyl Albums or EPs and Singles in color or special sleeves, (ii) fifteen percent (15%) of the Base Price for non-single pocket vinyl Albums, (iii) twenty percent (20%) of the Base Price for Records in analog prerecorded tape form, and (iv) twenty-five (25%) of the Base Price for compact-disc Records, audiovisual Records, Records in digital prerecorded tape form, New Technology

341

Configurations and any other form or configuration of Record, and Records sold in any other form of package, container or box.

(l)   <u>Discounts</u>:   Notwithstanding anything to the contrary contained herein, the royalty payable to band/artist for Net Sales of Records (whether or not intended for sale by the recipient thereof) sold at a discount to distributors, sub-distributors, dealers, or others, whether or not affiliated with the Company, shall be reduced in the same proportion as the regular wholesale price of such Records is reduced on sales of such Records (except for Records sold at less than fifty percent (50%) of their regular wholesale price, for which no royalties shall be payable hereunder). Such discounts shall not in and of themselves result in reduction of greater than an additional five percent (5%) in its royalties hereunder.

(m)   <u>All-in Royalty</u>: For avoidance of doubt, the royalty payable to band/artist pursuant to this paragraph shall be inclusive of any and all royalties that may be required to be paid to any third-party producers, mixers, or engineers for any services they may render in connection with the Masters and of any and all royalties that may be required to be paid to any musicians or band/artist members that band/artist may hire or that may otherwise be engaged by band/artist or otherwise to perform on Masters hereunder. At Company's election, it may pay royalties directly to such third-party or to band/artist, in either case fully relieving itself of such obligation. Should Company, in Company's sole discretion, choose to make any such third-party payments, then Company shall have the right to deduct the amount of any such payment from any royalties or other sums otherwise due to the band/artist hereunder.

There are a number of important implications here. Of overarching importance is the fact that different royalties apply to different formats and a variety of territories. For example, there is a different royalty for sales of Albums in the United States versus Europe. In America, generally (as in this particular example) the royalty is twenty percent of the Suggested Retail List Price **(the "SRLP")**.

However, the royalty paid for Canada and the United Kingdom will be seventy-five percent of one hundred percent of the royalty payable in America. And in the rest of world, the rate will be fifty percent of the royalty payable in America. Also, keep in mind that foreign sales will generate currency issues. A band/artist must pay attention to these technical details given that an improper exchange rate can cost the band/artist hundreds of thousands of dollars.

Paragraph (c) reduces the royalty even further: for mid-price and budget records, the royalty is only fifty percent of the one hundred percent full royalty. Be aware of the definitions of "budget" and "mid-price." A Mid-Price album is one sold "at less than eighty percent, and more than sixty-six and two-thirds percent, of the then-prevailing top-line Suggested Retail List Price." A Budget album is "sold at less than sixty-six and two-thirds percent of the then-prevailing top-line Suggested Retail List Price."

Paragraph (d) sets the royalty rate for a "Premium" album - those sold at less than full price for promotions and giveaways. A note for the band/artist - the Company must get your authorization to sell such albums, so do not give it away cheaply.

Paragraph (e) sets the rate for sales to the government or educational institutions - again reduced to fifty percent of the SRLP. Paragraph (f) does the same for sales through record clubs.

Paragraph (g) addresses royalty issues related to new technology. Under sub-clause (i), the royalty for New Technology is seventy-five percent of the base royalty. Note that if such sales become twenty-five percent of the net sales of the band/artist, the royalty will be renegotiated.

Under sub-clause (ii)(A), the royalty for sales of digital transmissions is fifty percent of the base price. The base price is the wholesale price paid by retailers or distribution mediums. Also, there are no "container" charges, such as for a CD cover - which is only fair since there are no containers for a digital transmission.

An important case that dealt with the issue of whether a download was a sale or a license, was addressed in *In F.B.T. Prods. LLC v. Aftermath Records*, 621 F.3d 958 (9th Cir. 2010). F.B.T. and Aftermath disagreed on whether the recording agreement's "Records Sold" provision or "Masters Licensed" provision sets the royalty rate for sales of Eminem's records in the form of permanent downloads and mastertones.[486] The record label wanted to pay the royalty that applied to regular recordings, Twelve Percent and Twenty Percent of the adjusted retail price of all "full price records sold in the United States ... through normal retail channels." Eminem argued that the royalty rate should be 50% since the download was a "license," not a sale.

Consequently, the Court needed to determine whether the Masters Licensed provision applied. To do so, [the Court] had to decide whether Aftermath licensed the Eminem masters to third parties.[487]

The Court stated:

Pursuant to its agreements with Apple and other third parties, . . . Aftermath did not "sell" anything to the download distributors. The download distributors did not obtain title to the digital files. The ownership of those files remained with Aftermath, Aftermath reserved the right to regain possession of the files at any time, and Aftermath obtained recurring benefits in the form of payments based on the volume of downloads.[488]

The Court further stated:

> Under our case law interpreting and applying the Copyright Act, too, it is well settled that where a copyright owner transfers a copy of copyrighted material, retains title, limits the uses to which the material may be put, and is compensated periodically based on the transferee's exploitation of the material, the transaction is a license. *F.B.T. Prods. LLC v. Aftermath Records*, 621 F.3d 958 (9th Cir. 2010) *See, e.g., Wall Data Inc. v. Los Angeles County Sheriff's Dep't*, 447 F.3d 769, 785 (9th Cir.2006); *MAI Sys. Corp. v. Peak Computer, Inc.,* 991 F.2d 511 (9th Cir.1993); *United States v. Wise,* 550 F.2d 1180, 1190-91 (9th Cir.1977); *Hampton v. Paramount Pictures Corp.,* 279 F.2d 100, 103 (9th Cir.1960).

As a result, the Court held that since "Aftermath permitted third parties to use the Eminem masters to produce and sell records, in the form of permanent downloads and mastertones, F.B.T. is entitled to a 50% royalty under the plain terms of the agreements."[489] "In sum, the agreements unambiguously provide that "notwithstanding" the Records Sold provision, Aftermath owed F.B.T. a 50% royalty under the Masters Licensed provision for licensing the Eminem masters to third parties for any use."[490]

The case had a huge effect on the music industry with many artists suing for back royalties.

Paragraph (h) sets the royalty for instances where the

Company licenses any of the Master Recordings. In those situations, the band/artist receives fifty percent of the revenues received.

Paragraph (i) addresses the situation of a "mixed" record, *i.e.,* not all of the tracks are Masters of the band/artist, or another artist is also featured on the Album. In those instances, the band/artist's royalty is pro-rated in proportion to the number of tracks of the band/artist versus the total number of the tracks on the Album.

Paragraph (j) states the rather obvious condition that no royalties are paid on "free" items, such as promo giveaways. However, there is still a major nuance here - the band/artist must be aware of too much product being given away for free.

Paragraph (k) informs the band/artist that no royalties will be paid until the Recording Costs and other advances to the band/artist are paid off.

Paragraph (l) is one of the real doozies in the Recording Agreement - container costs! The Company will charge the band/artist for costs associated with packaging the Masters. The band/artist really must pay attention to these types of clauses, as the Company can quickly "nickel and dime" the band/artist into the "red." And even though the costs associated with packaging the Masters have dropped drastically, there is little negotiation for the band/artist in this area. And, of course, remember the Eminem case on container costs for downloads!

Paragraph (m) is another alert to the band/artist that the royalties payable under the Agreement for discounted records are deducted in relation to the amount of the discount of the retail price. Again, the band/artist should be aware of the Company's actions in discounting the Sound Recordings in order to prevent the Company from abusing the royalty structure.

Paragraph (n) is a "CYA" clause - "cover your assets." The Company is establishing that any third-party royalties are included within the royalties paid. Basically, the band/artist is on the hook for any payments to those parties.

Accountings.

The accounting clause works hand-in-hand with the royalty clause. Whenever there is a royalty involved there *must* be an accounting clause.

Accountings:

(a)   Statements as to royalties earned under this Agreement shall be sent by Company to band/artist semi-annually within ninety (90) days after the end of each semi-annual calendar period ending June 30th and December 31st. Concurrently with the rendition of each statement, Company shall pay band/artist all royalties shown to be due by such statement, after deducting all Recording Costs and other permitted charges paid or incurred hereunder.

(b)   The Company may maintain reasonable reserves from royalties otherwise payable for any particular accounting period. Such royalty reserves shall be liquidated after the first four (4) semi-annual accounting periods following the accounting period in respect of which such reserve was established.

(c)   Returns shall be apportioned between free goods and Records sold in the ratio that the number of free goods bears to the total number of Records distributed prior to any return.

(d)   Band/artist shall be deemed to have consented to all accountings rendered by band/artist under this Agreement and said accountings shall be binding upon band/artist and shall not be subject to any

objection by band/artist for any reason unless specific objection, in writing, stating the basis thereof, is given to Company within two (2) years after the date such statement was initially rendered to Company, and after such written objection, unless suit is instituted within the earlier of (i) six (6) months after the date upon which Company notifies band/artist that Company denies the validity of the objection, or (ii) three (3) years after the date such statement was initially rendered to Company. Band/artist shall have the right at its sole cost and expense to appoint a certified public accountant to examine and make relevant extracts from Company's books as same pertain to the Masters hereunder, provided that any such examination shall be for a reasonable duration, shall take place at Company's offices during normal business hours upon reasonable written notice and shall neither occur more than once in any calendar year nor more than once with respect to any particular statement. Notwithstanding anything to the contrary contained herein, it is specifically understood that band/artist shall have no right to audit any of Company's distributors, joint venture partners, affiliates, or licensees.

(e) If a discrepancy is found that is greater than ten percent (10%) in favor of band/artist, the Company shall bear the cost of any audit of the statement or statements in dispute.

Paragraph (a) establishes the payment schedule of the royalties earned by the band/artist - in this case, on a semi-annual basis. The paragraph also states that the actual statements and release of funds will occur within ninety days of the conclusion of the prior six-month period. It is very important for the band/artist to understand the payment schedule and to be aware of the compliance by the Company. It is also important for the band/artist to realize that he or she receives no actual monies until any Advances and other upfront expenses made by the Company are reimbursed.

Paragraph (b) alerts the band/artist to the fact that the Company may keep a "reserve" from the royalties, in case of returns or in case there is an issue with the royalty to be paid. The band/artist should attempt to negotiate the amount of the reserve - something that is fair to both the Company and to the band/artist.

Paragraph (c) is a rather arcane provision stating that the effect on royalties will be rationed between free goods (records given away) and actual records sold. So, if 1,000 records were given away, and 1,000 records were sold, and 500 were returned, the 500 would be split between the free goods and the records sold. The bottom line is that 250 would be deducted from the total of sold records, thus affecting the royalty to the recording artist.

While paragraph (c) is relatively unimportant, paragraph (d) is paramount! The band/artist must be aware of the right to audit the statements delivered by the Company – remember our "brother/sister clauses." In this case, the band/artist has two years to contest a statement. If the Company denies the validity of the dispute of the statement, the band/artist then has six months in which to bring suit, or up to three years from the date of the original notice to the Company, *whichever is earliest*. It means that the band/artist must actively review each statement received from the Company and be aware of the deadlines in bringing suit. If the band/artist fails to timely bring suit, the statement is deemed accepted and the band/artist cannot dispute that particular statement again.

Paragraph (e) is a very important provision that is sometimes left out of agreements: if the discrepancy in the audit is greater than ten percent (10%) in favor of the band/artist, the Company will have to absorb the cost of the audit. For a band/artist, this is a very important provision because the cost of the audit could easily erase any of the gains from the audit.

Licensing of Musical Compositions.

One of the major revenue streams for a Company is the licensing of the Musical Compositions and the Masters' generated under the Agreement. The following clause is termed a "Controlled Musical Composition Clause," and relates to the Mechanical Royalty paid to the band/artist for the pressing/streaming of any Sound Recording or rights granted for "covers."

Licensing Of Musical Compositions:

(a)   Band/artist hereby agrees that Company shall have the right to license all Controlled Musical Compositions to Company (i) for the United States at a rate equal to seventy-five percent (75%) of the minimum United States statutory Copyright royalty rate and for Canada at a rate equal to seventy-five percent (75%) of the minimum compulsory rate in Canada (the "Controlled Rate") for top-line Albums, singles and EPs sold through normal retail channels, (ii) at seventy-five percent (75%) of the Controlled Rate for Records sold as Mid-priced Records, "premiums," New Technology Configurations, Government Sales and/or Direct Sales, and (iii) at fifty percent (50%) of the Controlled Rate for Records sold as Budget Records. Such Controlled Rate for any Controlled Musical Composition shall be calculated without regard to playing time and as of the earlier of (i) the date of its Delivery to Company of the Album concerned; or (ii) the date that band/artist were required to Deliver to Company the Album concerned.

(b)   Notwithstanding the foregoing, the maximum aggregate mechanical royalty rate which Company shall be required to pay in respect of any Album, regardless of the total number of Musical Compositions contained thereon, shall not exceed ten (10) times the rate specified above; nor two (2) times such amount for Singles; nor five (5) times such amount for EPs. The Company shall have the right to reduce the amounts payable to band/artist in connection with Controlled Musical Compositions and/or to charge as an advance against its royalties hereunder any amounts in excess of such sums. All mechanical royalties payable hereunder shall be paid on the basis of Net Sales of Records hereunder for which royalties are payable to Company pursuant to this Agreement. The Company may maintain reasonable reserves with respect to the payment of mechanical royalties that shall be liquidated in accordance with paragraph 10 above. In the event that any Controlled Musical Composition is embodied on a particular Record more than once, Company shall not be obligated to pay the above rate more than once in respect of such Controlled Musical Composition.

(c)   In respect of Controlled Musical Compositions performed in Videos, Company shall have the right to grant to Company an irrevocable perpetual worldwide license, to record, perform and reproduce such Musical Compositions in such Videos and to distribute, reproduce, publicly perform, and otherwise exploit such Videos and to authorize others to do so. The Company will not be required to make any additional payment in connection with those uses (other than as set forth herein), and that license shall apply whether or not Company receives any payment in connection with those Videos.

(d) If any Master embodies one or more Musical Compositions that are not Controlled Musical Compositions, band/artist shall upon Company's request obtain for Company's benefit mechanical licenses covering such Musical Compositions in a form no less favorable to Company than those contained in the then-current standard form Harry Fox Agency license. The Company shall work with band/artist and cooperate with band/artist in an effort to obtain such licenses. band/artist will cause the issuance of effective licenses, under Copyright or otherwise, to reproduce each Controlled Musical Composition on Records and distribute those Records outside the United States and Canada, on terms not less favorable to Company or Company's licensees than the terms generally prevailing in the country concerned with respect to the use of Musical Compositions on Records.

(e) For the avoidance of doubt, if the package for any Record shall be comprised of an audio-only copy of a Master together with Video copies of such Master, Company shall have no obligation to pay any additional mechanical or other payment in regard to the inclusion on such Record of the Video copy, it being understood and agreed that Company's sole obligation is to account to band/artist for the mechanical license in the audio only version of the Record in accordance with the provisions hereof.

The licensing of the Controlled Musical Compositions involves complicated provisions and formulas. As discussed previously, the owner of the Copyright has the exclusive right to publicly perform the Musical Composition. One exception to that right is the Mechanical Royalty - once a song is published (*i.e.,* offered for sale), anyone can then make their own version of that song. However, the person making the new version still has to pay a royalty - in this case, the mechanical royalty from the mechanical license usually obtained from the Harry Fox Agency, the leading provider of rights management, licensing, and royalty services for the music industry in the United States. Harry Fox is an agency that licenses, collects, and distributes mechanical royalties on behalf of musical Copyright owners, issuing mechanical licenses among other things.[491]

Pursuant to paragraph (a) of this Licensing provision, the Company has the right to license the Controlled Musical Compositions to itself but will only have to pay seventy-five percent of the applicable statutory royalty. The mechanical royalty is currently 12¢ per copy, or 2.31¢ per minute, whichever is greater.

Consequently, if paying the 12¢ per copy, the Company only has to pay approximately nine cents per copy. Additionally, the compensation is reduced further for budget records, or other cut-rate sales.

Paragraph (b) further limits the compensation owed by the Company by establishing a cap on the number of Musical Compositions for which the Company will pay. In this case, the Company will pay the mechanical royalty on only ten Musical Compositions, even if the Album contains more. The same will apply for EP's, singles, and other bargain offerings. Also, if a Musical Composition is on multiple albums, the Company will only pay one royalty.

Paragraph (c) gives the Company the right to use the Controlled Musical Compositions in a video without any further compensation, *other than what is included in the Video clause.*

Under paragraph (d), the Company requires the band/artist to gain permission of the Composer of any song the band/artist records that is not a Controlled Musical Composition. Thus, for example, if the band/artist does a "cover" of another artist's song, the band/artist must get the third-party Composer to allow the Company to license the Musical Composition under the same terms and conditions as if it was the band/artist's original song.

Paragraph (e) is another "CYA" clause - in this case making it clear that if a package contains both a Controlled Musical Composition and a Video, the Company will only have to pay compensation on the song, and not on the video as well.

One important development in this area is that Bertelsmann Music Group **("BMG")** will voluntarily refrain from applying the reductions to any new record deals and remove them from its entire catalogue over the coming years. In a statement from BMG, "The move forms part of BMG's ongoing program to rebalance the music industry in favor of artists and songwriters by abandoning longstanding practices designed to reduce the incomes of musicians." Also, the company, which was founded in 2008, pledged to review the record contracts from catalogs it has acquired for signs of racial bias.[492]

Videos.

Indicative of the ever-changing landscape of the music industry, videos were once the be-all and end-all for bands/artists in promoting their songs. Now, however, videos are merely one small part of a band/artist's overall marketing plan. Michael Jackson could spend $1 million dollars on a video in the late '80s and early '90s - no more. Now, a major recording artist is lucky to receive $100,000.00 to create a video. More often, however, videos are made with a budget of less than $10,000.00.

Videos:

(a)   Band/artist agrees to perform for the purpose of creating Video content that may be used by Company for *commercial purposes* in connection with the sale of Records hereunder, such as, for example, including any Album distributed hereunder, a companion DVD embodying its audiovisual performances. The term "Video" shall mean an audiovisual Recording embodying one or more Masters. The costs of any such Video content shall constitute Recording Costs and shall be fully recoupable from its royalties hereunder.

(b)   In addition, band/artist shall, at Company's request, appear and perform for the production of one or more *promotional Videos* that are intended to be used to market Records hereunder.

(c)   The elements (*e.g.,* director, concept, and storyboard) of any such Video shall be determined by band/artist in consultation with Company.

(d)   The Company agrees to pay the production costs of such promotional Videos made at Company's request under this Agreement, provided such costs have been previously approved by Company in writing.

(e)   All sums paid by Company in connection with each Video shall be deemed a Recording Cost and shall be recoupable by the Company out of all royalties becoming payable to band/artist pursuant to this Agreement, except that Company shall not recoup more than fifty percent (50%) of such sums from royalties becoming payable to Company in respect of audio-only Records; provided however, that in the event the costs incurred by band/artist in respect of any one particular Video shall exceed Thirty Thousand Dollars ($30,000.00), then any and all amounts paid by the Company in respect of such video in excess of Thirty Thousand Dollars ($30,000.00) shall be fully recoupable from its royalties hereunder. It is specifically understood that the Company shall have the right to recoup one hundred percent (100%) of all sums paid by the Company in connection with Videos from royalties' payable in respect of Videos to the extent that such sums are not recouped from royalties' payable in respect of audio-only Records. Notwithstanding the foregoing, if the aggregate production costs of any such promotional Video shall exceed the approved budget therefore due to band/artist's acts or omissions, band/artist shall reimburse the Company for such excess, failing which the Company shall have the right to deduct such excess from any monies payable to Company which shall include, without limitation, the right to recoup one hundred percent (100%) of such excess from any royalties becoming payable to band/artist hereunder.

(f)   Notwithstanding the above, band/artist's royalty in respect of Records embodying solely Videos (and not audio only Masters) shall be computed in accordance with the provisions of paragraph 9, except that: (i) the royalty rate pursuant to 9(a) shall be deemed to be ten percent (10%) for this purpose; (ii) royalties payable to band/artist in respect of Records solely embodying Videos shall include, without limitation, any royalty obligations to any producers of audio-only Masters used in connection with Videos and all third parties rendering services in connection with Videos (including, without limitation, the Video director); (iii) Company shall have the right to use and allow others to use each Video for advertising and promotional purposes for records

and Company's company with no payment to Company or any third parties; and (iv) with respect to Records embodying Videos made hereunder together with other material, royalties payable to band/artist shall be computed by multiplying the otherwise applicable royalty by a fraction, the numerator of which is the aggregate amount of playing time of all of the Videos embodied in such Record, and the denominator of which is the total playing time of all material (including, without limitation, Videos) embodied in such Record. Band/artist hereby acknowledges and agrees that Company shall have the right to couple Videos with audiovisual Recordings of other artists.

Paragraph (a) deals with the archaic notion that the videos will make money, *i.e.,* have a "commercial" use. The key word in paragraph (a) is therefore *commercial,* and it is important to note that the costs of the Video are recouped from the band/artist's royalties. Currently, however, videos have little impact on an artist's bottom line. While concert videos may be the exception, a concert video is different from a video that illuminates one song.

Paragraph (b) requires the band/artist to make *promotional* videos to help promote the Album. There is a difference - first, the promotional videos are not used to make money; second, the promotional videos may be broader in subject matter than just a particular Musical Composition. Again, the costs associated with the videos are recoupable from the band/artist's royalties.

Under paragraph (c), artistic elements such as director and the storyline of the video are decided upon in consultation between the parties. There is a balancing of interests at play in this short clause: the band/artist wants to be able to control the people and the look of the Video, but the Company wants to make sure the product has commercial potential. It is in both parties' best interests to compromise: the band/artist must acknowledge the investment of the Company, and the Company does not want an unhappy band/artist.

Paragraph (d) and (e) work hand-in-hand: paragraph (d) gives the Company the right to set the budget and pay the costs of the video; and paragraph (e) gives the Company the right to recoup the costs of the video. A key point is that the Company will only take up to fifty percent of the recoupment from royalties on records. In other words, the Company will look to recoup costs from the video *and* the Sound Recordings *but* will only take up to fifty percent from the royalties of the Sound Recordings. Hopefully, the Video will pay for itself, but, as mentioned above videos do not generate the revenue streams like in the past. Also, if the Video goes over budget, the Company can take up to one hundred percent of the royalties from the Sound Recordings until it has recouped its costs.

Similarly, Paragraph (f) makes clear that the Company can take one hundred percent of the royalties from the Videos until the Company has recouped its costs. It also restates that the Company can look to the royalties of the Sound Recordings, and even to the band/artist, if the Video goes over budget.

Paragraph (g) reduces the royalty on a record that just embodies videos. In this case, the royalty is reduced to 10% and the Company can allow others to use the videos for promotional purposes.

Independent Marketing, Press and Promotion Expenses and Tour Support.

The Company will commit to supporting the band/artist on tour. However, the amount of support and the use of that support (*i.e.,* how the money is spent) is often contentious.

Independent Marketing, Press and Promotion
Expenses and Tour Support:

(a)   Subject to band/artist's full and faithful
performance of all the material terms and conditions
hereof, Company shall expend the following minimum
recoupable amounts for independent promotion,
independent marketing, publicity and so-called "tour
support", which such "tour support" shall include the
costs of Company's providing band/artist with
reasonable ground transportation (*e.g.*, van or bus) to
and from its "live" performances within the
continental United States, with respect to each Album
recorded and delivered in satisfaction of its Minimum
Recording Commitment as follows:

Album 1: $150,000

Album 2: $250,000

Album 3: $350,000

In addition, without band/artist's prior written
consent, Company shall not recoup in excess of the
following amounts for independent marketing,
independent promotion, publicity, and so-called
"tour support" with respect to each Album recorded
and delivered in satisfaction of its Minimum
Recording Commitment:

Album 1: $50,000

Album 2: $60,000

Album 3: $70,000

For the avoidance of doubt, the Company shall have

the right to recoup such amount from royalties otherwise payable to band/artist hereunder and such amount shall count towards Company's satisfaction of the minimum recoupable amount to be expended by Company for Album 1.

Under paragraph (a), the Company will give the band/artist $150,000.00 in tour support for the first year. For each subsequent year, the tour support is increased by $100,000.00.

Paragraph (b) allows the Company to recoup up to $50,000.00 in expenses, but *only* if the band/artist has agreed to the expenditure of those amounts. This notice and approval concept is very important: it prevents a Company from pouring money into a tour without telling the band/artist, who would then find itself stuck in a black hole of debt.

Paragraph (c) merely restates that the costs expended by the Company are recoupable.

Inducement Letter.

Many times, the Company may wish to enter into an agreement with another label to promote and market the Album.

Inducement Letter/Dovetail Agreement:

Band/artist acknowledges and agrees that the Company may, at the Company's election, enter into an agreement with one or more third-party so-called major record companies (herein below a "Major" and each such agreement is referred to as a "Major Agreement") pursuant to which the Company may authorize any such Major to release Records embodying Masters subject hereto. The band/artist and the Company acknowledge that in connection with each such Major Agreement as the Company may

elect to enter into, the applicable Major may desire that band/artist execute and deliver to such Major a so-called inducement letter (herein an "Inducement Letter") confirming that band/artist will agree to fully perform hereunder and under the applicable Major Agreement and band/artist agrees to promptly execute and deliver to Company copies of any such Inducement Letter as Company may request. Band/artist and Company further acknowledge and agree that the terms of any such Major Agreement may vary from terms specified herein in certain ways, such as, for example, having to do with the manner and calculation of royalties, and that Company shall have the right, by notice in writing to band/artist, to modify the applicable terms hereof in order to insure that they shall comply with the terms and conditions of the applicable Major Agreement.**

Under this clause, the Company has the right to enter into agreements with third-party record companies, *i.e.,* "major" record companies.

Record Company Credit.

It is worth mentioning that the Company is going to want to get credit for creating and promoting the Album.

<u>Record Company Credit</u>:

The Company shall have the right to accord " _____ " an appropriate credit on all labels, in liner notes, back covers or inner sleeves of Albums, and on any single(s) in all configurations, embodying a Master, and in all one-half (1/2) page or larger paid advertisements placed band/artist or under Company's control in so-called "nationwide"

trade and consumer publications in the United States that pertain exclusively to commercial singles embodying a Master or which pertain to an Album.

The clause is straightforward and not controversial.

Trademarks.

The following paragraph will give the Company the right to apply for Trademark protection for the band/artist.

Trademarks:

On band/artist's behalf, Company shall have the right, at Company's sole election, to seek and secure Trademark registrations in and to the name "_____" throughout the world. Any costs paid or incurred by Company with respect to all such efforts shall be fully recoupable from royalties payable to band/artist hereunder.

The band/artist must be very careful in allowing the Company to secure any type of rights for Intellectual Property, particularly Copyrights and Trademarks. Artists are notorious for not taking care of the *business* side of the entertainment industry, and the Company is trying to protect itself and the artist. However, as discussed earlier, the Company should not be the *owner* of the Trademark. It is imperative for the band/artist to maintain constant vigilance as to the status of the Intellectual Property. Thus, while the Company may take charge of filing for a Trademark or Copyright, the band/artist should be listed on the papers as the owner. That way, if the band/artist and the Company ever part ways, the band/artist still owns the Copyrights and Trademarks to the music and the brand and can bring them to a new label to the extent otherwise permitted under the Agreement. This is important, as the band/artist will naturally want to maintain continuity under the same brand or band/artist name.

Band/artist's Promotional Activities.

The Company will require the band/artist to participate in activities that help promote the Record.

Band/artist's Promotional Activities.

(a) From time to time, at Company's request and at no expense to Company, band/artist shall appear at photographic sessions in connection with the creation of artwork, poster, and cover art to be used in connection with the advertising, marketing, and promotion of Masters hereunder; appear for interviews with representatives of the press and the Company's publicity personnel; and advise and consult with band/artist regarding its performances hereunder. At the Company's request and subject to band/artist's prior professional commitments, band/artist shall make personal appearances on radio and television and elsewhere and to record taped interviews, spot announcements, trailers, and electrical transcriptions, all for the purpose of advertising, exploiting and/or promoting Masters hereunder. Band/artist shall not be entitled to any compensation for such services, except as may be required by applicable union agreements; provided, that Company shall either promptly reimburse band/artist or advance band/artist the costs of reasonable travel and living expenses incurred by band/artist pursuant to a budget approved by band/artist in advance in connection with its rendition services rendered at Company's direction pursuant to this paragraph.

Under paragraph (a), the band/artist is obligated to remain available to help promote the Record, such as photo shoots and interviews. The band/artist will receive no extra compensation for the promotional work. However, the Company will cover the expenses of the band/artist in making the promotional appearances.

Website.

The Company will give itself the right to create and maintain a website for the band/artist. But, just as with any aspect of Intellectual Property, the band/artist must maintain vigilance so that the rights are not stolen or misappropriated.

Website.

(a)   Subject to paragraphs 16(b) and 16(c) below, Company and Company's licensees shall have the exclusive right, throughout the world, to create, maintain and host, and authorize others to create, maintain, and host any and all websites relating to the band/artist and to register and use the name "_____" and any variations thereof which embody band/artist's name (or the name of any individual member of band/artist), together with such suffixes (e.g., ".com". or ".co.uk") as the Company determine in the Company's reasonable judgment, as Uniform Resource Locators ("URLs"), addresses of domain names (each an "Band/artist Site"). Furthermore, the Company and the Company's licensees shall have the exclusive right in perpetuity throughout the world to use its name, photographs, likenesses, biography and any and all related rights granted to Company hereunder in connection with Company's own internet website at the URL

"www._____.com" or any variation thereof as the Company shall determine ("Label Site") to promote, among other things, Records embodying Masters hereunder. All such websites created by the Company or Company's licensees, and all elements thereof, and all rights thereto and derived therefrom, shall be the Company's property throughout the Territory and in perpetuity, such to the otherwise applicable provisions hereof. Band/artist agrees that band/artist shall at all times cooperate with the Company and actively promote and support the Company's Sites and/or the Label Site, including, without limitation, by providing current pictures, graphics, and editorial content in connection with the initial release of each Album, by engaging in a reasonable number of activities whereby band/artist shall interact with website visitors, and by participating in other online and e-mail promotions.

(b)   Notwithstanding anything to the contrary in paragraph 16(a), during and after the Term, the band/artist may continue to own, maintain and host its independent internet website at the URL "www._____.net" ("Independent Site") for the sole purposes of continuing the activities on the Independent Site in existence as of the date hereof, provided (i) the Independent Site includes on the band/artist's homepage a prominent link to the homepage of the Label Site or, if any, the band/artist Site, and (ii) the Independent Site is not used for the purpose of selling or otherwise distributing or transmitting of Records embodying Masters hereunder or any other materials owned or controlled without Company's prior written approval thereof.

(c)   Notwithstanding anything to the contrary in paragraph 16(a), after the expiration of the Term, but in no event sooner than seven (7) months following the delivery to the Company of the last album

delivered in satisfaction of its entire recording commitment, the Company shall, promptly following its request, transfer to band/artist on a quitclaim basis Company's rights in and to the URL "www._____.com" or any variation thereof, assuming Company has at that time the registration to such site.

The clauses together give the Company the right to create, host and maintain a website for the band/artist. The Company also has the right to let third-party licensees, such as professional website designers, create the website. In this case, the band/artist already has a website, so the clauses allow the band/artist to continue to use that website. However, the band/artist has to coordinate the activities of the independent website with the website hosted by the Company.

Seven months after the Agreement is over, the band/artist may take over the website from the Company.

There is one additional consideration that may be warranted. The band/artist may want to make clear in these clauses that the Copyright(s) in the website content and appearance, remains with the band/artist.

Injunctive Relief.

Given a breach by the band/artist, an important remedy for the Company is injunctive relief. An injunction is an order preventing the enjoined party (here, the band/artist) from doing something.

Injunctive Relief:

(a) Band/artist expressly acknowledges that its services hereunder are of a special, unique, and

intellectual character which gives them peculiar value, and that in the event of a breach, or threatened breach, by band/artist of any term, condition, or covenant hereof, Company will be caused immediate irreparable injury. Band/artist expressly agrees that Company shall be entitled to seek injunctive and other equitable relief, as permitted by law, to prevent a breach, or threatened breach, of this Agreement, or any portion thereof, by band/artist, which relief shall be in addition to any other rights or remedies, for damages or otherwise, available to Company.

One of the major remedies that the Company can turn to in the event of a breach by the band/artist is injunctive relief. When issued by the court, an injunction orders the parties to stop what they are doing and not take any further action. For the band/artist, this can be very damaging. The injunction will prevent the band/artist from recording any further material and even from performing. Effectively, the band/artist is on the sidelines until the controversy is resolved.

There are two types of injunctions. *Preliminary* injunctions are entered at the beginning of a lawsuit, in order to stop the offending conduct while the dispute is being resolved. A *permanent* injunction is entered if the requesting party (the Company) prevails in the dispute. If the Company loses the suit, then the preliminary injunction is lifted. Preliminary injunctions are difficult to obtain, as the Company is generally required to prove (a) that it is likely to succeed on the merits of the underlying dispute; (b) there is "irreparable harm" to the Company in the conduct continuing without an injunction; (c) the balance of hardships weighs in the Company's favor rather than the band/artist's; and (d) the public interest favors granting the injunction.[493] The first two factors are the most important. It is not easy to demonstrate a likelihood of success early on in a case before evidence is exchanged or depositions have occurred.

However, in many jurisdictions the more irreparable harm a Company can show, the less evidence of likelihood of success on the merits is needed, and vice versa.

Force Majeure; Defaults; Remedies.

In addition to injunction relief, the Company will also have the following remedies available.

Force Majeure; Defaults and Remedies:

Notwithstanding anything to the contrary contained in this Agreement:

(a) If Company's performance hereunder is delayed or becomes impossible or commercially impracticable by reason of any force majeure event, including, without limitation, any act of God, fire, earthquake, strike, civil commotion, act of government or any order, regulation, ruling or action of any labor union or association of artists affecting the Company and/or the phonograph record industry, Company, upon notice to band/artist, may suspend Company's obligations hereunder for the duration of such delay, impossibility or impracticability, as the case may be. During any such suspension Company shall not withhold the payment of royalties unless the force majeure event materially impairs Company's ability to calculate and/or pay royalties. No such single period of suspension shall extend for a period in excess of six (6) consecutive months unless the events giving rise to such suspension shall affect substantially all the United States recording industry.

(b) Each of the following shall constitute an event of default hereunder:

(i) Band/artist's voice and/or playing ability becomes impaired for a period in excess of ninety (90) consecutive days, as determined by a physician reasonably designated by Company, or band/artist ceases to seriously pursue its career as an entertainer, or band/artist attempts to assign this Agreement other than as permitted hereunder;

(ii) Band/artist commences a voluntary case under any applicable bankruptcy, insolvency or other similar law now or hereafter in effect or consent to the entry of an order for relief in any involuntary case under such law or consent to the appointment of or taking possession by a receiver, liquidator, assignee, trustee or sequestrator (or similar appointee) of band/artist or any substantial part of its property or band/artist make an assignment for the benefit of creditors or take any act (whether corporate or otherwise) in furtherance of any of the foregoing;

(iii) A court having jurisdiction over band/artist's affairs or its property enters a decree or order for relief in respect of band/artist or any of its property in an involuntary case under any applicable bankruptcy, insolvency or other similar law now or hereafter in effect or appoints a receiver, liquidator, assignee, custodian, trustee or sequestrator (or similar appointee) of band/artist or for any substantial part of its property or orders the winding up or liquidation of its affairs and such decree or order remains unstayed and in effect for a period of fifteen (15) consecutive days;

(iv) Band/artist fails to timely Deliver all Masters, Albums and other material required to be Delivered by band/artist hereunder; provided however, that in the case of late delivery Company shall provide band/artist with notice of such failure and provide band/artist with a thirty (30) day period within which band/artist shall have the right to cure such late delivery; or

(v) Band/artist fails to timely fulfill any of its material obligations hereunder. On the occurrence of any event of default set forth herein, the Company, without limiting its other rights or remedies, may, by notice to band/artist, elect to (i) suspend Company's obligations to band/artist hereunder for the duration of such event and/or (ii) terminate the Term by notice to band/artist given at any time (whether or not during a period of suspension based on such event or based upon any other event), and thereby be relieved of all liability other than any obligations hereunder to pay royalties in respect of Masters Delivered prior to such termination. It is specifically understood that in the event of any such termination all of band/artist's obligations that would remain in effect after the natural expiration of the Term (including, without limitation, its obligation to indemnify the Company and the re-recording restriction contained herein) shall remain in full force and effect as if the Term had expired naturally as of the date of such termination.

Paragraph (a) of this clause outlines what are termed *"force majeure"* events, *(i.e.,* an unexpected and disruptive event that may operate to excuse a party from a contract.) Under these situations the law feels that it is not fair to enforce an agreement because it would impose an unacceptable burden on that party.

Some types of *force majeure* events are earthquakes, fires, floods, and other natural disasters. Political events can also be a *force majeure,* *(e.g.,* an invasion or a strike by a labor organization). Finally, a court order might be *force majeure*, (*e.g.,* a court determines that a song is obscene). In these cases, the party obligated to pay or perform is excused while the condition continues.

Paragraph (b) outlines certain events considered to be a *default*, which will lead to a *breach*. A major event that would be considered a breach is if the band/artist is unable to perform. A band/artist's body and voice are part of the tools used by the band/artist to create the product. The Company, rightly, wants the band/artist to keep those tools in good working order. If they become broken, the Company does not have to pay the band/artist.

Part of keeping the tools in order is also the band/artist's mental state. If the band/artist is adjudicated incompetent (not able to understand reality), the Company can consider that a breach.

A clause seen in almost every agreement is a "bankruptcy clause." If the band/artist declares bankruptcy, the Company can terminate the Agreement. *However,* such clauses are considered non-operable in bankruptcy court and will not be recognized.

A final breach is if the band/artist does not deliver the Masters in a timely manner.

Under paragraph (c), in all of these cases, the Company can, rather than terminate the Agreement, "toll" the Agreement and not pay the band/artist. As one example, the Company might toll the Agreement while the band/artist is attending rehab for drug addiction. Consequently, a three-album deal can become a deal that might take years to complete. Bottom line to the band/artist - deliver the Masters. Paragraph (d) gives the Company the "nuclear option," *i.e.,* blow the Agreement up. The Company, in its sole discretion, can terminate the Agreement and not pay any further compensation. Under this scenario, one issue will be whether the band/artist is due any past royalties, and, if so, whether these will be retained by the Company for damages.

Representations and Warranties.

Although many people will quickly move past the Representations and Warranties section of an Agreement, it is imperative to pay close attention to what is written within these clauses in order to avoid problems later.

Representations and Warranties.

Band/artist represents and warrants that:

(a) Band/artist is under no disability, restriction, or prohibition, whether contractual or otherwise, with respect to its right to execute this Agreement and perform band/artist's terms and conditions;

(b) Band/artist is over eighteen (18) years of age;

(c) The Company shall not be required to make any payments of any nature for, or in connection with, the rendition of band/artist's services or the acquisition, exercise, or exploitation of rights by the Company pursuant to this Agreement, except as specifically provided herein;

(d) No materials hereunder, nor any use thereof, will violate any law or infringe upon or violate the rights of any third-party. "Materials," as used in this Agreement, shall include: (i) all Musical Compositions and other material embodied in the Masters, (ii) each name used by band/artist in connection with Masters, and (iii) all other materials, ideas, other intellectual property, or elements furnished or selected by band/artist and embodied in or used in connection with any Masters or the packaging, sale, distribution, advertising, publicizing or other exploitation thereof; and, Without limiting the foregoing, with respect to the Masters hereunder, band/artist will not "sample" or otherwise incorporate into the Masters (for convenience "Sample" or "Sampling" herein) or permit any other party to Sample any copyrighted or otherwise proprietary material ("Proprietary Material") belonging to any person, other than band/artist (such non-party herein referred to as the "Owner") without having first secured from the Owner a written agreement, in a form satisfactory to Company, that Company shall have the perpetual right to use such Proprietary Material in the Master(s) and to exploit the Master(s) in any manner permitted hereunder, all either without any payment whatsoever to the Owner or upon payment to the Owner of a payment approved by the Company. The Company shall not have an obligation to approve any such payment, and Company's approval of any such payment shall not constitute a waiver by Company of its rights of reimbursement from band/artist of Recording Costs in excess of the recording budget. Subject to the provisions hereof and unless otherwise agreed in writing, band/artist shall pay and be responsible for the clearance of any Sample (or removal of any uncleared Sample). In the event Company makes any payments to secure any license in connection with any Sample, then, without limiting any other rights or remedies that Company may have, band/artist shall reimburse Company for, or (at Company's election) Company shall have the right to deduct from any sums payable to band/artist hereunder, all costs incurred by band/artist in connection with any such Sample (including, without limitation, the costs incurred in connection with re-

recording, re-mixing, or otherwise re-editing any Master hereunder as a result of having to delete any uncleared Sample embodied thereon), and Company shall have the right to reduce any Copyright interest in the Musical Composition to which band/artist might otherwise be entitled by the full amount of any such Copyright interest that Company may be required to assign to any third-party in connection with the clearance of such Sample. Without limiting any of Company's other rights or remedies, Company shall be entitled to deduct its share of any reimbursable costs not promptly reimbursed by band/artist from any monies payable to band/artist hereunder. Any payment made by band/artist for the Sampling of any Proprietary Material shall constitute additional Recording Costs.

(e)   During the Term band/artist shall not, without Company's prior written consent in each instance, perform for the purpose of making Recordings for any person, firm, or entity other than the Company (a "Third Party" herein), nor shall band/artist allow any performance by band/artist to be recorded by any Third Party for any purpose during the Term, nor shall band/artist allow any Third Party to release any Record(s) embodying its performance(s) during the Term and within twelve (12) months after the Term; and

(f)   Band/artist shall not perform any selection recorded hereunder and commercially released hereunder for the purposes of making a Recording for anyone other than the Company for use in the Territory until the later of (i) 5 years after the date of the initial commercial release of the respective Record containing such selection or (ii) 2 years after the expiration or other termination of the Term.

Each of these Representations and Warranties is very important. Under paragraph (a), for example, the band/artist is assuring the Company that the band/artist can enter into this Agreement free and clear of any other encumbrances. Among other things, the purpose of this provision is the Company wants to make sure that the band/artist does not have any other recording commitment that would conflict with the delivery of Masters under this Agreement.

Indemnification.

Indemnification will work hand-in-hand with the Representations and Warranties section.

Indemnity:

(a) **Band/artist agrees to and does hereby indemnify, save, defend, and hold the Company harmless from any and all loss, liability and damage (including court costs and reasonable attorneys' fees) arising out of, connected with or arising as a result of any inconsistency with, failure of, or breach or threatened breach by band/artist of any warranty, representation, agreement, undertaking or covenant contained in this Agreement including, without limitation, any and all claims by any third-party inconsistent with its representations, warranties and covenants hereunder, which such claims are reduced to final adverse judgment in a court of competent jurisdiction or are settled with its prior written consent. The Company shall give band/artist notice of any claim to which the foregoing indemnity applies, and band/artist shall have the right to participate in the defense of any such claim through counsel of its own choice and at its expense; provided that Company shall control the defense of the claim.**

Pending the determination of any such claim, Company may withhold payment of all monies under this Agreement in an amount reasonably related to such claim. If an action or other proceeding shall not have been instituted within one (1) year after Company shall have withheld monies in respect of any such claim, then upon band/artist's request Company shall release any monies so withheld, but Company shall have the right to resume withholding if an action or proceeding shall later be instituted. Furthermore, in the event the band/artist shall post a bond in an amount, with a surety and in all other respects reasonably satisfactory to Company, Company shall no longer withhold monies hereunder in respect of the applicable claim.

Indemnification is a fancy word for saying, "I will protect you; I will shift the risk from you to me." In relation to the Representations and Warranties section, the band/artist is saying to the Company, "If any of my representations and warranties turn out to be false, I will defend you if you are sued." It is a very important clause and must be in any Agreement to protect the parties against false representations and warranties.

There are three other nuances in this paragraph: (i) the Company must give notice to the band/artist if any claim is made against the Company; (ii) the Company can withhold royalties until the claim is settled; and (iii) if no action is commenced within one year of the withholding, the band/artist can give notice to the Company for the release of the withheld royalties.

Definitions.

Definitions are key to any agreement. What a particular word means in a given context is critical to the proper interpretation of the Agreement. Here are some common terms that are defined within a Sound Recording Agreement.

Definitions:

As used herein, the following defined terms shall have the meanings set forth below:

(a) "Advance(s)" shall mean a prepayment of royalties otherwise payable to Company hereunder.

(b) The term "Delivery" and permutations thereof used in connection with Masters and/or Albums shall mean delivery to _____ at the Company's offices at the address above of all of the following: a two-track sequenced, completed, fully-edited, leadered, equalized, fully-mixed and mastered digital audio tape and/or U-matic 1630 tape and/or approved digital media equivalent in proper form for the production of the parts necessary to manufacture Records therefrom together with all consents, approvals, copy information, artwork, credits, licenses, mechanical licenses for all Musical Compositions and other material recorded in those Masters and/or Albums and other material and documents required by band/artist to release Records embodying those Masters and/or Albums and to manufacture album covers or other packaging therefore. The Company's election to pay to band/artist any monies which were otherwise required to have been paid upon or promptly after its Delivery to band/artist of Masters and/or Albums or Company's election to release any Record derived from any Master(s) and/or Album(s) shall not be deemed to be an acknowledgment by the Company that Delivery to Company of such Master(s) or Album(s) has been completed in accordance with the provisions of this subparagraph. Further, in either event, Company shall not be deemed to have waived Company's right to require band/artist's complete and proper performance thereafter of its obligation to Deliver to Company any Master(s) or any of Company's remedies for its failure to do so in accordance with the provisions hereof.

(c)   "EP" shall mean a Record embodying not less than five (5) nor more than seven (7) Recordings.

(d)   "Maxi-single" shall mean a Record embodying more than two (2), but not more than four (4) Recordings.

(e)   "Net Receipts" shall mean the flat-fee (or royalty, as the case may be) specifically attributable solely to one (1) or more Masters and received by the Company in the United States in U.S. dollars from a person, firm or corporation in respect of the exploitation by that person, firm or corporation of rights in those Masters, less (i) all costs paid or incurred by band/artist, Company's licensees and/or affiliates in connection with the exploitation of those rights and the collection of those monies, (ii) all taxes and adjustments; and (iii) all royalties or other sums payable by the Company to any person, firm or corporation in connection with the exploitation of those rights, including, without limitation, royalties for the mechanical reproduction of the Musical Compositions and other materials embodied in those Masters, but excluding the royalties or other sums payable to those third parties (e.g., producers, engineers, and mixers) for which band/artist is responsible under the terms of this Agreement.

(f)   "Net Sales" shall mean one hundred percent (100%) of Records sold which are paid for and not returned.

(g)   "New Technology Configurations" shall mean Records in any form, configuration, format, or technology, which is now known but not widely distributed (*e.g.,* DCC, mini disc, mp3, or "ipod") or which hereafter becomes known.

(h)   "Recording Costs" shall mean all wages, fees, advances and payments of any nature to or in respect of all musicians, vocalists, conductors, arrangers, orchestrators, engineers, producers, mixers, and copyists; payments to a trustee or fund based on wages to the extent required by any agreement between Company or Company's licensees, affiliates, or assigns and any labor organization or trustee; all studio, tape, editing, mixing, re-mixing, mastering and engineering costs; all costs of travel, per diems (other than any travel and/or per diems for any of Company's employees), rehearsal halls, non-studio facilities and equipment, dubdown, rental and transportation of instruments; all costs occasioned by the cancellation caused by band/artist or in respect of its actions or inactions of any scheduled recording session; and all other costs and expenses incurred in producing and mixing the Masters which are then customarily recognized as recording costs in the recording industry.

(i)   "Recording(s)" shall mean all forms, now known or hereafter devised, by which sound, whether or not accompanied by visual images, graphics, or other information, may be recorded, or fixed for reproduction or playback.

(j) "Record(s)" shall mean all forms or devices now known or hereafter devised, by which Recordings whether embodying (i) sound alone or (ii) sound synchronized with visual images, (e.g., "sight and sound" devices), may be manufactured or sold primarily for home use, including, without limitation, digital transmissions intended primarily for home use by the recipient thereof.

(k) "Single" shall mean a Record embodying up to two (2) Recordings.

(l) "Suggested Retail List Price" shall mean:

1. With respect to Records sold for distribution in the United States: Other than with respect to Compact Discs, Digital Compact Cassettes, Mini-Discs, other digital configurations, Electronic Transmission, and any and all new technologies; Company's Principal Company's published suggested retail list price in the United States during the applicable accounting period for the computation of royalties to be made hereunder, it being understood that a separate calculation of the suggested retail list prices will be made for each price configuration of Records manufactured and sold.

2. With respect to Compact Discs, Digital Compact Cassettes, Mini-Discs, other digital configurations, and any and all new technologies, including Electronic Transmissions not sold directly to a consumer; one hundred thirty percent (130%) of the lowest published wholesale price by band/artist or Company's Principal Company in the category of sale concerned. In the event such wholesale price changes during an accounting period, the applicable wholesale price for the entire accounting period shall

be deemed to be the average lowest daily price during the period.

3. With respect to Electronic Transmissions sold directly to a consumer; the price paid by the consumer for such Records, less any referral fees, commissions or similar fees paid to any person, firm, or corporation who, through their website, electronic mail, or other means, refers or otherwise facilitates the purchase by any consumer of a Record through an Electronic Transmission.

4. In the event that no Suggested Retail List Price is provided by Company's Principal Company, the Suggested Retail List Price shall mean one hundred twenty six percent (126%) of the lowest published wholesale price by band/artist or Company's Principal Company in the category of sale concerned.

5. With respect to Records sold for distribution outside the United States; the retail equivalent price utilized by Company's licensees outside the United States in computing monies to be paid to Company for the Record concerned; provided that in any country where there is no actual suggested retail list price or applicable retail list price, the SRLP shall be deemed to be the price established by band/artist in conformity with the general practice of the recording industry in such country.

Some of the key terms include:

"Advances," "Net Receipts," and *"Recording Costs"* - These may be the most important provisions and definitions in the Agreement. Why? Because they directly determine when and how the band/artist will make money. The band/artist must

be on top of what is being charged to its account *and* how will the Company determine profitability.

"Delivery" - The band/artist must be clear about what the requirements are in delivering the Masters to the Company. If the band/artist does not strictly comply with the requirements, the band/artist may deliver a Master but still be in default under the Agreement.

"EP," "Maxi-Single," and *"New Technology Configurations"* - With the ever-changing technological advances in how to record and how to deliver music, the band/artist needs to be aware of how technology may impact the Sound Recording Agreement.

"Records" and *"Recordings"* - The band/artist must understand what is considered a record or a recording. Usually, just about anything laid down in the studio is considered a record or recording. The result is that the Company will have a claim to all of the recordings.

"Suggested Retail Price" - As discussed, there are a variety of factors that impact how the Suggested Retail Price (the "SRP") is set. For example, there is a different SRP for recordings sold in the United States versus those sold in foreign countries. Also, there is a different SRP for records, CDs, and for digital transmissions. It is imperative for the band/artist, or its management, to have a clear grasp of the royalty structure to avoid either being underpaid or overpaid.

Miscellaneous (Boilerplate).

The Recording Agreement will close with standard "boilerplate" clauses that we have seen before.

Miscellaneous Provisions:

(a) **Approvals or Consents:** Except as otherwise

expressly set forth in this Agreement, wherever in this Agreement band/artist's approval or consent is required, such approval or consent shall not be unreasonably withheld. The Company may require band/artist to formally give or withhold such approval or consent by giving the band/artist written notice requesting same and by making the information or material in respect of which such approval or consent is sought available to band/artist. Band/artist shall give the Company written notice of approval or disapproval within five (5) business days after such notice (unless a shorter period of time is provided elsewhere in this Agreement as to such approval), and in the case of its disapproval, band/artist shall state the reasons therefor. Failure to give such notice to Company as aforesaid shall be deemed to be consent or approval. After the Term, the Company shall not be obligated to secure band/artist's consent to any matter as to which its consent is otherwise required hereunder if band/artist has died or during any period in which band/artist is not reasonably available to respond to Company's requests for consent.

(b)   Amendment. This Agreement may be amended, renewed, or continued only by a writing signed by both parties.

(c)   Attorneys' Fees. Should either party hereto, or any heir, personal representative, successor, or assignee of either party hereto, resort to legal proceedings in connection with this Agreement or Company's relationship with band/artist, the prevailing party shall be entitled to its costs, attorneys' fees, and litigation related expenses.

(d)   Assignment. Band/artist shall have the right to assign this Agreement to a partnership in which band/artist or an entity controlled by band/artist is a general partner; to a joint venture in which band/artist is one of the joint venturers; or to a corporation in which band/artist is one of the controlling principals. Any other assignments will require the Company's approval in writing.

(e)　**Construction**. The headings and captions of this Agreement are provided for convenience only and are intended to have no effect in construing or interpreting this Agreement. The language in all parts of this Agreement shall be in all cases construed according to its fair meaning and not strictly for or against either party.

(f)　**Execution**. Facsimile signatures shall be deemed the original signatures of the parties. The Agreement may be signed in counterparts.

(g)　**Entire Agreement**. This Agreement contains the entire agreement and understanding between the parties hereto and supersedes any prior or contemporaneous written or oral agreements, representations, and warranties between them respecting the subject matter hereof.

(h)　**Governing Law; Venue**. This Agreement shall be governed by and construed in accordance with the laws of the State of New York without regard to conflict of law principles with venue and jurisdiction in New York County, New York.

(i)　**Notices:** All notices to the Company shall be in writing and shall be sent postage prepaid by registered or certified mail, return receipt requested, addressed to:

To the Company: at the address first above written,

with a courtesy
copy to:

Stephen Wade Nebgen, Esq.
The Law Offices of Stephen Wade Nebgen, PLLC
3370 N. Hayden Road,
Suite 123-565
Scottsdale, Arizona 85251

And to band/artist: at the address first above written,

with a courtesy
copy to: [INSERT NAME AND ADDRESS]

Notwithstanding the foregoing, all royalty statements, and payments due hereunder shall be sent to band/artist at such address as set forth above by regular mail.

j.   <u>Rights Cumulative</u>. The rights and remedies provided by this Agreement are cumulative, and the exercise of any right or remedy by either party hereto (or by its successor), whether pursuant to this Agreement, to any other agreement, or to law, shall not preclude or waive its right to exercise any or all other rights and remedies.

k.   <u>Severability</u>. If any term, provision, covenant or condition of this Agreement, or the application thereof to any person, place, or circumstance, shall be held to be invalid, unenforceable, or void, the remainder of this Agreement and such term, provision, covenant, or condition as applied to other persons, places, and circumstances shall remain in full force and effect.

l.   **Waiver**. The failure of a party to exercise a right or remedy or a party's acceptance of a partial or delinquent performance shall not operate as a waiver of any party's rights or obligations under this Agreement and shall not constitute a waiver of the non-defaulting party's right to declare an immediate or a subsequent default.

m.   **No Act Against the Law**. Nothing herein contained shall be construed so as to require the commission of any act contrary to law and wherever there is any conflict between any provision of this Agreement and any present or future statute, law, ordinance or regulation, the latter shall prevail, but in such event the provision of this Agreement affected shall be curtailed and limited only to the extent necessary to bring it within legal requirements.

"Boilerplate" is the first thing that a client will request to be deleted. Yet, it is one of the *last* things that should be deleted. The reader should review the comments on "boilerplate" clauses. In addition to the important clauses such as "attorneys' fees," and "choice of law," some other important clauses are: (i) Notice - there is no way to start the clock ticking, if there is no proper notice; (ii) Execution - the Agreement allows the party to execute the Agreement by Facsimile, which is a very important provision to help facilitate the transaction; and (iii) Entire Agreement - this provision is a nod to the Parol Evidence Rule and also to the Statute of Frauds. Also, electronic signatures are considered legally binding and sufficient.

A very important clause in such boilerplate is the "Assignment" clause. It may seem rather pro forma but it can have huge ramifications. Without this clause, a Company may have trouble in accomplishing a sale of its assets. Similarly, a band/artist may at some time create a new company structure and style of business. In both cases, the Agreement can be assigned to the new entity.

Conclusion.

As is seen, a Sound Recording Agreement is absolutely slanted in favor of the record company and is complex. It is *imperative* that a recording artist get proper legal counsel as to the nuances of any agreement that is presented. Now you can see why Prince acted so passionately in response to Warner Brothers controlling the release of his albums!

CHAPTER 14

MUSIC PUBLISHING AGREEMENT

"The world of music begins with creative effort – the song.
What happens next with that song is the business of music."
-   Todd Brabec & Jeff Brabec[494]

After the band or artist has picked a Personal Manager, chose a producer, and are writing and recording material, it becomes imperative to get a Publisher to exploit the Musical Compositions. What does a Publisher do? As the Brabecs' describe it:

> the role of the Publisher is to exploit the song (get artists to record it; get the song placed in motion pictures, television series, videogames, advertising commercials, ringtones and

ringbacks, dolls and toys, musical greeting cards, etc.); to negotiate the deals with all of those who want to use the song (film and TV producers, advertising agencies, videogame companies, etc.); to protect the song (copyright the song, sue infringers, register the song with ASCAP, Harry Fox Agency, foreign country collection societies, etc.); and to collect all of the song's earnings from all sources (with the exception of the writer's share of performance monies) and pay the songwriter his or her share according to the songwriter/Publisher contract.[495]

There are a variety of music publishing agreements including:

i.   Single Song Agreement

ii.   Exclusive Song Writer Agreement

iii.   Co-publishing Agreement

iv.   Administration Agreement

v.   Collection Agreement

vi.   Sub-Publishing Agreement

vii.   Purchasing Agreement.[496]

In this chapter we will look at a Music Publishing Agreement which will be for a limited term and also is exclusive.

Term.

1. Term:

(a) The term (the "Term") of this Agreement shall commence on the date hereof and shall continue for a period of five (5) years, unless otherwise terminated or extended pursuant to the terms of this Agreement.

Under this provision, the Composer agrees to assign for a limited time, in this case five years, the rights in certain Musical Compositions to the Publisher. But _only_ those Musical Compositions that are listed on the Schedule "A."

A quick point here: if the grant of rights is for a term over forty years, the songwriter should be aware of the power of Section 203 of the Copyright Code, which will allow a grantor the right to terminate the agreement during a limited window beginning 35 years from the date of the grant and closing at 40 years from the date of the grant.[497] Another possibility is to have a reversion clause which will allow the grantor to regain the rights if certain goals or "benchmarks" have not been met.

After the term, the territory of the agreement needs to be addressed.

Territory.

Territory:

The territory covered under this Agreement is the universe (the "Territory").

As is usual, the territory will be the universe.

Subject Compositions.

The next provision addresses what Musical Compositions are covered by the Agreement.

Subject Musical Compositions:

(a) Subject Musical Compositions: Publisher shall have the exclusive rights to the administration of the Subject Musical Compositions (described with more particularity on the attached Exhibit "A") for the length of the Term, and any applicable extensions thereof, in the Territory for each Subject Musical Composition.

(b) With respect to the Subject Musical Compositions that are co-written or Subject Musical Compositions that are co-owned by a party other than Composer, Publisher's rights hereunder shall only extend to the portion of such Subject Musical Compositions written, owned, or controlled by Composer.

(c) With respect to any co-written Subject Musical Compositions, Composer shall cause any co-writer to confirm in writing the division of the percentage ownership interests between Composer and such co-writer(s) and deliver such writing to the Publisher, within five (5) business days of receipt of the document outlining the authorship shares of the co-written Subject Musical Compositions.

Clause (a) addresses what specific Musical Compositions will be covered by the Agreement. Generally, as in this case, the individual Musical Compositions will be listed on an attached Exhibit "A." There are a variety of reasons to do it this way but two come to mind right away: (i) it is better for drafting not to have a long list of Musical Compositions written out in the body of the Agreement, because (ii) you might leave a Musical Composition out or have to change the list from time-to-time.

Clause (b) deals with what happens if there are two or more co-writers of a Musical Composition. In that case, the Publisher's rights only extend to the percentage of the Musical Composition that the Composer has in that particular co-written Musical Composition.

Clause (c) requires the Composer to provide a chart of the division of the percentages on the co-written Musical Composition. Often, this will be in the form of a Song Authorship Agreement or a Split Letter.

In order to be clear of the Musical Compositions at issue, the next paragraph deals with excluded Musical Compositions.

Excluded Musical Compositions:

(a) Composer has written Musical Compositions prior to the execution of this Agreement that will not be considered Musical Compositions and will not be included under this

Agreement (the "Excluded Musical Compositions"). The Excluded Musical Compositions are listed on Exhibit "B" attached to this Agreement.

This paragraph is pretty straight forward – the listed Excluded Musical Compositions will not be subject to this Agreement and the Composer is free to enter in any other agreement regarding the Excluded Musical Compositions.

Now we come to one of the most important paragraphs of the entire Agreement – what are the rights and powers you are giving to the Publisher. As you will see, the grant is broad and powerful.

Rights Granted:

(a) **Publisher shall have the sole and exclusive right to act throughout the Territory as the exclusive publisher and administrator of all rights in and to the Subject Musical Compositions. Such grants shall include, but not be limited to, the following rights:**

(ix) **The right to secure copyright registration and renewal copyright registration with respect thereto under any law now in effect or hereinafter enacted;**

(ii) **All rights of control, including but not limited to, mechanical or other reproduction, synchronization, publication, printing, performances, derivative works, and dispositions, now or hereafter known;**

(iii) **The right to use the name, photograph, likeness, and/or biographical material of the Composer for the purposes of trade or otherwise in connection with the Subject Musical Compositions;**

(iv)   All rights to license, assign, and enter into agreements to or with any person or entity, including but not limited to affiliates of Publisher, with respect to all or a part of the rights contained in this Agreement;

(v)   to execute forms (and other routine copyright documents) in Composer's name and on Composer's behalf as attorney-in-fact (which appointment is coupled with an interest and is therefore irrevocable) and shall give immediate notice of any such use of the power granted under this paragraph to the Composer;

(vi)   All rights to collect any and all monies accruing or earned therefrom other than Composer's shares of performance fees;

(vii)   authorize any fundamental change in the English-language title and/or English-language lyric of a Subject Musical Composition, only with the Composer's approval, not to be unreasonably withheld. If no answer is received from Composer within five (5) days of notification, it will be deemed that approval has been given by Composer;

(viii)   alter the fundamental character of the melody of a Subject Musical Composition;

(ix)   grant any license for the use of any Musical Composition in any commercial or advertisement relating to political parties or candidates, social causes, tobacco, religious matters, or armed forces or in a theatrical motion picture that Publisher has been advised at the time of the applicable license request bears a rating of "NC-17" or a more restrictive rating; or

(x) authorize the so-called "grand rights" (the "Grand Rights") use of any Subject Musical Composition (i.e., the dramatization of the storyline of any Subject Musical Composition).

(b) This statement of exclusive rights is only in clarification and amplification of the rights of Publisher and not in limitation thereof.

(c) Publisher may exercise any right it deems necessary or desirable in connection with the administration, exploitation, or protection of the Subject Musical Compositions.

(d) Publisher and Publisher's foreign subsidiaries, affiliates and licensees have the fullest possible rights to administer and exploit the Subject Musical Compositions, to print, publish, dramatize, use and license any and all uses of the Subject Musical Compositions, to execute in its own name any and all licenses and agreements whatsoever affecting or respecting the Subject Musical Compositions, including but not limited to licenses for mechanical reproduction, public performances, dramatic uses, synchronization uses and sub-publication, and to assign or license such rights to others.

(e) Notwithstanding anything to the contrary contained herein, Publisher shall have no obligation to seek Composer's approval regarding any license for:

(i) any licenses of the Subject Musical Compositions which licenses are subject to the provisions of so-called blanket industry agreements, statutory compulsory licensing requirements, local society rules and regulations, and any current or future blanket licensing agreements

applicable to any portion, or all, of Publisher's catalog of Musical Compositions (and Publisher shall have the unrestricted right, at all times, to enter into any such agreements). Any and all monies derived from the Subject Musical Compositions that are contained within a blanket license shall be paid on a pro-rata basis.

(ii)   Publisher's inadvertent failure to obtain Composer's consent for a license which requires Composer's consent pursuant to this paragraph shall not constitute a breach of this Agreement.

(f)   Droit Morale. Composer waives any so-called "moral rights" which may now be or may hereafter be recognized, as well as any and all claims which it has or may have against Publisher, its sub-licensees, successors, and assigns, by use of the Subject Musical Compositions (attached herein below Exhibit "A"). As such, Composer waives approval rights for the licensed use of the Subject Musical Compositions, by any client, sub-licensee or third-party.

As you can see from the list above, the Composer gives the Publisher a broad grant of rights to do whatever the Publisher believes is the best way to exploit the Musical Composition.

Under Clause (a)(i), the Composer allows the Publisher to file copyrights on behalf of the Composer. Such a right can be of great benefit since you can turn a newly finished song over to the Publisher and they will file the copyright for you.

Under Clause (a)(ii), you grant the Publisher the right to control publication, printing, performance, mechanical or other reproduction, synchronization, sale, exploitation, revision, arrangement, adaptation, translation, use, and disposition. It is so important for the Composer to be aware of the broad grant under this provision.

Under Clause (a)(iii), the Composer grants the Publisher the right to use the likeness of the Composer in exploiting the Musical Composition. Furthermore, the Publisher can portray the Composer in any way the Publisher chooses.

Under Clause (a)(iv), the Publisher can assign the rights related to the catalogue of the Musical Compositions to anyone else or to another entity. Of course, this could be very upsetting to a Composer that has had a special relationship with the Publisher, and now suddenly, the Composer is being handled by someone that the Composer had no prior relationship with.

Under Clause (a)(v), the Publisher is granted the power to execute documents to help facilitate the exploitation of the Musical Compositions. Generally, it is important to have language stipulate that if the Publisher does execute any agreement, the Composer gets notice of the exercise of this right.

Under Clause (a)(vi), the Publisher will receive the royalties from the exploitation of the Musical Composition and then forward the appropriate portion to the Composer. It is important to remember that certain royalties, such as those from performing rights organizations, go directly to the Composer. Another key consideration will be to have an accounting clause to ensure that the Composer receives all the monies that are owed.

Under Clause (a)(vii) and Clause (a)(viii), the Publisher can change the lyrics and/or the music! Obviously, this can be very upsetting to a Composer or lyricist. The creators work hard to craft the harmonies and the lyrics, only to be arbitrarily changed by the
Publisher.

Under Clause (a)(ix), the Publisher has the power to grant licenses, the most common being a "synchronization license" –a license that allows the licensee to use the Musical Composition and "synch" it to a visual image. The key consideration is to try and control how the Musical Composition is "placed." For example, the Composer might try to forbid the Musical Composition being used in an R-Rated or X-Rated film. Also, the Composer might not want the Musical Composition used in a violent movie, television series, or video game.

Under Clause (a)(x), the Publisher can license the "grand rights" – a license to use the Musical Composition for use in a theatrical production. Again, this can be very lucrative to the Composer with royalties from a hit Broadway production.

Clause (b) makes it clear that the list of rights outlined in Clause (a) are not exhaustive and merely an initial statement of rights. However, the Publisher can change this at its discretion.

Clause (c) allows the Publisher to exercise any rights and authorizations in order to exploit the Musical Compositions. Again, it is important for the Composer to negotiate that the Publisher will notify the Composer of any use of this grant.

Clause (d) gives all the powers granted to the original Publisher to any of the Publisher's foreign subsidiaries, affiliates and licensees and they will have the full rights to administer and exploit the Musical Compositions.

Clause (e) states when the Publisher does *not* have to ask for consent: (i) for any license for an Acquired Musical Composition; or (ii) any licenses for blanket licenses under statutory compulsory licensing requirements. The Publisher shall have the unrestricted right, at all times, to enter into any such agreements.

Clause (g) states that, where the Composer's consent *is* needed, any inadvertent failure to gain the consent will not be cause for a breach. Such a clause gives the Publisher a little wiggle room regarding notice. The burden of giving notice usually will be on the Composer to bring it to the Publisher's attention. The Publisher will endeavor to correct the breach in a certain time frame.

Under Clause (h), if the Composer's consent is required for a particular use of the Musical Composition, the Composer's consent shall be deemed to have been granted if Composer does not object to such use within seventy-two (72) hours after Publisher's written request to the Composer for approval. The moral here is for a composer to be aware of any time restrictions and stay aware of the use of the Musical Composition.

A critical issue to remember, although this Agreement is for a limited term, is that most publishing agreements will be much longer, even for the life of the copyright term! But with Section 203 of the Copyright Code, the Composer may terminate the grant during a window beginning in 35th year after the grant and ending during the 40th year after the grant. However, that is still a long time. The better solution is to insert a "reversion clause." A "reversion clause" allows the Composer to get the rights back if certain "benchmarks" are not met. For example, the Publisher must get the Musical Composition recorded by a major artist or generate a certain amount of performance royalties during a stated time frame. If the "benchmarks" are not met, the Composer can file a notice of termination of the grant pursuant to the "reversion" clause.

Another major issue will be the ownership of the copyright of the Musical Compositions.

Assignment and Transfer of Copyright:

(a)   Composer hereby conveys, grants, and assigns exclusively to Publisher, its successors, and assigns, an undivided one hundred percent (100%) of Composer's entire right, title, and interest throughout the Territory for the Term, plus any applicable renewals and/or extensions thereof, including,

without limitation, the copyright, the right to secure copyright registration, and any applicable copyright renewal rights, in and to each of the Subject Musical Compositions.

(b)   Accordingly, without limiting the foregoing, Composer agrees and acknowledges that upon execution of this Agreement, Publisher shall have the sole and exclusive right to (i) administer and exploit the Musical Compositions in any manner or media now known or hereinafter devised, (ii) enter into and execute all agreements regarding the exploitation of the Musical Compositions, and (iii) the right to receive and collect all monies derived from the use and exploitation of the Musical Compositions (except for the "writer's share" of public performance payments).

(c)   Additionally, without limiting the foregoing, Publisher may, in its sole discretion, substitute a new title or titles for the Musical Compositions, make changes, arrangements, adaptations, translations, dramatizations, and transpositions of the Musical Compositions, in whole or in part, and in connection with any other musical, literary, dramatic, or other material, and add new lyrics to the music of the Musical Compositions or new music to the lyrics of the Musical Compositions, provided that Composer is still credited as a writer and still receives a "writer's share" of public performance payments.   Composer agrees and acknowledges that in the event an additional writer contributes to a derivate work of the Musical Compositions, Composer's "writer's share" may be decreased for such work by such additional writer(s) as negotiated in good faith by Publisher.

Composer hereby conveys, grants, and assigns exclusively to Publisher, its successors, and assigns, an undivided one hundred percent (100%) of Composer's entire right, title, and interest throughout the Territory for the Term, plus any applicable renewals and/or extensions thereof, including, without limitation, the copyright, the right to secure copyright registration, and any applicable copyright renewal rights, in and to each of the Subject Musical Compositions.

(d) Accordingly, without limiting the foregoing, Composer agrees and acknowledges that upon execution of this Agreement, Publisher shall have the sole and exclusive right to (i) administer and exploit the Musical Compositions in any manner or media now known or hereinafter devised, (ii) enter into and execute all agreements regarding the exploitation of the Musical Compositions, and (iii) the right to receive and collect all monies derived from the use and exploitation of the Musical Compositions (except for the "writer's share" of public performance payments).

Clause (a) and (b) give the Publisher a broad grant of rights. First, the Composer is granting to the Publisher 100% of the Copyright throughout the Territory for the Term of the Agreement. By doing so, the Composer has given the Publisher carte blanche to do whatever the Publisher wants to do with the Musical Compositions.

The Publisher will be the exclusive entity to administer and exploit the rights connected to the Musical Compositions. But do note that the Composer will retain the "writer's share" of public performance revenue.

Clause (c) gives further rights to the Publisher. Among

other things, the Publisher can change the title, make new arrangements, and can change the lyrics!

What Musical Compositions are being transferred by the Composer to the Publisher is a substantive provision of the agreement.

The next clause deals with an important aspect – Compensation! There are a variety of revenue streams, and each might have a different applicable royalty.

Compensation:

(b)　No advances shall be paid pursuant to this Agreement.

(c)　Publisher agrees to exert reasonable effort to commercially exploit the Musical Compositions and shall pay the following royalties to the Composer:

(i)　Sheet Music. Fifteen (15¢) cents for each sheet music copy, choral parts, instrumentals, or orchestrations thereof manufactured by Publisher and sold and paid for in the U.S.;

(ii)　Songbooks. Twelve and a half percent (12 ½%) of any and all gross sums actually received by Publisher for all songbooks or collections including said Musical Compositions manufactured by Publisher and sold and paid for in the U.S.;

(iii)　International Sales. Fifty percent (50%) of any and all net sums actually received by Publisher from printed uses of the Musical Compositions originating in countries other than the U.S.;

(iv) **Licensing Rights.** Fifty (50%) percent of any and all net sums actually received by the Publisher from the electrical transcription and reproducing rights, motion picture and television synchronization rights and all other rights (excepting public performing rights) therein, including the use thereof in print form, whether sheet music, choral parts, instrumental parts, orchestrations, song books, collections, song lyric folios, magazines, or other special syndications;

(v) **Performance Rights Royalties – Composer's Portion.** Composer shall receive One Hundred Percent (100%) of the Composer's portion of the performance royalties received from any performance rights organization;

(vi) **Performance Rights Royalties – Music Publisher Portion.** Publisher shall receive One Hundred Percent (100%) of the musical publishing portion of the performance royalties received from any performance rights organization;

and

(vii) **Mechanical Royalties.** Fifty (50%) percent of any and all sums actually received by Publisher or its agent, after deduction of collection fees if any charged by such agent, from the exploitation of the mechanical royalty right of the Musical Compositions.

Under Clause (a), the Publisher states that it will use its best efforts to exploit the Musical Compositions. Upon exploitation, the Publisher will pay to the Composer the following royalties:

(i) **Sheet Music.** Fifteen (15¢) cents per sheet;

(ii) **Songbooks.** Twelve and a half percent (12 ½%) of the price of the songbook;

(iii) **International Sales.** Fifty percent (50%);

(iv) **Licensing Rights.** Fifty (50%) percent of the license fee;

(v) **Performance Rights Royalties – Composer's Portion.** Composer shall receive Fifty Percent (50%) of the performance royalties;

(vi) **Performance Rights Royalties – Music Publisher Portion.** Publisher shall receive fifty percent (50%) of the performance royalties; and

(vii) **Mechanical Royalties.** Fifty percent (50%).

As can be seen, there are a variety of royalty rates. The percentages are pretty standard but are subject to negotiation. Taylor Swift will get a better royalty structure than Taylor Slow.

The next clause will deal with the collection of the revenue generated by the exploitation of the Musical Composition.

Collection of Income:

(a) **Publisher will receive and collect all gross receipts (the "Gross Receipts") derived from the Musical Compositions.**

(b) **"Gross Receipts" is defined as any and all revenue, income and sums derived and actually received by Publisher in the United States (after** deduction of any collection or other fees charged by The Harry Fox Agency, Inc., or any other such collection agent which may be used by Publisher anywhere in the United States and Canada, and after deduction of any collection fee or share of royalties charged by any collection agent or sub-publisher used by Publisher outside the United States and Canada) from the exploitation of the Subject Musical Compositions, including without limitation, mechanical royalties, synchronization fees, dramatic use fees, printing income and the Publisher's share of public performance fees.

(c)   In the event Publisher or Publisher's subsidiaries or affiliates in the United States or Canada shall print and sell any printed editions of any of the Musical Compositions, Gross Receipts with respect thereto, for the purposes of this Agreement, shall be deemed to be a royalty on the net paid sales of each printed edition, which royalty shall be equal to the then current royalty generally being paid by print licensees in the United States to unrelated Publishers.

Clause (a) gives the Publisher the right to receive the "Gross Receipts" from the exploitation of the Musical Composition. It is a standard arrangement. "Gross Receipts" will be defined in the next clause. But one important consideration is to have an "Accounting" clause so that the Composer can receive timely statements, a reasonable time to review the statements, the ability to look at the books and records, and to have an accounting.

Clause (b) defines "Gross Receipts." Be aware of how broad the definition is of "Gross Receipts." "Gross Receipt" will include all revenue, income and sums derived and actually received by the Publisher from the exploitation of the Musical Compositions, and will include, among other things, mechanical royalties, synchronization fees, dramatic use fees, printing income and the Publisher's share of public performance fees.

Clause (c) will bring sheet music into the definition of "Gross Receipts."

The next important clause deals with the collection of performance royalties. As mentioned above, performance royalties earned by the Composer come from the right to publicly perform the Musical Composition. The performance royalties are tracked by the performance rights organizations such as ASCAP, BMI, and SESAC.

Under the next section, the collection of the performance royalties is addressed.

Collection of Performance Royalties:

(a)   Public performance rights in and to the Musical Compositions for the United States of America and Canada shall be assigned to, and licenses shall be issued by, the performing rights society with which each party is affiliated.

(b)   Said society shall be and is hereby authorized to collect and receive all monies earned from the public performance of the Subject Musical Compositions in the United States and Canada and shall be and is hereby authorized to collect and receive all monies earned from the public performance of the Subject Musical Compositions in the United States and Canada and shall be and is hereby directed to pay directly to Publisher the entire amount allocated by said society as the publisher's share of public performance fees for the United States

and Canada.

(c)   Publisher is hereby authorized to collect and receive the Publisher's share of all monies earned or payable from the public performance of the Musical Compositions. The payments made by the performing rights society as described above shall be based on the respective agreements between the society and the parties hereto. Composer hereby warrants and represents that it has no un-recouped salaries, advances, compensation, or fees outstanding or recoupable from any other performing rights society.

(d)   If any Musical Composition acquired in whole or in part by Composer during the term hereof or by Publisher under the provisions of this Agreement shall have been written or co- written by a member of a performing rights society other than the society to which the Parties hereto belong, said Musical Composition or the appropriate share thereof shall be a Musical Composition hereunder, co-owned by an affiliate of Composer which shall be a member of said other society, and administered by Publisher's affiliate.

(e)   Annexed hereto as Exhibit "B" is the form of letter of direction and assignment from Composer to ASCAP which shall effectuate the provisions of this paragraph. Composer shall sign and deliver to Publisher copies of said letter simultaneously herewith, and in default thereof Publisher is hereby authorized and empowered by Composer to sign copies of this letter for and on behalf of Composer and submit same to the appropriate society.

Clause (a) states that the performance royalties will be collected by the appropriate performance rights organization **(the "PROs")** and the PROs will issue licenses.

Clause (b) and (c) state that the PRO will pay the Publisher's portion to the Publisher and that the Publisher is entitled to receive its portion.

Clause (d) addresses the issue of new Musical Compositions that are created and if there are multiple composers. Also, it speaks of the situation where one Composer is a member of a performing rights society other than the society to which the Composer that is a party to this agreement belongs. In that case, the co-Composer's PRO will administer that share.

Clause (e) will require the Composer to sign a form of letter of direction and assignment to effectuate the provisions of the clauses above.

The prior clause addressed the collection of performance royalties. The next clause addresses the collection of mechanical royalties.

Collection of Mechanical Royalties:

(a)   Mechanical royalties for the Subject Musical Compositions for the United States and Canada may be collectible by The Harry Fox Agency, Inc. or any other collection agent which may be designated by Publisher, provided, however, that Publisher shall, in the case of any record company in the United States or Canada affiliated with Publisher, issue the mechanical licenses directly to said record company at the then current statutory rate (with such reduced rates for special types of sales or distribution for which Publisher customarily grants reduced rates to nonaffiliated record companies) and collect mechanical royalties directly therefrom, in which case there shall be no collection fee as referred to above.

Pursuant to this clause, mechanical royalties for the Musical Compositions subject to the agreement will be collected by The Harry Fox Agency, Inc. But note that the Publisher, when it comes to a record company, can issue the mechanical licenses directly at the statutory rate, considering the record company's deductions.

Often, a Publisher will assign its rights to a sub-publisher. Here is a typical clause:

Sub-Publishing Agreements:

(a)   Publisher may enter into sub-publishing or collection agreements with, and license or assign this Agreement and any of its rights hereunder and delegate any of its obligations hereunder to, any persons, firms, or corporations in the Territory. If Publisher is or shall be a party to any sub-publishing, collection or administration agreement for any country of the world with a subsidiary or affiliate, such agreement shall be deemed to be an agreement with an unrelated third party and, for the purposes of this Agreement, such agreement shall be deemed to be on a basis no less favorable to Publisher than an agreement providing for the American publisher to receive fifty percent (50%) of the mechanical royalties computed at the source, fifty percent (50%) of public performance royalties computed at the source and ten percent (10%) of suggested retail selling price on printed editions.

The Publisher can enter into a sub-publishing agreement for a variety of activities including collection and administration. However, the terms of any agreement with a third-party will be on terms that are no less favorable for the Publisher.

The next clause is one of the most important in the whole agreement – the "Accounting Clause." A way to look at an Accounting Clause is that it is the "sister" to any royalty provisions. It is imperative that when there is any form of contingent compensation that there is an "Accounting Clause." The reason is simple – you want to be able to make sure you are receiving the royalties to which you are entitled.

Accounting:

(a) Publisher shall compute royalties payable to Composer hereunder as of June 30th and December 31st for each preceding 6 (six) month period during which royalties are received. Publisher will render a statement and pay any royalties, less any recouped advances and any other amounts Composer may owe Publisher and applicable taxes, if any, within sixty (60) days of the end of said period. All royalties shall be paid in United States of America currency. If no royalties are earned by Composer during any given six (6) month period, Publisher shall not be required to render any statement(s) until Composer has earned royalties so that a statement reflecting such royalties is rendered pursuant to this paragraph. Notwithstanding the foregoing, the Parties agree that Composer shall not be entitled to any statement or payment until total accumulated royalties due exceeds Seventy-five Dollars ($75.00). All royalty statements and payments shall be deemed conclusive, final, and binding unless specific objection in writing is given to Publisher within two (2) years after the statement was rendered.

(b) Composer shall have the right to audit the books and records of Publisher with respect to any statement rendered pursuant to this agreement, no more than once during each calendar year. If

Composer chooses to conduct such an audit, Composer shall give Publisher thirty (30) days prior written notice of its desire to conduct said audit and said audit shall be conducted by a certified public accountant or attorney. All royalty statements rendered by Publisher to Composer shall be binding upon Composer and not subject to any objection by Composer for any reason unless specific written objection, stating the basis thereof, is submitted by Composer to Publisher within two (2) years from the date rendered. Composer will not have the right to sue in connection with any accounting or for royalties due during said accounting period unless such suit is commenced not later than one (1) year after the end of that two (2) year period. Initially, the Composer shall bear the costs and expenses of said audit. However, if there is a discrepancy in the accounting equal to or greater than ten percent (10%) in favor of the Composer, the Publisher shall bear the costs of the accounting.

(c) No royalties shall be payable to Composer by Publisher, or any of Publisher's Licensees, until payment of said royalties has been received by Publisher.

(d) Royalties received or credited to Publisher's account outside of the United States shall be computed in the national currency in which Publisher is paid by Publisher's Licensees and shall be credited to Composer's royalty account hereunder at the same rate of exchange as Publisher is paid and shall be proportionately subject to any transfer or comparable taxes which may be imposed upon Publisher's receipts.

The "Accounting Clause" is one of the most important clauses in the agreement. As mentioned above, when there is a royalty involved the Composer will want to make sure that he/she is properly receiving the royalties owed.

Clause (a) requires the Publisher to provide timely statements regarding the status of royalties. Under this agreement, the statements are semi-annual. It is common to have quarterly statements. Note that print royalties will only be paid to the Composer once a year – a reason could be that there are only insignificant amounts generated by print sales.

Clause (b) contains an important provision regarding contesting a statement. Under this agreement, the statement will be considered binding unless the Composer brings an objection within two years from the date it is rendered. So, it is especially important to be aware of this time period. Also, it can be a point of negotiation – many times the Publisher will want a period of only one year. Try to negotiate out of such an abbreviated period – it does not give the Composer a reasonable time to review the statement.

Clause (b) also states that the Composer can audit the books and records of the Publisher. The Composer must give thirty days' notice to the Publisher. The initial cost of the accounting will be paid by the Composer, but in many agreements there will be a clause that says that if there is a discrepancy of ten percent (10%) or more, the Publisher will have to pay for the audit.

Clause (c) states that no royalties will be paid until the Publisher has actually received the royalty. For a Composer, this can be particularly frustrating when the Musical Composition is a hit, but the revenue takes months to flow in.

Clause (d) is necessary as the globalization of the music market is growing. Consequently, the royalties outside the United States will be computed in the national currency in which Publisher is paid by licensees. The savvy Composer will be aware of this clause and its effect on the actual royalty receive

Breach; Cure; Termination.

Another important clause is how to terminate the Agreement if the relationship between the Composer and the Publisher goes sour.

Breach; Cure; Termination:

(a)   Breach and Cure. Neither Party will be deemed in breach unless the other Party gives notice and the notified Party fails to cure within thirty (30) days after receiving notice (15 days, in the case of a payment of money); provided, that if the alleged breach does not involve a payment of money and is of such a nature that it cannot be completely cured within thirty (30) days, the notified Party will not be deemed to be in breach if the notified Party commences the curing of the alleged breach within such thirty (30) day period and proceeds to complete the curing thereof with due diligence within a reasonable time thereafter.

(b)   Injunctive Relief. Neither Party shall have the right to seek injunctive relief to prevent a threatened breach of this Agreement by the other Party. All payments required to be made by Publisher hereunder shall be subject to any rights and/or remedies that may otherwise be available to Publisher in the event of a breach of this Agreement on Composer's part not cured in the manner prescribed above, and to any withholding that may be required by the rules and regulations of any taxing jurisdiction having authority.

(c)   Termination – Cause. Either Party may terminate the Agreement if:

(i)   A Party defaults on any payment obligation hereunder and does not cure such default within thirty (30) of receiving written notice thereof; or

(ii)   Immediately for "Cause." "Cause" shall be defined as any of the following:

b.   intentional act of fraud, embezzlement, theft, or any other material violation of law that occurs during or in the course of the Term of this Agreement;

c.   intentional damage by one Party to other Party's assets;

d.   intentional disclosure of either Party's confidential information; or

e.   willful conduct by either Party that is demonstrably and materially injurious to the other Party's reputation or company, monetarily or otherwise.

(d)   Effect of Termination for Cause.

(i)   If the termination of the Agreement is for Cause, the Agreement shall be immediately terminated. The Party causing the breach for Cause shall:

A.   forfeit any and all monies due to that Party for the period prior to the breach; and

B. forfeit any and all monies that may be due subsequent to the breach.

(ii) The non-breaching Party shall be allowed to continue to use the intellectual property of the breaching Party without further compensation to the breaching Party.

It is so important to address the issue of termination. In clause (a) the Agreement states the requirements of giving notice and allowing the breaching Party time to "cure," i.e., time to make good on the broken promise.

Clause (b) will deny the Party that has been harmed to file for injunctive relief. The only relief to the Party that has been harmed is to seek money damages. There are pluses and minuses to this clause, depending upon which side of the dispute you are on. But this is a clause that is standard and not subject to negotiation.

Clause (c) addresses the grave issue of when the breach is for Cause. A simple example is when you find out the Publisher has been improperly holding or even spending monies owed to the Composer. In that case, the Composer will want to terminate immediately – there will be no "cure" period for a breach of Cause. Think about it – do you really want to stay in business with someone who stole from you?

Clause (d) outlines the penalties that can be imposed upon the breaching party, among them, no more money to the Publisher and any rights given to the Publisher are terminated.

The Breach and Cure provisions will tie in with the next important clause – the "Reversion Clause."

Reversion Clause.

(a) Composer shall have the following reversion rights:

(i) In the event that Composer has not earned _____ U.S. Dollars ($_____) collectively for a Subject Musical Composition as a direct result of Publisher's efforts within five (5) years from the Effective Date, Publisher agrees to transfer ownership of such under earning Subject Musical Composition back to Composer, provided that Composer provides at least sixty (60) days' notice to Publisher. Notwithstanding the foregoing, such reversion notice may only be given within two (2) years after such five (5) year period.

(b) Without limiting the foregoing, the Parties agree and acknowledge that if Composer fails to provide notice within the time periods specified above for any under earning Subject Musical Compositions, then Publisher shall remain owner of such Subject Musical Compositions and this Agreement as it pertains to such Subject Musical Composition shall continue with full force and effect;

(c) Notwithstanding the foregoing, Publisher may, within either of the above sixty (60) day periods, elect to pay Composer the difference between the above mentioned applicable minimum earnings and the actual earnings, if any, for each under earning Subject Musical Composition, in which case Publisher shall remain owner of such Subject Musical Composition and this Agreement as it pertains to such Subject Musical Composition shall continue with full force and effect;

(d)   All payments made by Publisher in fulfillment of the minimum earning requirement shall be considered advances against future royalties and recoupable therefrom. Publisher shall in good faith have final say over whether earnings are a direct result of Publisher's efforts.

(e)   Without limiting the foregoing, the Parties agree and acknowledge that direct payments to Composer of the "writer's share" of public performance payments, along with all payments from Publisher in connection with a Subject Musical Composition, shall be counted toward the accrual of earnings required to achieve the minimum earning requirements;

(f)   Upon the reversion of a Subject Musical Composition as provided above, all rights in and to such Subject Musical Composition, including all copyrights, shall revest in and become the sole property of Composer, free of any and all encumbrances, except that Publisher shall still be entitled to collect and retain one hundred percent (100%) of the "publisher's share" of public performance income from the Subject Musical Composition in perpetuity throughout the Territory only for placements or other opportunities that Publisher procured. Publisher shall in good faith have final say over whether Publisher procured a placement or other opportunity. Without limiting any other rights herein, prior to reversion of a Subject Musical Composition and/or Publisher executing any document transferring copyright in a Subject Musical Composition back to Composer, Composer shall sign and deliver a letter of direction to BMI, ASCAP, and

417

SESAC (as applicable) instructing direct and perpetual payment to Publisher of one hundred percent (100%) of the "publisher's share" of public performance income throughout the Territory for placements of such Subject Musical Composition that Publisher procured; and

(g) Notwithstanding the foregoing, for the avoidance of doubt, reversion of the rights in and to the Subject Musical Compositions are (i) subject to the terms of any and all licenses already granted to third parties pursuant to this Agreement, and (ii) shall in no way affect any licenses entered into in accordance with this Agreement, including, without limitation, Publisher's right to receive and collect monies derived from such licenses.

Clause (a) grants the Composer to terminate the Agreement and have his/her rights "revert" back – they will get all their rights back. Clause (a)(i) is especially important. The clause refers to goals the Publisher must meet, or the Composer can terminate the Agreement. Such goals referred to as "benchmarks." If the Publisher does not meet the "benchmarks," the Composer can terminate the Agreement by giving notice.

Clause (b) puts the duty on the Composer to give proper notice of the termination and reversion. If proper notice is not given then the clause will not be enforced.

Clause (c) does give the Publisher a chance to cure; namely, by giving the Composer an amount of money that would meet the benchmarks.

Clause (d) is interesting. If the Publisher does make a payment to meet the benchmarks, it will be deemed an "advance" against what is owed to the Composer!

Clause (e) states that the "writer's share" of royalties will count towards the benchmarks.

Clause (f) addresses what happens after the reversion clause has been exercised. All rights will revert to the Composer, *but* the Publisher still retains the "publisher's" share of any revenue from efforts of the Publisher. As we saw in the context of a Personal Manager, if possible, it is good to get a "sunset" clause. But Clause (f) in this Agreement states that the Publisher will receive its share of monies that result from the efforts of the Publisher during the Term in perpetuity.

Clause (g) protects any third-party that the Publisher has entered in an agreement or granted a license. The termination and reversion of the Agreement will not affect the third-party agreements.

The balance of the Agreement will be comprised of the "boilerplate" language we discussed above in the chapter on Contracts. Key ones will be Warranties and Representations, particularly that the Composer has all the rights in the Musical Compositions and there are no claims against the Musical Compositions. And another key one is Indemnification in case a Warranty or Representation turns out to be false. A final key provision is the Notice provision – how and where do you tell the other party to the Agreement that something is wrong? If proper notice is not given, then the other party has a defense against any action that the other party might take.

And any comment on "boilerplate" must mention an "Attorneys' Fees" clause. It is so important to have this clause that in some jurisdictions, if you do not have the clause, the attorney can open to a claim of malpractice! Please review the comments on an Attorneys' Fee Clause in the section on Contracts.

Attached to many music publishing agreements will be an Assignment. It will be something similar to the following.

Assignment

ASSIGNOR:

ASSIGNEE:

PORTION CONVEYED: An undivided 50% of Copyright, Plus 100% of Administration Rights.

For valuable consideration, ASSIGNOR hereby assigns, transfers, sets over, and conveys to ASSIGNEE an undivided 50% interest in ASSIGNOR's share of the Musical Compositions listed on the annexed Schedule, together with the exclusive worldwide administration rights in such share in accordance with the terms and conditions of the Music Publishing Agreement between the Parties of even date herewith.

This assignment includes the copyrights and proprietary rights in said Musical Compositions and in any and all versions thereof, and any renewals and extensions thereof (whether presently available or subsequently available as the result of intervening legislation) in the United States of America and elsewhere throughout the world, and further including any and all causes of action for infringement of the same, past, present, and future, and all proceeds from the foregoing accrued and unpaid and hereafter accruing.

IN WITNESS WHEREOF, the undersigned has executed the foregoing Assignment as of the _____ day of _____, 20____

Conclusion

For song writers/composers, the Music Publishing Agreement is of tremendous importance – the money to be earned from songwriting is considerable. In 2021, and continuing into 2022, huge artists have sold the catalogues of their songs (note the difference between the Sound Recordings and the Music Publishing separation of revenue sources). Some examples include Sting selling his catalogue of Musical Compositions to Universal Music Publishing Group for Three Hundred Million Dollars ($300,000,000.00)[498]; Bruce Springsteen selling *both* the rights to his recorded music and the song rights to Sony Music for Five Hundred Million Dollars ($500,000,000.00)[499]; and Bob Dylan selling his catalog of recorded music for One Hundred Fifty Million Dollars ($150,000.000.00)[500]. That is a nice payday for the songwriters!

Another aspect to music publishing is the longevity of the revenue streams generated by the Musical Composition. A great recent example is the song "It's a Lovely Day" by *Bill Withers*. By an unofficial count, through 2021 and into 2022, the song has been used in at least four national commercials, was covered by Demi Lovato on live national television during President Biden's Inauguration; and used for the "in and out's" of the commercials run during the NBA playoffs of 2021. Conservatively, that song made hundreds of thousands of dollars and yet the Sound Recording came out in 1977. With the recent use of the Musical Composition, sales and streams have increased exponentially through the renewed interest in the Musical Composition.

To the greatest extent possible, a songwriter/band should try to control their music publishing rights. But here, the key element will be leverage - Taylor Swift gets a music publishing deal that Taylor Slow does not. The infamous "360 Deal" of a Record Label Contract will require the recording artist to give the music publishing to the music publishing division of the label. So, the label makes money on the sale of the Sound Recordings *and* the revenue streams from music publishing.

As mentioned above under Revenue Streams, music publishing in a major source of the monies to be made in the music industry. Try at all costs to keep as much control of the music publishing as possible.

CHAPTER 15

ON TOUR

"A lot of people can't stand touring but to me it's like breathing - I do it because I'm driven to it."
- Bob Dylan

"On the road again. Just can't wait to get on the road again."
- Willie Nelson[501]

Now we get to some really fun stuff! The stories, legends, and apocryphal myths of bands on the road are legion. Some of the more outrageous ones that *are* true are:

Ozzy Osbourne: Ozzy has two heads on his wall - in 1981, he bit off the head of a dove after a signing a record deal; in 1982, a bat flew near the stage and he bit

423

its head off. He thought the bat was a plastic toy - afterwards he had to be treated for rabies.[502]

Vanilla Fudge/Led Zeppelin (the "mudshark incident"): This story has a central core - a groupie was allegedly defiled with a mudshark in a hotel room in Seattle, Washington. However, both Vanilla Fudge and Led Zeppelin were in the hotel and both bands claim the story.[503]

The Who (Keith Moon's birthday): on August 23, 1967, Keith Moon and The Who were celebrating Moon's 21st Birthday at the Holiday Inn in Flint, Michigan. By the end of the night, Moon had blown up a toilet in his room, chipped a tooth running from the Sheriff's Department, and drove a car into the pool.[504]

On a serious note, there are three sides to the issue of live performances: (i) the Place; (ii) the Promoter; and (iii) the Performer. We will call it the Tour Triangle. And like another famous triangle - the Bermuda Triangle - it may seem easy to get in, but it can be a nightmare to escape.

In this chapter, we will focus on the Performer side of the Triangle.

As mentioned in Chapter 3 regarding the various revenue streams, touring is a gold mine. Often acts continue to generate significant revenue long after having any type of popular hit. Throughout this chapter, The Rolling Stones are a model of the lucrative revenue of touring. In almost every significant area of touring, the Rolling Stones were the first, or among the first, to exploit and monetize it.

One of the biggest things the Stones did was to recruit tour sponsors.[505] The Rolling Stones developed a mobile app for the "50 and Counting" tour, in conjunction with Citibank.[506] Other major sponsors such as Budweiser, Citibank, and Ameriquest have put their names on a Stones tour. Rascall Flatts wears the clothes of JC Penney's brand, American Living.[507] In 2006, the value of tour sponsorships in North America reached $1.38 billion.[508] It has only increased since.

Another example: in May of 2010, The Rolling Stones re-released "Exile on Main Street." The Stones surrounded the re-release with a huge merchandising avalanche of more than one hundred items. The items included baseball caps, boxes containing signed lithographs, album-cover T-shirts, and "as worn by" clothing items.[509]

Speaking of clothing - it is *de riguer* for recording artists to have their own clothing label. And those clothes are going to be worn on stage and then sold at the concert for even more money than "new" versions of the clothes would cost.

The Market.

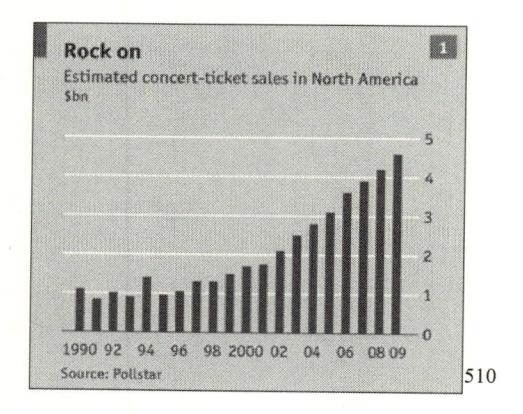

Rock on
Estimated concert-ticket sales in North America
$bn

Source: Pollstar
510

However, there is a big caveat to these figures - it is not that more people came to the concerts. Rather, fewer people paid more money for a ticket. Pollstar tracks ticket sales for the concert industry. According to their research, in 1996 a ticket to one of America's top 100 concert tours cost $25.81. By 2009, the actual cost of a ticket had risen to $62.57.[511] The Rolling Stones concert in 1970 in Toronto cost approximately $8. Tickets for the 50th anniversary tour in Toronto started at $166.50, with the priciest spots listed for upwards of $600 a seat.[512]

Another nuance to ticketing is the concentration of power in a limited number of ticket sellers. With the merger of Ticketmaster and Live Nation, Live Nation is now the major ticket seller for live concerts. Pearl Jam famously took on Live Nation prior to the merger but has now had to make peace with the ticket giant and allows Live Nation to sell its concert tickets.

The effects of the merger are already being made known. Most recently, tickets for Taylor Swift's new Eras Tour went on sale in November 2022 for verified fans with a pre-sale code. This is a practice designed to allow "real people" to obtain tickets before scalpers start buying them in large numbers during the public sale. But due to Swift's popularity, 3.5 million people pre-registered – the largest registration in history. Heavy traffic almost immediately crashed Ticketmaster's site – both from the substantial number of verified fans as well as from bot attacks. Ticketmaster was not loading, would not allow the verified fans to access tickets, and to the extent they did, even took away tickets in their shopping cart if a second party purchased them while the first was attempting to pay. Two days later, Ticketmaster called off the sale to the general public due to the high demands on the system and the extraordinarily low number of remaining tickets in inventory – leaving thousands, if not millions, disappointed. As of this writing, the *New York Times* reports that the Department of Justice has opened an antitrust investigation into Live Nation, regarding whether it had abused its power over the live music industry via monopoly.

No matter the state of the economy, there is still a large amount of money spent by concert goers to see the "Show." Variety reports that, "[t]he global concert business scored a record year (2013) with the top twenty tours, earning $2.43 billion in primary ticket sales. It generated $1.96 billion in 2012.[513]

However, it will be interesting to see how the numbers rebound after the Covid pandemic shut down live performances.

The Agreements.

Two different documents come into play regarding a live performance: (i) the Appearance or Performance Agreement; and (ii) the Rider. The Appearance Agreement is a straightforward document that establishes the time and dates for the band/artist to perform. The Rider is a document from the band/artist to the promoter of the show, indicating what the band/artist needs to put on the performance.

Dates.

Performance Dates:

Date(s) of Performance: **From:** ___/___/___

To: ___/___/___

Time of Performance: **From:** _____a.m./p.m.

To: _____a.m./p.m.

The first thing the Agreement does is establish the date and time of the performance or performances. Sometimes the performance may be a single appearance; at other times, it might be a "run" of performances. It is important to make it clear what is expected from the performer.

Description of Performance:

See the attached Exhibit "A" and attendant Rider.

Another overlooked item in the Agreement is to describe with particularity just what type of performance is expected from the band/artist. For example, is it a "solo" concert or with a full band/artist? An "electric" concert or an "acoustic" set; a full "set" or "bare bones?" All these questions must be addressed to avoid any controversy later.

Place.

Place of Event/Performance:

Name of Venue:

Address: City, State Zip

Phone Number for Venue Contact:

Another item that needs to be explicitly stated is, "Where are we going to play?" This fact needs to be addressed with specificity since many large venues have multiple performance areas. If you play at a large casino, it makes a significant difference between playing a large "showroom" versus a small "lounge." In one case, one of the authors had a client who was hired to play at a major college football game. However, it became a huge issue whether the client would play inside or outside the stadium. The performer cannot assume anything.

Compensation and Payment.

The most important clauses of all, to the performer are the ones that answer the questions "_How much_ am I going to make?" and "_When_ do I get paid?"

Compensation: _____ **Dollars**
($_____)
(the "Compensation").

Payment.

The Venue shall pay to the Performer the

agreed upon Compensation for performance of the Services within thirty (30) days after the Performance, upon the Venue's approval of Services in accordance with Federal and State law.

The issue of Compensation has many nuances. For example, compensation might be dependent upon attendance figures, (*e.g.,* if 10,000 people, then the band/artist gets $100,000.00, if there are 20,000, the band/artist gets $200,000.00). Compensation might also include both a "flat fee" component and a "contingent" component. Other important nuances could include profit participation in "streaming" revenue from the broadcast of the concert, or participation in the sales of DVD's and CD's from the concert.

For small clubs, many of the club owners will require the band/artist to sell a certain number of tickets. The band/artist will then be allowed to keep a certain percentage as compensation. In effect, the band/artist is creating the means to pay itself!

The currency the performer will receive can also become a major problem. Performers, and particularly American performers, want to be paid in American dollars. So, an issue arises regarding the exchange rates of currency where, for example, the concert is taking place in Europe: what is the conversion rate to convert a Euro into an American dollar, and what fees are associated with the conversion?

When the performer gets paid is also of great contention. The band/artist obviously wants to be paid before the gig, and no later than the conclusion of the gig. The promoter wants to have a grace period to make sure there is time to account for any problems in the box office. A happy balance between the two points of view can sometimes be hard to strike.

Check In.

The Performer or the Road Personal Manager shall call the Venue:

    Office phone: _____

    Home phone: _____,

    Or cell phone: _____,

between the hours of ____ a.m. and _____ p.m. preceding the performance, stating time of arrival, place of lodging, mode of transportation, and name under which lodging will be registered. Within forty-eight (48) hours of the event, the Performer or its Representative shall provide Venue with information regarding time of arrival, if available. A good quality show is predicated on excellent communication between Performer and Venue.

If a rehearsal or sound check is required, the Performer must be at the performance site no later than four (4) hours before scheduled performance. If no rehearsal or sound check is necessary, the Performer may be present sixty (60) minutes prior to performance. All rehearsals and sound checks must be completed at least sixty (60) minutes prior to performance.

A common concern is that musicians do not have the greatest reputation for reliability and punctuality. Consequently, a proper performance agreement will require the performer, or her representative, to check in and make sure the band/artist is on time. The promoter will also want the performer to show up in a timely manner regarding a sound check and other logistical issues.

Responsibility of Performer's Equipment.

(a) The Venue is not responsible for any equipment or service not specifically stated in this Agreement.

The promoter is not going to take responsibility for the performer's equipment. It is up to the performer to get insurance on the equipment. The performer has the responsibility for the equipment on tour, *and,* also once it enters the performance venue.

Force Majeure.

(a) The Performer will not be liable for failure to appear, present, or perform, if such failure is caused by or due to the disability or illness or accident of Performer, or acts or regulations of public authorities, labor difficulties, civil tumult, strike, epidemic, interruption, or delay of public transportation service, acts of God, or any cause beyond the reasonable control of either party. It is also agreed that both parties are to make their "best efforts" in order to present the program as scheduled.

As commented on earlier, a *force majeure* clause is particularly important to both parties. The promoter does not want to have to pay a performer if the concert hall burns down. And, conversely, the performer does not want to have liability for a performance if a snowstorm prevents them from getting to the gig.

Tour Rider Agreement.

The Tour Rider (the "Rider"), although often overlooked, is of great importance. The Rider tells the promoter what the performer is going to need to put on a first-class show. Most Riders are straight-forward . . . but then there are the types that make the tabloids. One of the most famous (infamous?) is the Rider of Iggy Pop. It is a long, rambling document that, along with important technical and backstage provisions, contains commentaries on a multitude of topics, various doodlings and drawings, and inside humor. For example, in describing how to set up Iggy's dressing room, the directions to the staff read as follows: "just let someone loose with a little bit of artistic flair...Er, do you know any homosexuals?" You can find the Rider at http://www.thesmokinggun.com/documents/crime/lust-laughs.

On a more serious note, the Rider will be broken into two sections: (i) a section on technical requirements; and (ii) a section on what is needed backstage and, if applicable, lodging, transportation, and food.

Technical Requirements.

The first part of the Rider will address the technical requirements of the performer in putting on the show.

SECTION A: TECHNICAL RIDER PROVISIONS

Personnel

Please provide the following minimum personnel:

Head Sound Technician: One qualified person to run the board and be in charge of the sound. This person should be familiar with in-ear monitor systems, and multi-channel wireless headset systems.

Lighting Technician: The lighting technician will also be required to follow cues from the script for some basic lighting changes.

(Optional: If available, a stagehand to assist with opening the curtain and firing the fog machine would be helpful.)

Sound System

The Group will require either the house system or a system provided by a professional third-party. The system must be approved by _____ Entertainment (_____) thirty (30) days in advance of the show.

Note: The Promoter and Venue must make provisions for sound to be mixed from Front of House (i.e., not from the side of the stage or from a sound booth but from the middle or directly in back of the audience - lower level if multi-level seating).

Speakers:

• A two- or three-way system sufficient to provide full coverage of the venue with 110 decibels at the mixing console.

• Frequency response of 40 to 20k hertz

• Appropriate power

Console:

A 24 channel (4 aux, 2 pre, 2 post, or all pre-faders) professional quality (Yamaha, Sound craft, Soundtracs). The console must be capable of at least two separate monitor mix sends. Note: if other bands are present, console should have enough capacity to meet the needs of the Group's rider on separate, discrete tracks so that once sound check is completed, their channels are not adjusted for other bands.

Rack:

- 3 - 1/3 octave graphic equalizers (Klark Technic, Ashley)

- 1 revs (spx 90 or 9000, lexicon)

- 2 stereo or 4 single compressors (dbx, Rane, bss only)

- If the system is in stereo, one more equalizer is required.

Monitors:

In Ear System:

The Group usually arrives with their own wireless in-ear monitor system. The sound tech should be familiar with such systems. At the time of printing, the Group is using _____ In Ear Monitors. The transmitter rack is usually located on stage in the wing. The Group use the system in mono mode. The transmitters require an XLR in. The system is multiple frequency, UHF.

_____ will require a separate monitor mix from the board (delivered to the stage via a balanced, unpowered monitor return line).

_____ in-ear monitor is usually handled by the Group and does not go through the board.

Stage Monitors:

• Two monitors are required in case of technical problems with the Group's in-ear system, as well as to provide sound to the stage for any guest audience members that appear on stage.

• 12 and horn or 15 and horn

• Sufficient power to drive monitors undistorted to 110 decibels

• Frequency response 40 to 20k hertz

• 2 Monitor mixes

Wireless Mics:

In most cases, the Group will arrive with their own wireless headset system. The system is racked with the in-ear monitor system and is usually kept on the stage in the wing. The system provides a balanced XLR output. At the time of printing, the system is a UHF Sennheiser system.

Please also provide a minimum of one quality hand-held wireless microphone system as a backup. This mic will be located on a boom stand, downstage center and can be used by the announcer/emcee where applicable.

Wireless Guitar System:

In most cases, the Group will arrive with their own wireless guitar system. At the time of printing, this system is a UHF Samson Airline Guitar system operating at a frequency of 804.75 MHz. Please ensure that this frequency is kept clear.

CONTACT US ASAP IF THIS IS A PROBLEM.

Other Microphones and Stands:

As per Microphone Chart and Stage Plot

CD Player:

The Group will arrive with their own CD player which is controlled by a foot pedal remote control from the stage. Another CD player should be available at the board to roll pre-roll music and as an emergency backup for the Group's system.

Misc:

- All necessary cables and cords (snake, mic cables, speaker cables, and power cables)

- Sufficient power to console, rack, and amplifiers

- Stage AC power drop of at least one 15-amp circuit as indicated on plot

- Staging

Stage:

The stage must be sturdy and safe, with no gaps or sags.

SANDBAGS: IMPORTANT!!!!

For concerts outside of the _____ area, Promoter must supply 2 large or four small sandbags which will be used for the "Boom Box" prop. This can alternatively be stage weights. 4 x 15-pound sandbags would be perfect.

Risers:

If available, two 4' x 8' riser at a height of roughly 24" will be used to hold the Boom Box prop (no people will be on this riser). These measurements are somewhat flexible. We will do our best to make it work with what you have available. PLEASE call us if you have questions.

Tables:

Two small tables are usually required: (one to hold the wireless gear and one which will be used as a stage prop). We are very flexible with the specifications of these tables; however, ideally, the stage prop table will be covered with a dark cloth, will be approximately 3 or 4 feet long and will be on rollers. Prop tables will likely also be required in the wings.

Stairs:

The Group usually brings one or more members of the audience up onto the stage. Also, the Group often ventures into the audience during the show. Wherever possible, stairs should be provided to the stage from the audience to facilitate this.

Lighting and Effects:

Please have a few different washes available. It is usually helpful to have amber-gelled specials on _____, _____, and the _____ (see stage plot). The Boom Box requires a special, tightly focused lens at its mouth. The lighting technician will flicker this light as the Boom Box talks (according to a script which will be provided at the time of the show). The show will usually end with a "discomania-like" megamix. Please be prepared to give us as wild a chase as you can (including the house, if possible). Any moving lights will be appreciated for this final medley. Also, a hazer, if available, will be used for this part of the show.

Smoke Machine:

Stage left wing which can be fired from the lighting board or by a stagehand.

IMPORTANT: Promoter is responsible for ensuring that smoke machine will not trigger a false fire alarm.

Call Time / Sound Check:

Call time will be arranged with the Group prior to the date of the concert.

Load-in for sound, lights, and staging should be well underway before the Group arrives so that the crew can concentrate on loading in the Group's gear and assisting them with setup when they arrive. The Group typically arrives approximately 2.5 hours before curtain. Sound check typically commences approximately 60-90 minutes before curtain.

Stage Plot and Mic Chart:

The Stage Plot and Mic Chart (on the following page) form part of this Rider. Please contact us immediately if you have not received the entire Tech Rider.

Keyboard Note:

Please note that you need not provide a keyboard. A keyboard is sometimes part of the show and sometimes not at the Artists discretion. However, if a keyboard is used, the band/artist will provide one unless other arrangements have been made.

CHOIR NOTE:

For some shows, a children's choir will accompany the Group. Usually this will mean a few extra microphones for the choir (hanging, if possible), plus one or two solo choir mics. Also, the choir set-up benefits from an extra pair of monitors in a sidewash configuration. Usually, the presenter is aware as to whether or not the Group will be bringing a choir; however, if you are unsure,

please do not hesitate to contact
_____.

Standard Stage Plot:

Note: For special shows, please add 3-4 choir mics mid-stage canter (hanging if possible) and an additional pair of monitors. Two additional standard vocal mics on stands would also be needed for choir solos.

MICROPHONE/CHANNEL CHART (STANDARD DUO):

Channel Description   Type: Snake Insert

- 2 Vox Wireless headset (provided by artist) Compressor

- Key (not in every show) DI

- Acoustic DI Compressor

- Spare MicWireless Beta 58 or better Compressor

- CD Left Ch. XLR Out

- CD Right Ch. XLR Out

- (Plus, extra mics for choir if applicable)

Monitor Mixes: Please note: If necessary, wedges can be the same mix. However, _____ will require a separate mix for an in-ear monitor. _____ in-ear monitor mix will be handled

directly by the band/artist and will not go through the board.

Regarding technical requirements, the first thing that the performer is going to demand is professional and competent sound and light personnel. There is nothing more frustrating to BOTH the performer and the audience than not being able to see or hear the performance. So, the band/artist is rightfully demanding a "Head Lighting Technician" and a "Sound Technician."

The performer has to list the sound and light equipment with specificity. It is imperative that the band/artist tell the venue what its technical needs are. If the venue is unable to meet those needs, the band/artist needs to be aware of the shortcomings so that it may take steps to correct the insufficiencies.

In this rider, the band/artist is requesting certain types of speakers, sound board, rack, and monitors. For example, the sound board must be 24-channel, the rack must be able to take certain types of equipment, and the band/artist will bring its own "in-ear" system while the venue must supply the on-stage monitors.

An important item addressed in this Rider is that of wireless guitars. Such guitars are common now and allow the band/artist to be more mobile, both on stage and even moving out into the audience. If such guitars will be used, it is essential for the band/artist to let the venue know so that the proper technical steps are accomplished by the venue.

The Rider will list special items that the band/artist will need on stage, such as a CD player and a smoke machine. Again, it is important to give a heads up to the venue regarding any "specialties." In today's world people take CGI (computer generated imagery) and special effects as rote, a band/artist often wants to put on a flashy technological accompaniment - electric sparks, flames, lasers, etc. Local governing agencies and venues may have rules about what is and is not permitted due to size, fire hazards and other issues. The last thing a band/artist wants is to arrive at a venue only to find out that the special effects they use are not allowed.

The Rider will also deal with issues related to the stage - it must be of a certain width and depth and be secure in its construction. Also, the Rider makes it clear that the stage should have no holes or weak spots. It is amazing the conditions (or lack thereof) that the authors' own clients have encountered. The band/artist must make it clear that safe conditions are a mandatory condition for doing the show. Put it in writing - it will make an enormous difference when you have to fight over the condition of the stage.

In this particular Rider, the performance will include a choir. Consequently, the band/artist is requesting risers for the choir, tables for certain items on the stage, and a staircase for when the band/artist may wish to bring an audience member up on stage. The last item is of special note - if the band/artist is going to do some special staging, it must let the venue know. There are fire regulations that must be followed and other nuances that must be acknowledged. Also addressed here are the requirements for lighting - in this case, the request to make sure there are a variety of light effects available.

The Rider then turns to the stage plot and microphone chart. Each band/artist should have a diagram of how the stage needs to be set up. It is also important to give an indication of the number of microphones needed on stage and how they are to be deployed. Also, the Rider addresses a special need regarding the keyboards - in this case, the band/artist will bring a keyboard if one is needed. However, many times the venue will be required to provide an instrument, usually a grand piano.

The band/artist does not want to have to travel with an expensive grand piano, so it will make the venue rent one for the performance.

The technical requirements conclude in this Rider with the layout of the microphones and the chart of microphone lines. It establishes the channel, the type of connection, and the snake insert needed, if any.

The Rider then turns to the Backstage requirements.

SECTION B: GENERAL RIDER PROVISIONS

Accommodations:

If the contract stipulates that the Promoter is to provide accommodations, then they must be provided according to the following guidelines: Accommodation must be at a four-star facility in a no-smoking and pet hair free room (_____ has a severe allergy to pet hair). Promoter will be responsible for all room charges and tax; however, band/artist will be responsible for any incidentals. Where accommodation is for longer than two nights, room must be a suite equipped with kitchen facilities. Any exceptions to these guidelines must be approved in advance by the Artists.

Transportation:

If the contract stipulates that the Promoter is to provide air transportation, then it must be provided according to the following guidelines: Flights within Canada should be booked on Air Canada, an Air Canada affiliate, or WestJet whenever possible. Flights times and details must be

coordinated with the office of All Together Now Entertainment (see below). Please note that we avoid some airlines, such as Jetsgo, which has baggage requirements that will not allow for the Artists' equipment without major additional expenses. If Promoter insists on such an airline, then Promoter may be responsible for these additional baggage charges. For ground transportation, unless otherwise agreed to in advance, Promoter will provide a minivan rental (no smoking) for the Artists to be picked up and returned at the airport. Promoter will be responsible for all rental charges including mileage, taxes, and insurance; however, artist will be responsible for all fuel charges (unless venue is greater than 150 miles from airport).

Hospitality:

We understand that you are a busy concert presenter and not a caterer. We prefer to leave hospitality up to your discretion, rather than as a contractual matter. The Group are vegetarians. _____ also cannot eat garlic, onions, wine, peppers, bananas, or MSG. If we do not hear otherwise, the Group will assume that they need to take care of their own meals. The following would be greatly appreciated, though not necessary: bottled water, fresh fruit, hot water, chamomile tea, honey.

Promoter will provide:

- An adequate and acceptable performance space, clean, safe, dry and in good order, with adequate stage lighting and electrical power.

• A private, lockable room to be used as a dressing room, including, if possible, a mirror, bathroom, and a place to hang costumes. If a shower is available, please provide three fresh towels and soap.

The following from load-in until load-out:

• Full access to performance and dressing areas.

• Parking immediately adjacent to venue for band/artist vehicle(s).

• Two responsible, capable persons for assisting in load-in, set-up, and load-out.

• Security for Artists and their equipment.

• Where applicable and upon request, Promoter agrees to provide Artists with a reasonable number of tickets or passes for the event (typically no more than eight tickets per performance).

Merchandise Sales:

Promoter will supply a booth or table for the sale of band/artist's merchandise before and after the performance(s). The booth will be staffed with volunteers/employees of the Promoter unless otherwise agreed to by the band/artist. For shows of four hundred or fewer patrons, two sellers and two banquet tables will be required (one for selling and another, adjacent, for autographs). For shows over four hundred patrons, a second sales location with one additional banquet table and a minimum of one additional staff will be required. Promoter must provide a cash box with a cash float (i.e., "petty cash").

Canada: This should consist of two rolls of $1 coins and one roll of $2 coins.

USA: This should consist of $50 in $1 bills and $50 in $5 bills.

For shows in excess of eight hundred patrons, please double this amount.

Please read and familiarize your sales staff with the separate instruction sheet regarding sales of

merchandise.

Merchandise Sales Instruction Sheet:

Please familiarize your front of house staff and/or merchandise salespeople with this information well in advance of the show. If you have any questions or concerns, please do not hesitate to contact _____.

SET-UP / STAFF (see illustration on next page)

Primary sales location:

The primary sales location will consist of one or two banquet tables (approx. eight foot) for sales plus an adjacent banquet table for autographs. The primary sales location should be located in such a way as to capture the most possible visibility and traffic from patrons as they leave the auditorium. The primary sales location should be staffed with a minimum of two salespersons and two ushers. One usher's job will be to direct the flow of the line such that patrons line up in front of the merchandise table and proceed to the autograph table. A second usher's job will be to stand adjacent to the autograph table to help ensure traffic flow and to discourage "cutting in line." If available, stanchions should be used to help direct the flow of traffic.

Secondary sales location:

For audiences in excess of four hundred patrons, a second sales location will be required. This sales location can be staffed with a single person. The location can consist of a single banquet table and should be located away from the first location, and preferably by a major exit door.

The secondary sales location will help provide a way for patrons to purchase merchandise without having to wait in the long sales/autograph line.

FLOAT / CASH BOX:

Each sales location should have a cash box with a cash float. The float should consist of $50 in $1 bills and $50 in $5 bills. For shows in excess of eight hundred patrons, please double this amount. Please make sure that the float is counted before sales begin and that the boxes are used ONLY for sales of the Group merchandise (*i.e.*, not ticket sales).

PRICING:

A price list and sign will be provided with the merchandise for each show. Prices are always round figures and always include all applicable taxes. Discounts are often offered for multiple purchases (Ex. for example, $18 per CD or $15 each for multiple CDs). These discounts are applicable PER FAMILY.

SCHEDULE:

Merchandise will generally arrive with the artists at load-in. Set up should begin well in advance of the how such that sales may begin as audience starts to arrive (generally 60 minutes prior to show time.)

Sales will take place before the show, during any intermission (if any) and after the show. The Group will generally sign autographs after the show, adjacent to the primary sales location. After sales have concluded, merchandise will be re-packed and financial settlement will take place immediately. Merchandise and cash boxes must be kept safe at all times and should never be left alone (for example, during the show).

FORMS OF PAYMENT:

- CASH

- VISA, MC, AMEX

Note: All of these cards can be processed on the same slips (*i.e.,* even if it says "Visa" on the slip, it is ok to use the slip with an Amex card, or other cards). No other cards than Visa, MasterCard, or Amex can be accepted.

IMPORTANT: For every credit card transaction, please:

1. Swipe the card with the machine provided.

2. Confirm that the full card number is legible on the back slip.

3. Obtain a signature and a legible PHONE NUMBER.

CHECK:

If the patron has no other form of payment, we will accept personal checks made payable to "_____". The check must include a phone number. For checks over $50, please obtain ID and record the relevant number on the back of the check (for example: "State Driver's License - _____").

The Promoter will not make any audio or video recordings or broadcasts of the performance(s) nor will it knowingly allow the same, without the prior written consent of _____.

Promotional Materials to help you promote the concert can be found at:

_____ .com. Additional promotional materials can be obtained by contacting our office.

THANK YOU for taking the time to carefully read this Rider. Please do not hesitate to contact us should you have any questions or if there is anything we can do to help ensure a successful event.

As important as the technical requirements for the show are the hospitality needs of the band/artist. A hungry or angry performer does not make for a good show. So, the performer will give detailed instructions on what needs to be provided by the promoter for the band/artist's backstage needs, in order to be fed and relaxed for a good show.

The first item addressed is lodging. If the band/artist is to perform for more than one night, the promoter will have to provide lodging. In this Rider, and as is common, the lodging must be in a hotel with a rating of four-stars or above. The worst thing in the world is to be on the road and have the promoter place the band/artist in a "fleabag" motel.

The next item is transportation. Depending on the type of tour and the length of the stay in the promoter's city, the band/artist will need transportation. Again, depending upon the type of tour and length of stay, the promoter may need to pick the band/artist up at the airport and arrange for local transportation - a driver or a car, or possibly both.

The next item is food - and this is not to be taken lightly. The band/artist will make specific requests for types of water, fruit, vegan or non-vegan, or even macrobiotic needs. Everyone has heard the stories of "only green M&M's." But the requests can be deadly serious. Food allergies can stop a performance as surely as a snowstorm. Also, failure to follow the request for "green m&m's" can indicate that the promoter has not read the Rider carefully.

The Rider then turns to some general backstage requirements - an area that is safe, clean, and secure for the band/artist to sit and relax. In the next paragraph, the band/artist is requesting, from load-in to load-out, full access to the venue, some assistance in loading in and out, convenient parking for the band/artist, and a certain number of "comps" or free tickets.

The final part of the Rider concerns the needs of the band/artist in selling their merchandise. The band/artist will want a certain number of places to sell merchandise, depending upon the size of the crowd. It will not sit well with the band/artist if its merchandising booths are relegated to the outskirts of the venue where it is difficult to see, and sales will be low. It is important to keep this in mind - the band/artist does not want to have inadequate sales staff or insufficient outlets and fail to serve its fans. The band/artist will want the promoter to provide a "float box" or "cash box" for cash sales. Also, the band/artist will provide the promoter with a price list of the merchandise and instructions on how to sell the merchandise. A final note in the Rider regards the availability of the band/artist after the performance - in this case, the band/artist will be available after the show to sign autographs and meet fans.

Conclusion.

A Rider is a very, very important document and the band/artist must be thorough in putting one together and in enforcing it when they go on the road. Without a proper Rider, the band/artist can have a disastrous performance or tour, and be left penniless, in a roach-filled motel room, and with no way to get home.

<u>CONCLUSION</u>

The music business is ever changing and evolving. And the pace of that change might be unique to the music industry. The computer industry might be the only other industry with a similar dynamic of change - and ironically, one feeds the other. The changes in computer technology have resulted in an enormous impact on the recording business.

Today, iPads and iPhones carry iTunes. Streaming services like Pandora make your smart TV a music delivery system. Spotify allows you to create your own playlist – in essence becoming your own radio station. And with all of these, *you* control the content. No more buying a full album to get one hit single - simply go to Spotify and put it on your playlist. No more searching for a channel that played "your kind of music" - program Pandora and off you go.

The only way for artists to survive today is to stay on top of how technology has already changed, and will continue to change, the way their music is distributed and monetized. This, in turn alters their various legal rights, intellectual property rights, and sources of revenue. And the change will only increase. So, artists must stay abreast of the changes in order to always protect their rights.

INDEX

End Notes.

[1] MICK JAGGER & KEITH RICHARDS, IT'S ONLY ROCK 'N ROLL (Rolling Stones Recs. 1974).

[1] John Noble Wilford, *Flute's Revised Age Dates the Sound of Music,* N.Y. TIMES (May 29, 2012), http://www.nytimes.com/2012/05/29/science/oldest-musical-instruments-are-even-older-than-first-thought.html?_r=0.

[2] LARRY J. HOEFLING & NILS THOR GRANLUND: SHOW BUSINESS ENTREPRENEUR AND AMERICA'S FIRST RADIO STAR (2010).

[3] Ian Whitcomb, *THE FIRST CROONERS: Volume 3: 1935-1940,* PICKLEHEAD, https://www.picklehead.com/ian/ian_txt_firstcrooners3.html (last visited May 7, 2021).

[4] "I think I'm much more a singer than I am a crooner. In the days of Russ Colombo and Rudy Vallée, I think that they were rightly termed 'crooners' because they had very small, soft voices. They were very good at it, but when Bing came along he was more of a 'singer,' and I think through the years most of us have begun to execute more singing than we did crooning. (Rather than being nasal or making cow-like sounds of 'moos' or those utterances, you know.)" *Sinatra: Off the Record* (CBS television broadcast Nov. 16, 1965).

[5] Jessica Reaves, *Person of the Week: Elvis Presley*, TIME (Aug. 15, 2002), http://content.time.com/time/nation/article/0,8599,337778,00.html#ixzz2rq2OWRWA.

[6] PETER GURALNICK, LAST TRAIN TO MEMPHIS: THE RISE OF ELVIS PRESLEY 645-48 (1994).

[7] "Girls were fainting, screaming, rushing the field, and peeing themselves." Willie Simpson, *The Beatles, Live at Shea Stadium,* http://www.williesimpson.com/the-beatles-live-at-shea-stadium (last visited May 7, 2021).

[8] *History*, AM. FED'N MUSICIANS, http://www.afm.org/about/history (last visited May 7, 2021).

[9] *Id.*

[10] Abdul Malik Al Nasir, *Jalal Mansur Nuriddin: Farewell to the 'grandfather of rap'*, THE GUARDIAN (June 6, 2018), https://www.theguardian.com/music/2018/jun/06/jalal-mansur-nuriddin-last-poets-obituary-grandfather-of-rap.

[11] Kyle Anderson, *Michael Jackson's* Thriller *Set to Become Top-Selling Album of All Time*, MTV NEWS (July 20, 2009), http://www.mtv.com/news/1616537/michael-jacksons-thriller-set-to-become-top-selling-album-of-all-time/.

[12] Monica Herrera, *Michael Jackson: King of Billboard's Pop Charts,* BILLBOARD (June 25, 2009), http://www.billboard.com/articles/news/268281/michael-jackson-king-of-billboards-pop-charts.

[13] *Gold & Platinum,* RECORDING INDUS. ASS'N AMERICA, https://www.riaa.com/gold-platinum/ (last visited May 7, 2021).

[14] Ben Sisario, *Music Sales Drop 5% as Habits Shift Online*, N.Y. TIMES (Sept. 25, 2014), https://www.nytimes.com/2014/09/26/business/media/music-sales-drop-5-as-habits-shift-online.html.

[15] Lars Brandle, *U.S. Vinyl Album Sales Up by 53% in Q1,* BILLBOARD (Apr. 17, 2015), http://www.billboard.com/articles/business/6538585/us-vinyl-album-sales-up-by-53-in-q1.

[16] Amy Watson, *LP/Vinyl album sales in the United States from 1993 to 2019,* STATISTA (Jan. 8, 2021), https://www.statista.com/statistics/188822/lp-albumsalesintheunitedstatessince2009/#:~:text=Data%20on%20vinyl%20album%20sales%20in%20the%20United,sold%2C%20up%2014.5%20percent%20from%20the%20previous%20.

[17] *Global Recorded Music Revenues Reached $28.8bn in 2021, Says Midia,* MUSIC BUS. WORLDWIDE (Mar. 22, 2022), https://www.musicbusinessworldwide.com/global-recorded-music-revenues-hit-25-9bn-in-2021-up-18-5-yoy/.

[18] *With $15bn in Revenue, 2021 Was the Biggest EVER year for the US record industry (kind of...),* MUSIC BUS. WORLDWIDE (Mar. 9, 2022).

[19] *Universal Music Group Generated $2.7 Billion in Q2; Recorded Music Subscription Streaming Revenue Grew 7.0% Yoy,* MUSIC BUS. WORLDWIDE (July 28, 2022), https://www.musicbusinessworldwide.com/universal-music-group-generated-2-7-billion-in-q2-recorded-music-subscription-streaming-revenue-grew-7-0-yoy/.

[20] *Sony Generated Over $2bn from Recorded Music and Publishing in Calendar Q2; Recorded Music Revenues Were Up 11.2% Yoy,* MUSIC BUS. WORLDWIDE (July 29, 2022), https://www.musicbusinessworldwide.com/sony-generated-over-2bn-from-recorded-music-and-publishing-in-calendar-q2-recorded-music-revenues-were-up-11-2-yoy/.

[21] *Warner Music Group Revenues Up 12.1% in Calendar Q2; Recorded Music Streaming Up 2.7%,* MUSIC BUS. WORLDWIDE (Aug. 12, 2022), https://www.musicbusinessworldwide.com/warner-music-group-revenues-up-12-1-in-calendar-q2-recorded-music-streaming-up-2-7/.

[22] *The US Music Publishing Industry Generated $4.7bn Last Year – But The Record Industry Grew Twice As Fast*, MUSIC BUS. WORLDWIDE (Aug. 25, 2022), https://www.musicbusinessworldwide.com/the-us-music-publishing-industry-generated-4-7bn-last-year-but-the-record-industry-grew-twice-as-fast/#:~:text=Here%20is%20one%20of%20those,the%20calendar%20year%20of%202021.

[23] 17 U.S.C. § 102(a).

[24] *Id.* § 106.

[25] *Copyright Registration for Sound Recordings*, U.S. COPYRIGHT OFF., https://www.copyright.gov/circs/circ56.pdf (last visited May 10, 2021).

[26] 17 U.S.C. § 101.

[27] *Benefits of Copyright Registration*, COPYRIGHT ALL., https://copyrightalliance.org/education/copyright-law-explained/copyright-registration/benefits-of-copyright-registration/ (last visited May 10, 2021).

[28] *How Long Does Copyright Last?*, U.S. COPYRIGHT OFF., https://www.copyright.gov/help/faq/faq-duration.html (last visited May 10, 2021).

[29] *What is a trademark?*, U.S. PAT. TRADEMARK OFF., https://www.uspto.gov/trademarks/basics/what-trademark (last visited May 10, 2021).

[30] *What is a Patent?*, U.S. PAT. TRADEMARK OFF., https://www.uspto.gov/trademarks/basics/what-trademark (last visited May 10, 2021).

[31] Andrew Flanagan, *A Music Industry Peace Treaty Passes Unanimously Through Congress*, NPR (Sept. 19, 2018, 5:17 PM), https://www.npr.org/2018/09/19/649611777/a-music-industry-peace-treaty-passes-unanimously-through-congress.

[32] *Id.*

[33] *Id.*

[34] *The Music Modernization Act*, U.S. COPYRIGHT OFF., https://www.copyright.gov/music-modernization/ (last visited May 6, 2021).

[35] *Id.*

[36] *Id.*

[37] William F. Patry, *Copyright Law and Practice*, DIGIT. L. ONLINE, http://digital-law-online.info/patry/patry7.html (last visited May 6, 2021).

[38] *Flo & Eddie, Inc. v. Sirius XM Radio, Inc.*, 821 F.3d 265, 265 (2d Cir. 2016).

[39] Dani Deahl, *The Music Modernization Act has been signed into law*, VERGE (Oct. 11, 2018, 12:08 PM),

https://www.theverge.com/platform/amp/2018/10/11/17963804/music-modernization-act-mma-copyright-law-bill-labels-congress.

[40] *Circulars 56 and 56a*, U.S. COPYRIGHT OFF., http://www.Copyright.gov/circs (last visited May 7, 2021).

[41] *See* 17 U.S.C. § 102(b).

[42] *Copyright FAQs: Copyright in General*, U.S. COPYRIGHT OFF., https://www.copyright.gov/help/faq/faq-general.html#:~:text=When%20is%20my%20work%20protected,of%20a%20machine%20or%20device (last visited on Sept. 15, 2022).

[43] 17 U.S.C. § 106.

[44] *GROSSES – BROADWAY IN NYC*, BROADWAY LEAGUE, http://www.broadwayleague.com/index.php?url_identifier=nyc-grosses-11 (last visited May 7, 2021).

[45] Steve Vondran, *The 9th Circuit Court and Music Copyright Infringement* – de minimis *Exception*, VONDRAN LEGAL (Aug. 11, 2019) https://www.vondranlegal.com/de-minimis-use-in-copyright-music-law#:~:text=In%20the%20context%20of%20copyright,listener%20cannot%20%20recognize%20the%20appropriation.

[46] *See Bridgeport Music, Inc. v. Dimension Films*, 230 F.Supp.2d 830 (Mid-Tenn 2002), *rev'd*, 401 F.3d 647 (6th Cir. 2004), *amended by*, 410 F.3d 792 (6th Cir. 2005).

[47] *See Bridgeport*, 410 F.3d 792.

[48] *See id.* at 798

[49] *See id.* at 800.

[50] *See id.* at 801.

[51] *See id.* at 802.

[52] *See VMG Salsoul, LLC v. Madonna Louise Ciccone*, 824 F.3d 871, 875 (9th Cir. 2016).

[53] *Id.* at 875-76.

[54] *Id.* at 877; *see also Ringgold v. Black Entm't Television, Inc.*, 126 F.3d 70, 74-75 (2d Cir. 1997).

[55] *See VMG Salsoul, LLC*, 824 F.3d at 874.

[56] *Id.* at 877.

[57] *See id.* at 888.

[58] *See id.* at 889; *see also Bridgeport*, 410 F.3d at 798 n.6, 801-02 & n.13.

[59] Janet Fries and Jennifer T. Criss, *Debunking Copyright Myths*, A.B.A. (Aug. 5, 2019), https://www.americanbar.org/groups/intellectual_property_law/publications/landslide/2018-19/july-august/debunking-copyright-myths/.

[60] *Copyright Registration for Sound Recordings*, *supra* note 26.

[61] *Copyright Registration for Sound Recordings*, *supra* note 26.

[62] *About*, SOUNDEXCHANGE, http://www.soundexchange.com/about/ (last visited May 7, 2021).

[63] *See* 17 U.S.C. § 114(d)(2).

[64] 17 U.S.C. § 101.

[65] *Copyright Crash Course: Who Owns It?*, UNIV. TEX. LIBRS., https://guides.lib.utexas.edu/copyright/whoowns (last visited May 7, 2021).

[66] *See Childress v. Taylor*, 945 F.2d 500, 505 (2d Cir. 1991); H.R. REP. NO. 94-1476, at 120 (2d Sess. 1976), *as reprinted in* 1976 U.S.C.C.A.N. 5659, 5736 (stating that words and music of a song is an example of interdependent parts of a joint work); *see also* S. Rep. No. 94-473, at 103-04 (1st Sess. 1975).

[67] *Childress*, 945 F.2d at 507-08.

[68] *Id.* at 507.

[69] *Copyright Crash Course, supra* note 66.

[70] *Copyright Crash Course, supra* note 66.

[71] David Rabinowitz, *Work Made For Hire Agreement Cannot Be Retroactive*, MOSES & SINGER, LLP. (June 2013), https://www.mosessinger.com/articles/work-made-hire-agreement-cannot-be-retroactive.

[72] *Id.*

[73] *Copyright Registration for Sound Recordings, supra* note 26.

[74] 17 U.S.C. § 411(a).

[75] *Fees*, U.S. COPYRIGHT OFF., http://www.Copyright.gov/docs/fees.html (last visited May 7, 2021).

[76] *Circulars*, U.S. COPYRIGHT OFF., http://www.Copyright.gov/circs (last visited May 7, 2021).

[77] *Les Scott Interview* (Mar. 1, 2022).

[78] *Group Registration for Unpublished Works (GRUW)*, https://www.copyright.gov/gruw/ (last visited Mar. 22, 2022).

[79] Timothy Lee, *Senate passes copyright bill to end 140-year protection for old songs*, ARS TECHNICA (Sept. 19, 2018, 2:29 PM), https://apple.news/AtA6FqgiQSzOiYEjXkdXrKg.

[80] *Id.*

[81] *The Music Modernization Act, supra* note 35.

[82] 17 U.S.C. § 302(a).

[83] *How Long Does Copyright Protection Last?*, U.S. COPYRIGHT OFF., https://www.copyright.gov/help/faq/faq-duration.html#:~:text=As%20a%20general%20rule%2C%20for%20works%20created%20after,of%20the%20author%20plus%20an%20additional%2070%20years (last visited May 7, 2021).

[84] Larry Rohter, *Record Industry Braces for Artists' Battles Over Song Rights*, N.Y. TIMES (Aug. 15, 2011), https://www.nytimes.com/2011/08/16/arts/music/springsteen-and-others-soon-eligible-to-recover-song-rights.html.

[85] *Id.*

[86] Larry Rohter, *A Copyright Victory, 35 Years Later*, CNBC (Sept. 11, 2013, 8:48 AM), http://www.cnbc.com/id/101025467.

[87] Robert Mclean, *Paul McCartney sues to get Beatles songs back from Sony*, CNN BUSINESS (Jan. 19, 2017, 4:35 AM), https://money.cnn.com/2017/01/19/media/paul-mccartney-sony-lawsuit/index.html.

[88] *Id.*

[89] *Id.*

[90] *Paul McCartney Finally 'Gets Back' His Beatles Copyrights*, PACE INTELL. PROP. SPORTS & ENT. L.F., (Oct. 29, 2018).

[91] Ashely Cullins, *Paul McCartney Reaches Settlement With Sony/ATV in Beatles Rights Dispute*, HOLLYWOOD REP., (June 29, 2017, 6:29 PM), https://www.hollywoodreporter.com/thr-esq/paul-mccartney-reaches-settlement-sony-atv-beatles-rights-dispute-1018100.

[92] *Id.*

[93] Jonathan Bailey, *The Problem with the Fifth Fair Use Factor*, PLAGIARISM TODAY (Mar. 24, 2011), https://www.plagiarismtoday.com/2011/03/24/the-problem-with-the-fifth-fair-use-factor (last visited Mar. 1, 2022). "Are you evil?" or, "Does the judge like you?"

[94] *Sampling*, OXFORD DICTIONARY (2021).

[95] *Mashup*, DICTIONARY.COM (2021).

[96] *Scott Interview*, *supra* note 78.

[97] *Campbell v. Acuff-Rose Music, Inc.*, 510 U.S. 569, 578 (1994).

[98] *Parody*, MERRIAM-WEBSTER DICTIONARY (2021).

[99] *Id.*

[100] *Campbell*, 510 U.S. at 569.

[101] *Id.* at 579.

[102] *Id.* at 584.

[103] *Id.* at 580-81.

[104] *Measuring Fair Use: The Four Factors*, STANFORD LIBRS., http://fairuse.stanford.edu/ Copyright_and_Fair_Use_Overview/chapter9/9-b.html (last visited May 6, 2021).

[105] *Id.*

[106] *Id.*

[107] *Id.*

[108] *Id.*

[109] *Id.*

[110] *Id.*

[111] *Id.*

[112] *"About the Creative Commons,"* https://creativecommons.org/about/cclicenses/. (last visited Mar. 21, 2022)

[113] *What Is the Public Domain?*, COPYRIGHTLAWS.COM (Nov. 13, 2020), https://www.copyrightlaws.com/what-is-the-public-domain/.

[114] *Id.*

[115] *See N.Y.C. Image Int'l, Inc. v. RS USA, Inc.*, No. 19-CV-10355, 2020 U.S. Dist. LEXIS 193016, at *6 (S.D.N.Y. Oct. 16, 2020).

[116] Federal Copyright law does not cover Sound Recordings made prior to 1972. Rather, these recordings are protected by state common law on Copyright infringement. 17 U.S.C. § 301(c).

[117] *Arista Records, LLC v. Lime Grp.*, LLC, 715 F.Supp. 2d 481, 507 (S.D.N.Y. 2010) (citing *Island Software & Comput. Serv., Inc. v. Microsoft Corp.*, 413 F.3d 257, 260 (2d Cir. 2005)).

[118] *Three Boys Music Corp. v. Bolton*, 212 F.3d 477, 481 (9th Cir. 2000) , cert. denied, 531 U.S. 1126 (2001) (citing *Smith v. Jackson*, 84 F.3d 1213, 1218 (9th Cir. 1996)).

[119] *See Antonick v. Elec. Arts, Inc.*, 841 F.3d 1062, 1065-66 (9th Cir. 2016); *see also Williams v. Gaye,* 885 F.3d 1150, 1163 (9th Cir. 2018).

[120] *See* 17 U.S.C. § 504.

[121] *See id.* § 504(c)(1).

[122] *See id.* § 504(c)(2).

[123] R.J. Lehmann, *'Blurred Lines' decision offers blurry conception of copyright*, R STREET (Mar. 11, 2015), http://www.rstreet.org/2015/03/11/blurred-lines-decision-offers-blurry-conception-of-copyright/.

[124] Mike Masnick, *Court Won't Rehear Blurred Lines Case, Bad News For Music Creativity,* TECHDIRT, (July 12, 2018, 1:29 PM), https://www.techdirt.com/articles/20180711/18065840222/court-wont-rehear-blurred-lines-case-bad-news-music-creativity.shtml.

[125] Kal Raustiala & Christopher Jon Sprigman, *Squelching Creativity: What the "Blurred Lines" team copied is either not original or not relevant*, SLATE (Mar. 12, 2015, 12:27 PM), https://slate.com/news-and-politics/2015/03/blurred-lines-verdict-is-wrong-williams-and-thicke-did-not-infringe-on-marvin-gaye-copyright.html.

[126] *UMG Recordings, Inc. v. Shelter Cap. Partners, LLC*, 667 F.3d 1022, 1022 (9th Cir. 2011).

[127] *Id.*

[128] 17 U.S.C. § 501.

[129] *Id.* § 512(a)-(d).

[130] *Id.* § 512(c)(1)(B), (d)(2).

[131] *The History of Symbols*, GRAPHIC DESIGN HIST., http://www.designhistory.org/Symbols_pages/symbols.html (last visited May 7, 2021).

[132] ASHLEY PACKARD, DIGITAL MEDIA LAW 162 (2010).

[133] *Stella Artois Nanno 1366 Trademark Information*, TRADEMARKIA, https://trademark.trademarkia.com/stella-artois-anno-1366-77003422.html#:~:text=The%20USPTO%20has%20given%20the%20STELLA%20ARTOIS%20ANNO,CONTINUED%20USE%20NOT%20FILE

D%20WITHIN%20GRACE%20PERIOD%2C%20UN-REVIVABLE (last visited May 6, 2021).

[134] *The local history of Burton upon Trent*, BURTON ON TRENT, http://www.burton-on-trent.org.uk/category/miscellany/bass-logo (last visited May 7, 2021).

[135] *What is a trademark?*, U.S. PAT. TRADEMARK OFF., https://www.uspto.gov/trademarks/basics/what-trademark (last visited May 7, 2021).

[136] *Qualitex Co. v. Jacobson Prods. Co.*, 514 U.S. 159, 164 (1995).

[137] *Trademark, patent, or copyright*, U.S. PAT. TRADEMARK OFF., https://www.uspto.gov/trademarks/basics/trademark-patent-copyright (last visited May 7, 2021).

[138] *Id.*

[139] 15 U.S.C. § 1052(f).

[140] *Matal v. Tam,* 137 S. Ct. 1744, 1751 (2017).

[141] *Id.* at 1753.

[142] *Id.* at 1753-54.

[143] *Id.* at 1751.

[144] *Iancu v. Brunetti*, 139 S. Ct. 2294, 2294 (2019).

[145] *In re Brunetti*, 877 F.3d 1330, 1336 (Fed. Cir. 2017).

[146] *Id.*

[147] *Iancu*, 139 S. Ct. at 2298.

[148] *Id.* at 2299.

[149] *Id.* at 2302.

[150] SIEGRUN D. KANE, KANE ON TRADEMARK LAW: A PRACTITIONER'S GUIDE 2-3 (5th ed. 2007).

[151] *Id.*

[152] *Id.*

[153] Jonathan Mahler, *If the Word 'How' Is Trademarked, Does This Headline Need a TM?*, N.Y. TIMES (Oct. 5, 2014), https://www.nytimes.com/2014/10/06/business/chobani-and-dov-seidman-wrestle-over-use-of-how-trademark.html.

[154] *Id.*

[155] *Id.*

[156] *Id.*

[157] *Id.*

[158] *See U.S.P.T.O. v. Booking.com B.V.*, 140 S. Ct. 2298, 2301 (2020).

[159] U.S. PAT. TRADEMARK OFF., EXAMINATION GUIDE 3-20: GENERIC.COM TERMS AFTER USPTO V. BOOKING.COM (Oct. 2020), https://www.uspto.gov/sites/default/files/documents/TM-ExamGuide-3-20.pdf?utm_campaign=subscriptioncenter&utm_content=&utm_medium=email&utm_name=&utm_source=govdelivery&utm_term=.

[160] *Id.*

[161] *Id.*

[162] KANE, *supra* note 151, at 2-10.

[163] KANE, *supra* note 151, at 2-10.

[164] KANE, *supra* note 151, at 2-10.

[165] KANE, *supra* note 151, at 2-10.

[166] *Six Prods., Inc. v. United Merchs. & Mfrs., Inc.*, 295 F. Supp. 479, 488 (S.D.N.Y. 1968).

[167] KANE, *supra* note 151, at 2-10.

[168] KANE, *supra* note 151, at 2-10.

[169] KANE, *supra* note 151, at 2-10.

[170] *Basic Facts About Trademarks videos*, U.S. PAT. TRADEMARK OFF., https://www.uspto.gov/trademarks/basics/basic-facts-about-trademarks-videos (last visited May 7, 2021).

[171] 15 U.S.C. § 1051(a).

[172] *Id.* § 1051(b).

[173] *Basic Facts*, *supra* note 171.

[174] *Basic Facts*, *supra* note 171.

[175] *Basic Facts*, *supra* note 171.

[176] *Basic Facts*, *supra* note 171.

[177] *Basic Facts*, *supra* note 171.

[178] *Basic Facts*, *supra* note 171.

[179] *Basic Facts*, *supra* note 171.

[180] *Basic Facts*, *supra* note 171.

[181] *Basic Facts*, *supra* note 171.

[182] *Basic Facts*, *supra* note 171.

[183] *Basic Facts*, *supra* note 171.

[184] *Basic Facts*, *supra* note 171.

[185] *Basic Facts*, *supra* note 171.

[186] *Basic Facts*, *supra* note 171.

[187] *Basic Facts*, *supra* note 171.

[188] *Rockin' the Trademark*, U.S. PAT. TRADEMARK OFF., https://www.uspto.gov/trademark/laws-regulations/rockin-trademark#consent (last visited May 7, 2021).

[189] *Id.*

[190] *See* 15 U.S.C. § 1114(1).

[191] *See id.*

[192] *See id.*

[193] Eriq Gardner, *Van Halen Sues Drummer's Ex-Wife for Using Famous Last Name*, BILLBOARD (Oct. 17, 2013), https://www.billboard.com/articles/news/5755807/van-halen-sues-drummers-ex-wife-for-using-famous-last-name.

[194] *Mortellito v. Nina of Cal., Inc.*, 335 F. Supp. 1288, 1296 (S.D.N.Y. 1972).

[195] *Ameritech, Inc. v. Am. Info. Techs. Corp.*, 811 F.2d 960, 965 (6th Cir. 1987).

[196] *See* 15 U.S.C. § 1117.

[197] JOHNNY BURKE & ARTHUR JOHNSTON, PENNIES FROM HEAVEN (Columbia Pictures 1936).

[198] *Scott Interview, supra* note 78.

[199] *See Scott Interview, supra* note 78.

[200] *See Scott Interview, supra* note 78.

[201] *Artist Revenue Streams*, FUTURE MUSIC COAL., (Oct. 10, 2010), http://futureofmusic.org/article/research/artist-revenue-streams.

[202] ARI HERSTAND, HOW TO MAKE IT IN THE NEW MUSIC BUSINESS 410 (2020).

[203] David Balto, *Opinion: DOJ Got It Right On ASCAP, BMI Consent Decrees*, LAW360 (Aug. 8, 2016, 11:30 AM), http://www.law360.com/articles/825684/opinion-doj-got-it-right-on-ascap-bmi-consent-decrees.

[204] H.R. No. 94-1476, at 121 (2d Sess. 1976).

[205] Balto, *supra* note 204.

[206] Balto, *supra* note 204.

[207] 17 U.S.C. § 301(c).

[208] Robert Clarida, *Who Owns Pre-1972 Sound Recordings?*, ROY ROSENZWEIG CTR. FOR HIST. AND NEW MEDIA (Nov. 13, 2000), https://chnm.gmu.edu/digitalhistory/links/cached/chapter7/link7.55b.pre-1972recordings.html#:~:text=Pre-1972%20sound%20recordings%20can%20be%20protected%20either%20by,the%20record%20producer%20by%20express%20or%20implied%20agreement.

[209] *See* 17 U.S.C. § 101.

[210] Caitlin Dewey, *You have 12 hours to watch astronaut Chris Hadfield cover 'Space Odyssey' in space before the video goes offline forever*, WASHINGTON POST (May 13, 2014, 12:41 PM), http://www.washingtonpost.com/news/the-intersect/wp/2014/05/13/you-have-12-hours-to-watch-astronaut-chris-hadfield-cover-space-oddity-in-space-before-the-video-goes-offline-forever/.

[211] *Scott Interview, supra* note 78.

[212] *Scott Interview, supra* note 78.

[213] Heather McDonald, *Paying and Collecting Mechanical Royalties: What Artists, Labels, and Publishers Need to Know*, BALANCE CAREERS (June 27, 2019), https://www.thebalancecareers.com/mechanical-royalties-2460503.

[214] *Id.*

[215] *The MLC Process*, MECH. LICENSING COLLECTIVE, https://themlc.com/how-it-works (last visited May 7, 2021).

[216] *Id.*

[217] Steven Lackenau, *Untangling the Bundle: Grand Rights vs. Small Rights,* MUSICAL AM. WORLDWIDE (June 3, 2014), https://www.musicalamerica.com/news/newsstory.cfm?storyid=31868&categoryid=7.

[218] Jason P. Baruch, *Acquiring Music Musical Composition Rights for Stage Plays*, SENDROFF & BARUCH, LLP (Jan. 1, 2005), http://sendroffbaruch.com/acquiring-music-Musical Composition-rights-for-stage-plays/.

[219] *Id.*

[220] *Tribute band/artist*, DICTIONARY.COM (2021).

[221] *Is it Legal to be a Tribute Band*, BRADLEY LEGAL GRP., P.A. (Dec. 23, 2011), https://bradleylegalgroup.com/is-it-legal-to-be-a-tribute-band/artist/.

[222] *Id.*

[223] *Id.*

[224] *Id.*

[225] Ben Sisario, *As Music Streaming Grows, Artists' Royalties Slow to a Trickle*, N.Y. TIMES (Jan. 28, 2013), https://www.nytimes.com/2013/01/29/business/media/streaming-shakes-up-music-industrys-model-for-royalties.html.

[226] Sean Fitzjohn, *Streaming Payouts Per Platform (+Royalties Calculator),* PRODUCER HIVE, https://producerhive.com/music-marketing-tips/streaming-royalties-breakdown/ (last visited May 7, 2021).

[227] *Id.*

[228] William Glanz, *music tech: understanding the growth of streaming,* SOUNDEXCHANGE (July 25, 2018), https://www.soundexchange.com/2018/07/25/music-tech-understanding-the-growth-of-streaming/.

[229] *SoundExchange Hits $9 Billion Milestone, Completes 150th Royalty Distribution* (Mar. 24, 2022), https://www.soundexchange.com/news/soundexchange-hits-9-billion-milestone-completes-150th-royalty-distribution/#:~:text=SOUNDEXCHANGE%20HITS%20%249%20BILLION%20MILESTONE%2C%20COMPLETES%20150TH%20ROYALTY%20DISTRIBUTION&text=WASHINGTON%20%E2%80%93%20March%2024%2C%202022%20%E2%80%93,to%20music%20creators%20since%202003.

[230] Sisario, *As Music Streaming Grows, supra* note 226.

[231] Sisario, *As Music Streaming Grows, supra* note 226.

[232] HERSTAND, *supra* note 203, at 6.

[233] Doug Gross, *Songwriters: Spotify doesn't pay off . . . unless you're a Taylor Swift,* CNN BUSINESS (Nov. 13, 2014, 11:58 AM), http://www.cnn.com/2014/11/12/tech/web/spotify-pay-musicians/index.html?iref=allsearch.

[234] Cristina Alesci & Frank Pallotta, *How much did Taylor Swift really make off Spotify?*, CNN MONEY (Nov. 12, 2014, 9:36 PM), http://money.cnn.com/2014/11/12/media/taylor-swift-spotify/index.html.

[235] Andrew Urias, *What Is The Value of Digital and Streaming Music?*, ANDREW W. URIAS PLLC (July 18, 2018), https://www.uriaslaw.com/music-business/2018/07/18/what-is-the-value-of-recorded-music/.

[236] Ben Sisario, *Sirius's Move to Bypass a Royalty Payment Clearinghouse Causes an Uproar*, N.Y. TIMES (Nov. 6, 2011), https://www.nytimes.com/2011/11/07/business/media/siriuss-move-to-bypass-royalty-agency-causes-uproar.html.

[237] Ben Sisario, *Fight Builds Over Online Royalties*, N.Y. TIMES (Nov. 4, 2012), https://www.nytimes.com/2012/11/05/business/media/fight-growing-over-online-royalties.html.

[238] *Id.*

[239] *H.R. 6480 (112th): Internet Radio Fairness Act of 2012*, GOVTRACK, https://www.govtrack.us/congress/bills/112/hr6480#summary/libraryofcongress (last visited May 7, 2021).

[240] *Id.*

[241] *See* Trevir Nath, *How Pandora and Spotify Pay Artists*, INVESTOPEDIA (Feb. 10, 2021), https://www.investopedia.com/articles/personal-finance/121614/how-pandora-and-spotify-pay-artists.asp (stating that Pandora's 2020 royalty rate of 0.00133 cents per play was so low that it would take an artist 1.1 million plays to earn the monthly minimum wage of $1,472).

[242] Kristin Vartan, *Breaking Down the Legal Terms in Taylor Swift's Music Ownership Dispute*, EW (Nov. 15, 2019, 5:23 PM), https://ew.com/music/2019/11/15/taylor-swift-song-ownership-legal-terms/.

[243] Satoshi Nakamoto, *Bitcoin Open Source Implementation of P2P Currency*, P2P FOUNDATION (Feb. 11, 2009, 10:27 PM), https://satoshi.nakamotoinstitute.org/posts/p2pfoundation/1/.

[244] Steven Buchko, *How Long Do Bitcoin Transactions Take?*, COINCENTRAL (Dec. 12, 2017), https://coincentral.com/how-long-do-bitcoin-transfers-take/#:~:text=The%20average%20time%20it%20takes%20to%20mine%20a,minutes%20to%20over%2016%20hours%20in%20extreme%20cases.

[245] One non-exhaustive list includes: Mediachain, Ujo, Choon, Musicoin, Mycelia, Viberate, Blokur, eMusic, Voise, MusicLife, Bitsong, Digimarc, Blockpool, Audius, and Inmusik. Sam Daley, *17 Blockchain Music Companies Reshaping a Troubled Industry*, BUILTIN (last updated

May 3, 2021), https://builtin.com/blockchain/blockchain-music-innovation-examples.

[246] *Overview of Bittunes 2.0*, BITTUNES, https://music.bittunes.com/overview/ (last visited Mar. 10, 2021).

[247] *Core Processes in Bittunes 2.0*, BITTUNES, https://music.bittunes.com/core-processes/ (last visited Mar. 10, 2021).

[248] *Id.*

[249] *Scott Interview, supra* note 78.

[250] *Scott Interview, supra* note 78.

[251] *Core Processes, supra* note 248.

[252] *Micro-Earnings in the Bittunes Platform*, BITTUNES, https://music.bittunes.com/micro-earnings/ (last visited Mar. 10, 2021).

[253] Roneil Rumburg, Sid Sethi & Hareesh Nagaraj, *Audius: A Decentralized Protocol for Audio Content* (last updated Oct. 8, 2020), https://whitepaper.audius.co/AudiusWhitepaper.pdf.

[254] *Id.*

[255] Grace Muthoni, *SOUNDAC Is Using Blockchain to Solve a Major Problem in the Music Industry*, BLOCKTELEGRAPH (Sep. 11, 2018, 9:00 AM), https://blocktelegraph.io/soundac-using-blockchain-solve-major-problem-music-industry/.

[256] John Bartmann, *PeerTracks: Blockchain Music Streaming Platform*, JOHN BARTMANN: AUDIO AND MUSIC PRODUCTION, https://johnbartmann.com/blog/peertracks-blockchain-powered-beta-music-streaming-platform/ (last visited Mar. 10, 2021).

[257] *Id.*

[258] *Trending*, AUDIUS, https://audius.co/trending (last visited Mar. 10, 2021).

[259] Samantha Hissong, *Kings of Leon Will Be the First Band to Release an Album as an NFT*, ROLLING STONE (Mar. 3, 2021), https://www.rollingstone.com/pro/news/kings-of-leon-when-you-see-yourself-album-nft-crypto-1135192/.

[260] Jacob Kastrenakes, *Beeple Sold an NFT for $69 Million*, VERGE (Mar. 11, 2021), https://www.theverge.com/2021/3/11/22325054/beeple-christies-nft-sale-cost-everydays-69-million.

[261] Hissong, *supra* note 260.

[262] Katrina Nattress, *Kings of Leon Have Generated $2 Million on NFT Sales of Their New Album*, IHEART RADIO (Mar. 14, 2021), https://www.iheart.com/content/2021-03-14-kings-of-leon-have-generated-2-million-on-nft-sales-of-their-new-album/.

[263] Tim Ingham, *NFTs for Copyrights: Why Non-Fungible Tokens Could Transform Who Gets Paid from Music Rights, and How*, MUSIC BUS. WORLDWIDE (Mar. 15, 2021), https://www.musicbusinessworldwide.com/nfts-for-copyrights-why-non-

fungible-tokens-could-transform-who-gets-paid-from-music-rights-and-how/.

[264] *Id.*

[265] *Blockchain for Ticketing: A Complete Guide*, EVENT MANAGER BLOG (Oct. 29, 2020), https://www.eventmanagerblog.com/blockchain-ticketing.

[266] *Id.*

[267] *Id.*

[268] Andrea Tinianow, *When Blockchains Crash, Who Can You Sue?*, FORBES (Feb. 7, 2019, 2:32 PM), https://www.forbes.com/sites/andreatinianow/2019/02/07/when-blockchains-crash-whom-can-you-sue/?sh=7226dc827775.

[269] *See id.*; *see also* Chairman Jay Clayton, *Statement on Cryptocurrencies and Initial Coin Offerings*, U.S. SEC. & EXCH. COMM'N (Dec. 11, 2017), https://www.sec.gov/news/public-statement/statement-clayton-2017-12-11#:~:text=It%20has%20been%20asserted%20that%20cryptocurrencies%20are%20not,the%20characteristics%20and%20use%20of%20that%20particular%20asset.

[270] Tinianow, *supra* note 269.

[271] Tinianow, *supra* note 269.

[272] Tinianow, *supra* note 269.

[273] Andy Gensler, *How Ed Sheeran's 2018 Divide Tour Set the All-Time Touring Record*, POLLSTAR (Dec. 17, 2018), https://www.pollstar.com/article/exclusive-ed-sheerans-divide-tour-to-break-u2s-all-time-touring-record-tonight-138597, (last visited May 10, 2021).

[274] *Id.*

[275] Rashad, *Ed Sheeran's 'Divide' Tour Is Now the Highest Grossing Tour of All Time,* THAT GRAPE JUICE.NET (Aug. 2, 2019), https://thatgrapejuice.net/2019/08/sheerans-divide-tour-now-the-highest-grossing-tour-time/.

[276] Sam Greenspan, *11 Music Superstars Who are Technically No-Hit Wonders*, 11 POINTS (Mar. 12, 2018), https://11points.com/11-music-superstars-technically-no-hit-wonders/.

[277] *Publicity*, LEGAL INFO. INST., http://www.law.cornell.edu/wex/publicity (last visited May 7, 2021).

[278] *See Midler v. Ford Motor Co.*, 849.F.2d 460, 463 (9th Cir. 1988).

[279] *Statutes & Interactive Map*, RIGHT OF PUBLICITY, http://rightofpublicity.com/statutes (last visited May 7, 2021).

[280] Scott Zamost & Poppy Harlow, *The most recognizable band/artist on Earth? Inside the world of KISS Inc.*, CNN MONEY (Oct. 24,

2011, 8:32 AM),
http://money.cnn.com/2011/10/18/news/kiss_products/index.htm.

[281] Steve Strauss, *Gene Simmons of Kiss Says This 1 Word Made Him a Millionaire*, INC. MAGAZINE (Nov. 30, 2017), https://www.inc.com/steve-strauss/the-one-simple-word-that-gene-simmons-says-made-kiss-a-billion-dollar-business.html.

[283] James C. McKinley, Jr., *Exhuming the Last of Hendrix's Studio Sessions*, N.Y. TIMES (Mar. 6, 2013), https://www.nytimes.com/2013/03/07/arts/music/people-hell-and-angels-the-last-of-hendrix.html.

[283] Rich Stim, *The Right of Publicity*, NOLO, http://www.nolo.com/legal-encyclopedia/the-right-publicity.html (last visited May 7, 2021).

[284] Dorothy Pomerantz, *Michael Jackson Leads Our List Of The Top-Earning Dead Celebrities*, FORBES (Oct. 23, 2013, 9:56 AM), http://www.forbes.com/sites/dorothypomerantz/2013/10/23/michael-jackson-leads-our-list-of-the-top-earning-dead-celebrities/.

[285] *Id.*

[286] *Id.*

[287] Nick Hall, *These Dead Celebrities Made More Money Than You This Year*, (Nov. 7, 2021), https://manofmany.com/lifestyle/highest-paid-dead-celebrities-2021.

[288] THERE'S NO BUSINESS LIKE SHOW BUSINESS (Twentieth Century-Fox Film Corp. 1954).

[289] *Crowdfunding*, OXFORD DICTIONARY (2021).

[290] Nickolas C. Jensen, *Fundraising on the Internet: Crowdfunding, Kickstarter and the JOBS Act,* ARIZ. ATT'Y, March 2013, at 22.

[291] *Id.*

[292] *Invest*, INVESTOR.GOV, http://investor.gov/glossary/glossary_terms/invest (last visited May 7, 2021).

[293] *Registration Under the Securities Act of 1933*, INVESTOR.GOV, http://www.sec.gov/answers/regis33.htm (last visited May 7, 2021).

[294] 17 C.F.R. § 230.504(b)(iii).

[295] *Accredited Investors*, INVESTOR.GOV, http://www.sec.gov/answers/accred.htm (last visited May 7, 2021).

[296] 17 C.F.R. § 230.506(b)(2)(i)-(ii).

[297] Georgia Quinn & Anthony Zeoli, *The Definitive Guide: Intrastate Crowdfunding Exemptions,* CROWDFUND INSIDER (July 15, 2014, 8:28 AM), http://www.crowdfundinsider.com/2014/07/44088-the-definitive-guide-intrastate-crowdfunding-exemptions/.

[298] 15 U.S.C. § 77d(a)(6)(B)(i)-(ii); Jensen, *supra* note 291.

[299] § 77d(a)(6)(B)(i)-(ii).

[300] *SEC Adopts Rules to Permit Crowdfunding*, SEC Press Release 2015-249, (Oct. 30, 2015), https://www.sec.gov/news/pressrelease/2015-249.html.

[301] BRUCE BROWN, THE HISTORY OF THE CORPORATION, VOL. 1 (2015).

[302] *Id.*

[303] *Id.*

[304] Uniform Limited Partnership Act, 14 U.S.C. §§ 171.10-.90 (2021); ROBERT W. HAMILTON, CORPORATIONS INCLUDING PARTNERSHIPS AND LIMITED PARTNERSHIPS 146 (5th ed. 1994).

[305] HAMILTON, *supra* note 305, at 146.

[306] HAMILTON, *supra* note 305, at 146.

[307] *See* N.Y. PARTNERSHIP LAW §§ 20-28

[308] *Id.* § 121-303(a).

[309] Sandra Feldman, *The LLC handbook*, WOLTERS KLUWER (Mar. 30, 2021), https://www.wolterskluwer.com/en/expert-insights/the-llc-handbook.

[310] *Id.*

[311] HAMILTON, *supra* note 305, at 160.

[312] HAMILTON, *supra* note 305, at 160.

[313] E. ALLAN FARNSWORTH, CONTRACTS 3 (2d ed. 1990).

[314] *Id.* at 5.

[315] *Id.* at 4.

[316] *Id.* at 13.

[317] *Id.*

[318] *Id.* at 10.

[319] *Id.* at 11.

[320] *Id.*

[321] *Id.* at 12.

[322] *The Common Law and Civil Law Traditions*, U.C. BERKELEY, SCH. LAW., https://www.law.berkeley.edu/wp-content/uploads/2017/11/CommonLawCivilLawTraditions.pdf (last visited May 7, 2021).

[323] *Id.*

[324] *Id.*

[325] MARVIN A. CHIRELSTEIN, CONCEPTS AND CASE ANALYSIS IN THE LAW OF CONTRACTS 30 (2d ed. 1993).

[326] FARNSWORTH, *supra* note 314, at 114.

[327] CHIRELSTEIN, *supra* note 326, at 29.

[328] CHIRELSTEIN, *supra* note 326, at 51.

[329] FARNSWORTH, *supra* note 314, at 170.

[330] CHIRELSTEIN, *supra* note 326, at 34.

[331] *Lucy v. Zehmer*, 84 S.E.2d 516, 516 (Va. 1954).

[332] *Donald Trump Drops Bill Maher Lawsuit*, HUFFINGTON POST (Apr. 2, 2013, 12:04 PM), http://www.huffingtonpost.com/2013/04/02/donald-trump-drops-bill-maher-lawsuit_n_2999605.html.

[333] *Lefkowitz v. Great Minn. Surplus Store*, 86 N.W.2d 689, 689 (Minn. 1957).

[334] CHIRELSTEIN, *supra* note 326, at 37.

[335] CHIRELSTEIN, *supra* note 326, at 160.

[336] FARNSWORTH, *supra* note 314, at 115.

[337] FARNSWORTH, *supra* note 314, at 118-19.

[338] FARNSWORTH, *supra* note 314, at 119.

[339] CHIRELSTEIN, *supra* note 326, at 38.

[340] FARNSWORTH, *supra* note 314, at 143.

[341] FARNSWORTH, *supra* note 314, at 155.

[342] FARNSWORTH, *supra* note 314, at 52.

[343] RESTATEMENT (SECOND) OF CONTS. § 71 (A.L.I. 1981).

[344] FARNSWORTH, *supra* note 314, at 44-45.

[345] Chappell v Nestlé [1960] AC 87 (Eng.) ("A peppercorn does not cease to be good consideration if it is established that the promisee does not like pepper and will throw away the corn"). As an example of literal usage, a peppercorn was used as consideration over 200 years ago when the Old State House in St. George where parliamentary sessions were held was leased to the Freemasons for a rent of only one peppercorn. Bermuda holds a traditional and festive "Peppercorn Ceremony" every year in memoriam. *See, e.g.*, Bermuda Attractions, *Bermuda Peppercorn Ceremony*, http://www.bermuda-attractions.com/bermuda_000106.htm (last visited May 7, 2021).

[346] FARNSWORTH, *supra* note 314, at 45.

[347] Raffles v. Wichelhaus (1864) 159 Eng. Rep. 375 (Ex Ch).

[348] FARNSWORTH, *supra* note 314, at 499.

[349] FARNSWORTH, *supra* note 314, at 693.

[350] FARNSWORTH, *supra* note 314, at 694-95.

[351] FARNSWORTH, *supra* note 314, at 683.

[352] *Sherwood v. Walker*, 33 N.W. 919, 919 (Mich. 1887).

[353] FARNSWORTH, *supra* note 314, at 684 (citing RESTATEMENT, *supra* note 344, § 152)

[354] FARNSWORTH, *supra* note 314, at 684.

[355] CHIRELSTEIN, *supra* note 326, at 60.

[356] CHIRELSTEIN, *supra* note 326, at 59.

[357] FARNSWORTH, *supra* note 314, at 272-73.

[358] *Chase Manhattan Bank v. N.Y.*, 787 N.Y.S.2d 155, 157 (N.Y. App. Div. 2004).

[359] FARNSWORTH, *supra* note 314, at 282.

[360] *See Austin Instrument v. Loral Corp.*, 324 N.Y.S.2d 22, 25 (N.Y. 1971).

[361] FARNSWORTH, *supra* note 314, at 269.

[362] FARNSWORTH, *supra* note 314, at 249.

[363] FARNSWORTH, *supra* note 314, at 249.

[364] FARNSWORTH, *supra* note 314, at 257.

[365] FARNSWORTH, *supra* note 314, at 260.

[366] FARNSWORTH, *supra* note 314, at 250.

[367] *See Small v. Lorillard Tobacco Co.*, 94 N.Y.2d 43, 57 (1999); *P.T. Bank Cent. Asia, NY Branch v. ABN AMRO Bank N.V.*, 301 A.D.2d 375, 376 (1st Dep't 2003).

[368] *Scienter*, BLACK'S LAW DICTIONARY (6th ed. 1994).

[369] *See* CAL. FAM. CODE § 6751.

[370] *See* CAL. LAB. CODE § 1700.37.

[371] *Id.* § 2855.

[372] *Berg v. Traylor*, 56 Cal. Rptr. 3d 140, 144 (Cal. Ct. App. 2007).

[373] *Id.* at 145.

[374] CHIRELSTEIN, *supra* note 326, at 59.

[375] FARNSWORTH, *supra* note 314, at 238.

[376] FARNSWORTH, *supra* note 314, at 239.

[377] FARNSWORTH, *supra* note 314, at 240.

[378] FARNSWORTH, *supra* note 314, at 240.

[379] FARNSWORTH, *supra* note 314, at 243.

[380] FARNSWORTH, *supra* note 314, at 243.

[381] *SBRMCOA, LLC v. Bayside Resort, Inc.*, 707 F.3d 267, 271 (3d Cir. 2013).

[382] RESTATEMENT, *supra* note 344, § 110.

[383] RESTATEMENT, *supra* note 344, § 110.

[384] FARNSWORTH, *supra* note 314, at 412.

[385] FARNSWORTH, *supra* note 314, at 412.

[386] FARNSWORTH, *supra* note 314, at 445.

[387] FARNSWORTH, *supra* note 314, at 450.

[388] RESTATEMENT, *supra* note 344, § 209.

[389] FARNSWORTH, *supra* note 314, at 470.

[390] FARNSWORTH, *supra* note 314, at 470.

[391] FARNSWORTH, *supra* note 314, at 470.

[392] FARNSWORTH, *supra* note 314, at 472.

[393] FARNSWORTH, *supra* note 314, at 472.

[394] FARNSWORTH, *supra* note 314, at 479.

[395] FARNSWORTH, *supra* note 314, at 473 (quoting Arthur L. Corbin, *The Parol Evidence Rule,* 53 YALE L.J. 603, 630 (1944)).

[396] FARNSWORTH, *supra* note 314, at 840.

[397] FARNSWORTH, *supra* note 314, at 840.

[398] FARNSWORTH, *supra* note 314, at 842.

[399] FARNSWORTH, *supra* note 314, at 843.

[400] FARNSWORTH, *supra* note 314, at 844-45.

[401] FARNSWORTH, *supra* note 314, at 845.

[402] FARNSWORTH, *supra* note 314, at 840.

[403] CHIRELSTEIN, *supra* note 326, at 142.

[404] CHIRELSTEIN, *supra* note 326, at 143.

[405] *Parker v. Twentieth Century-Fox Film Corp.*, 474 P.2d 689, 690 (Cal. 1970).

[406] *Id.* at 693.

[407] FARNSWORTH, *supra* note 314, at 842.

[408] FARNSWORTH, *supra* note 314, at 843.

[409] FARNSWORTH, *supra* note 314, at 843.

[410] FARNSWORTH, *supra* note 314, at 850.

[411] FARNSWORTH, *supra* note 314, at 854.

[412] *Injunction*, MERRIAM-WEBSTER DICTIONARY (2021).

[413] FARNSWORTH, *supra* note 314, at 855.

[414] FARNSWORTH, *supra* note 314, at 855.

[415] *Lumley v. Wagner* (1852) 604, 42 Eng. Rep. 687 (Ch).

[416] *Id.* at 683.

[417] CHIRELSTEIN, *supra* note 326, at 173.

[418] CHIRELSTEIN, *supra* note 326, at 173.

[419] CHIRELSTEIN, *supra* note 326, at 173.

[420] CHIRELSTEIN, *supra* note 326, at 173.

[421] A NIGHT AT THE OPERA (Metro-Goldwyn-Mayer Studios 1935).

[422] *Wood v. Lucy, Lady Duff-Gordon*, 118 N.E. 214, 214 (N.Y. 1917).

[423] *Id.*

[424] *Id.* ("The law has outgrown its primitive stage of formalism when the precise word was the sovereign talisman. . . . [I]t takes a broader view today.").

[425] FARNSWORTH, *supra* note 314, at 569.

[426] RESTATEMENT, *supra* note 344, § 224.

[427] FARNSWORTH, *supra* note 314, at 565.

[428] FARNSWORTH, *supra* note 314, at 566.

[429] Wayne Schiess, *"shall" vs. "will"*, LEGALWRITING.NET (May 16, 2005), http://www.utexas.edu/law/faculty/wschiess/legalwriting/2005/05/shall-vs-will.html.

[430] *See Reed, Roberts Assocs., Inc. v. Strauman*, 353 N.E.2d 590, 593 (N.Y. 1976).

[431] *BDO Seidman v. Hirshberg*, 712 N.E.2d 1220, 1223 (N.Y. 1999).

[432] *Trade secret*, LEGAL INFO. INST., http://www.law.cornell.edu/wex/trade_secret (last visited May 7, 2021).

[433] *Id.*

[434] CHIRELSTEIN, *supra* note 326, at 113.

[435] *Boilerplate*, WEST'S ENCYCLOPEDIA OF AM. L. (2d ed. 2008).

[436] In New York, the right to recover attorneys' fees "must be statutory or contractual." *Greco v. GSL Enters., Inc.*, 521 N.Y.S.2d 994, 994 (N.Y. Civ. Ct. 1987); *Hooper Assocs., Ltd. v. AGS Computers, Inc.*, 548 N.E.2d 903, 904 (N.Y. 1989) (An award of attorneys' fees to the prevailing party in a litigation must be "authorized by agreement between the parties, statute or court rule. . . .").

[437] Gene Maddus, *IATSE Members Vote to Ratify Contract, Ending Strike Threat,* VARIETY MAGAZINE (Nov. 15, 2021, 11:16 AM)

[438] *History, supra* note 9.

[439] *History, supra* note 9.

[440] *History, supra* note 9.

[441] *History, supra* note 9.

[442] *History, supra* note 9.

[443] *History, supra* note 9.

[444] *History, supra* note 9.

[445] *History, supra* note 9.

[446] *History, supra* note 9.

[447] *History, supra* note 9.

[448] *Teamsters Union*, ENCYCLOPEDIA BRITANNICA (2021).

[449] *Id.*

[450] *Teamster History*, TEAMSTER, https://teamster.org/about/teamster-history/ (last visited May 7, 2021).

[451] *Id.*

[452] *Id.*

[453] *Id.*

[454] TEAMSTERS LOCAL 399, https://www.ht399.org/ (last visited May 7, 2021).

[455] *ABOUT THE IATSE*, INT'L ALL. THEATRICAL STAGE EMPS., http://www.iatse-intl.org/about-iatse (last visited May 7, 2021).

[456] *Id.*

[457] TEAMSTERS LOCAL 399, *supra* note 455.

[458] TEAMSTERS LOCAL 399, *supra* note 455.

[459] *About Local One*, THEATRICAL STAGE EMPS. LOC. ONE, http://iatselocalone.org/Public/About_Local_One/About_Local_One.aspx (last visited May 7, 2021).

[460] *About SAG/AFTRA,* About | SAG-AFTRA (sagaftra.org), (last visited Mar. 21, 2022).

[461] ROGER WATERS, HAVE A CIGAR (Harvest Recs. & Columbia Recs. 1975).

[462] Eric R. Danton, *Roger Waters Regrets Pink Floyd Legal Battle*, ROLLING STONE (Sept. 19, 2013, 12:40 PM), https://www.rollingstone.com/music/music-news/roger-waters-regrets-pink-floyd-legal-battle-191084/.

[463] *Id.*

[464] James Mckinley, *The Wall Goes On, and Grows Even Longer*, N.Y. TIMES (July 5, 2012), http://www.nytimes.com/2012/07/06/arts/music/rogers-waters-talks-about-the-wall-and-pink-floyd.html?pagewanted=all.

[465] *Scott Interview, supra* note 78.

[466] NEIL SEDAKA, BREAKING UP IS HARD TO DO (Rocket Recs. 1962).

[467] JAMES L. DICKERSON, COLONEL TOM PARKER: THE CURIOUS LIFE OF ELVIS PRESLEY'S ECCENTRIC MANAGER 72 (2001).

[468] Telephone interview with Pete Angelus, Personal Manager (Dec. 5, 2016).

[470] *Id.*

[471] BOB SPITZ, THE BEATLES: THE BIOGRAPHY 717 (2005).

[472] Dorian Lynskey, *John Fogerty: 'I had rules. I wasn't embarrassed that I was ambitious'*, Guardian (May 29, 2013, 7:58 AM), https://www.theguardian.com/music/2013/may/29/john-fogerty-creedence-clearwater-interview.

[472] *Id.*

[473] *Id.*

[474] *Id.*

[475] *Id.*

[476] Kory Grow, *Flashback: John Fogerty Wins Rare Self-Plagiarism Suit in 1988*, ROLLING STONE (Nov. 9, 2018, 11:53 AM), https://www.rollingstone.com/music/music-news/john-fogerty-self-plagiarism-lawsuit-creedence-clearwater-revival-752805/.

[477] *Phil Ramone*, GRAMMY AWARDS, https://www.grammy.com/grammys/artists/phil-ramone/6534 (last visited May 7, 2021).

[478] *George Martin*, INT'L MOVIE DATABASE, https://www.imdb.com/name/nm0552326/ (last visited May 7, 2021).

[479] SPITZ, *supra* note 471, at 301.

[480] SPITZ, *supra* note 471, at 784.

[481] ROGER WATERS, WELCOME TO THE MACHINE (Columbia Recs. 2000).

[482] *Roger Waters Says He Shouldn't Have Sued Pink Floyd*, RTTNEWS (Sept. 20, 2013, 7:35 PM), http://www.rttnews.com/2191702/roger-waters-says-he-shouldn-t-have-sued-pink-floyd.aspx.

[483] 17 U.S.C. § 203(a)(5).

[484] Rohter, *supra* note 87.

[485] Mary Ermel, *Exclusive band/artist Recording Agreement - Getting Started in the Music Business*, TEX. MUSIC OFF., https://gov.texas.gov/music/page/tmlp_contractsextra (last visited May 7, 2021).

[486] *See F.B.T. Prods., LLC v. Aftermath Recs.*, 621 F.3d 958, 962 (9th Cir. 2010).

[487] *Id.* at 964.

[488] *Id.* at 965.

[489] *Id.* at 966.

[490] *Id.* at 967.

[491] *FAQs*, HARRY FOX AGENCY, https://www.harryfox.com/#/faq (last visited May 7, 2021).

[492] Jem Aswad, *BMG Eliminates 'Poisonous,' 'Anachronistic' Controlled-Musical Composition Clause From U.S. Label Contracts*, Variety, https://variety.com/2020/music/news/bmg-eliminates-controlled-Musical Composition-clause-1234797547/ (last visited Apr. 24, 2022).

[493] *See, e.g., Marlyn Nutraceuticals, Inc. v. Mucos Pharma GmbH & Co.*, 571 F.3d 873, 877 (9th Cir. 2009).

[494] Todd Brabec & Jeff Brabec, *SONGWRITER AND MUSIC PUBLISHER AGREEMENTS; A Relationship Necessary For Success*, https://www.ascap.com/help/music-business-101/200809, (last visited Oct. 10, 2021).

[495] *Id.*

[496] *Music Publishing Agreements*, https://www.songstuff.com/music-business/article/music_publishing_contracts/#:~:text=This%20is%20an%20agreement%20between,pay%20royalties%20to%20the%20songwriter (last visited Aug. 26, 2022).

[497] *See* 17 U.S.C. § 203.

[498] *Sting Sells Song Catalog to Universal for $3000 m+;* https://www.musicbusinessworldwide.com/sting-sells-song-catalog-to-universal-for-300m/ (last visited Sept. 3, 2022).

[499] *Bruce Springsteen's $500 million-plus catalog sale to Sony Explained; https://www.musicbusinessworldwide.com/the-important-detail-of-bruce-springsteens-500m-plus-catalog-sale-to-sony-music-group/* (last visited Sept. 3, 2022).

[500] *Sony Music acquires Bob Dylan's recorded music catalog;* https://www.musicbusinessworldwide.com/sony-music-acquires-bob-dylans-recorded-music-catalog11111/ (last visited Sept. 4, 2022).

[501] WILLIE NELSON, ON THE ROAD AGAIN (Columbia Recs. 1980).

[502] Bryan Johnson, *Top 10 True Rock Music Stories*, LISTVERSE (June 18, 2014), http://listverse.com/2012/09/11/top-10-true-rock-music-stories/.

[503] Andy Greene, *The 10 Wildest Led Zeppelin Legends, Fact-Checked*, ROLLINGSTONES (Oct. 16, 2019, 4:20 PM), http://www.rollingstone.com/music/lists/the-10-wildest-led-zeppelin-legends-fact-checked-20121121/led-zeppelin-once-defiled-a-groupie-with-a-mud-shark-19691231.

[504] Raul, *Keith Moon Drove A Car Into A Pool at The Holiday Inn On His 21st Birthday*, FEEL NUMB (May 4, 2011), http://www.feelnumb.com/2011/05/04/keith-moon-drove-a-car-into-a-pool-on-his-21st-birthday/.

[505] *Having a Ball*, ECONOMIST (Oct. 7, 2010), http://www.economist.com/node/17199460/print.

[506] IEG, WHAT SPONSORS WANT AND WHERE THEIR DOLLARS WILL GO IN 2016, https://www.sponsorship.com/Resources/What-Sponsors-Want-and-Where-Dollars-Will-Go-in-20.aspx (last visited May 7, 2021).

[507] *Having a Ball*, *supra* note 506.

[508] *Having a Ball*, *supra* note 506.

[509] *Having a Ball*, *supra* note 506.

[510] *Having a Ball*, *supra* note 506.

[511] *Having a Ball*, *supra* note 506.

[512] Michael Rushton, *Why are tickets for rock concerts so expensive?*, ARTSJOURNAL (Apr. 24, 2013), http://www.artsjournal.com/worth/2013/04/why-are-tickets-for-rock-concerts-so-expensive/.

[513] *Bon Jovi Has 2013's Top-Grossing Tour*, HOLLYWOOD REP. (Dec. 31, 2013, 12:33 PM), http://www.hollywoodreporter.com/earshot/bon-jovi-has-2013s-top-668105.

Made in the USA
Middletown, DE
04 June 2023

31727355R00291